BIRDING THE HUDSON VALLEY

Kathryn J. Schneider

Birding

THE HUDSON VALLEY

University Press of New England

Hanover and London

University Press of New England
www.upne.com
© 2018 Kathryn J. Schneider
All rights reserved
Manufactured in the
United States of America
Typeset in Calluna

For permission to reproduce any of the
material in this book, contact Permissions,
University Press of New England,
One Court Street, Suite 250, Lebanon NH
03766; or visit www.upne.com

PHOTO CREDITS:

Page xvii Kettle of hawks.
© Deborah Tracy-Kral.

Page 316 Snow Geese showing
their mountainous flight formation in
the background. © Deborah Tracy-Kral.

*This book was published with the
generous support of Furthermore:
a program of the J. M. Kaplan Fund.*

Library of Congress Cataloging-in-
Publication Data available upon request

Names: Schneider, Kathryn J., author.

Title: Birding the Hudson Valley /
Kathryn J. Schneider.

Description: Hanover: University Press
of New England, [2018] | Includes
bibliographical references and index. |

Identifiers: LCCN 2018002993 (print) |
LCCN 2018006649 (ebook) |
ISBN 9781512602678 (epub, pdf, & mobi) |
ISBN 9781611687187 (pbk.)

Subjects: LCSH: Bird watching—Hudson
River Valley (N.Y. and N.J.)—Guidebooks. |
Bird watching—New York (State)—
Guidebooks. | Birds—Hudson River Valley
(N.Y. and N.J.)—Identification. | Birds—New
York (State)—Identification. | Birding
sites—Hudson River Valley (N.Y. and N.J.)—
Guidebooks. | Birding sites—New York
(State)—Guidebooks. | Hudson River Valley
(N.Y. and N.J.)—Guidebooks.

Classification: LCC QL684.N7 (ebook) |
LCC QL684.N7 S36 2018 (print) |
DDC 598.072/347471—dc23

LC record available at
https://lccn.loc.gov/2018002993

5 4 3 2 1

TO BILL, WHO UNDERSTANDS MY PASSION
FOR BIRDS AND LOVES ME ANYHOW

Contents

Preface

According to a 2011 US Fish and Wildlife survey, roughly forty-six million Americans, or about 15 percent of the US population, consider themselves to be birdwatchers. These numbers suggest that more than four hundred thousand Hudson Valley residents feed, observe, or photograph birds. However, this same survey indicated that the vast majority of New Yorkers enjoy their wildlife-watching activities primarily around their homes. A mere 27 percent actually travel to watch birds. While some birds can be seen anywhere, even the best backyards have a limited number of species. The only way to truly appreciate the depth and diversity of bird life in our valley is to explore new sites and see new birds. This book provides the guidance for bird enthusiasts of all levels to break out of their comfort zones and expand their birding horizons.

The Hudson Valley is full of beautiful places to go birdwatching. Conservationists and land-use planners have worked hard to identify and protect important wildlife habitats and natural communities that support the region's biodiversity. Public and private funds have been used to purchase these lands and to provide amenities that welcome visitors and enhance opportunities to see wildlife. The parks, preserves, and conservation areas of the Hudson Valley contribute greatly to the valley's richness and natural beauty, and you can enhance your birding experience by exploring some of these areas.

I see this book as more than a bird-finding guide. These pages include history, ecology, bird biology, and tourism. The first chapter, on land-use history and biogeography, attempts to provide a framework for understanding the Hudson Valley landscape and the distribution of the birds that live here. The next three chapters, on birdwatching skills and bird biology, begin as many authors have begun before, with the basics of choosing binoculars, feeding birds, and bird identification. But, because my goal is to entice birdwatchers to move beyond their bird feeders, Chapters 3 and 4 focus on making the transition to birding "in the field." These sections describe bird behavior, habitats, and the seasonality of birding with a focus on the Hudson Valley, and include ways for beginners to hone their skills to become better birders and see more birds.

However, no amount of written guidance can substitute for spending time watching birds, and the majority of this book is about the places to see them. The collection of sites in Chapters 6 through 9 tries to identify birding destinations that capture all the different kinds of birds that each county has to offer. These sites take birders to a variety of habitats, including farms, grasslands, old fields, wetlands, orchards, city parks, rocky summits, mountaintops, rivers, lakes, and salt marshes. Emphasizing diversity forced me to make hard choices and leave out some great birding spots, so these sites are merely an introduction. In many ways, I have used birds to create a tour of the ten-county region that lets birdwatchers sample the natural history of the Hudson Valley. If I have done this well, the orientation will whet your appetite to visit more places and see more birds.

Acknowledgments

Writing this book was one of the most difficult things I have ever done, and it would never have happened without the support and assistance of so many people. First and foremost, I thank the birding community of the Hudson Valley. Major parts of this work rely on decades of data contributed by birders and assembled into Breeding Bird Atlases, Waterfowl Counts, Christmas Bird Counts, eBird, and other repositories. This cumulative knowledge laid the foundation for this book, and I believe its very existence speaks to the remarkable willingness of birders to share their data, time, and expertise. In many ways, I owe a debt of gratitude to every Hudson Valley birder, but a few deserve to be named specifically.

I thank Bob Budliger, who encouraged University Press of New England to take a chance on this first-time author. He critiqued my book proposal and offered helpful suggestions during the book's formative stages. Ted Murin and David Strayer encouraged me and patiently answered my questions about the writing and publication process. Gilbert (Wray) Rominger soothed my concerns about administrative matters. It was he who suggested that University Press of New England approach Furthermore grants in publishing for financial backing that ultimately supported this work.

Birders up and down the Hudson Valley helped select sites for this book. When I asked about their favorite birding destinations, birders were eager to share their knowledge and lobby for their most beloved areas. I am grateful to Janet Allison, Scott Baldinger, Mike Bochnik, Barbara Butler, Steve Chorvas, Bill Cook, Jim de Waal Malefyt, Richard Guthrie, Tait Johansson, John Kent, Carena Pooth, Charlie Roberto, Ann Swaim, Larry Trachtenburg, Chet Vincent, Alan Wells, Phillip Whitney, Tom Williams, and Will Yandik for their input, and I am sorry I could not include all of their wonderful birding places. Thanks also to Tom Burke, Barbara Butler, Steve Chorvas, Elijah Goodwin, Alan Mapes, Carena Pooth, Charlie Roberto, and Ann Swaim, who answered endless questions about sites, maps, and bird distributions in the Hudson Valley. I especially appreciate the contributions of Della Wells, Alan Wells, Jane Graves, Deborah Langford, Brad Smyth, and Rachel Schneider, who read drafts of the manuscript and offered helpful suggestions that improved it greatly.

I am indebted to the bird clubs and their field trip leaders, who welcomed me on their outings and introduced me to their local preserves. Alan and Della Wells, John Kent, Tom Williams, Richard Guthrie, and Robert Lewis set aside time to take me on guided tours of their favorite birding spots. I am grateful to Marian Sole, birding companion extraordinaire, for her birding insights, her uncomplaining attitude, and especially her good sense of direction.

From the very beginning, I wanted this book to be beautiful. Photos draw people to a book, and more than anything, I want this book to be read. I thank talented photographers Alan Wells, Deborah Tracy-Kral, Bruce Dudek, Denise and Scott Stoner, Carena Pooth, Naomi Lloyd, John Hershey, Tom Williams, and Joan Collins, who gave permission to use their images. I am also grateful to Tristan Lowery, who worked evenings, weekends, and holidays to create respectable reference maps, sometimes from notes, GPS tracks, and blurry photos. John Kent, Kara Caputo, Trish Miller, and Matt Young provided much-needed technical help with figures and permissions.

Finally, special thanks to my husband Bill for his patience, support, and encouragement.

BIRDING THE HUDSON VALLEY

BIRDING THE HUDSON VALLEY

Least Sandpiper. © Naomi Lloyd.

1   The Hudson Valley Landscape

The birds of the Hudson Valley live in a place that has been shaped by both nature and humans. Indeed, it is the combination of natural beauty and rich cultural heritage that makes the Hudson Valley unique and sets it apart from the rest of New York State. Though picturesque and scenic, most of the area is no longer "natural." Pristine ecosystems have been replaced by a mosaic of altered lands and waters to create a modern natural and cultural landscape.

This chapter explains how glaciers formed the rivers, lakes, cliffs, drumlins, waterfalls, and soils of the Hudson Valley. It briefly explores how the activities of Native Americans and European settlers changed the Hudson River, its shoreline, its forested uplands, and its wildlife. Finally, this chapter describes the present-day landscape of the Hudson Valley, looking first at the river and then at large biophysical regions distinguished by their geology, climate, topography, and soils. This broad overview provides a sense of how the land has changed and sets the stage for understanding the distribution of birds in the Hudson Valley.

A Land Shaped by Glaciers

During the last ice age, the Hudson Valley was covered by glaciers. As the massive ice sheets advanced from north to south, they scoured and scraped the land below, destroying any living organisms in their paths. Glaciers gouged out and deepened the Hudson River channel. They robbed the ocean of water as they advanced, converting liquid water to ice and lowering sea level so much that most of the continental shelf near New York City was actually dry land. The Hudson Canyon, a deep-water gorge in the continental shelf favored by pelagic birds, is part of the river's now submerged ancient riverbed.

Ice advanced and retreated over the Hudson Valley many times during the

Pleistocene Epoch, reaching a thickness of nearly half a mile in some places. As the glaciers passed, the ice ripped off loose masses of bedrock, shaping the escarpments and cliff faces visible today on the west side of the Hudson. Underneath, the ice piles of coarse sediments were left in egg-shaped hills called drumlins, which dot pastoral farmlands throughout the Hudson Valley. The glaciers cut drainage channels to the Hudson River, forming future waterfalls. The great ice sheets bulldozed rocks and boulders ahead of them, and wherever they stopped, they deposited massive ridges of boulders, gravel, silt, and sediment known as glacial moraines.

After the last glacial advance, about twenty-two thousand years ago, the ice sheet began to melt faster than it grew; this resulted in a northward retreat. As it melted, the ice sheet carried sand and silt down its face, leaving a smooth, flat, outwash plain. The slow-moving, melting glaciers formed lakes and wetlands by scooping out areas of soft rock. Chunks of ice broke off and became buried in the sandy outwash. When this ice melted, the water-filled depressions became the valley's kettle-hole ponds and bogs.

In the Hudson River drainage, a moraine blocked the rush of melting ice water on its way to the sea. When the thick ice was present, its sheer weight depressed the land, but its retreat northward allowed land south of the ice front to rebound, forming a large depression around the Hudson River between Glens Falls and Newburgh. The depression filled with water from the melting glacier, and created a 160-mile-long body of water called Glacial Lake Albany, which covered most of the Hudson Valley for the next four thousand to five thousand years. Ten streams flowed into the lake, forming sandy deltas at their mouths. The Mohawk River, an especially large tributary to the west, deposited the sandy sediments of the Albany Pine Bush, an inland pine barrens community that still has remnants of ancient sand dunes sculpted by winds thousands of years ago. Over time, the flat bottom of Glacial Lake Albany accumulated deep sediments of clay and loam. As the glacier continued to melt northward and the land rose with its retreat, the lake eventually drained into the sea through the Hudson River channel. It left behind rich soil for productive farmland and clay banks that provisioned a thriving brickmaking industry in the 1800s.

Beyond the shores of the ancient lake, the ice sheets left poor soils derived from ground-up rocks. The glaciers left thin layers of rocky soil on hilltops and somewhat deeper deposits in the valleys, where the ice sheets were thicker and moved more slowly. Rocks, along with the picturesque water-

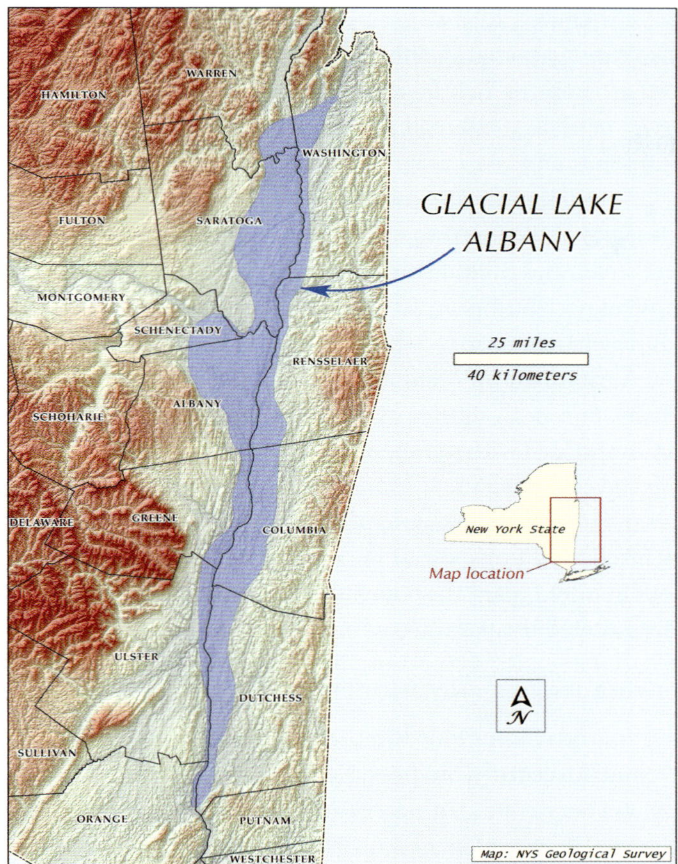

Glacial Lake Albany. Courtesy of New York State Museum, Albany, NY.

falls, escarpments, farmland, lakes, ponds, and drumlins, are the legacy of glaciation in the Hudson Valley.

A Land Changed by Humans

Humans have lived in the Hudson Valley for at least seven thousand years. At first, their impacts were small. In 1609, when Henry Hudson traveled up the river that now bears his name, he encountered Native Americans living along its shores. In spring, summer, and fall, the Native Americans lived in small seasonal settlements that were close to the river. Here they fished from seasonal fish runs, gathered shellfish, and grew crops of beans, maize, pumpkin, and tobacco on the rich floodplain soils. In winter, they moved away from the river to more sheltered inland sites, where they practiced ice fishing on frozen ponds and lakes, trapped beaver, and hunted small game and deer. While it is well known that the indigenous people of the Hudson Valley burned clearings in the forest to plant crops and attract wildlife, their populations were small, and their disturbances were minor and temporary compared to those of post-European settlement.

That all began to change in 1623, when the Dutch established the settlements of New Amsterdam on Manhattan Island and Fort Orange near modern-day Albany. European settlers came to the Hudson Valley to trade and make money. Impressed with the abundant wildlife and fertile soil, they began harvesting and exporting the "commodities" of the New World. They established permanent settlements along the river and its tributaries, and exploited the rich soils and transportation routes the waterways provided. Over the next four hundred years, the population of the Hudson Valley grew, and its inhabitants altered the natural communities dramatically.

THE RIVER, ITS TRIBUTARIES AND SHORELINE

The Hudson River of today is nothing like the river that Henry Hudson explored in the seventeenth century. Studies have shown that the river between Athens and Troy was once a braided waterway with many secondary channels. It was dominated by intertidal and shallow water habitats of less than two meters in depth that included more than sixty islands (Miller, Ladd, and Nieder 2006). This river must have teemed with waterfowl, shorebirds, and waders. However, these shallows impeded navigation. Like many a modern boater, Hudson himself ran aground on a bank of ooze in the middle of the river near Castleton and had to wait for the next high tide to continue his journey.

After completion of the Erie Canal in 1825, efforts to improve the channel to Albany began in earnest. The state tried to reduce erosion from the riverbanks by constructing spur dikes that projected out from the shoreline into the current. The construction also blocked secondary channels to increase flow and scour a single narrow but deeper channel, through dredging where necessary. The federal government took over in 1831, and the Army Corps of Engineers built longitudinal dikes, still visible at low tide, parallel to the current to constrict the flow and increase scour (Collins and Miller 2011). Dredging increased, and the spoils were placed behind the dikes. Shallow areas were filled, and former islands were joined to each other or to the mainland, where they became part of the river's floodplain. Today, periodic dredging continues on parts of the river between New York City and Albany to maintain the shipping channel at a depth of a little over thirty feet. The price for maintaining the Upper Hudson River estuary as a major commercial shipping channel has been the loss of nearly three thousand acres of shallows, many miles of shoreline, and more than forty islands, all natural communities that undoubtedly provided important habitat for many birds.

Like the Native Americans, European settlers lived close to the river to take advantage of the fertile soils and efficient transportation. Residential development, agriculture, industry, and transportation concentrated on the river's shorelines. By the mid-1800s, the railroads linked Manhattan and Albany. Dependable year-round transportation made it possible to export more goods to New York City; this fueled industries such as ice harvesting and brickmaking, which further altered or degraded natural habitats.

Before refrigeration, from the early 1800s until about World War I, ice companies cut blocks of ice from the frozen river in winter. Steam-powered conveyors moved the large blocks into icehouses for storage and later distribution to consumers by boat, rail, or wagon. At its peak, the ice industry employed thousands of seasonal workers (Calandro 2005; Harris and Pickman 2000). Remnants of the more than one hundred icehouses that dotted the shoreline between New York and Albany, mostly on the middle and upper parts of the river, are still evident today.

The Hudson Valley brickmaking industry began in the mid-seventeenth century, but boomed in the mid-1800s, when horrific fires in New York City destroyed hundreds of wooden structures, and building codes required the use of more fireproof materials. Brick production made use of the clay left behind by Glacial Lake Albany along the shores of the river from Mechanicville to Haverstraw. The old clay pits are marked on topographic maps. On the landscape, the pits appear as deep hollows; and when explored, some remain littered with bricks from the past. Brickmaking continued in the Hudson Valley for nearly three and a half centuries, but declined as profits decreased when new building materials became available (Hutton 2003).

Harvesting ice on the Hudson River circa 1912.
New York State Archives.

THE UPLANDS

At the time of European settlement, land away from the river was heavily forested, except perhaps for small tracts burned by Native Americans for agriculture and wildlife (Day 1953). The warmer valley forests were dominated by oak and chestnut, while northern hardwood forests, composed of beech, maple, yellow birch, hemlock, and white pine, covered cooler sites including the Taconics and the Catskills. Some of the highest elevations supported extensive stands of spruce, fir, and paper birch (Cronon 1983).

When the Dutch and later the English arrived, they set about clearing the land for agriculture. They built dams on tributary streams, used waterpower to run sawmills, and then exported ship masts and firewood to Europe. Oak, chestnut, and especially hemlock, which grew in dense stands on north-facing slopes in the Catskills, were cut for their bark and used in the tanning industry through most of the nineteenth century. After the Civil War, farms were abandoned as agriculture moved west into the more fertile prairies of the central United States. The first farms to be abandoned were the least productive: those located on thin, marginal soil and steeper north-facing slopes. The more profitable homesteads on better soils hung on longer, but by the turn of the twentieth century, nearly all the forests in the Hudson Valley had been cut over at least once and sometimes two or three times (Swaney, Limberg, and Stainbrook 2006).

Because of farm abandonment, forest cover in the valley has increased over the last 150 years. However, because of their historic land use and past disturbance, the mature forests of today are very different from the relatively undisturbed primary forests that greeted European settlers. In today's Hudson Valley, chestnut oak and northern red oak forests dominate the steep, rocky sites that were selectively cut but probably never used for agriculture. Poorer soils at lower elevations that were once pasture now support white and black oak and pignut hickory. Areas with the best soils, the ones used for cultivated crops, typically succeeded to woods of red maple and white pine woodlands (Glitzenstein et al. 1990).

Natural succession following farm abandonment took place in a world influenced by human activities. Abandoned farms were sometimes reforested with plantations of trees provided by government-sponsored programs. Chestnut blight and Dutch elm disease led to the decline and near elimination of the American chestnut and elm, trees that were common in the original forests. Today's forests also contain nonnative plants that were not present on this continent before European settlement. Norway maple, tree of heaven, Japanese barberry, multiflora rose, Oriental bittersweet, and garlic mustard are all introduced exotics that are now common in many Hudson Valley forests.

Humans have also interfered with natural processes that play a key role in maintaining some kinds of forest communities. Natural fires fueled by oak leaves were important in maintaining the species composition of some forest types, especially pine barrens and oak-dominated ridges in the Hudson Highlands and Shawangunk (pronounced shawn-gum) Mountains. The elimination of fire has altered the species composition of these fire-dependent forest communities, which now favor red maples and black locust.

Along with the flora, forest wildlife has also changed. For example, without natural predators, which were removed in part by hunting activities and habitat loss, white-tailed deer populations have exploded. These herbivores devour tree seedlings, and this impedes natural regeneration of the existing forest habitat. Conversely, beaver population densities are likely lower now than during presettlement times, although these populations are on the rebound. Open beaver meadows in forest ecosystems significantly increase bird diversity (Smith and Marks 2008).

The Physical Setting of Today's Hudson Valley

For practical reasons, the birdwatching sites in this book are chosen from the ten counties that border the Hudson River between the Troy Dam and New York City, but the Hudson River watershed extends well beyond these counties. The Hudson River collects water from a 13,326-square-mile area that includes not only most of the land in eastern New York, but also small parts of Vermont, Massachusetts, and New Jersey. The river travels 315 miles from its origins in the high peaks of the Adirondacks to the Atlantic Ocean in New York City.

THE RIVER

During this journey, the Hudson River changes dramatically. In the Adirondacks north of Glens Falls, the watershed is heavily forested. The water is cold, clear, shallow, fast moving, and filled with whitewater rapids. Below Glens Falls, the Hudson becomes a different river. Now lower, slower, and wider, its movement is controlled by a series of dams as it passes through a mostly rural landscape of pastures and farmland.

The federal dam at Troy, 154 miles north of New York City, marks another transition. From this point south, there are no more dams. The river is open to the sea, and freshwater draining the land mixes with salt water from the ocean. South of Troy, the river becomes an estuary, one of the most productive ecosystems on earth. The amount of salt water in the Hudson River increases along a gradient from north to south. Because salt water is denser than freshwater, it moves north up the Hudson from the ocean along the bottom of the river. How far seawater intrudes depends on the amount of freshwater flowing in from the watershed. The location of this "salt front" changes, depending on rainfall or snow melt. In dry summers, it sometimes reaches as far north as Newburgh. Between Troy and Newburgh, the Hudson River water is considered freshwater, while south of Newburgh, its salinity makes it brackish.

Another feature of the Hudson River estuary is that it is tidal. Like tides on the oceans, tides on the Hudson River result from the gravitational pull

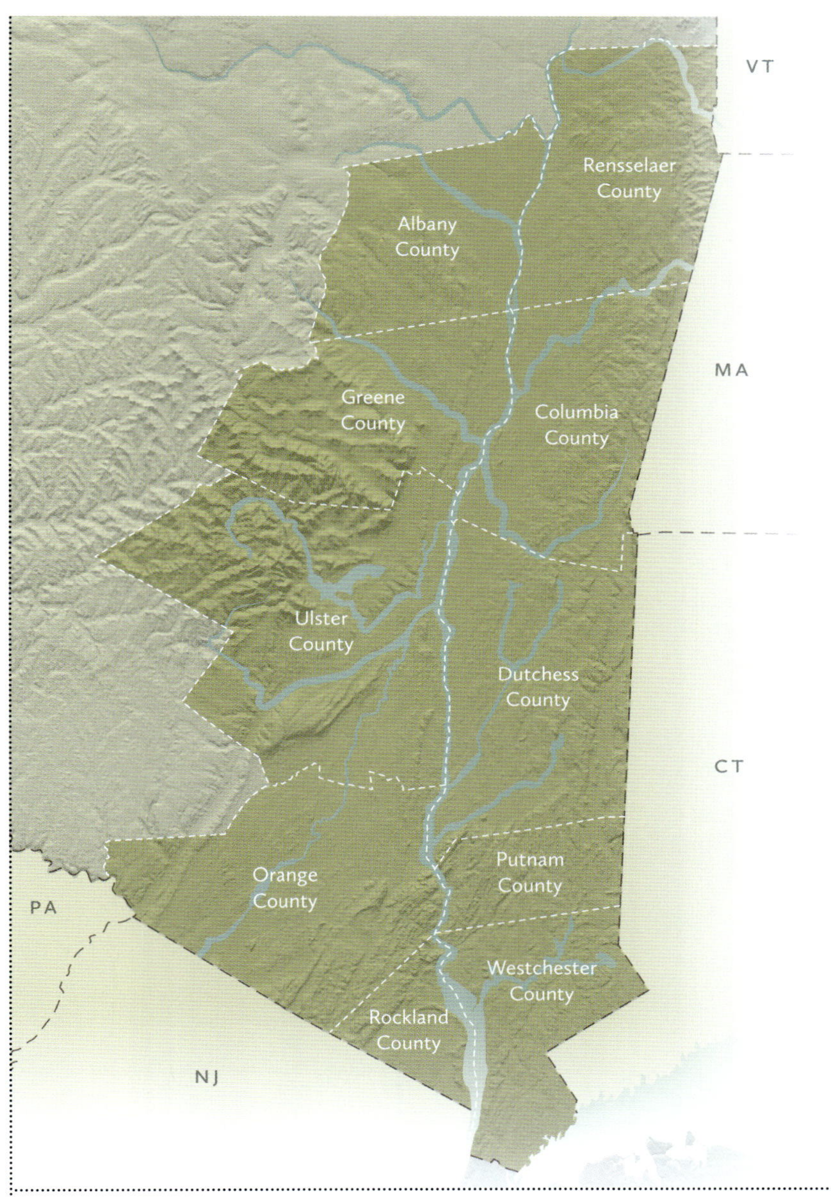

COUNTIES OF THE HUDSON VALLEY

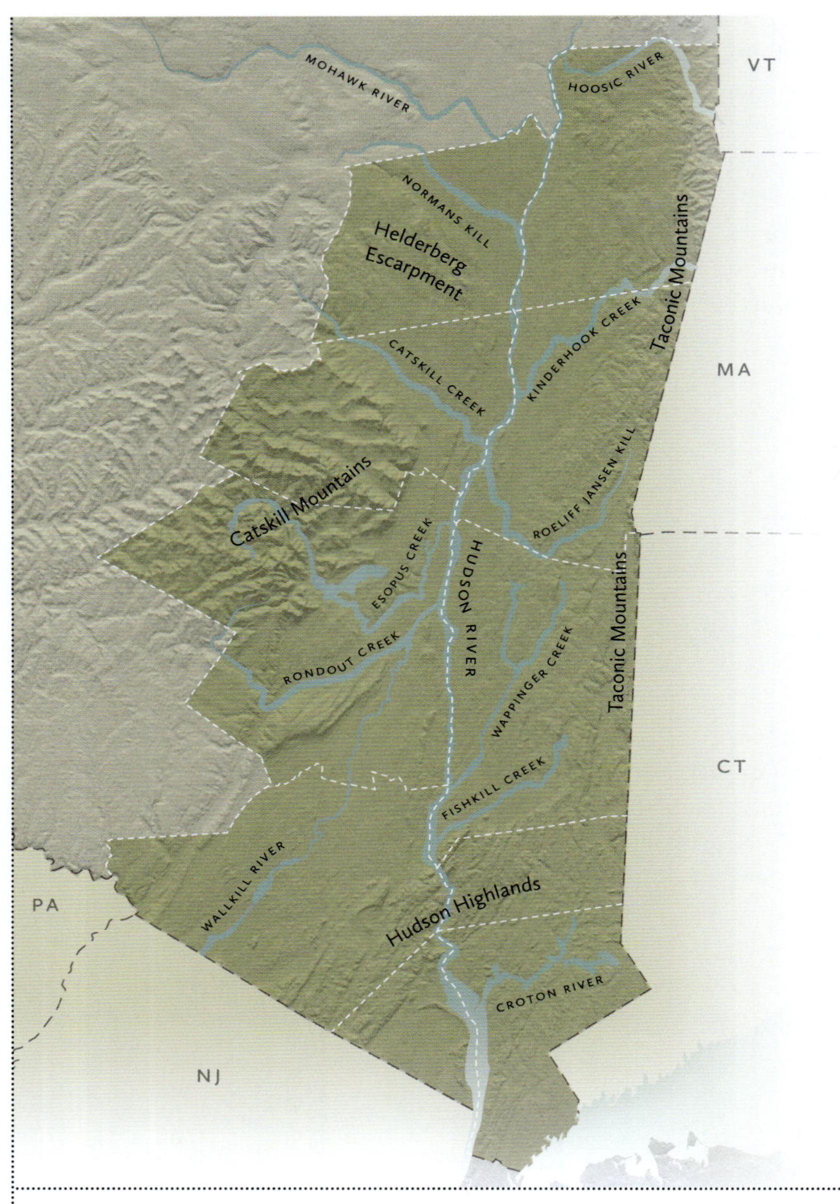

THE HUDSON RIVER AND ITS MAJOR TRIBUTARIES

of the moon and the sun. The river has two high and two low tides every twenty-four hours and fifty minutes, with the timing changing from day to day. The tide travels up the river like a wave from the ocean, taking nine hours to reach Troy, so the timing of the tide also varies with location. High tide at Newburgh occurs earlier than high tide further north at Troy. The tide deposits sediments on the shore and washes them back into the river as it recedes. As a result, the water in the tidal Hudson River is never clear, but the turbidity is actually the rich organic matter suspended in the water column that makes the estuary so productive for fish and wildlife.

The difference in water level between high and low tides changes with the phase of the moon and the shape of the river channel. Tides tend to be more extreme when the earth, sun, and moon are in alignment, as they are during full or new moons. These are called spring tides, a confusing term that has nothing to do with the season, but instead refers to the tide's tendency to "spring forth" under this orientation. Tides are weaker when the sun and moon are at right angles to each other, as they are during half moons, when their gravitational pulls partially cancel each other out. These "neap" tides have a smaller tidal range (Strayer 2012).

For birders along the Hudson River, tides are important because they change the depth of the water. Canoeists in a tidal marsh need to know what to expect from the tide, and it is wise to check a reliable online tide table (for example, those provided by the National Oceanic and Atmospheric Administration, NOAA) before heading out on the river. Some shallow areas are accessible only at high tide, and a falling tide can leave one stranded. Moreover, at low tide, gulls, shorebirds, waders, and other water birds feed on exposed mudflats, rocks, and shallows along the shores, but these birds hide in the marshes out of sight during high tide. Planning around the tides can make the difference between seeing birds and not seeing birds. Just remember that freshwater inflows are important, and tides are not always as predictable as tide tables might have you believe.

THE LAND

The terrestrial landscape of the Hudson Valley is wonderfully diverse. One of the easiest ways to describe the land is to group it into regions that share similar ecological characteristics. New York State has several different landscape classification systems, but the ecozones used here were developed by the New York State Department of Environmental Conservation (NYSDEC or the DEC) to map and describe areas with comparable natural and cultural features (Dickinson 1979, 1983). The land within each ecozone has a common geological origin and climate, so the topography, vegetation, and wildlife tend to be similar. The descriptions for these six ecozones are a framework for understanding the Hudson Valley landscape.

APPALACHIAN PLATEAU On the west side of the Hudson River, the northwestern edge of the Appalachians reaches into the Hudson Valley to form the Helderberg Highlands, the Catskill Mountains, the Schoharie Hills, and the Neversink Highlands. This region features flat-topped mountains and rolling hills with steep escarpments, deep ravines, and fast-moving streams that form a large part of the western Hudson River watershed. The high peaks of the Catskills in western Greene and Ulster Counties have the highest elevations in the ten-county area, reaching altitudes over thirty-five hundred feet. These uplands have cold, snowy winters and cool summers. The land is more than 75 percent forested. Northern hardwood forests of beech, maple, and hemlock dominate, but oaks are prevalent on south-facing slopes, hemlocks occupy cool ravines, and patches of mountain spruce-fir forest occur at elevations over three thousand feet.

HUDSON VALLEY Once covered by Glacial Lake Albany, the land immediately west and east of the Hudson River is now a lowland of gentle, rolling plains bordered by low hills that generally rise only a few hundred feet above sea level. The climate is relatively moist and mild, with warm summers, cold winters, and moderate rainfall that is evenly distributed throughout the year. Because of this combination of flat topography, rich soils, and mild climate, the region is largely agricultural. Transportation infrastructure is well developed here, and population densities in this region have always been high compared to surrounding areas. The presettlement hardwood forests have been cleared many times, and successional forests and fields of red cedar dominate today's abandoned farmlands. The streams in this region are tributaries of the Hudson that are tidal near their confluence with the river.

TACONIC HIGHLANDS The spine of the Taconic Ridge forms much of the eastern border of New York State with Massachusetts and Connecticut. These low mountains, with elevations under three thousand feet, descend into rolling foothills toward the Hudson Valley. The Rensselaer Plateau, a

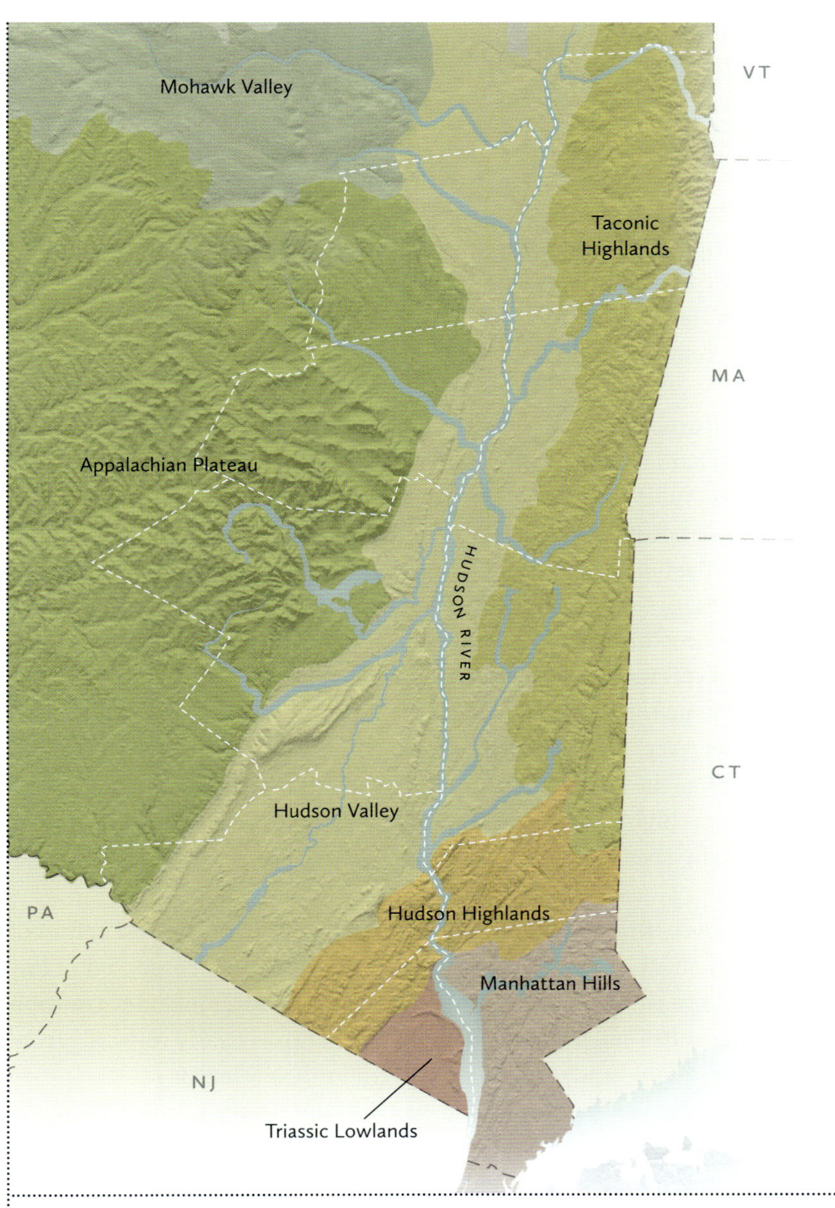

ECOZONES OF THE HUDSON VALLEY

high-elevation area in central Rensselaer County, has escarpments on all sides and thin, rocky, poorly drained soils that are not suited for agriculture. With an average elevation of about fifteen hundred feet, this hilly landscape has cold, snowy winters. The plateau is more than 80 percent forested, with many areas of spruce and balsam, while the Taconic Mountains have extensive woodlands dominated by northern hardwoods.

The Taconic foothills are far less wooded, with a considerable amount of agriculture, many old fields, and woodlands in various stages of succession. Population densities in the Taconics are generally low, but are increasing with the recent rise in development of vacation properties.

HUDSON HIGHLANDS Geologically, the Hudson Highlands are composed of a strip of hard igneous and metamorphic rock that cuts diagonally across the Hudson Valley and forms low mountains, under two thousand feet in elevation, on both sides of the river in the vicinity of West Point. The highlands form the border between Orange and Rockland Counties, and occupy most of Putnam County on the east side of the river. Rising steeply from the shoreline along this narrow part of the river, the rocky outcrops form some of the most spectacular scenery in the Hudson Valley.

On this steep topography, the soils are thin and acidic. Oaks interspersed with smaller tracts of northern hardwoods dominate forested land. A significant portion of the land in the Hudson Highlands is publicly owned. Population density is high so close to New York City, and much of the unprotected land has been developed for homes and industry.

TRIASSIC LOWLANDS This small ecological zone in the southwest corner of the study area covers southern Rockland County. Mostly composed of low hills, its eastern edge on the west side of the Hudson River includes a portion of the famous Palisades, a large escarpment that rises nearly vertically from the river's shoreline and extends southward into New Jersey.

Warm, humid summers and mild, wet winters are the norm. The region is only 23 percent forested, and more than 60 percent of the land has been altered by development. The remaining forests are dominated by oak and northern hardwoods.

MANHATTAN HILLS The hilly topography and bare rock outcrops of the Manhattan Hills give Westchester County its distinctive, rugged appearance.

Elevations range from sea level near Long Island Sound and the Hudson River to about seven hundred feet. Oak forests predominate in undeveloped tracts and occupy about 35 percent of the land, nearly half of which is developed.

Similar to the Triassic Lowlands in climate, the region has wet, mild winters and warm, humid summers.

2 In the Beginning, There Was Birdwatching

Millions of people worldwide call themselves birdwatchers, but not all of them are birders. Both love birds, and nearly all birders start out as birdwatchers, but somewhere along the line, some birdwatchers undergo a transformation that makes them passionate about their interest in birds. No longer content to sit home and watch birds at a feeder or note the birds in the backyard, they begin to seek out birds in new and different places.

More than anything else, it is this desire to see more that separates birders from birdwatchers. What triggers this transformation varies from one individual to another. For many, it is an unforgettable up-close-and-personal experience with a particular bird. Sometimes a teacher or mentor plays a key role in igniting the passion, but birdwatchers and birders are different creatures. Birders study the birds they hope to see. They keep data and lists, and they travel seeking particular species.

Why don't more birdwatchers become birders? Partly, it may be an image problem. Historically, the term birdwatcher conjured up images of dweebs and retirees with binoculars, oblivious to the world around them. However, that view is rapidly changing. While the demographics are still skewed toward older Americans who have more free time and disposable income, today's birders are a diverse group that includes students, professional scientists, well-educated amateurs, outdoor enthusiasts, photographers, and ardent conservationists. They wear their binoculars with pride and mingle with others who do the same. Moreover, birders are friendly and passionate about their pastime. They love sharing their knowledge and turning others on to birding.

This chapter is aimed at the backyard birdwatcher who is interested in birds and likely has a bird feeder, but is not yet a true birder. Almost every accomplished birder started out at a feeder and graduated to more exciting birdwatching adventures. Done well, backyard birding provides a way for novices to develop their observation, identification, and documentation skills in a comfortable environment—a very good place to start. The advice that follows is designed to send backyard birdwatchers into the world of birding with a solid foundation for building new skills.

Tools for Getting Started

Basic birdwatching requires only binoculars and an identification guide, but these tools of the trade are constantly changing. We live in a world of technological innovation, where scientific advances make fine optics better every year, and new software applications (apps) are quickly replacing books and CDs. Beginners do not need the latest and greatest (and often the most expensive) tools to get started, but having the right basic equipment is crucial because it prevents frustration and makes birdwatching more fun.

BINOCULARS FOR BIRDING

A surprising number of beginning birdwatchers do not have the binoculars they need to see birds well. Binoculars are made for many different purposes. The type that works best for birdwatching is not the same as the types needed for boating, sports, operas, backpacking, astronomy, butterfly watching, or hunting. Unfortunately, beginners usually start out with borrowed binoculars, and these are often poorly suited for viewing birds. It's fine to start with inferior optics, but honing your birding skills and making the transition from birdwatcher to birder require binoculars that are appropriate for the task.

Obtaining the proper equipment does not have to be expensive. Used equipment is fine, and most longtime birders will tell you that they have owned more than one pair of binoculars during their birding careers. Most birders buy up as their skills mature and new models become available. Beginners can buy a fine pair of brand-new birding binoculars for $200 to $500, and used ones for significantly less. The key is knowing which binocular features are most important for watching birds.

MAGNIFICATION AND FIELD OF VIEW
Binoculars come with printed numbers such as 7x42, 8x32, or 10x50. The first number is the magnification or power of the binoculars. Though it seems counterintuitive, higher magnification is not always better, because small differences in magnification are barely perceptible to many people. Plus, there is a trade-off between magnification

and the field of view, or the area you can see. A larger field of view that covers a bigger three-dimensional area makes it easier to find a moving bird, a key consideration in birdwatching. Most birders favor binoculars with 7x or 8x magnification instead of 10x because of the larger field of view. Compact or "mini" binoculars are not recommended for beginning birders, because they have a very small field of view that makes it difficult to locate birds.

BRIGHTNESS The second number written after the magnification is the objective diameter in millimeters; that is, the width of the lens farthest from your eye. The size of this lens and the magnification work together to determine how much light reaches your eyes. Brightness is an important consideration for birding under low-light conditions, which might be encountered in deep woods, on cloudy days, or at dawn and dusk. While bigger objectives let in more light, they also add size and weight. Nonreflective coatings also help deliver more light to the eyes. To maximize brightness, look for binoculars where all the glass elements are "fully multicoated."

RESOLUTION AND FOCUS Resolution is the ability to distinguish two objects; but more simply, it relates to the sharpness of the image. You can test the resolution of binoculars by focusing them on a newspaper tacked to a wall. Resolution is a function of the quality of the glass used in binoculars. Good glass is expensive and contributes greatly to the cost of high-end binoculars. Glass quality is usually adequate with binoculars that sell for at least $200.

Because birds move, birding binoculars need to focus quickly and efficiently. A center-focus wheel that falls within easy reach of your index finger is best. If possible, it's a good idea to hold several different models to see how they feel in your hands and to test your ability to focus them quickly. Avoid inefficient zoom binoculars.

EYE RELIEF If you wear glasses, or especially if you switch between glasses and contacts, be sure that your binoculars have adjustable eye relief. Glasses prevent the user from holding the lenses against the eyes. With glasses, the ocular lenses sit fifteen to twenty millimeters away and reduce the field of view. Birding binoculars should have adjustable eyecups that can be rolled or screwed down to compensate for the increased distance.

OTHER CONSIDERATIONS Binoculars usually come with a neck strap. A wider strap is generally more comfortable, but hanging even the most lightweight

Birding with binoculars, the tools of the trade. © Carena M. Pooth.

binoculars from your neck for more than a few hours can be hard on your neck and back. For this reason, many people invest in an inexpensive binocular harness that distributes the weight more comfortably and has the added advantage of holding the binoculars close to the body, where they are less likely to be damaged. It takes some practice to put a binocular harness on efficiently, but many birders like to use them.

Birders are tough on binoculars. Because binoculars are fine pieces of optical equipment, they are vulnerable to shocks, which can knock the lenses out of alignment. Dirt damages the coatings and glass, and if water infiltrates the housing, the image becomes foggy. These vulnerabilities are the reason that expensive, top-of-the-line binoculars are armored with a hard rubber outer shell and are waterproof. Until you can afford these features, try to avoid dropping your binoculars or knocking them into things unnecessarily. Never leave them on the roof or seat of a car. Put them on the floor instead, and keep them out of the rain as much as possible. If you drop your binoculars in water, they will need an expensive professional cleaning.

It is a good idea to clean binoculars once in a while to remove pieces of vegetation, dust, crumbs, and fingerprints. However, improper cleaning can do more harm than good. The first step should always be to gently remove particles of grit and grime with a camel's hair brush, the brush of a lens pen, or a can of compressed air. Removing debris before wiping the lenses prevents the coatings or glass from being scratched. Nearly all spots and fingerprints come off by gently rubbing them with lens-cleaning paper or a microfiber cloth specifically designed for cleaning lenses. If spots still remain, use a small amount of water or isopropyl alcohol–based lens cleaning solution on lens paper or a microfiber cloth, and rub gently. Do not use any lens cleaner that contains ammonia, because it can damage the coatings.

FIELD GUIDES

Besides binoculars, a field guide is the only other essential birding tool. Field guides are books or apps that are carried in the field and used to identify birds, but birdwatchers also use field guides indoors as textbooks to study bird identification. Most birders own more than one field guide or identification app, but if they take a hard-copy guide into the field, they carry only one. Cell phones, with their ability to store field data and bird identification apps, may one day replace books for bird identification in the field. Today's apps use a lot of storage space, and the GPS features sap battery strength, especially if the weather is cold, so it's a good practice to keep a traditional field guide on hand as a backup. Hard-copy field guides still have their place for at-home bird study.

There are dozens of field guides on the market, and new books and apps are produced every year. There are also specialized taxonomic guides for difficult groups such as warblers, gulls, shorebirds, and hawks in flight. To some extent, choosing a field guide is a matter of personal taste, and the one that is right for you today may not fill your needs when your birding skills mature. That said, here are some things to consider when selecting your first field guide.

COVERAGE A good field guide must include all of the birds you are likely to see. If you do most of your birding in the eastern United States, then a guide to the birds of eastern North America is a good choice, but you will need to buy another book for your trip to California. Beginners often like books and apps with smaller geographic coverage because they contain fewer birds to sort through, but beginners almost always graduate to guides that cover more ground. Most bird identification apps can be set to cover various states and provinces, a flexibility that books cannot offer.

PORTABILITY The best field guides are small enough to fit into an easily accessible pocket; this leaves your hands free to hold your binoculars. Digital apps are, of course, as portable as your cell phone and are accessible for as long as the battery holds out.

ORGANIZATION AND LAYOUT A good field guide puts all the information you need to home in on a correct identification in one place, including pictures, seasonal distribution and range, and text. It is difficult to fit all this information on one page or two facing pages of a small book, but some guides do this fairly well. The amount and quality of the text varies greatly.

Historically, the books used for bird identification have presented the birds in roughly phylogenetic order, putting the most primitive birds first and the more recently evolved species toward the end. Although evolution is not linear, most North American guides did their best to straighten out the tree of life by adopting the scientific order of the American Ornithological Society's (AOS; formerly the AOU) *Checklist of North and Middle American Birds* and its supplements. This order has the advantage of grouping together birds with shared traits, such as webbed feet or hooked bills. It also taught students some of the characteristics of bird families, to show how woodpeckers differ from thrushes, for example. While taxonomic order was never transparent to beginners, with such guides it was fairly easy to learn.

New field guides may be organized differently. Recent editions of the AOS *Checklist* have shuffled the orders and families of birds based on discoveries in molecular biology. It is unclear if the authors of future field guides will organize their books around the new evolutionary relationships, or choose a user-friendly method of organization that groups similar birds together.

Bird identification apps, because they are digital, can and do contain a lot more information than books, including additional images and vocalizations. These auditory cues are frequently helpful and sometimes essential in making an ID. The best apps help you pin an ID on your bird by doing some of the sorting for you, using the date, your GPS location, and smart search tools to narrow down the choices. However, the number of species and the amount of material is sometimes overwhelming for beginners, and its accessibility varies greatly from one application to the next.

BOOKS AND APPS Traditional field guide books are widely available at local book and bird stores, and apps can be found online. Some apps are free, and others have "lite" versions that let you test out the program. As a starting point, here are a few widely used general field guides and apps to consider:

The Sibley Field Guide to Birds of Eastern North American (2016) by David Sibley. Packed with illustrations, including birds in flight and seasonal plumages, Sibley's guide and accompanying app feature remarkable artwork and rich text that makes for fascinating reading.

Peterson Field Guide to the Birds of Eastern and Central North America (2010) by Roger Tory Peterson. This book, first published in 1934, is best known for the "Peterson arrows" that point to "field marks" that are useful in identification.

National Geographic Field Guide to the Birds of North America (2011) by Jon Dunn and Jonathan Alderfer. Available in the smaller split eastern and western versions, this book covers all of North America and includes many rare species not found in other field guides.

Merlin Bird ID by Cornell Lab of Ornithology. Free and designed for the true beginner, this app arrives at an ID by asking questions about size, color, and habitat, and then using GPS location and date to create a photographic lineup of potential species. A great starting point for novices, the app currently covers nearly all the most likely species, and the latest version can even identify birds from photos.

iBird by Mitch Waite Group. The first bird app on the market, this popular guide now comes in different versions with increasing levels of sophistication and cost.

Audubon Bird Guide: North America by National Audubon Society (NAS). This free app covers more than eight hundred North American species, includes a rich variety of vocalizations for each bird, and links to eBird data (an online checklist detailed later in this chapter).

Bird Feeders as a Stepping-Stone to Birding

Feeding birds is a great way to start birdwatching. Many nature lovers feed birds to "help them out" in winter when food is scarce, but the reality is that wild birds do not need our help. There is little scientific evidence that bird feeding increases winter survival, or that letting feeders go empty increases winter mortality (Brittingham and Temple 1988). Bird feeding should be viewed as a practice that increases our enjoyment of birds because it offers

A bird feeder is a good way to start birdwatching. © Denise Hackert-Stoner, Naturelogues.

the opportunity to view birds at close range. That said, feeding birds comes with responsibilities. Improper bird feeding can actually harm birds.

FEEDING BIRDS RESPONSIBLY

Bird feeders should be located in a place that is easy to see and close to low shrubs that birds can use to escape from free-ranging cats and bird-eating raptors like Cooper's Hawk and Sharp-shinned Hawk. Window crashes are a significant source of mortality at feeders, and locating a feeder within three feet of a window makes the birds slow down enough to prevent harm. An alternative is to place feeders at least thirty feet away from windows. The right location can also help you avoid feeding squirrels, who clean out feeders and prey on bird's eggs and nestlings. Try to place feeders at least ten feet from tree branches. If that is not possible, these varmints can usually be deterred with a well-designed squirrel-proof feeder or the addition of baffles, either

An immature Cooper's Hawk hunting small birds at a bird feeder. © Scott Stoner, Naturelogues.

stovepipe or eighteen-inch tilting baffles, above and below the feeder.

The bird-feeding operations that attract the greatest bird diversity provide a variety of foods in different settings, with black oil sunflower seed as the primary offering. Presenting food at different levels, from the ground to the treetops, and using hopper, platform, tube, nectar, and suet feeders, attracts a nice mix of birds. While nearly all birds like black oil sunflower, some species are also enticed by other fare, such as safflower (Northern Cardinal); nyjer, a.k.a. thistle (American Goldfinch, Pine Siskin, Common Redpoll); white proso millet (Dark-eyed Junco, White-throated Sparrow); cracked corn (Wild Turkey, Mourning Dove); suet (woodpeckers, nuthatches); sugar water (hummingbirds); and fruit (Baltimore Oriole, Gray Catbird).

Poor feeder hygiene can spread disease. Feeders should be scrubbed and washed periodically with a 10 percent bleach solution to remove feces and old caked seed, and to destroy pathogens. It is best to store seed in a metal can to keep it dry and protected from rodents. Because sunflower seed is mostly fat, it sometimes turns rancid. Wet or moldy food should never be used. The accumulated shells under feeders should be raked up and removed from time to time because they harbor pathogens and attract pests such as rats, skunks, raccoons, or bears.

Bears like bird seed. If you live in bear country, you should probably not feed birds between the first of April and the end of November. Once bears raid a feeder, they are inevitably attracted to others, so the only long-term solution to avoid conflicts between humans and bears is to remove the attraction (New York State Department of Environmental Conservation). Feed the birds in winter when the bears are hibernating.

LEARNING TO BIRD AT A FEEDER

A bird feeder is a good place to begin learning some of the skills needed to become a real birder. A feeder brings birds into a seminatural setting where you can practice using binoculars to see them. The birds are easier to identify because even the best feeding operations usually attract only a limited number of common species. Finally, feeder birds offer an opportunity to learn how to record data, including date, time, species, behaviors, and other information that would otherwise be lost and forgotten. When bird observations are properly documented, they can be studied, analyzed, listed, compared, and shared with others.

GETTING ON THE BIRD Finding and actually seeing birds through binoculars takes some practice. Birds are moving targets, but a feeder brings birds to predictable perches. To see a bird through your binoculars, hold them with both hands and lift them off your chest, so that they are under your eyes.

Bird feeders that attract black bears should be removed from April through November.
© Carena M. Pooth.

Purple Finch or House Finch? An identification challenge to master at a bird feeder.
© Bruce Dudek; © Deborah Tracy-Kral.

Choose a bird to look at with your naked eye. Keeping your eyes on the bird, bring the binoculars up to your eyes and focus. If you are lucky, the bird will be there, but it's easy to be off target, and sometimes the bird moves. Wait a few seconds, and if the bird does not come into your field of view, lower the binoculars away from your eyes just a little and look over the top. Spot the bird with your unaided eyes, and try again. Sometimes an obvious reference point, like a dead leaf or broken twig that is near the bird, can help you find your target. Scanning large areas with binoculars is rarely the best way to find a bird. Disciplined birders fix their gaze on the target and bring the binoculars to bear on the bird. Once you have learned to find a bird at a feeder, make it harder by choosing birds that are on the ground among shrubs or in nearby foliage. Mastering the skill of "getting on the bird" is fundamental to birding.

SEEING WHAT IS IMPORTANT A bird feeder is a good but imperfect place to learn bird identification. Because the birds are usually viewed from indoors, important outdoor bird identification clues, such as vocalizations and habitat, are lost. Nevertheless, feeder birds are a good place for beginners to start because the birds are easy to see and they make repeat appearances. A feeder offers a chance to develop careful observation skills, to learn how to use your field guide, and to become intimately familiar with a few common species before ever setting foot in the field.

Because birds move, it is critically important to keep an unfamiliar bird in view as long as possible, making mental notes of everything that might help in identification. Try to avoid taking your binoculars off the bird. Wait until it disappears from sight or until you have a complete mental picture of it. Since many birds are seen only briefly, the trick is to note as much information as possible, before it is gone forever.

Start with shape, size, and posture. It is surprisingly difficult to judge the size of a lone bird, but thinking of size in relative terms makes it easier. Try to determine how big the bird is compared to a chickadee, robin, crow, or Canada Goose. Next, take note of its shape. Is it chunky like a Blue Jay or slender like a Red-winged Blackbird? Does it perch upright like a woodpecker or crouch like a sparrow?

Look closely at the bird, working your way from head to tail. The shape and length of the beak is especially useful. Is it needlelike, hooked, swollen at the base, or conical? Note the length of the bill relative to the size of the bird's head, because this dimension can distinguish look-alikes such as Hairy and Downy Woodpeckers. How long is the tail relative to the bird's body, and how far down the tail do the tips of the wings project? On long-winged birds, the tips reach far down the tail or even beyond the end.

Look closely at the plumage for details, or field marks. Does it have wing bars, an eye ring, or a line over the eye? Note the location of each color and how far each pattern extends. For example, does the streaked breast continue down onto the abdomen and flanks?

Pay attention to behavior and numbers. Does the bird stay on the ground or perch in trees or shrubs? Does it actually take food from the feeder, and if so, what does it eat? Is the bird all by itself, or is it part of a flock of similar birds? Try to count how many there are. At a feeder, a good way to get a decent estimate of the number of individuals of one species is to determine the maximum number present at any one time.

IDENTIFYING THE BIRD AND RECORDING OBSERVATIONS Once the bird is gone or you have all the information you can get, it is time to use your field guide, book, or app to try to pin an ID on the bird you saw. How you use your guide will depend on its design, but no matter which tool you use, your ability to identify birds will be greatly improved if you take the time to read its introduction. Arriving at an ID is basically a process of narrowing down the possibilities based on various criteria such as date, location, and all of the characteristics that you observed. Apps have filters that can substitute for leafing through a book. When you think you know what you've seen, read the text, make note of the field marks, look at the range map, listen to the vocalizations (even if you did not hear any), and study the information. See if you can determine if your bird was male or female, adult or immature. You may not be able to identify every bird you see, but you can probably narrow things down and figure out what features to look for the next time you encounter the same bird.

Record the birds you identify and other observations as soon as possible. There are many good reasons to document bird sightings, but the most important is that keeping records makes you a better birdwatcher. Noting what you see forces you to look closely and hone your observation skills. The very act of writing it down helps commit the bird to memory by allowing you to review and reconsider what you saw, gain new insights, or catch mistakes. Keeping track of birds by date calls attention to their seasonality, because arrivals and departures become more evident.

At one time, birders kept all their observations in notebooks and journals, but modern birders can use eBird (ebird.org), an online checklist program launched in 2002 by the Cornell Lab of Ornithology and the National Audubon Society. EBird is free and simple to use, and the online instructions are straightforward. You simply record where, when, and how you went birding, and then fill out an online checklist to record all the birds you saw and heard, making use of as many data fields as possible to record all of your observations. Local experts review the sightings to ensure that errors do not enter the system; in this way, beginners have a chance to learn from their mistakes. For birders, the beauty of eBird is that it uses technology to instantly create cumulative bird lists such as life lists, yard lists, county lists, year lists, and the like. By entering data in eBird, the birding community has helped create a huge database that is used to share sightings and study bird populations.

3   From Birdwatcher to Birder

Backyard bird feeding is a gateway to the bigger and better world of birding. Feeders can provide a good introduction to birds, a chance to sample what birding has to offer; but feeder watching is no substitute for the real thing, and some people get tired of feeding birds once the bird diversity stabilizes into a group of regular visitors. Bird-feeder fatigue is the perfect reason to start looking for birds beyond your backyard. Discovering what birding has to offer involves actually "going birding," that is, taking your binoculars and field guide out of the house and into the world in search of birds.

This chapter is about going birding and looking for birds in new and different places. Bird feeders attract only a limited clientele. There are many new birds to see, but most of them will never come to feeders. They live in a variety of places, and the only way to see them is to go to where they are. Chasing birds is an adventure: a chance to discover not only new birds, but new places. Birding lets Mother Nature lead you on an exploration of the natural areas around you.

Birding is a form of outdoor recreation, a hobby, or even a sport that offers the opportunity to breathe fresh air, hike, and experience nature. Seeing birds in their natural habitat, where they find food, avoid predators, defend territories, mate, and raise young, provides an opportunity to learn about their behavior and understand how they live and survive. Birds are fascinating creatures, and watching them in the context of their natural environment helps us appreciate how birds make a living using the resources of forests, wetlands, grasslands, and other Hudson Valley ecosystems.

Before You Go—Staying Safe While Birding the Hudson Valley

Newly hatched outdoor enthusiasts sometimes forget that venturing into nature requires preparation. In addition to binoculars and a field guide,

A birder with her pants tucked into her socks to guard against ticks.
© Carena M. Pooth.

birders also need appropriate clothing and footwear for the weather and terrain, and enough food, water, and sun protection for the time in the field. A more thorough introduction to outdoor recreation is beyond the scope of this book, but it is important to note that Mother Nature deserves respect. Although most of the Hudson Valley is not far removed from civilization, a few safety issues deserve special mention.

From April to October, be prepared to encounter mosquitoes, ticks, and other biting creatures. A variety of debilitating tick-borne diseases have become more prevalent and worrisome in recent years, but even mosquitoes can carry disease. The best defense is to avoid being bitten by wearing long pants and long sleeves, and by using insect repellent. Ticks live in low vegetation and shrubbery and attach to unsuspecting humans who walk through these areas. Once on board, the tick climbs upward until it finds bare skin. Light-colored clothing makes ticks easier to see, and tucking your pants into your socks or wearing gaiters blocks the route up your legs. Avoiding encounters with ticks is a good reason to stay on the trails. A careful tick check, a hot shower, and washing your clothes after a day in the field are recommended. It is best to find ticks and remove them before they become embedded and have an opportunity to transfer bacteria to you, their host (Centers for Disease Control and Prevention 2017).

Two species of venomous snake, timber rattlesnake and northern copperhead, have small, isolated populations in the Catskills, the Hudson Highlands, and the Taconics. They live in dens in rocky ledges and are active from late April to mid-October. These snakes are naturally camouflaged and blend in with their surroundings, so it is important to watch for them, especially in open sunny areas where they bask in the sun on cold mornings. Closed footwear and protective clothing provide some protection, but the best strategy is to be vigilant in areas where snakes are present, and always give them a wide berth.

Timber Rattlesnake.
© Carena M. Pooth.

Poison ivy is a native plant that thrives in edge habitats in the Hudson Valley, especially along the river. Its clusters of three leaves grow as both a ground cover and a vine, sometimes hidden among other harmless vegetation. About 85 percent of humans are allergic to the oil, called urushiol, found in all parts of the plant, including the leaves, stems, roots, and berries. Any direct contact can result in a red, itchy rash that is not contagious, but is definitely miserable. Even people who think they are not allergic can become sensitized to poison ivy by repeated contact. The oil can also be transferred to the skin from clothing, pet fur, and tool handles. My unhappiest experience with poison ivy occurred when I removed my boots after a day in the field and walked around barefoot. The oil on the hems of my pants transferred to my feet, and the resulting rash made it impossible to wear shoes for a solid week! Learn what this plant looks like, and avoid it. Protect your skin with long sleeves and long pants, and wash any clothes that have come in contact with poison ivy before wearing them again. If your skin does come in contact with poison ivy, the oil can be removed with rubbing alcohol or vigorous and thorough washing with grease-cutting soap and water, but this needs to be done as soon as possible after contact. I carry alcohol wipes in my pack for poison ivy emergencies.

Birding by canoe or kayak is a great way to visit unique bird habitats, but

A particularly healthy
poison ivy vine.
© Alan W. Wells.

boating on the Hudson River is not to be taken lightly. New York State law requires personal floatation devices for all passengers, and these must be worn from November 1 to May 1. The main channel of the Hudson supports a major shipping route with tankers and barges that throw big wakes, and summer weekends see plenty of recreational boat traffic. Fortunately, birders can avoid most of these hazards by spending their time in the quiet marshes and coves where interesting birds are most likely to be seen, but it is imperative to check the tides before venturing into these areas. Many of the Hudson's outstanding tidal marshes are easily accessible on a rising tide, but low tide can leave boaters mired in mud with no easy way out when the water recedes.

Hunting for turkey, waterfowl, bear, deer, and other game is permitted and even encouraged at many of the sites described in this book. In the absence of natural predators like wolves, hunting is needed to reduce overbrowsing by deer, so that trees can reproduce. The New York State Department of Environmental Conservation sets specific hunting seasons annually, and these vary by location, but current information is always available at the agency's website (www.dec.ny.gov). In general, most hunting takes place in the fall, but the statewide spring turkey season in May overlaps with spring migration. It is wise to avoid birding sites where hunting is permitted during those seasons, especially the main big-game season for deer in late November.

The Annual Cycle

A bird is a finely tuned machine. Flying is energetically expensive, so every aspect of a bird's physiology is designed to use energy efficiently. Birds get their energy from the food they eat, and they need calories for everything they do. A bird can find only so much food, so any energy that is used for flight or heat production cannot be used for other energetically demanding activities, such as territorial defense, egg production, growing new feathers, or migrating. The birds of the Hudson Valley operate in a climate where day length, temperature, and food availability vary seasonally. Their ability to survive and reproduce depends on finding adequate food in a changing environment.

In the Hudson Valley and throughout the temperate zone, spring brings warm temperatures, longer days, and a flush of new insect life. Spring and summer are times of plenty for birds. Migrants move north, following the growing seasonal food supply. Temperatures are warm and food is abundant, so birds can allocate energy to reproduction. Most songbirds, regardless of what the adults eat, feed their rapidly growing young protein in the form of insects and other animal matter. These foods are reliable, widespread, and abundant in summer.

When the energetic demands of the breeding season are past, most adult birds replace all or most of their feather coat in a process called molt. Molt is a costly endeavor that takes place over a period of weeks and involves shedding and regenerating thousands of feathers. Birds generally do not have enough energy to molt and breed or migrate at the same time. Shorebirds and other birds that breed in the arctic, where summer is very short, often start molting on the breeding grounds, pause the molt during migration, and then complete it after they reach their wintering areas.

After the summer solstice, the days begin to get shorter, leaving birds with less time to find food. Cooler temperatures increase their energy demands, but because feathers are such wonderful insulators, birds are well equipped to deal with cold temperatures as long as they have enough food. Freezing temperatures kill most insects, greatly reducing the food supply. Some birds, like our resident Black-capped Chickadee, are able to shift their diet to include insect eggs, pupae, seeds, and fruits, but those that depend on insects, such as swallows, warblers, and vireos, migrate to the warmth of the Neotropics. For the birds that stay, winter is all about avoiding predation and getting enough food to survive until the next breeding season.

Find the Food, Find the Bird

Food is vitally important to birds. Ultimately, it is food availability that drives the seasonality of breeding and migration and the selection of habitat. A

Common Nighthawk, a Neotropical migrant that feeds on flying insects.
© Scott Stoner, Naturelogues.

good way to find birds, especially outside the breeding season when food sources are limited, is to focus on what birds eat and where they find it. Many birders keep notes on the foraging behavior of birds and learn to recognize the larvae, insects, flowers, fruits, and seeds that make up their seasonal food supplies. Some birds have exquisite adaptations that allow them to specialize. Crossbills, for example, use their unusual beaks to loosen seeds from spruce and hemlock cones. But many birds, especially those that spend the winter in the Hudson Valley, have a more generalized diet that changes with the season and the availability of various foods.

Neotropical migrants, like warblers, time their spring migration to the availability of insects. The adult insects die when winter temperatures dip below freezing, but the next generation overwinters as dormant eggs and pupae. When warm temperatures return, the eggs hatch into caterpillars that feed on the new soft, emerging leaves of trees and shrubs. This is where the warblers find caterpillars; the birds use their sharp bills to pick them off the vegetation. Hummingbirds, which feed on nectar, time their return to spring-flowering plants such as azaleas. Common Nighthawks wait until the streams warm up enough to trigger huge hatches of aquatic insects, and then they wend their way north over water, feeding as they go.

Fruits and seeds ripen in late summer and fall. Grapes, cherries, pokeweed, and dogwoods are among the first to go. They are devoured by the young of the year and by migrants, but some fruits persist into winter, and a few become more desirable after they have been frozen and softened a bit. Energy-rich poison ivy berries are eaten by Tufted Titmouse, Downy Woodpecker, Yellow-rumped Warbler, and Black-capped Chickadee. Near the coast, Tree Swallows survive on waxy bayberries. A stand of multiflora rose covered with rose hips can support a Northern Mockingbird all winter long. Pine Grosbeak likes the long-lasting fruits of mountain ash, and staghorn sumac attracts European Starling, American Robin, Cedar Waxwing, and Eastern Bluebird in late winter. When snow covers the ground, overwintering finches and sparrows find seeds along roadsides, where snowplows scrape the shoulders

Yellow-rumped Warbler
eating energy-rich
poison ivy berries.
© Deborah Tracy-Kral.

down to bare ground. Horned Lark, Snow Bunting, and sometimes Lapland Longspur pick corn or seeds from manure spread on agricultural fields.

In winter, many small birds that prefer animal matter find eggs and pupae on plants. Black-capped Chickadees tear apart goldenrod galls for the wasp larvae inside, and also search dried oak leaves for moth eggs. Downy Woodpeckers split open the stems of common reed to find stem borers. Hawks and owls hunt the open grassy fields, where small mammals spend the winter in tunnels under grass and snow. When rivers and large bodies of water freeze over, some gulls take to landfills and parking lots, where they survive on garbage. Birds are opportunists. Their survival depends on this, and the more you learn about what birds eat throughout the year, the easier it is to find them.

Birds, Migration, and Weather

Although food is the ultimate factor driving the distribution of birds from season to season, weather plays a key role in fine-tuning their presence, especially during spring and fall migration. Most birds are either diurnal (daytime) or nocturnal (nighttime) migrants. Diurnal migrants include an interesting mix of species. Raptors, for example, travel during the day on thermals, the rising columns of warm air created by the heat from the sun. Aerial insectivores, such as swifts and swallows that catch insects on the wing, can eat en route. Woodpeckers, crows, jays, robins, cardinals, and a variety of other species also migrate during the day. Daytime migrants generally stay over land, and tend to follow topographic features such as ridges, rivers, and coastlines. The vast majority of songbirds, however, migrate at night, when they pay no attention to landforms. Nocturnal migration allows birds to take advantage of a cooler, more stable atmosphere, leaves time to forage during the day, and helps small birds avoid day-flying falcons and hawks, their main predators.

Spring and fall migrations are fundamentally different; there is an urgency to spring migration. Males of most species move north first because early arrival on the breeding grounds helps them get prime territories that confer a significant reproductive advantage. Females arrive later, but most of the migrants make the journey north over a period of about six weeks. Fall migration, on the other hand, is a more leisurely affair. The first shorebirds, usually failed breeders, start south as early as late June. Most insectivores depart in late summer while there is still plenty to eat, but some birds that depend on open water for food linger into winter and stay until the water ices over.

Migratory behavior has evolved in response to drastic seasonal changes in the food supply. Shorter days in the fall or longer days in the spring trigger a host of physiological changes that culminate in migration. Weather, especially temperature and wind direction, are crucial factors that influence the timing and rate of migration. Earth's weather is caused by uneven heating of the atmosphere, which creates air masses with differing temperatures and pressures. Fronts are the boundaries between two different air masses, and they tend to be associated with areas of rain or snow. In spring, warm air masses from the Gulf of Mexico begin to reach north, and spring migrants use the warm southerly winds on the west side of the warm front to power their trip north. Similarly, in fall, polar air masses from Canada produce cold fronts, and strong northerly winds behind these fronts carry birds south. Each spring and fall, birders eagerly anticipate the arrival of new migrants with the passage of these weather fronts that can be used to predict migration events over large geographic areas. The Cornell Lab of Ornithology's BirdCast webpage (birdcast.info) uses the latest scientific data to make real-time predictions of bird migration. However, local winds can have a huge influence on what we see on the ground.

Birds may migrate in great numbers when tailwinds blow them in the right direction. Nocturnal migrants typically lift off and begin their exodus thirty to forty-five minutes after sunset. How long they fly once they begin to move depends on their food reserves, weather conditions, and the proximity of good habitat. Some birds make long, nonstop flights to their destinations, but while they are over land, most songbirds will fly about two hundred miles before coming down at dawn to rest, feed, and restore their fat reserves for their remaining journey (Able 2004). In spring, the migration takes place along broad fronts; and because land warms up before water, the birds choose inland forests for stopover sites where they can find caterpillars and other insects. Fall migrants, on the other hand, tend to stopover near water, which retains heat longer. In fall, birds are more likely to be found along coastlines and the shores of rivers and lakes, where temperatures are more moderate and insects more plentiful.

The importance of a tailwind to migrating birds cannot be overstated. Sometimes birds traveling north hit a cold-front boundary, or southbound migrants encounter a warm front advancing from the south. Both of these conditions present birds with unfavorable headwinds that stop migration in its tracks, and birds seem to "fall out" of the skies. Fallouts can also occur when birds encounter fog or heavy rain. If this happens when the birds are over unsuitable habitat like the open ocean, it can spell disaster; but on land, this can make for spectacular birding, when hundreds of exhausted, hungry birds are forced to land all at once in a small area.

Two other types of wind-related migration phenomena bear mentioning here. The first is what is known as a "spring overshoot," which can occur in early spring when birds are on the move from the Caribbean and the southern United States, and a cold front stretches across the Florida peninsula deep into the Gulf of Mexico. If the front moves east offshore overnight, birds that would normally breed to our south may get caught up in the strong southerly/southwesterly winds ahead of the front and find themselves displaced far northeast of where they should be (Farnsworth and Van Doren 2013). These conditions delight birders by bringing southern rarities such as Summer Tanager, Blue Grosbeak, Little Blue Heron, Mississippi Kite, and Yellow-throated Warbler into the northeastern United States.

A second type of event takes place when fall bird migration is affected by hurricanes and tropical storms that come roaring north from the warm waters of the tropics. Storm birding can be dangerous, and birders should never put themselves in peril to see a bird; but with proper precautions, hurricanes can offer the opportunity to see rarities and vagrants. These cyclonic disturbances rotate counterclockwise and sometimes bring tropical seabirds

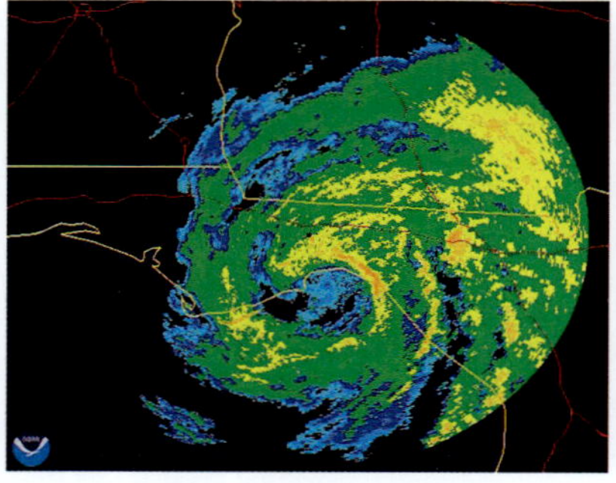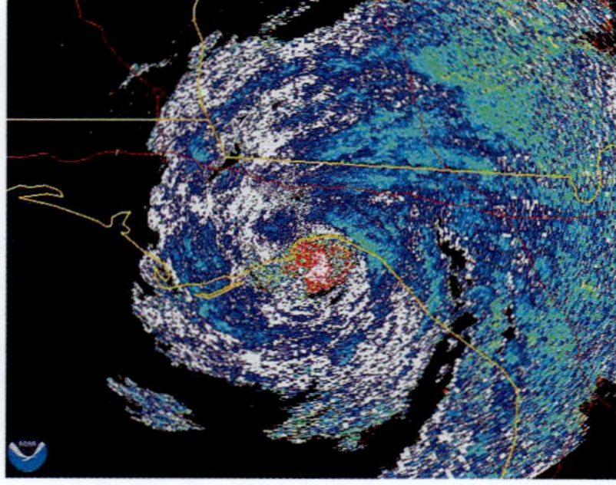

Red dots in the image on the right show birds caught in the eye of Hurricane Hermine as it makes landfall on Florida's Gulf Coast. National Centers for Environmental Information, Ashville, NC, 2016.

If you know what to look for, it is possible to observe birds migrating on radar. The radar images produced by the National Weather Service are developed from a national network of radar installations across the country. These radar installations use NEXRAD (next generation radar), a Doppler radar system that uses microwaves to measure the reflectivity of things in the atmosphere. Rain and snow as well as birds, bats, insects (dragonflies), and dust reflect microwaves, and the amount of reflected energy can be used to estimate the density of these objects. Reflectivity is displayed on the radar screen in colors ranging from most reflective (purple/red) to least reflective (green/blue). Radar can also track the velocity and direction of movement of targets.

On a night in spring or fall, when the wind and weather conditions seem right for migration, use the link http://weather.cod.edu/satrad/nexrad/index.php to go to the single-site radar image for Albany, which covers the entire Hudson Valley. The radar site map tab on the top right shows radar installations for the country. Use the tab on the left for the product menu, and view an animated radar loop of base reflectivity beginning around dusk. Birds reflect in the 5 dbZ to 25 dbZ range, which appears as light blue to light green. Birds beginning their exodus thirty to forty-five minutes after sunset start as diffuse blue images close to the center of the radar circle. Over time, the blue color grows out from the center and increases in reflectivity, becoming greener as more birds take to the air. By choosing base velocity on the product menu, it is possible to see the direction of movement, because green images are moving toward the radar and red ones are moving away.

The product menu for this site also allows you to select hydrometeor classification, a display that uses an algorithm to separate out different types of radar echoes. This is a handy feature because it separates precipitation and ground clutter from "biologicals," or BI on the legend. The biologicals are most likely birds, but dragonflies and bats create similar images. These can usually be sorted out by time of year, velocity, or the shape of the image. Bats emerging from roosts start out with a high reflectivity immediately. Bats also have a higher velocity than birds, while insects are slower (Clemson University).

inland from the Atlantic. The size, strength, speed, and track of the storm are all important in determining which birds are displaced. Typically, observation sites north and east of the storm's center are most productive. The northeast quadrant of the advancing storm has winds from the southeast that can pin birds against the shoreline that would prefer to be at sea. The period after the storm's eye passes can be a great time to see vagrant seabirds such as frigatebirds, storm-petrels, skuas, jaegers, and southern terns. In August of 2011, Hurricane Irene tracked up the Hudson Valley into central Massachusetts and brought at least a dozen White-tailed Tropicbirds to inland sites (Hurricane Irene Redux 2011). There are many hurricane birds among the long list of Hudson Valley vagrants in the Appendix.

Some Important Bird Habitats in the Hudson Valley

Birds do not exist in a vacuum. Birds belong to natural communities that include groups of plants, animals, and other living things that interact with each other and tend to occur together in recognizable and predictable ways. For example, on moist, acid soils at middle elevations, deciduous hardwood forests in the Hudson Valley are dominated by sugar maple and beech with lesser amounts of basswood, red maple, hop hornbeam, and yellow birch. The understory includes seedling trees, striped maple, witch hazel, and viburnums, while the ground layer has plants such as Christmas fern, blue cohosh, baneberry, and false Solomon's seal. Some of the animals associated with these communities are just as predictable as the plants. It would be unusual to visit these woods in summer and not see Black-capped Chickadee, Red-eyed Vireo, Ovenbird, and American Redstart as well as eastern chipmunk and red-backed salamander.

Birders do not talk much about natural communities, but they do recognize bird habitats, the parts of the natural communities that a bird uses to survive and reproduce. The Ovenbird mentioned here, for example, does not use just any deciduous hardwood forest. It generally chooses especially large tracts of woods with a closed canopy and deep leaf litter where it can forage for invertebrates. Habitat choice is driven by the need to find food and produce young, so it is not surprising that birds with special needs, like the Pileated Woodpecker, breed in older woods where they can find large dead trees suitable for the large nest holes required to raise their young. Similarly, you would not expect to find ground-nesting grassland birds like

Ovenbird prefers large tracts of deciduous forest with plenty of leaf litter.
© Deborah Tracy-Kral.

Bobolink in a forest, because this habitat does not provide enough ground cover to conceal them.

Ecologists classify birds as either habitat specialists, who have very specific habitat requirements, or generalists, whose habitat needs can be met in many different kinds of natural communities. Broadly speaking, birds tend to be much more habitat-specific during the breeding season than at other times of the year. When freed of the requirements of nesting, year-round residents tend to wander more and show up in areas where they might not breed. Food is so important to migrating birds that many species feed wherever they can find nourishment, though most still prefer areas with familiar plants and substrates. For example, during migration, a spruce budworm specialist like Cape May Warbler is most likely to be found foraging in spruce trees, but the bird can also be seen in other habitats.

Good birders have at least a rudimentary understanding of bird habitats. They recognize the structure and plant composition of natural communities that are important to birds. This insight allows birders to go into an area knowing which birds to expect and which ones to hope for. A good way to begin studying habitats is to pay attention to the bird's surroundings. Note what the bird is eating and where it is feeding. The following discussion focuses on some of the more significant natural and cultural bird habitats in the Hudson Valley.

Forest communities are the most common ecosystems in the Hudson Valley. By definition a forest is dominated by trees, but all forests are not the same. They vary in species composition, age, plot size, and condition. Oddly, studies have shown that many birds do not show strong preferences for the particular tree species that compose a forest, but they do make a distinction between deciduous and coniferous woods. Deciduous forests lose their leaves in winter and are home to birds such as Rose-breasted Grosbeak and Red-eyed Vireo. Coniferous woods are dominated by evergreens; Red-breasted Nuthatch, Golden-crowned Kinglet, Purple Finch, Blackburnian Warbler and Yellow-rumped Warbler, and Barred Owl are a few of the species more likely to be found in these areas. Mixed woods have many birds that are found in both deciduous and coniferous forests.

A mature, undisturbed forest has layers that include the canopy, midstory, understory, and ground layer. The age of the trees is uneven, with plenty of young trees, saplings, and seedlings waiting to replace their parents. Mature forests have trees that are old enough to produce nuts and seeds, essential food for birds and other wildlife. These forests have gaps in the canopy from tree falls, as well as standing dead trees (snags). Dead trees host borers and other invertebrate prey, and also provide nest cavities.

Unfortunately, undisturbed forests are rare in the Hudson Valley. Nearly all our forests have been cut several times, as evidenced by old stumps in some of today's woodlands. The presence of rock walls provides further proof that many forests were once farmland or pasture. These postagricultural forests have undergone succession, but have grown back in even aged stands. Over-abundant deer consume much of the shrub layer and prevent many trees from regenerating, and sometimes the understory is replaced by thorny invasive plants like barberry or multiflora rose that are unpalatable to deer.

All kinds of forests have birds, but a large, mature tract with a well-developed canopy is more likely to have Scarlet Tanager and forest-nesting raptors. Woodpeckers and other cavity nesters favor woods with standing dead trees. Birds that nest on or near the ground, including Ovenbird, Hooded Warbler, Wood Thrush, and Ruffed Grouse, need the cover of a well-developed ground layer and understory. Young, open forests dominated by short trees and saplings are favored by Chestnut-sided Warbler, American Redstart, and Eastern Towhee.

GRASSLANDS, PASTURES, AND AGRICULTURAL LANDS

The grasslands of the Hudson Valley are not natural. They exist because humans cleared the forests for agriculture. Left to nature, open land would quickly succeed to forest. When farming dominated the valley, grassland birds found good breeding sites in hayfields and lightly grazed pastures. Today there are fewer farms, and modern agriculture is far less bird-friendly than it was centuries ago. Many of today's pastures are so intensively grazed that they provide inadequate cover for ground-nesting birds. Grass-dominated hayfields start out as great habitat in early May for Bobolink, Eastern Meadowlark, Savannah Sparrow, and Grasshopper Sparrow that move in and defend territories. However, most modern dairy farmers take three cuttings of hay each year, and the second cutting in early June destroys the nests and young. The failure to reproduce successfully is one of the reasons that many grassland bird populations in the Northeast have declined by 70 percent to 90 percent in the last thirty years (US Department of Agriculture 2010).

In the Hudson Valley, grassland bird species diversity is highest at sites that are specifically managed for these birds, sites like the Shawangunk Grasslands National Wildlife Refuge. The best fields for birds are large, open landscapes that are planted with a mixture of grasses and mowed after the nesting season is over to keep the site grassy year after year. These fields incorporate

Eastern Meadowlark, an obligate grassland breeding bird.
© Alan W. Wells.

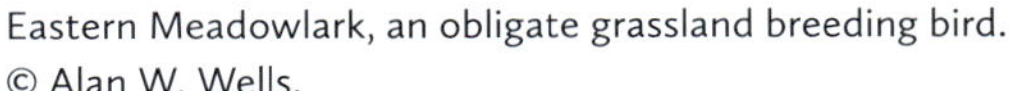

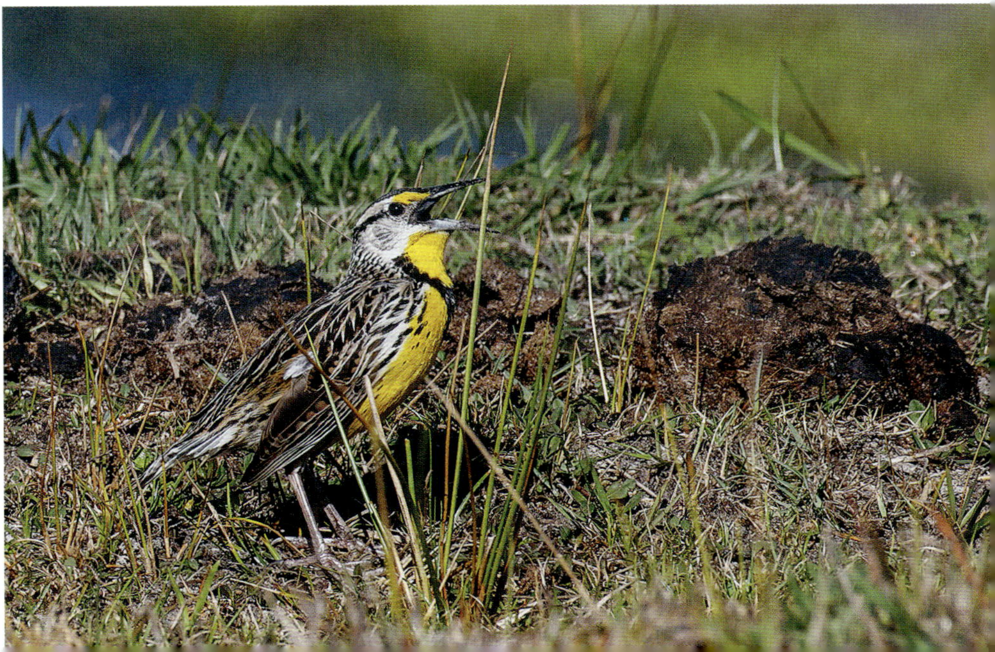

habitat diversity with areas of short, medium, and tall grass, patches of low wet vegetation, areas of bare ground, thatch, deep litter, and song perches. Only the largest, most dense grasslands seem to have enough meadow voles to support Northern Harrier and Short-eared Owl.

Some agricultural settings are attractive to birds. In the Hudson Valley, Vesper Sparrow is often found in strawberry fields that have the bare ground and low vegetation the birds need for nesting. In winter, Horned Lark, Snow Bunting, and Lapland Longspur search for seed in fresh manure that farmers spread on fields. During migration, Canada Goose, American Pipit, Killdeer, and other shorebirds use recently cut cornfields and row crops, especially if these are wet. After the growing season, seed-rich spent crops and fallow plots in community gardens make terrific sparrow habitat.

SCRUBLANDS AND SUCCESSIONAL OLD FIELDS

Scrublands and old fields are early successional, ephemeral habitats that typically form on old clear-cuts or abandoned fields. These habitats, sometimes called thickets, are characterized by dense shrubs and saplings under ten feet tall and by the absence of a closed canopy layer. As the Northeast has become more forested, thickets have become less common. At one time, ornithologists thought that edge and shrubland species were the same; however, recent research has shown that shrubland birds avoid edges and are a unique assemblage of species adapted to using these short-lived natural communities (Schlossberg and King 2008). The species that occupy shrublands change as the habitat is transformed by succession.

As habitat develops on a site that has been cleared and plowed, it is first dominated by grasses and annual plants such as goldenrod, milkweed, and spotted knapweed. In the absence of disturbance, woody shrubs including multiflora rose, shrub dogwood, and brambles move in, followed by red cedar, serviceberry, sumac, and choke-cherry. Field Sparrow, American Woodcock, Gray Catbird, Brown Thrasher, Blue-winged Warbler, Prairie Warbler, Chestnut-sided Warbler, Indigo Bunting, and Eastern Towhee use these thickets until they develop into forests with closed canopies.

WETLANDS

Wetlands, classified broadly by ecologists as either marshes or swamps, are important bird habitats. Marshes are open wetlands that are dominated by grasses and reeds, while swamps are wooded wetlands with trees and shrubs.

The wetlands along the shores of the Hudson River are tidal. These tides, which cause water levels to rise and fall twice a day, add complexity and richness to the wetlands that border the river.

Marshes are home to secretive and seldom-seen birds that live among the cattails, rushes, and sedges that dominate the emergent vegetation. In many parts of the Hudson Valley, once-pristine marshlands have been invaded by nonnative common reed and purple loosestrife, which degrade the habitat for breeding marsh birds. The bird diversity of a marsh depends on its size, the amount of open water, and the complexity of the vegetation, among other factors. Marsh birds are more likely to be heard than seen. Patient birders are sometimes rewarded with glimpses of Marsh Wren, Virginia Rail, American Bittern, Least Bittern, Sora, Pied-billed Grebe, Common Gallinule, and American Coot around the marsh edge.

Bogs, beaver meadows, and fens are other types of open wetlands that are defined by their hydrology and soil chemistry. Depending on their size, these areas may be home to some of the same birds found in marshes, and old beaver meadows and some bogs may have peat mats and standing dead trees that can be used by cavity nesters such as woodpeckers, swallows, Eastern Kingbird, Wood Duck, and Hooded Merganser. Green Heron, Common Yellowthroat, Acadian Flycatcher, and Northern Waterthrush may also be present.

Swamps are forested wetlands, and in a few places along the tidal Hudson, they take the form of floodplain forests where high seasonal tides periodically inundate the riverside terraces. Floodplain forests in our area are characterized by tall cottonwoods, silver maples, and an open understory with poison ivy, Virginia creeper, jewelweed, and ferns. Away from the river, swamps occur in poorly drained depressions. The most common swamps in the Hudson Valley are dominated by red maple and hardwoods, with an understory of spicebush and ferns. These habitats are good places to find migrating Rusty Blackbird and breeding Red-shouldered Hawk, Yellow-throated Vireo, Great Crested Flycatcher, Brown Creeper, and many woodpeckers.

OPEN WATERS AND MUDFLATS

Open water is where waterfowl, waders, Bald Eagle, Osprey, gulls, and terns find their food. During migration, this habitat provides aquatic invertebrate hatches for aerial insectivores such as Common Nighthawk, swallows, and swifts. The mudflats and shorelines have prey including worms, crabs, and other invertebrates that fuel the journeys of transient shorebirds, especially plovers, yellowlegs, and sandpipers. In the Hudson Valley, open water comes in many forms: from rivers, creeks, streams, and lakes to reservoirs, impoundments, and farm ponds.

Aquatic habitats are especially good for waterfowl. The vast majority of the ducks, geese, and swans that can be seen here breed in northern and western North America and migrate to areas with open water to spend the winter. Some continue on to the Chesapeake Bay and the Atlantic Ocean, but others stay in the Hudson Valley as long as there is enough open water for them to find food. As winter progresses and temperatures drop, small bodies of water freeze, but open water persists below dams and waterfalls, on swift-moving streams, and any place with warm water inflows from springs or industrial operations. The brackish southern parts of the Hudson River also tend to stay open late into the winter. When aquatic habitats start to freeze, waterfowl and gulls begin to concentrate in the ever-decreasing number of open-water sites. These are great places to find rarities that move into our area when the Great Lakes freeze in harsh, cold winters.

COASTAL HABITATS

The only coastal habitats in the ten counties covered in this book occur in Westchester County along the shore of Long Island Sound. This unique habitat holds some species that are extremely unlikely to be observed anywhere else in the Hudson Valley. Because the open salt water of the sound does not freeze in winter, it is an important wintering area for many birds that migrate from the Great Lakes, including grebes, loons, scoters, and other waterfowl. The offshore waters also provide regular sightings of Northern Gannet, Brown Pelican, and Black Skimmer. The rocky shores are a good place to see Purple Sandpiper (in winter), Ruddy Turnstone, and American Oystercatcher. Sandy beaches and mudflats support a variety of shorebirds.

Salt marshes and mudflats form in the tidal areas at the shore's edge. These habitats are dominated by salt-tolerant grasses such as salt-meadow grass and cordgrass, and are home to Black-crowned Night-Heron, Yellow-crowned Night-Heron, Clapper Rail, Saltmarsh Sparrow, Seaside Sparrow, and migrating and overwintering Nelson's Sparrow.

Great Horned Owl begins nesting in January. It sometimes adopts the old stick nests of Great Blue Herons. © Naomi Lloyd.

A Monthly Guide to Birding the Hudson Valley

There are always birds to be found in the Hudson Valley, but whereas May brings great birding almost everywhere, some months make bird finding a little more challenging. Foul weather and cold temperatures make us want to stay indoors, but nearly every experienced birder has a story of a fantastic bird seen under horrendous weather conditions. Birding year-round keeps your skills sharp, broadens your experience, and deepens your bird lists. The goal of this section is to suggest places to see birds twelve months of the year. Just remember the saying, "There is no such thing as bad weather, only unsuitable clothing."

JANUARY This is typically the coldest and snowiest month in the Hudson Valley. Keep the feeder filled, and check carefully for irruptive winter finches. If the river freezes, look for concentrations of waterfowl and gulls in areas of open water around dams and waterfalls. The weekend of Martin Luther King Day is when most local bird clubs visit rivers, lakes, and ponds to count ducks, geese, swans, loons, and grebes for the New York State Ornithological Association (NYSOA) statewide winter waterfowl count. Listen at night for Great Horned Owls starting their courtship. Overwintering raptors and Short-eared Owl numbers reach their peak at Coxsackie Creek, Shawangunk Grasslands, and Croton Point.

FEBRUARY A snowshoe hike on a moonlit night is a fun way to listen for owls. In severe winters when some of the Great Lakes freeze over, grebes and loons make their way to open areas on the Hudson River. February is when Audubon and the Cornell Lab of Ornithology hold the Great Backyard Bird Count, where participants collect data and submit it to birdcount.org to create a snapshot of winter bird populations. Visit gbbc.birdcount.org to participate. Horned Lark, Snow Bunting, and Lapland Longspur forage in cornfields and along the edges of roads scraped clear of snow. The first Red-winged Blackbirds return to the Upper Hudson.

MARCH Waterfowl diversity increases as birds begin moving north. Look along the Hudson and on open lakes, ponds, and reservoirs. Bald Eagle is nesting, and because the leaves are still off the trees, this is a good time to spot perched adults and locate nests. Killdeer, Wilson's Snipe, and American Woodcock begin to return. March is a great time to visit birding sites along Long Island Sound in Westchester County, where spring arrives earlier than at other sites in the Hudson Valley. Look for Purple Sandpiper, American Oystercatcher, Northern Gannet, Red-necked Grebe, and Red-throated Loon.

APRIL American Woodcock displays reach their peak in April, so this is a good time to join a field trip to witness this annual spectacle. Early migrants begin to arrive in earnest, and birders compete to find the first of the season (FOS) Tree Swallow, Rusty Blackbird, Osprey, Eastern Phoebe, Blue-headed Vireo, Blue-gray Gnatcatcher, Louisiana Waterthrush, and other early warblers. Spring shorebird migration is also the best time to see Solitary Sandpiper and Greater Yellowlegs. To prepare for a day in the field, follow electronic mailing lists known as listservs to learn what birders are seeing.

MAY May is the peak of spring migration and the most wonderful time of the year for birders. Spring and fall are the only opportunities to see and study migrants that do not stay to breed in our region. This is the time to see Tennessee Warbler, Cape May Warbler, Palm Warbler, Bay-breasted Warbler, and Wilson's Warbler. The uncommon breeders, including Cerulean Warbler, Mourning Warbler, and Canada Warbler, are also more abundant during migration and easiest to find in May when they are singing and the leaves are still sparse. Common Nighthawk migrates late in the month. Look for them feeding on insects at dusk over rivers and streams, and sometimes

Eastern Phoebe fledglings. © Carena M. Pooth.

around streetlights. Big Days, Birdathons, and other birding competitions to find the most species in twenty-four hours take place in May. Consider joining a team, and learn how to plan a route to maximize species, support a worthy cause, and share in the fun.

JUNE By June, many species are nesting and the woods become quiet. However, because breeding tends to start later at high elevations, June is the best time to seek out the boreal specialists such as Swainson's Thrush and Bicknell's Thrush, Blackpoll Warbler, and Yellow-bellied Flycatcher. Areas of spruce-fir forest might also have Magnolia Warbler and Yellow-rumped Warbler. Eastern Whip-poor-will, rare and local in the Hudson Valley, is sometimes heard calling from open woodlands on moonlit nights in June. This is also a good time to find nests, because many adults are feeding their young. Breeding Bird Surveys are conducted in June when migration has ended.

JULY Young birds, fledglings, and birds in juvenile plumage are abundant in midsummer, posing identification challenges for beginners. Youngsters beg incessantly from protected areas near the nest, and parents feed them for a while; but in some species, the adults stop feeding the first offspring to produce a second brood. This is a good time of year to learn to recognize juvenile robins, blackbirds, sparrows, and other common species that often look quite different from full adults.

AUGUST A few late breeders such as American Goldfinch and Cedar Waxwing may still be nesting, but once the young are fledged, many birds begin to wander and start migrating south. Shorebirds, especially the failed breeders, begin their journey south. Great Egret and Brant appear on the Hudson and in large wetlands. Common Nighthawk is seen and heard peenting at dusk over waterways. Most songbirds molt before they migrate, and some acquire a new and often significantly different feather coat for the winter. Wild Turkey is conspicuous and easy to see in August, when groups of growing poults (young turkeys) follow the parents around open fields.

SEPTEMBER In September, migration is in full swing for shorebirds, warblers, and raptors. The Broad-winged Hawk migration usually peaks in this region during the second or third week, bringing hundreds to thousands of birds a day soaring over hawkwatches in spectacular kettles. Some migrants that are more common and most easily seen in fall in the Hudson Valley include Black-bellied Plover, Semipalmated Plover, Buff-breasted Sandpiper, Pectoral Sandpiper, Philadelphia Vireo, Connecticut Warbler, and Orange-crowned Warbler. Visit Jean Iron's website (www.jeaniron.ca) for Ron Pittaway's Winter Finch forecast, which predicts the likelihood of northern finches and other species moving south (and coming to feeders) based on cone crops in Canada and northern New York.

OCTOBER The bulk of the fall sparrow migration takes place in October. Look for Lincoln's Sparrow and White-crowned Sparrow to arrive early, followed by Fox Sparrow and White-throated Sparrow, Dark-eyed Junco, and finally American Tree Sparrow at the end of the month. Both Golden-crowned Kinglet and Ruby-crowned Kinglet become abundant in October. Winter waterfowl begin to arrive, and their numbers increase.

NOVEMBER The majority of North American waterfowl breed in Canada and winter along the coast, often far south of the Hudson Valley; but in late fall on their way to Long Island Sound, the Chesapeake Bay, and the Atlantic Coast, many of them stop to feed on our lakes, reservoirs, and rivers. November is the time to see grebes, scoters, scaup, loons, and Snow Geese. Do not delay, because many of these birds will leave and continue to the coast as winter sets in and inland bodies of water freeze over.

DECEMBER Each year, the National Audubon Society coordinates Christmas Bird Counts between December 14 and January 5. The goal is to do a twenty-four-hour census of all the birds in a fifteen-mile diameter count circle. Anyone can join a Christmas Count by finding one nearby and contacting the compiler prior to count day. Go to nybirds.org/ProjCBC to find a count near you. If you are a beginner, you can expect to be paired with an experienced team, and you should plan to attend the compilation (a.k.a. roundup) after the count to learn what everyone saw.

4 Step Up Your Birding Game

For beginning birders, much of the excitement of birding comes from seeing new birds. Sadly, the more we bird, the harder it becomes to find new species. It is this quest for new birds that drives birders to explore new places, travel farther afield, and join birding tours. Often, however, there are interesting birds to be seen close to home, but we simply do not see them. The ability to detect and recognize new birds is a skill that develops with study, learning, and especially experience. There are no shortcuts, but there are things you can do to build your birding expertise.

Listen to the Birds—Learning Songs and Calls

Bird vocalizations not only increase our ability to find birds, but also provide important identification clues. Nocturnal birds, such as owls, for example, are much more likely to be heard than seen, but even birds that are active by day become difficult to see once the trees leaf out. Others, like Fish Crow and American Crow or the Empidonax flycatchers, are difficult to identify to species by using only their appearance. In situations like these, knowing bird vocalizations can make the difference between a confident ID and a potentially great bird that got away.

Ornithologists have traditionally separated bird sounds into songs, the typically complex vocalizations that male and some female birds use to defend territories and attract mates; and calls, which are shorter and simpler and used in other contexts. Because of their length and complexity, songs are easier for birders to learn than calls, but birds sing very little once the breeding season ends. Most calls, on the other hand, are given by both sexes and used year-round. Flight calls are given at night during migration, and are now being recorded and used in conjunction with radar to monitor bird movements. High-pitched alarm calls warn other birds that there are predators in the area, but savvy birders use these calls to find raptors and owls. Chip calls, which are given during the day throughout the year, can be extremely useful in bird identification.

Training your auditory memory, so that you can hear a sound and recognize it again, is the key to learning bird vocalizations. Scientific research has shown that individuals vary greatly in their ability to create auditory memories, but one thing is clear: repetition is a key component of every learning strategy. Many birders admit that they forget songs over the winter and need a refresher every spring. There is also general agreement that the very best way to learn a song is to track down the source of a new sound in the field. There

A Wood Thrush belting out its song.
© Alan W. Wells.

is something about the process of tracking down the source of the song and discovering the songster prominently perched on territory, throwing back its head and belting out the tune for all to hear, that cements the notes in our auditory memories. While there is no substitute for time in the field, there are a number of other approaches to learning vocalizations that birders find helpful.

MNEMONICS

For decades, birders have relied on these memory gimmicks to identify birds by song. For some bird songs, mnemonics are extremely helpful. For example, most beginners find it useful to associate the Indigo Bunting's song with phrases like "fire, fire, where, where, here, here," or a Tufted Titmouse with a loud "peter, peter, peter." Many field guides and online sources have lists of helpful bird song mnemonics that can reinforce the unique elements and phrases for some species.

However, there are a number of problems with mnemonics. First, the songs of some birds just don't seem to fit catchy, easy-to-remember phrases, and many birds sing more than one song or variable songs that mix elements and phrases, in differing combinations. Second, what sounds like "peter, peter, peter" to one person may sound like "here, here, here" to someone else. And finally, mnemonics don't work well on most calls, which are typically short and difficult to learn, but are probably more useful for bird identification because they are given by both sexes all year long.

RECORDINGS AND APPS

There are a number of instructional audio recordings available to help beginners learn bird songs. The *Birding by Ear* (2002) series by Richard Walton and Robert Lawson has been around for a long time and is still widely used in ornithology classes across the country. The authors present the songs of common species in learning groups whose songs share similar characteristics, and the narration identifies "handles" and mnemonics that aid in bird identification. There are also apps available for learning bird songs: for example, Chirp (Spiny Software Ltd.) and Larkwire (Larkwire, LLC) allow you to create customized bird-song quizzes and score your progress.

Bird vocalizations can be downloaded for free from the Macaulay Library at the Cornell Lab of Ornithology and other online sources, and technically inclined birders can create their own customized playlists. In addition, nearly all the field guide apps on the market include an audio component that can be used to "check" a vocalization heard in the field against standard recordings for a particular species. Unfortunately, some birders play these recordings in the field to lure birds into the open. The use of playbacks to see birds is a controversial practice because it disturbs their behavior and can confuse birders who think they are hearing a real bird. If playbacks are used at all, they should be used responsibly, sparingly, and at low volumes (Sibley 2011).

DESCRIPTION AND VISUALIZATION

Recently, the authors of *The Warbler Guide* (2013), Tom Stephenson and Scott Whittle, have advocated for a new system for learning bird vocalizations based on descriptions that are derived using three objective criteria: sound quality, pitch trend, and number of sections. While I doubt their system will ever replace the well-known, beloved mnemonics of some species, their technique holds promise for songs and chips that are difficult to characterize.

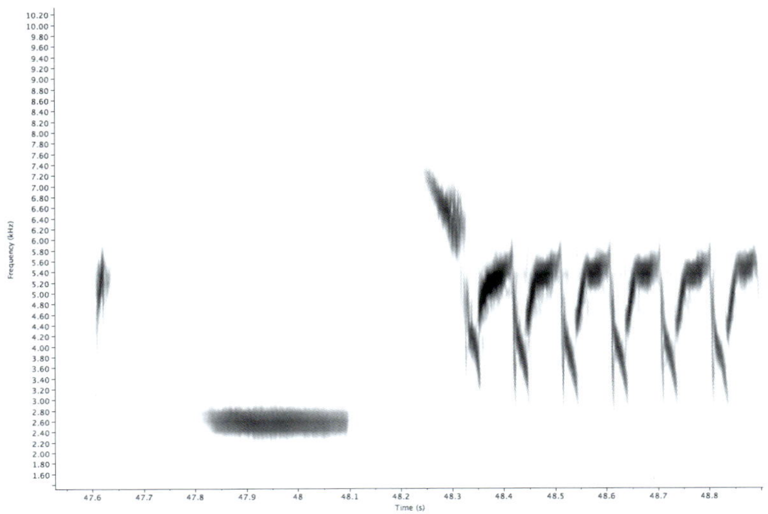

A sonogram for the familiar "drink your tea" song of the Eastern Towhee, showing time on the x-axis and frequency or pitch on the y-axis. Macauley Library at the Cornell Lab of Ornithology, recorded by Robert A. Bethel.

Eastern Towhee (male). © Carena M. Pooth.

Briefly, the system asks the listener to describe song quality as buzzy, clear, trilled, or partly buzzy; and pitch trend as rising, falling, steady, or variable; and then to describe the number of sections or parts. These three answers are entered into the birder's Warbler Guide app (Princeton University Press) to determine the singer's identity. To teach their method, the authors make extensive use of sonograms, which are basically pictures of songs that plot pitch on the y-axis and time on the x-axis. Software such as Raven Lite 2.0 (Cornell Lab of Ornithology) can be used to further investigate bird sounds through sonograms. Stephenson and Whittle believe that their system, although still in its infancy, can be useful for many birds besides warblers (Stephenson and Whittle 2015).

TIPS FOR LEARNING BIRD VOCALIZATIONS

If you are just starting to learn bird sounds, buy an instructional CD or phone app so you have recordings to study, and learn the vocalizations of a small group of five to ten common birds in your area, ones that you can hear in your backyard. Don't limit yourself to songs. Pay attention to the chip calls as well. Find these birds outside, and observe them as they utter their vocalizations. Learn all the vocalizations of this core group really well.

Choose a system to describe the bird vocalizations you hear, and use it. Make up a mnemonic or learn an existing one, draw a primitive sonogram, or describe the sound quality, pitch, and sections. It doesn't really matter which method you choose. The process of trying to categorize and describe what you hear will help anchor that sound in your auditory memory.

Spend time in the field, and pay attention to bird vocalizations, especially those you have not heard before. If possible, find a mentor who knows birds sounds better than you do, and can help you learn. Try to track down any new songs and chips, and identify their sources. If you are unable to find the bird, write down a description of the vocalization; and then use habitat, season, distribution, and your recordings to narrow down the possibilities.

Each season before the migrants return, review the birds in your repertoire and relearn any songs you might have forgotten. Choose a small number of new species to add to your repertoire every year. Study recordings of their vocalizations, and commit them to memory. The hardest bird vocalizations to learn are those of rare species and transients that are in our area for only a short time each year. As your skills improve, focus on these birds seasonally.

For the truly committed, a baby monitor is a fun way to keep track of new arrivals. Buy a baby monitor at a yard sale, and then put the transmitter on your porch and the receiver in your bedroom. From the warmth of your bed, listen for owls at night and listen to the dawn chorus during the breeding season. Get out of bed, and track down and identify any sounds you do not recognize.

Tap into the Birding Community

The path to becoming an accomplished birder involves study. Any educator will tell you that students learn in different ways, and birders are no exception. Tools like books and recordings have their place, but learning birds requires the "hands-on" component that puts newly cultivated skills to work in the field with the birds themselves. Birding alone is the way to master the fundamentals of birding. Solo birders are forced to work out IDs on their own and develop their individual learning techniques, but they run the risk of "learning" an incorrect identification, especially for songs and calls. Birding with others is the equivalent of group work. Groups are a way to tap into decades of birding experience, to learn the tricks of the trade, and maybe even to find a mentor or birding buddy. People who are passionate about birds make up an active, growing community that exists in the real world in the form of clubs and organizations, and in cyberspace as members of social networks. No matter how you connect with others, joining the community of birders opens doors, and while birding alone is fun, birding with others is even better.

BIRD CLUBS AND FIELD TRIPS

Bird clubs are geographically based birding organizations whose members share a passion for birds. They exist at the local, state, national, and international levels. Although their missions vary, local bird clubs are usually involved in bird education and habitat conservation, organized birding events, citizen science, and record-keeping activities. Many hold monthly program meetings that feature interesting bird-related lectures and the opportunity to meet and interact with members of the birding community. Membership in a local bird club is an inexpensive way to connect to a friendly, interesting, and diverse group that includes people who enjoy birds in many different ways. My local bird club, for example, includes photographers, bloggers, bird banders, scientific researchers, international bird tour travelers, conservation

Birding Organizations in the Hudson Valley

STATEWIDE

New York State Ornithological Association (NYSOA) www.nybirds.org
New York State's ornithological society has both member organizations and individual members.

Audubon New York www.ny.audubon.org
New York State office of National Audubon Society (NAS) has affiliated chapters and individual members statewide.

New York State Young Birders Club www.nysyoungbirders.org
A special project of NYSOA, this club provides a community for birders between ages ten and nineteen.

REGIONAL AND COUNTY

Hudson-Mohawk Bird Club www.hmbc.net
Geographic base is the eleven counties around Albany; owns Henry Gerber Reist Sanctuary in Niskayuna.

Audubon Society of the Capital Region www.capitalregionaudubon.org
Capital region chapter of NAS.

Alan Devoe Bird Club www.alandevoebirdclub.org
Columbia County; owns Wilson M. Powell Sanctuary in Old Chatham.

John Burroughs Natural History Society www.jbnhs.org
Ulster County.

advocates, and competitive listers. In New York State, where most local bird clubs are members of the New York State Ornithological Association, these groups provide a way to connect to a whole state full of birders.

Bird clubs and other organizations up and down the Hudson Valley offer organized field trips that are open to the public. These trips are advertised in newspapers and published in the field trip calendars of bird club websites. Joining a field trip is a good way to meet other birders, and a great way to improve your birding skills. A group sees more birds than a single individual can, simply because it has more eyes. Field trips offer an opportunity to explore new sites with experienced birders who know where to find the birds, and can lead you to convenient free parking, the best viewing points, and

Ralph T. Waterman Bird Club www.watermanbirdclub.org
   Dutchess County.
Edgar A. Mearns Bird Club www.mearnsbirdclub.org
   Orange County.
Orange County Audubon Society www.orangecountynyaudubon.org
   Orange County NAS chapter; owns five small sanctuaries in Orange
   County.
Putnam Highlands Audubon Society www.putnamhighlandsaudubon.org
   Western Putnam County NAS chapter.
Rockland Audubon Society www.rocklandaudubon.org
   Rockland County NAS chapter.
Saw Mill River Audubon Society www.sawmillriveraudubon.org
   NAS chapter for northwestern Westchester County; owns eight
   sanctuaries and maintains a staffed office in Chappaqua.
Bedford Audubon Society www.bedfordaudubon.org
   NAS chapter for northeastern Westchester and parts of Putnam County;
   owns four sanctuaries in northeastern Westchester County and main-
   tains staffed office at Bylane Farm in Katonah.
Central Westchester Audubon Society www.cwasociety.org
   NAS chapter for central Westchester County.
Hudson River Audubon Society of Westchester www.hras.org
   NAS chapter for southwestern Westchester County.
Bronx River-Sound Shore Audubon Society www.brssaudubon.org
   NAS chapter for southeastern Westchester County.

even the nearest bathroom. The greatest benefit of group birding by far is the opportunity to learn from more experienced birders—a chance to tap into the cumulative knowledge and experience of everyone in the group.

Field trips are welcoming groups, but if you are new to group birding, it helps to know what to expect. A good field trip leader is knowledgeable about the site and shares the plan for the trip with the group at the start. If parking is limited, participants may be asked to carpool from the meeting place, and you should be prepared to join in as a rider or driver. Most field trips that are open to the public are easy-to-moderate walks, but if an outing is advertised as strenuous, be realistic about your ability to keep up, and skip trips that seem too ambitious. Wear appropriate footwear and clothing,

A field trip at the beach to look for shorebirds. © Carena M. Pooth.

and bring everything you need for the trip, including binoculars, field guide, water, food, insect repellent, and sunscreen. Often, someone in the group will keep a bird list for the trip and offer to share it via eBird, where you can delete any species you personally missed.

Bird walks are social affairs, but because songs and chip calls are critical to bird detection and identification, it is best to keep your voice low and choose the right moments to chat. Stay with the group, and let the leader lead and spot birds. Birding groups do their best to help everyone see the birds, but don't expect to see every bird on the trip, especially when there are leaves on the trees. During the breeding season, most of the birds will be identified by their vocalizations, season, and habitat. Ask others in the group to help you learn to use these identification clues.

A field trip also offers a special opportunity to see and test the latest and greatest birding equipment. At some sites, the trip leader will carry a spotting scope to view distant birds and will give everyone a chance to take a look. Do not miss the opportunity to see what a scope has to offer! Scopes and tripods are significant financial investments, but they open up a world of possibilities for seeing birds that are far away.

SOCIAL NETWORKING FOR BIRDERS

Birders who cannot join organizations can still connect to today's birding community via the internet and various types of social media. By reporting sightings to eBird for record-keeping purposes, users automatically become part of an online birding community where their data can be shared and used by other eBirders. The eBird site contains a wealth of bird information, much of it developed from eBird sightings. You can configure eBird to send daily or hourly email alerts for rare birds, or even for specific species reported in various geographic areas (ebird.org/ebird/alerts).

Many birders also subscribe to state and regional listservs, electronic mailing lists that distribute emails to subscribers via the internet. Listservs provide a convenient and timely way to share bird sightings with others in the group. These electronic mailing lists for birding are usually set up for a specific geographic region. In New York State, NYSBIRDS-L covers the entire state, but there are also regional lists established and managed by local birding groups. When a list is first set up, the owners draw up guidelines that describe its purpose, topics, geographic coverage, and rules about things like advertising and attachments. These rules are usually viewed onscreen during the subscription process or sent to new users via email when they subscribe. Most list guidelines ask members to sign their posts with their name and location. It is also important to remember that pretty much anyone can join an electronic mailing list, and some birders from outside your region will subscribe just to monitor bird sightings. These readers will not be familiar with local names, so it is helpful to describe locations thoroughly. When listservs report rare birds, competitive birders may jump in the car and go on a "chase" to add new life birds or make a vital addition to one of their lists.

Because of Facebook's emphasis on pictures, birders who take photos like to connect with birding friends and birding organizations through this site or other social networking websites. New York Birders, the New York State Ornithological Association, and many local bird clubs have active Facebook pages. Some bird clubs also use text-messaging applications such as Twitter and WhatsApp Messenger to share rare bird alerts.

Electronic Mailing Lists in the Hudson Valley

NYSBIRDS-L is an email list that deals with birds and birding in New York State. Its primary purpose is to disseminate information about wild bird sightings, although limited discussion on bird behavior, identification, conservation, and distribution are also welcomed. Subscription information and guidelines at www.northeastbirding.com.

HMBirds focuses on sightings and bird behavior in the eleven counties in NYSOA's Kingbird Region 8 near Albany. Reports of rarities outside the region are also welcome. Subscription information and guidelines at groups.yahoo.com/group/hmbirds.

MidHudsonBirds receives bird reports from Ulster, Dutchess, Greene, and Columbia Counties, including the Catskill and Shawangunk Mountains. Subscription information and guidelines at groups.yahoo.com/group /MidHudsonBirds.

Activities to Build Your Birding Skills

COMMIT TO REGULAR BIRDING. Go early if you can, and go often, whenever your schedule allows, but put it on the calendar and treat it like a dentist's appointment. If you make a date to go with someone else, you'll be less likely to cancel.

LEARN TO STUDY FLOCKS OF BIRDS. Even when birds fly over in huge numbers, many of them can be identified by shape, vocalizations, flight formation, behavior, date, and a knowledge of bird distributions. Scan those huge flocks of Canada Geese and pick out a Snow Goose!

FOCUS ON A DIFFICULT GROUP. If gulls, shorebirds, or sparrows give you trouble, study a small number that occur regularly in your area, and learn everything you can about them. Then find them in the field.

TAKE PICTURES (EVEN BAD ONES) OF BIRDS. The new, relatively inexpensive digital superzoom cameras with image stabilization and automatic focus make it possible for almost anyone to take pictures of birds. These cameras are small and lightweight, and even poor images can help in bird identification. When you review photos on a computer, you can sometimes see details

A rare Ross's Goose among Canada Geese. © Naomi Lloyd.

not evident in the field. With a bit of practice (and luck!), you might even get some good photos.

PARTICIPATE IN A CITIZEN SCIENCE PROJECT. These research projects use data gathered by volunteers to monitor bird populations and address scientific questions. The Cornell Lab of Ornithology, Vermont Center for Ecostudies, New York State Department of Environmental Conservation, and National Audubon Society are just a few of the groups in the Hudson Valley that are using citizen science data to study everything from boreal bird populations to turkey numbers.

JOIN A GROUP AND DO A BIG DAY DURING SPRING MIGRATION. The goal of these events is to see as many species as possible in twenty-four hours. Big Days are typically organized by local bird clubs, sometimes as fund-raisers. They are exhausting but exhilarating!

VISIT A MONITORED HAWKWATCH. Go in the fall when there is a northwest wind, or in spring when the winds are from the south, and watch as raptors soar by. More than any other kind of birding, hawk identification forces you to focus on season, size, shape, and behavior.

Immature Red-tailed Hawk in flight.
© Alan W. Wells.

American Woodcock on its nest.
© Scott Stoner, Naturelogues.

TAKE PART IN AN AUDUBON CHRISTMAS BIRD COUNT. A Christmas tradition since 1900, this twenty-four-hour bird winter census takes place each year between December 14 and January 5. It tallies the birds in fifteen-mile-diameter circles throughout the country. Find a count near you at www.audubon.org/join-christmas-bird-count or contact a local bird club to participate.

CHASE A BIRD. Monitor the listservs, and when a rare bird is reported, gather some friends and take a road trip to see it. At the destination, you are likely to find a mutually supportive group of birders who have traveled from far and wide to see the same bird. Even if you miss the bird, you are sure to meet nice people and learn a lot.

SEE AN AMERICAN WOODCOCK DISPLAY. Take a field trip with a local birding organization to a site where these birds breed. A sure sign of spring, these strange-looking shorebirds perform their bizarre courtship, complete with nasal peent vocalizations and twittering aerial flights, even when there is still snow on the ground.

Visiting a Hawkwatch

The migrations of large soaring birds, such as raptors, rely on lift from rising columns of air called thermals. These updrafts develop over land as the sun rises in the sky and heats the earth's surface unevenly. Thermals push the birds upward and allow them to glide effortlessly downwind on their journey north or south. Thermals do not develop over water, so big bodies of water form barriers to hawk migration and steer the birds inland. Updrafts also form where winds meet cliffs or ridges, funneling birds through the valleys below. These geographic features define the location of hawkwatch sites, established areas where observers count migrating birds to monitor raptor populations. The Hawk Migration Association of North America (HMANA) has an established network of about two hundred sites that collect hawk count data and report it on www.hawkcount.org. While several Hudson Valley hawkwatches are among the sites listed in this book, the HMANA website has locations, directions, and peak migration dates for hawkwatch sites throughout North America.

Hawkwatches offer magnificent, long-distance views of approaching raptors and the landscape below. Their locations on ridges and hilltops put the observers close to the migrating birds. HMANA sites welcome visitors, and during the count season they are staffed by one or more official counters trained in hawk identification. Some sites have observation decks or bleacher seating, but sometimes a comfortable rock is the only place to sit.

In the Hudson Valley, the majority of our raptors pass through between late August and early December. Broad-winged Hawk migration peaks during the second or third week in September, but big migration days depend on favorable weather—in fall, that means a northwest wind following the passage of a cold front. The majority of the raptors typically pass over between 10:00 a.m. and 2:00 p.m., when thermals are at their peak.

When they first come into view, the birds appear as distant specks over landmarks with local names or posted numbers that spotters use to help people get on the bird. Identification of migrating hawks relies less on field marks and more on size, shape, and manner of flight. As the bird moves along its predictable route, observers study the relative size and shape of the head, wings, body, and tail. How does it hold its wings? Are they flat or in a V-shaped dihedral? Are the wingbeats fast or slow, shallow or deep? Traditional field marks come into play only if the bird comes in close enough for them to be seen. It takes study and practice to identify migrating raptors, but no one ever forgets the thrill of thousands of hawks soaring overhead on a beautiful day.

ADD AGE, SEX, BREEDING CODES, AND COMMENTS TO YOUR BIRD LISTS.
Take the time to record these additional notes, even though eBird makes it
almost too easy to keep a bird list and nothing else. Good field data includes
breeding evidence and information that will help you find and recognize the
bird the next time you see it.

ADVOCATE FOR THE BIRDS. Get involved in bird habitat protection, either by
joining a conservation group or by acting to protect sites close to your home.
Advocacy is a chance to share your passion and teach others about birds.

Seeing, Finding, Reporting, and Documenting Rare Birds

The vast majority of birds we see are common, widespread species, but what
motivates many birders to watch birds day after day is the chance to see
something uncommon—that is, a "good bird." Good birds are different things
to different people. New life birds (lifers), ones you have never seen before,
are perhaps the most exciting; but a new bird for your home county, a new
yard bird, or even a first-of-the-season (FOS) sighting can be almost as much
fun. Birds that are unexpected because they are outside their normal range
or season are also considered good birds.

Keeping track of your sightings by location and date helps clarify what
is common and what is not. Listing is easy with eBird because the program
automatically generates life lists and year lists for states, counties, and other
geographic areas. Listing adds a fun new dimension to birding because it
allows you to see what you are missing and to target birds to build your lists
and fill those gaps. Many birders take listing very seriously and compete
against other birders to find the most birds. Each year the New York State
Ornithological Association sponsors a county and state listing competition
that is very popular in the New York birding community.

One of the easiest ways to see rare birds is to let others find them for you.
Birders are eager to share good birds and usually post their sightings to eBird
and listservs. When a rare bird is found, directions, details, and photos spread
quickly within the birding community via email, phone calls, and social media. Rare birds and vagrants usually do not stay in one place for long, so it's
best to chase them as soon as possible. At the site, parked cars, scopes, and
happy birders usually mark the good bird's location.

Finding a rare bird yourself is much more difficult. Most birders go into

Snowy Owl, a rare visitor to the Hudson Valley, is one bird worth chasing.
© Naomi Lloyd.

the field expecting to find certain species and therefore tend to write off all birds as something common. Finding rare birds requires a different mindset: knowing what could be seen, and being prepared for the unexpected. Some birders seem to be especially skilled at finding rare birds. These elite birders are intimately familiar with the common species and alert to subtle differences that may distinguish rarities. They study every bird they see in detail to be sure the more common Greater Yellowlegs isn't really a Lesser!

If you are lucky enough to see a really unusual bird, it is important to share the information. Some birds are so rare that they should be reported and documented for the New York State Avian Records Committee (NYSARC). Established in 1977, NYSARC maintains the official Checklist of Birds of New York State, and it has identified species that need NYSARC review. These include birds that are new to the state, new breeding records, and extreme out-of-range or out-of-season records. The list of reportable rarities, the reporting form, and instructions can be found at nybirds.org/NYSARC.

Rarities that many birders will want to see deserve special consideration. Before you post your great find to listservs or Facebook, it is important to think about whether the bird is vulnerable to disturbance because it is either nesting or possibly stressed by a lack of food. If the answer is yes, then

Crowd of birders and photographers ethically observing a rare Great Gray Owl that visited New York State in winter 2017. © Naomi Lloyd.

you should share your sighting with only your most trusted and ethically responsible birding friends. Also, consider entering the data in eBird without a detailed location, at least temporarily. If the bird is on private property or at a feeder, ask yourself if it can be viewed without trespassing or violating the privacy of the landowner. Imagine if hundreds of curious birders with cameras and spotting scopes came to your backyard! Some people who host rare birds are happy to have visitors, but this level of cooperation cannot be taken for granted. Good situations happen when someone from the birding community talks to the landowner, explains the importance of the bird, and negotiates workable visitation times and ground rules.

Ethical Birding and Conservation

When we venture into natural areas to experience nature, we are entering the homes of birds and other wildlife. They depend on these places for food and shelter, and our presence and activities affect their way of life. An action that seems harmless to us, like taking a shortcut through a field or cutting down a dead tree for firewood, could trample nests or remove a food source. When birding, our primary concern should be the welfare of birds and their habitats.

The American Birding Association's (ABA) Code of Birding Ethics provides excellent guidance along these lines (www.aba.org). The ABA asks birders to follow this code, and to distribute and teach it to others. In addition, many birders follow Leave No Trace Principles (www.lnt.org) to minimize their impact on the environment. Some of the best birding sites are natural areas removed from the trappings of civilization, including bathrooms. Human feces contain bacteria that harm the environment if not treated properly, so if a portable toilet or outhouse is provided, use it. If nature calls in the middle of nowhere, be prepared to use the woods properly. Choose a site at least two hundred feet from water and away from trails. Bury feces in a hole six to eight inches deep, and do not leave toilet paper in the field. Put it in a plastic bag, carry it out, and dispose of it like the trash it is.

Because we share public lands with an increasing number of outdoor enthusiasts who are not birders, I believe it is important for birders to do more than just model ethical behavior. We need to become educators and advocates for the birds and bird habitat by sharing our knowledge. The people we encounter in natural areas are all potential birders. They are already outdoors. Share your passion. Let people—especially children—look through your binoculars or spotting scope. Show them pictures, answer questions, and tell them about birds. Most people do not harm birds or damage habitat deliberately. They do it because they do not understand birds. For example, the man I encountered throwing a stick for his dog into a field filled with nesting Bobolinks had no idea that those pretty birds nested on the ground and that his dog might be trampling their eggs.

Birders also need to become involved in the management of their favorite birding sites. Too often, I hear birders complaining to each other about changes at a site instead of talking to the people in authority who can actually make a difference. We are just one of many constituencies that use most of these areas, and if local land managers do not know the birds are important, other interests will be served. It is best to get a seat at the table before there is a crisis, such as an "improvement" that will adversely affect bird habitat. Prior involvement opens the door to discussing alternative ways to accomplish similar goals. It also adds credibility to your side of the debate if you can bring bird data to the negotiating table.

American Birding Association Code of Birding Ethics

1. Promote the welfare of birds and their environment.
   a. Support the protection of important bird habitat.
   b. To avoid stressing birds or exposing them to danger, exercise restraint and caution during observation, photography, sound recording, or filming.

      Limit the use of recordings and other methods of attracting birds, and never use such methods in heavily birded areas or for attracting any species that is Threatened, Endangered, of Special Concern, or is rare in your local area.

      Keep well back from nests and nesting colonies, roosts, display areas, and important feeding sites. In such sensitive areas, if there is a need for extended observation, photography, filming, or recording, try to use a blind or hide, and take advantage of natural cover.

      Use artificial light sparingly for filming or photography, especially for close-ups.
   c. Before advertising the presence of a rare bird, evaluate the potential for disturbance to the bird, its surroundings, and other people in the area, and proceed only if access can be controlled, disturbance minimized, and permission has been obtained from private landowners. The sites of rare nesting birds should be divulged only to the proper conservation authorities.
   d. Stay on roads, trails, and paths where they exist; otherwise, keep habitat disturbance to a minimum.
2. Respect the law, and the rights of others.
   a. Do not enter private property without the owner's explicit permission.
   b. Follow all laws, rules, and regulations governing use of roads and public areas, both at home and abroad.
   c. Practice common courtesy in contacts with other people. Your exemplary behavior will generate goodwill with birders and non-birders alike.
3. Ensure that feeders, nest structures, and other artificial bird environments are safe.

a. Keep dispensers, water, and food clean and free of decay or disease. It is important to feed birds continually during harsh weather.

b. Maintain and clean nest structures regularly.

c. If you are attracting birds to an area, ensure the birds are not exposed to predation from cats and other domestic animals or dangers posed by artificial hazards.

4. Group birding, whether organized or impromptu, requires special care. Each individual in the group, in addition to the obligations spelled out in Items #1 and #2, has responsibilities as a Group Member:

a. Respect the interests, rights, and skills of fellow birders, as well as people participating in other legitimate outdoor activities. Freely share your knowledge and experience, except where code 1(c) applies. Be especially helpful to beginning birders.

b. If you witness unethical birding behavior, assess the situation and intervene if you think it prudent. When interceding, inform the person(s) of the inappropriate action and attempt, within reason, to have it stopped. If the behavior continues, document it and notify appropriate individuals or organizations.

Group Leader Responsibilities [amateur and professional trips and tours]:

c. Be an exemplary ethical role model for the group. Teach through word and example.

d. Keep groups to a size that limits impact on the environment and does not interfere with others using the same area.

e. Ensure everyone in the group knows of and practices this code.

f. Learn and inform the group of any special circumstances applicable to the areas being visited (e.g., no audio playback allowed).

g. Acknowledge that professional tour companies bear a special responsibility to place the welfare of birds and the benefits of public knowledge ahead of the company's commercial interests. Ideally, leaders should keep track of tour sightings, document unusual occurrences, and submit records to appropriate organizations. (American Birding Association)

Finally, birders put lots of money into local businesses near important birding areas, but much of this patronage goes unnoticed because we never let people know that we came to see the birds. Wear your binoculars into the restaurant, or tell the wait staff about the birds you saw. Land set aside and protected for outdoor recreation has real value to local economies. The contributions of birders need to be recognized like those of hunters, fishermen, snowmobilers, and other groups, who all do a better job of publicizing their use of managed areas than we do.

5 Introduction to Birding Sites

This book includes sites that welcome both birds and birders. Public lands are managed for many different purposes, including some that are not compatible with birdwatching, but they have the advantage of legal access, regular maintenance, interpretation, infrastructure, and facilities that make them pleasant places for birders to visit. The birding areas chosen here favor managed areas with substantial amounts of land dedicated to "passive recreational use." They typically have many acres with miles of trails, little development, and minimal environmental impact. In general, they tend to include areas where walking is encouraged, safe, and not too strenuous.

From these birder-friendly sites, I have tried to identify areas where birders can see a wide variety of birds. Just because an area has many acres of undeveloped land does not necessarily mean it will have good bird diversity or uncommon species. Birds tend to occur in predictable habitats that are scattered throughout the Hudson Valley landscape. Moreover, these bird communities change seasonally, so accurately cataloging the bird fauna of even a single site requires many visits. Fortunately, the skilled birders in the Hudson Valley have generously shared both their data and their opinions on the best sites for birds.

But birders will go anywhere to see birds, including landfills, sewage treatment plants, and parking lots that sometimes have food sources that birds can use. These areas can be good places to see birds, but they are not natural, and they are generally not nice places to spend a day, so they are not included here. The birding sites selected for this guide were chosen to showcase the spectacular scenery of the Hudson Valley as well as the birds. They are likely to include either a diversity of bird habitats in a small area or special environments that support rare species. My goal is to identify a suite of birder-friendly sites that captures the full range of habitats and bird diversity that each county has to offer.

Thousands of acres of land have been set aside for outdoor recreation in the Hudson Valley, but the ownership and management of these properties is a mix of government and private entities. In the collection of great birding areas presented here, there are lands owned by federal, state, and local government agencies as well as private conservation organizations. This mix of ownership clearly demonstrates that in an area like the Hudson Valley, which has been settled and developed for centuries, it takes much more than a village to preserve our natural heritage. It takes government working at many levels, often in partnership with private conservation organizations, to keep land open and accessible to everyone. The resulting mosaic of public land ownership means that birders and other outdoor enthusiasts who visit these sites encounter a confusing array of rules, permitted activities, hours, fees, and amenities. The birding sites chosen here are no exception, so it is important that first-time visitors take the time to read the signage posted at the entrance of nearly every reserve.

This guide includes two areas that are part of the National Wildlife Refuge System. Another federal agency, the National Oceanic and Atmospheric Administration, partners with the New York State Department of Environmental Conservation to manage four areas on the Hudson River that are part of the National Estuarine Research Reserve. These federal lands have no admission fees, but as a part of their mission to conserve and manage wildlife habitat, hunting and fishing are allowed in season with a valid permit.

Most of the state-owned recreational land in the Hudson Valley is administered by two different agencies: NYSDEC and the Office of Parks, Recreation and Historic Preservation (OPRHP), better known simply as "Parks." Statewide, NYSDEC manages over four million acres, most of it in the Adirondack and Catskill Forest Preserves, while OPRHP administers about 330,000 acres. Nearly half of the birding sites identified in this guide are owned by these two state agencies.

NYSDEC classifies its holdings into categories that determine how the land can be used. Wildlife Management Areas (WMA), for example, are protected primarily for the production and use of wildlife, so hunting, fishing, and trapping should be expected. NYSDEC State Forests (SF) are managed by professional foresters as working forests, but a wide range of consumptive and passive recreational activities, including birdwatching, are now major components of State Forest management plans. With the exception of campgrounds, NYSDEC lands generally do not have fees, and they usually do not have restrooms and other amenities unless they are associated with an environmental education center or campground.

OPRHP holdings include state parks (SP), historic sites, rail trails, marinas, beaches, pools, and golf courses, but despite all this infrastructure, nearly 85 percent of the park system is open space. Unfortunately, many state parks have strict hours of operation and charge a vehicle entry fee, which varies with location and season. Many people who like to bird in state parks regularly find it economical to invest in an Empire Pass, which provides unlimited vehicle entry into most parks for a modest annual fee. The majority of state parks in this guide, unless they are "undeveloped," have well-developed facilities, including restrooms. Park-specific fees, amenities, and access pass options are available at www.nysparks.com.

Some unique birding sites have such strong local support that they are protected by local governments. The amount of public land owned and managed by counties, towns, and cities varies dramatically in different parts of the Hudson Valley. Some, like Westchester County, which administers more than fifty parks including several nature centers, are able to devote substantial resources to land ownership and facilities maintenance. The more rural parts of the valley, however, with a smaller tax base to support public land, seem to rely more on private conservation organizations to protect open space. Fees, hours, and amenities vary considerably.

The Hudson Valley is fortunate to have many private nonprofit organizations committed to the conservation of natural areas. These groups include some large, well-known and well-staffed conservation groups such as The Nature Conservancy (TNC), National Audubon Society (NAS), and Scenic Hudson. Others, such as Vassar College, the Huyck Preserve, and the Cary Institute of Ecosystem Studies, own land to support their education and research activities, but they open it to the public for compatible recreational use. Local land trusts own and manage some of the wonderful birding sites in this guide. Unlike government agencies that depend on taxes to buy and manage land, these groups rely on grants and donations to do their good work. They need our support. Their ability to buy land and maintain it for public activities like birding depends on us.

Finally, this is a good place to mention that many of the birding sites that follow have received special recognition for their value to birds. The National

TABLE 5.1. Sites with Important Bird Area and/or Bird Conservation Area Status

Site	IBA	BCA
UPPER HUDSON		
Albany Pine Bush Preserve	•	•
Dyken Pond Environmental Education Center		•
Hunter Mountain	•	•
John Boyd Thacher and Thompson's Lake State Park	•	•
Schodack Island State Park	•	•
Stockport Flats	•	
MID-HUDSON		
Balsam Lake Mountain	•	•
Harriman State Park, Elk Pen	•	
Harriman State Park, Island Pond	•	
Harriman State Park, Lake Skannatati Pine Swamp Loop	•	
Mills Norrie State Park		•
Minnewaska State Park Preserve		•
Shawangunk Grasslands National Wildlife Refuge	•	
Sterling Forest State Park, Ironwood Drive	•	•
Tivoli Bays Wildlife Management Area	•	•
LOWER HUDSON		
Bear Mountain State Park, Doodletown, and Iona Island	•	•
Arthur W. Butler Memorial Sanctuary and Chestnut Ridge Hawkwatch	•	
Clarence Fahnestock State Park	•	•
Constitution Marsh Audubon Center and Sanctuary	•	•
Croton Point Park	•	
Edith G. Read Wildlife Sanctuary	•	
Hook Mountain	•	
Little Stony Point State Park	•	•
Marshlands Conservancy	•	
Rockefeller State Park Preserve	•	
Rockland Lake State Park		•
BEYOND THE TEN COUNTIES		
Bashakill Wildlife Management Area		•
Vischer Ferry Nature and Historic Preserve		•

Audubon Society, acting as the United States partner for BirdLife International, has used a rigorous scientific process to identify areas that deserve special protection. Important Bird Areas (IBAs) meet one of three criteria: (1) they support species of conservation concern or those with a restricted range; (2) they are places where birds congregate in large numbers at one time; or (3) they support groups of birds that are representative of certain habitats, such as grasslands, forests, shrublands, or wetlands. In addition, New York State has adopted the IBA criteria to recognize Bird Conservation Areas (BCAs), state-owned lands where birds deserve special protection. Statewide, there are more than 130 IBAs and 59 BCAs that have been classified as critical sites for birds. Some sites in areas of mixed ownership have received both designations. Table 5.1 lists the birding sites in this book that have received these significant recognitions.

About the Birding Sites

For convenience, the birding sites that follow are presented in four groups that have little to do with the ecology or geography of the Hudson Valley. These regions and the counties within them were chosen to ensure a fairly even distribution of birdwatching areas throughout the ten counties of the Hudson Valley. Within each county, the sites are organized moving from north to south and west to east, as if you were reading a book. The sites themselves vary in size from postage-stamp preserves to tracts covering tens of thousands of acres.

Directions lead from an easily accessible major road, intersection, or town to the main (or sometimes the birders') entrance. Websites for online trail maps are also given here. Use the website's search engine to locate the map. At large sites with multiple trailheads or parking areas, alternative entrances are mentioned in the text or shown on maps.

The description for each site begins with its landscape setting, history, and ownership. Though birds can be found anywhere, these sketches are designed to hit the highlights by leading birders to the best habitats and viewing areas for each site. This approach will work well for birders who can manage only one visit, but to be honest, my goal is to provide an introduction that will whet your appetite for each place and encourage you to come back again and again.

6 The Upper Hudson Valley

Best place to....	Site
SEE WATERFOWL	Tomhannock Reservoir
FIND GRASSLAND BIRDS	Ooms Conservation Area at Sutherland Pond
FIND SHOREBIRDS	Cohoes Flats
SEE MIGRATING WARBLERS	Five Rivers Environmental Education Center
FIND HIGH-ELEVATION BIRDS	Hunter Mountain
WATCH MIGRATING RAPTORS	John Boyd Thacher State Park
FIND A RARE BIRD	Coxsackie Creek Grassland Preserve
GO BIRDING IN LATE SUMMER	Taconic Crest Trail
GO BIRDING IN WINTER	Cohoes Flats
BIRD FROM A BOAT	Stockport Flats
HIKE AND BIRDWATCH	Beebe Hill and Harvey Mountain State Forest
TAKE THE KIDS	Five Rivers Environmental Education Center
EXPERIENCE BIRDS AND CULTURE	Olana
TAKE THE GRANDPARENTS	Greenport Conservation Area and Harrier Hill

The four counties in the Upper Hudson Valley include Albany and Greene on the west, and Rensselaer and Columbia on the east. Much of the population in this region is concentrated near the river in the state capital, Albany, and in the cities of Cohoes, Troy, Catskill, and Hudson. The Mohawk River, the largest tributary of the Hudson, enters from the west, cascading over Cohoes Falls before it joins the river at Peebles Island. Its connection to Glacial Lake Albany formed the pine barrens of the Albany Pine Bush, a rare natural community found nowhere else in the Hudson Valley. The Mohawk forms the boundary between Albany and Saratoga Counties to the north.

This part of the Hudson River is freshwater but still tidal as far north as the federal dam and lock at Troy. There are no tides north of the Troy dam, and above this barrier to the Rensselaer County line, the main stem of the Hudson River is regulated by four dams and locks. However, most of the freshwater tidal marshes in Greene and Columbia Counties are protected from development and have excellent bird habitat.

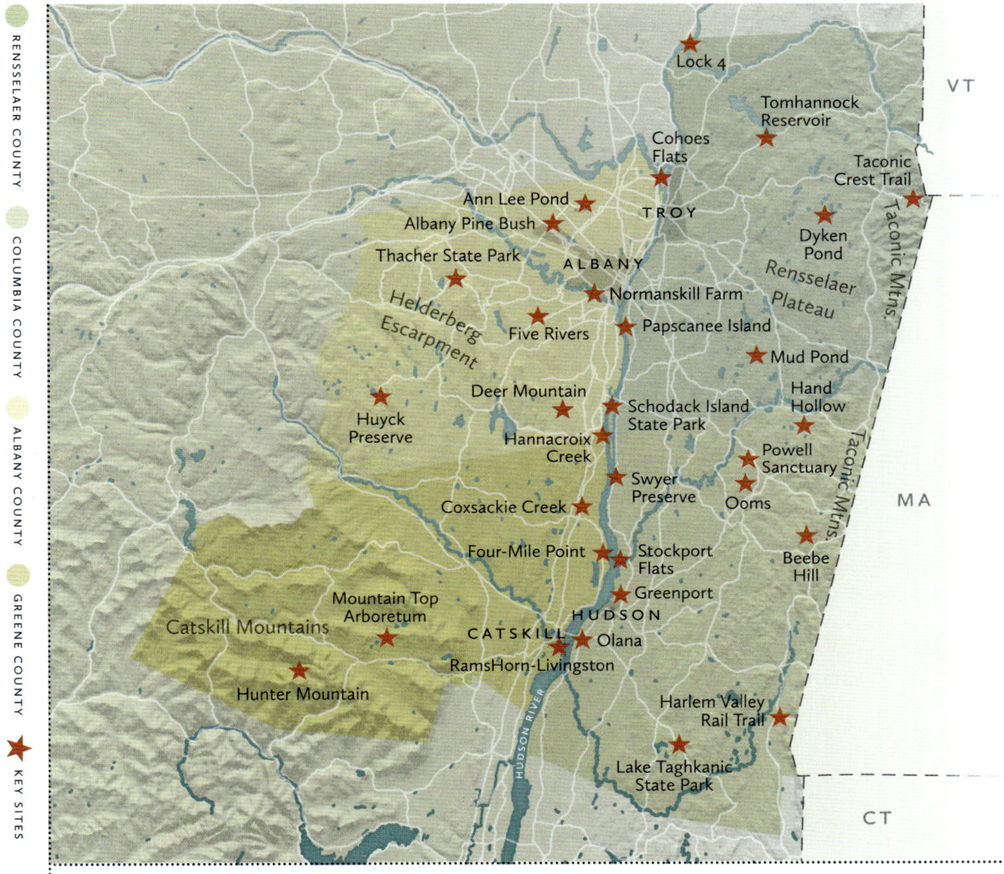

THE UPPER HUDSON VALLEY

The highest elevations in this region are found in the Catskill Mountains, which reach into the southwestern part of Greene County, including Hunter Mountain and a number of other mountains over thirty-five hundred feet. The Helderberg Escarpment in northwestern Albany County and the Taconic Mountains and Rensselaer Plateau in the eastern counties have habitat for birds that live at higher elevations. Between these highlands and the river, the undeveloped lands of the Upper Hudson Valley are mostly rolling hills with farms, pastures, and occasional small towns.

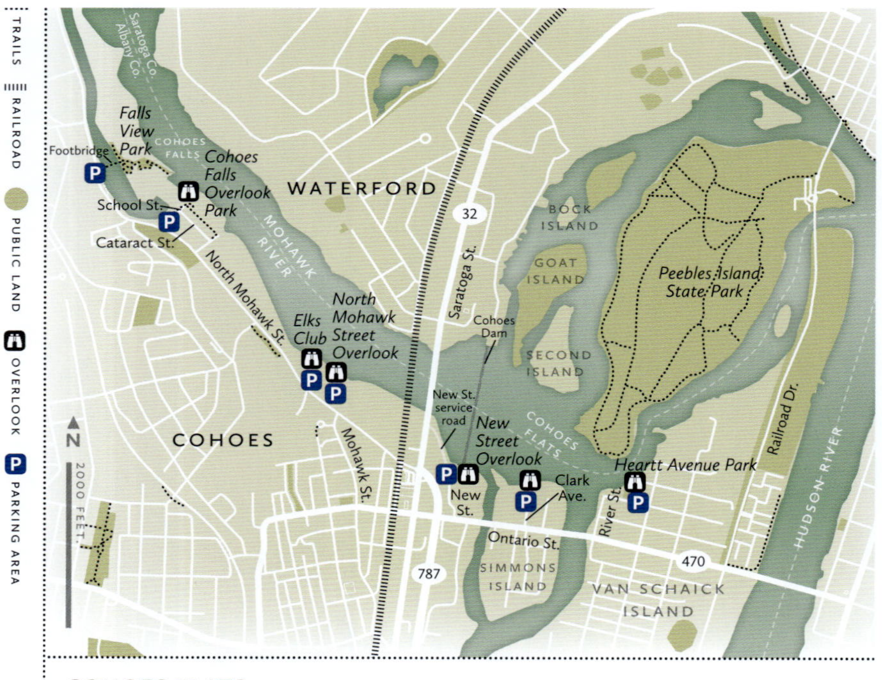

COHOES FLATS

ALBANY COUNTY

Cohoes Flats

GPS ADDRESS 1 Clark Avenue, Cohoes

LATITUDE/LONGITUDE 42.77492 −73.69260

DIRECTIONS From I-787 going north in Cohoes, turn east (right) onto NY 470/Ontario Street and continue across the bridge over the Mohawk River about 0.25 mile to Clark Avenue. Turn left onto Clark Avenue and proceed about 0.1 mile to the end, to a dirt parking lot on the left for the New York State Dam Recreation Area.

Cohoes Flats is an area of exposed rock ledges in the Mohawk River just below Cohoes Falls, a massive waterfall, second only to Niagara Falls in New York State. To early settlers, Cohoes Falls was a major barrier to navigation, but it generated power for the mills and turned Cohoes into a major manufacturing center in the 1800s. Today its water is diverted to turn turbines that generate electricity at the School Street Powerhouse. From May 1 to November 1, Falls View Park provides seasonal access to the waterfall and the river via a pedestrian bridge over the power canal, but the best birding is often below the falls from viewpoints and overlooks. Water levels are key. When the water is low, ten feet or less on the gauge at Cohoes (see water.weather.gov for real-time data), the exposed riverbed attracts wonderful birds that use the exposed rocks to feed. Low water levels also make it possible to walk out into the middle of the river and set up a spotting scope for a 360-degree view of river and shoreline. However, this fantastic birding comes with the caveat that water levels can change quickly on the Mohawk because of distant storms, snowmelt, and power plant activities upstream; and footing on the riverbed is rough, wet, and sometimes slippery.

Some of the access points shown on the map are closed or treacherous in winter. Falls View Park is gated, and the overlook from the Cohoes parking area on North Mohawk Street is not plowed. In winter, local birders tend to use Cohoes Falls Overlook Park at the junction of School and Cataract Streets, the access point on Clark Avenue behind the U-Haul dealership, or Heartt Avenue Park. Local birders have also been promised access to an overlook southeast of NY 32 at the top of the dam (New Street) that is currently blocked by bridge construction. Winter access is important because the falls and the current keep the river ice-free, and the open water attracts waterfowl and gulls. Common Goldeneye and both mergansers are regular, but in brutal winters when the Great Lakes freeze, this area has seen Long-tailed Duck, Redhead, and other uncommon waterfowl. Iceland, Glaucous, Bonaparte's, and Lesser Black-backed Gulls can sometimes be found among the Ring-billed, Herring, and Great Black-backed Gulls that congregate here in winter. Bald Eagle, Peregrine Falcon, and Merlin are often seen as well.

Willet at Cohoes Flats.
© Naomi Lloyd.

At other times of year, Cohoes Flats is known for its waders and shore-birds. Great Egret and Black-crowned Night-Heron have been seen in the fall during post-breeding dispersal. May and September are best for shorebirds, with around twenty species recorded, including Ruddy Turnstone, Pectoral Sandpiper, Stilt Sandpiper, Willet, Dunlin, Black-bellied Plover, and American Golden-Plover.

This is a good place to mention nearby Peebles Island State Park. Although technically in Saratoga County, it also has a view of Cohoes Flats. Peebles sits at the confluence of the Mohawk and Hudson Rivers between the municipalities of Waterford in Saratoga County and Cohoes in Albany County. Two branches of the Mohawk River wrap around the sides of Peebles Island and empty into the Hudson River at its northeast end. The landscape surrounding the island is dramatic, with panoramic views of the rivers, shoals, islands, cliffs, waterfalls, and dams. This site is accessed via Railroad Drive on Van Shaick Island.

Ann Lee Pond and Bauer Environmental Park

GPS ADDRESS Heritage Lane, Albany
LATITUDE/LONGITUDE 42.73892 −73.81440
DIRECTIONS From I-87, take Exit 4 and proceed toward Albany International Airport. Turn onto Wolf Road and then left onto NY 155/ Albany Shaker Road toward the airport, and go 1.6 miles to Heritage Lane. Turn south (left) onto Heritage Lane and continue to the second of two parking areas. Trail map at www.albanycounty.com.

Ann Lee Pond and nearby Bauer Environmental Park in northeastern Albany County are relatively small, adjacent preserves with surprising bird diversity given their proximity to Albany International Airport and suburban housing developments. Ann Lee Pond is part of the Shaker National Historic Site District, which includes buildings from the first settlement of the Shakers, a celibate Christian community known for simple living, architecture, and craftsmanship. Some of the buildings are used for offices, a gift shop, and programs, including three large craft fairs. The nature preserve occupies 170 acres on the south side of Heritage Lane, and there are plans to build a connector trail to Bauer, which is currently accessed from Sand Creek Road between Watervliet-Shaker Road and Wolf Road.

Both of these sites are exceptionally convenient and accessible, perfect spots for a quick birding fix during lunch, a layover at the airport, or a stop on the way home from work; but for anyone with more time, there is plenty to explore. The centerpiece of Ann Lee is the pond, created by the Shakers to drain nearby wetlands for farming. The red trail around the pond, level and about a mile long, crosses a small wetland near the road, cuts through a deciduous forest and swamp with a small Great Blue Heron rookery, and then crosses the pond on a floating bridge that offers an unobstructed view into open water to the north and the cattail marsh to the south. The woods are exceptionally good for warblers (more than twenty species recorded), thrushes, vireos, and flycatchers in spring. In the fall, look for sparrows in the shrubby areas on the west side of the pond. The pond is shallow and tends to freeze early, but it gets good waterfowl in early spring. Scarce species such as Horned Grebe, Gadwall, Redhead, both scaup, American Wigeon, and other rarities have put in an appearance. Common Nighthawk has been reported in late August, and open-country birds like mimids and Eastern Bluebird nest in the Shaker orchard across the street. Bauer is mostly wet woods and lacks the habitat diversity of Ann Lee Pond Preserve, but it has a half-mile-long boardwalk that is handicapped accessible.

Albany Pine Bush Preserve

GPS ADDRESS 195 New Karner Road, Albany
LATITUDE/LONGITUDE 42.71891 −73.86389
DIRECTIONS From I-87 Exit 2W, NY 5W/Central Avenue, go west 2.0 miles to NY 155/New Karner Road. Turn west (left) onto NY 155 and continue 1.2 miles to the Discovery Center. Detailed trail maps at www.albanypinebush.org.

Even if the Albany Pine Bush were not a great place to see birds, it would still be an important place to visit because the preserve protects the inland pitch pine-scrub oak barrens, a rare, fire-dependent natural community that is known from fewer than twenty sites worldwide. Twelve to fifteen thousand years ago, as the last glaciers melted and retreated northward, runoff drained down the Mohawk, forming a sandy delta at the edge of Glacial Lake Albany. This huge body of water eventually covered the Hudson Valley between Glens Falls and Newburgh. Today, deposits from that delta form the sloping dunes

ALBANY PINE BUSH PRESERVE

and sandy soil of the Albany Pine Bush. These hot, dry soils were colonized by drought-tolerant plants and animals capable of surviving periodic fires, and this resulted in a unique natural community dominated by tall pitch pines with a low understory of scrub oaks. The habitat features dozens of rare plants and animals, including the endangered Karner blue butterfly.

Because the Albany Pine Bush is situated on the edge of the City of Albany, two rapidly growing suburbs (Colonie and Guilderland), and two interstate highways (I-87 and I-90), its protection was a conservationist's nightmare. However, in 1988 the area's preservation became a possibility when the New York State Legislature created the Albany Pine Bush Preserve Commission to protect, manage, and restore the site. But by this time, development had already created a fragmented landscape, and years of fire suppression had altered the unique assemblage of plants and animals, allowing invasive species to degrade the rare natural community. It has taken decades of research, citizen education, mechanical management, prescribed burning, and land acquisition to restore, maintain, and protect the Albany Pine Bush Preserve.

Its very existence is a testimony to intergovernmental cooperation and the hard work of committed conservationists.

Any visit to the Albany Pine Bush should begin at the Discovery Center, a "green" building with solar panels and composting toilets, educational exhibits, a gift shop, and free trail maps. This is a good place to pick up a current trail map and check trail conditions, because they are constantly changing and sometimes closed for management activities such as tree thinning and prescribed burns. The thirty-two-hundred-acre preserve boasts a total of about eighteen miles of well-marked trails, but they are scattered over many parcels and originate at ten different trailheads. Travel on unofficial trails is not permitted, and following any unmarked trail is a good way to get lost.

The pitch pine-scrub oak barrens community includes a variety of bird habitats, but the preserve is a restoration work in progress, and fire-suppressed parts of the site include mixed forest. The more pristine parts of this ecological community have an understory of scrub oak with grassy openings and scattered pitch pine. Some areas include extensive patches of prairie-like grassland, filled with bluestem and wildflowers such as wild blue lupine, the food

The Prairie Warbler population is monitored at the Albany Pine Bush Preserve to evaluate the quality of its pitch pine–scrub oak barrens habitat. © Deborah Tracy-Kral.

plant of the Karner blue butterfly. Eastern Towhee is abundant in restored parts of the Albany Pine Bush along with good numbers of Prairie Warbler, Eastern Bluebird, Indigo Bunting, Chestnut-sided Warbler, Red-breasted Nuthatch, American Woodcock, Field Sparrow, Song Sparrow, and an occasional Brown Thrasher. As restoration continues, this habitat is likely to increase, and it is hoped that some historical breeders that are still reported, like Golden-winged Warbler, Mourning Warbler, and Eastern Whip-poor-will, will become more common. With its mixed ownership, this preserve has achieved both IBA and BCA status.

The Discovery Center and Karner Barrens East and West, which are connected by a trail under busy NY 155, are the most visited and well-known parts of the Albany Pine Bush. These areas contain a representative chunk of the iconic barrens habitat, a dune with views of the Helderbergs and the Berkshires, and some small ponds and marshes with viewing platforms. Common Nighthawks are counted over this part of the barrens in late August as part of a monitoring program. The eastern border of Karner Barrens East abuts the restored Albany Landfill, which has grasslands and fence posts where birds often perch. Similar but quieter barrens habitat is present in other parts of the preserve, especially at Kings Highway Barrens and Blueberry Hill, which is embedded in a quiet suburban neighborhood with no busy highways.

The Albany Pine Bush is so large and constantly changing that it only makes sense to discuss a few of the other landscape features that may be of interest to birders. Water features other than small ponds are uncommon in this environment. Rensselaer Lake in the Rapp Barrens is a disjunct, noisy portion of the preserve where waterfowl and shorebirds turn up during migration. Much of this buffer area consists of deciduous woods. The Madison Avenue Pinelands, once overgrown with hardwood, is being restored by cutting and fire and may become good habitat for Pine Warbler. The Great Dune is more than a mile long and fifty feet tall, the largest sand dune in the preserve. Breeding-bird surveys in this area have found Wild Turkey and Ruffed Grouse with young. A trail in this parcel crosses the Kaikout Kill, a small stream that might have interesting birds, especially during migration. Finally, the Hunger Kill Barrens parcel, though remote and disturbed, has closed canopy forests, a wooded creek, and ravines—habitat features not found elsewhere in the preserve.

John Boyd Thacher and Thompson's Lake State Parks

GPS ADDRESS 1 Hailes Cave Road, Voorheesville

LATITUDE/LONGITUDE 42.65539 −74.01926

DIRECTIONS From the junction of NY 85 and NY 157 in New Salem, take NY 157 2.0 miles to the main entrance of Thacher State Park. To get to Thompson's Lake State Park, stay on NY 157 through the park to CR 256/ Ketcham Road, and take it west about a mile to the nature center on the left. Trail maps at parks.ny.gov/parks.

These two birding areas include three disjunct parcels of public land in parts of four towns (New Scotland, Knox, Berne, and Guilderland) in the northwest corner of Albany County. They are owned and managed collectively by OPRHP. The north and south sections of John Boyd Thacher State Park

Dawn at the Helderberg Hawkwatch. Tom Williams.

sit on the edge of the three miles of shale and limestone cliffs known as the Helderberg Escarpment, while Thompson's Lake State Park is a few miles farther west. Historically and geologically significant, the first 350-acre parcel was donated by Emma Treadwell Thacher in 1914. Since that time, the protected area has grown to include about twenty-four hundred acres with spectacular vistas, thirty miles of trails, and large forested areas at elevations of twelve hundred to fourteen hundred feet.

The most accessible and well-studied bird viewing areas are found in the southern portion of Thacher State Park and at Thompson's Lake. The northern part of Thacher is somewhat remote, and the terrain is mostly wooded. Here, despite a well-developed trail network, all the escarpment overlooks are long hikes from the nearest parking areas on the western perimeter. However, NY 157 runs through the southern part of Thacher and provides easy year-round access to many areas, including a new four-season visitor center.

More than 170 species have been reported from various parts of Thacher State Park, and 102 are listed as probable breeders. Many of these birds have been seen during spring and fall migration at the Cliff Edge Overlook. Located on the edge of the escarpment, this spot is the perfect vantage point for watching migrating raptors as they soar overhead and make use of the cliff-generated updrafts. Though some raptors can be seen here at any time of year, Broad-winged Hawk numbers peak in mid-September. Most years, the park offers a guided hawkwatch for the uninitiated that explains how to identify raptors on the wing (see parks.ny.gov for dates and details). Common Ravens, resident and frequent at Thacher, soar among the raptors and scavenge roadkill on the park roads.

The Escarpment Trail and the popular Indian Ladder Trail run along the top of the cliffs and across and down the talus slopes. Shaded and icy in winter, the Indian Ladder Trail is closed from November 15 to May 1, and even in early spring, the cliff face is shaded until mid-morning; but once the sun reaches this area, the sparsely wooded cliff face teems with migrating songbirds. Winter Wren, Hermit Thrush, Black-throated Blue Warbler, Black-and-white Warbler, American Redstart, Ovenbird, and Dark-eyed Junco are common, and Worm-eating and Canada Warbler have been seen in the past.

On top of the escarpment and west of NY 157, the park is dominated by mature beech-maple forest with intermittent hemlock ravines and occasional stands of pine and plantings of spruce. This area has a complex network of trails that offers many options for loops of varying length. The nature trail from the Paint Mine parking lot is a good trail to explore to see what the top of the escarpment has to offer. Spruce plantings in this area draw boreal warblers such as Bay-breasted, Magnolia, and Cape May. The trail passes by streams and waterfalls where Louisiana Waterthrush is likely. Northern Goshawk nest in the park and vocalize to aggressively defend their nests, while Black-throated Green Warbler, Blackburnian Warbler, and Red-breasted Nuthatch are found in hemlock stands. Also on top of the escarpment is a wetland area accessible from the Hop Field parking lot via the yellow trail. This red maple swamp has a boardwalk.

No trip to this area would be complete without a stop at Thompson's Lake and the Emma Treadwell Thacher Nature Center. The nature center has good maps, interpretive programs, restroom facilities, and bird feeders. It is built on the west shore of the lake, which, though small, is sometimes used by uncommon water birds including migrating Osprey, Common Loon, and diving ducks. In winter, scoters are sometimes seen. During the summer, the campground and swimming area effectively exclude most waterfowl.

The trails around the nature center run through shrubby old fields and meadows and along forest edges. Eastern Bluebird and Tree Swallow use the nest boxes, and Wild Turkey are common. The brushy fields have Eastern Towhee, Brown Thrasher, Chestnut-sided Warbler, and Prairie Warbler, while the grassier sites are good for Field Sparrow, Savannah Sparrow, Eastern Meadowlark, and Bobolink.

Normanskill Farm

GPS ADDRESS 95 Mill Road, Albany

LATITUDE/LONGITUDE 42.63485 –73.80019

DIRECTIONS From the junction of I-787 and US 9W in Albany, take US 9W north 0.5 mile. Continue straight onto McAlpin when US 9W turns right, and continue another 0.25 mile to its junction with NY 443. Turn left and follow NY 443 0.4 mile to its junction with Mill Road just north of the bridge over the Normanskill. Turn north (left) onto Mill Road and follow it 0.25 mile, under a bridge, past its intersection with Normanskill Drive, to a dirt parking area with a kiosk.

This lovely patch of green is located on the Normans Kill Creek within the Albany city limits. Actively farmed since the 1800s, it was most recently home to Normanskill Dairy, which delivered milk and dairy products to local families until the late 1960s. In 1980 the City of Albany acquired the land to preserve open space and recreational opportunities for residents, and today this rural acreage serves that purpose and several others. The farm operates under a lease agreement with a local farmer, hay is produced on-site, and the main livestock building houses the horses of the Albany Mounted Police Unit. The farm is best known as a dog park, but it is also home to the Albany community gardens. Most of the land is open for hiking and wildlife observation, and because the property joins the Capital Hills Golf Course, there is lots of shared open space available for exploration. Local birders have observed more than 135 species in its mosaic of habitats, including such rarities as Yellow-throated Warbler and Mourning Warbler. While the woods along the creek are great for spring warblers, every habitat at the farm has its own surprises.

Two interesting old bridges, now closed, are just a short walk from the parking lot. The old bridge over the Normanskill still stands blocked off on the south side of Normanskill Drive, the road that intersects Mill Road just

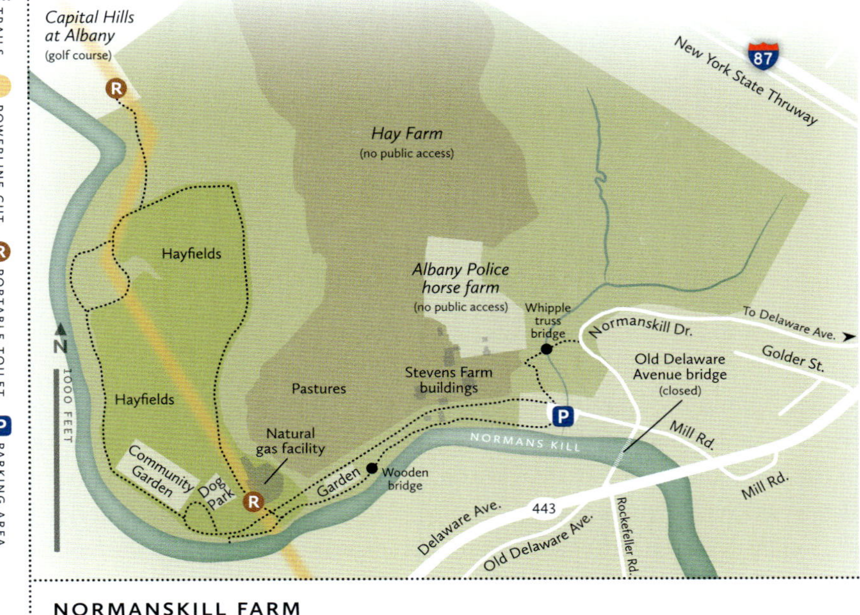

before the parking lot entrance. Pedestrians can walk out on the bridge for a spectacular long view of the "kill," across the flats toward where it empties into the Hudson River about a mile downstream. The creek's rocky outcrops are a good place to look for gulls, shorebirds, waders, waterfowl, and other birds that use this shallow water habitat. The old bridge includes a section of the original yellow-brick road surface that was used on the Delaware Turnpike to bring people and goods to Albany.

Across Mill Road from the parking lot, a pathway lined with logs leads up the hill through the woods to an old Whipple Cast and Wrought Iron Bowstring Truss Bridge that spans a deep ravine and a small tributary of the Normanskill. An interpretive sign describes its colorful local history, and the bridge provides an opportunity to study birds in the treetops and to search the area below for both waterthrushes and Winter Wren. The area beyond the bridge has restricted access, but it still provides glimpses of the active horse pasture where birds may be present.

From the parking area, a dirt road leads to the community garden plots, and the unmarked but fairly obvious Stevens Farm hiking trail begins in the

Cliff Swallow has nested on the buildings at Normanskill Farm. © Kathryn J. Schneider.

woods right at the kiosk along the edge of the Normanskill. The trail hugs the creek and parallels the road until the vehicle road dead-ends at the back of the community gardens. Staying on the hiking trail offers a nice view of a slower section of Normanskill Creek. Belted Kingfisher and various waterfowl are sometimes seen here, swallows feed on insects overhead, and shorebirds such as Spotted Sandpiper and Solitary Sandpiper forage on the muddy edges of the stream during migration. Pay special attention to the swallows at this site, because Cliff Swallows have built their distinctively shaped mud nests on the side of the barn and attempted to breed. Eastern Bluebirds use the nest boxes along the creek and are often seen in this area.

The road from the parking lot toward the community gardens passes by a steep, shrubby hillside used by shrubland specialists. This dirt road is also a wonderful place to study sparrows. In the fall especially, migrating sparrows feed on the seeds and fruits in the fallow garden plots. They sometimes perch on the wire fence or drink water from puddles in the road, thus providing an opportunity to study the defining characteristics of these sometimes frustrating little brown jobbers. Nine species of sparrow have been seen here on a single fall visit, including White-crowned Sparrow, Savannah Sparrow, Fox Sparrow, Field Sparrow, and Vesper Sparrow. Killdeer usually nest in the gravelly area around the gas distribution station. The dirt road ends at the back of the garden plots, but the hiking trail continues along the Normanskill near the edge of the open hayfields and on to the golf course. Bobolink and Eastern Meadowlark defend territories in these fields before mowing begins in the spring. A variety of raptors, including American Kestrel, Red-tailed Hawk, Cooper's Hawk, and occasionally Merlin have been seen hunting these fields.

The hiking trail joins the golf course at the fourteenth tee, where there is a portable toilet and a hiker's rest stop sign. From here it is 1.5 miles to the clubhouse and 1.2 miles back to the parking lot at the farm.

Five Rivers Environmental Education Center

GPS ADDRESS 56 Game Farm Road, Delmar

LATITUDE/LONGITUDE 42.60881 −73.89053

DIRECTIONS From the light at the junction of NY 52/Cherry Avenue and NY 443/Delaware Avenue in Delmar, go west 1.2 miles past Bethlehem High School to Orchard Street (Five Rivers Complex sign on corner). Turn west (right) onto Orchard Street and continue 0.4 mile to the first left, Game Farm Road. Follow Game Farm Road 0.2 mile to Vlomankill Road, and turn right into the visitor center parking lot. Trail map at www.dec.ny.gov/docs /administration_pdf/5rivermap.pdf.

Operated by the New York State Department of Environmental Conservation, Five Rivers is probably the best and most diverse birding site in Albany County. The cumulative bird list stands at about 225 species, and good finds are reported in every season. When the first pieces of property were purchased in 1933, NYSDEC used that land to research and propagate upland game birds, but today the facility focuses on environmental education, and the land is managed for wildlife habitat. The 450-acre facility is heavily used by school groups in the spring and early fall, and the property includes a number of indoor and outdoor classrooms as well as five interpretive trails with seasonal brochures. The visitor center has restrooms, classrooms, exhibits, and indoor and outdoor viewing areas for well-maintained bird feeders. There are short wheelchair-accessible trails close to the parking lot and visitor center.

There are twelve miles of trails at Five Rivers, so what follows are just a few highlights. The Beaver Tree Trail starts across from the parking lot entrance at a kiosk on the opposite side of Game Farm Road. This half-mile loop circles Beaver Pond with a boardwalk through cattail marsh, paths along an area of woods dominated by pines, and bridges at both ends. Ducks and marsh birds are the avian highlight of this trail, but look for shorebirds below the dam during migration.

The beautiful and popular Vlomankill Trail descends into a hemlock ravine and uses two bridges to create a 0.5-mile loop along both sides of a

Red phase Eastern Screech-Owl in its nest hole. © Deborah Tracy-Kral.

lovely stream featuring exposed bedrock outcrops. To reach the Vlomankill trailhead, walk to the back of the parking lot and follow the paved road west past its junction with Goose Lane to a kiosk. Both Carolina Wren and Winter Wren are seen along the Vlomankill, and Louisiana Waterthrush likely breeds here. Fordham Crossing, a side path off the Vlomankill Trail, leads to a slow-water area with mudflats that attract Solitary Sandpiper and Spotted Sandpiper. The Vlomankill can also be accessed via two side trails off the North Loop Trail, Big Pine Trail, and Jay's Home Run. Blackburnian Warbler, Pine Warbler, and Red-breasted Nuthatch are reported along these two approaches.

The Old Field interpretive trail begins at a kiosk just west of the two buildings at the north end of the parking lot. This half-mile figure eight passes through an old orchard, before entering old fields where American Woodcock display in spring. The trail loops between two ponds where Mallards are almost always present and other waterfowl should be expected.

The Wild Turkey Trail on the east side of the property begins at a kiosk at the back of the parking lot just past the Graded School Program Building. The first third of this 1.5-mile loop passes through an overgrown old field with fruiting shrubs that are attractive to Cedar Waxwing, Eastern Bluebird, and other thrushes. Blue-winged Warbler and Brown Thrasher occur in this area, and Carolina Wren is often heard singing from the tangles of vegetation. In fall, migrating sparrows feed on the mowed pathways. Continuing north, the trail follows the edge of a large field planted in cold-season grasses. One-third of the field is mowed each fall to preserve grassland habitat in various stages of succession. In the spring, Boblink, Eastern Meadowlark, and Savannah Sparrow nest here, and Short-eared Owl and Northern Harrier hunt these fields for rodents in winter. The trail turns right and enters the woods at the north edge of the field. Here, Foreman's Loop passes through an older forest dominated by oaks with dead snags that are good for woodpeckers, including Pileated Woodpecker and Yellow-bellied Sapsucker.

At slightly more than two miles, the North Loop Trail, which is used for hiking and cross-country skiing, is the longest trail at Five Rivers. It begins just north of the Old Field trailhead. From a birding perspective, the most interesting habitats are Wood Duck Marsh and Fox Marsh, where Great Blue Heron, Green Heron, other waders, waterfowl, Belted Kingfisher, and during migration, Northern Waterthrush can be found. Orchard Oriole has bred near the northern junction with the service road, and Wilson's Snipe is heard at dusk in early spring in the wet fields to the east. The northern side of the loop passes through sections of mature pine and hardwood forests, where woodpeckers are common and Ruffed Grouse have been seen.

Huyck Preserve and Biological Research Station

GPS ADDRESS 5052 Delaware Turnpike, Rensselaerville
LATITUDE/LONGITUDE 42.51562 −74.13926
DIRECTIONS From Delmar, take NY 85 west to Rensselaerville. Turn right onto Delaware Turnpike and continue less than 0.25 mile to the visitor center on the right. Trail maps at www.huyckpreserve.org.

Known locally as simply the Huyck Preserve, the Edmund Niles Huyck Preserve and Biological Research Station sits atop the Helderberg Plateau in the picturesque hill town of Rensselaerville. Though far from the county's major population centers, the site is beautiful and well worth a trip to this distant part of Albany County. The two-thousand-acre preserve is privately owned and managed, and has been open to the public for recreation, conservation, research, and education for more than eighty years. The preserve's cumulative bird list totals 194 species, including some birds that are hard to find in other, more accessible parts of the county.

Ten-Mile Creek, which runs through the preserve, is impounded in two places to form hundred-acre Lake Myosotis and Lincoln Pond. In the 1870s, the creek provided power to a family-owned papermaking felt woolen mill that was located at the foot of Rensselaerville Falls and employed much of the town's population. When the mill moved to Albany, the Huyck family kept the property for public recreation, eventually donating five hundred acres to establish the preserve in 1930. The research station supports academic research with summer fellowships and housing for scientists at the Eldridge Research Station near Lincoln Pond.

The growth of the preserve included the addition of land that is predominantly forested, and in fact, most of the property is hemlock-northern hardwood forest. Embedded within this landscape are pristine streams, a spectacular waterfall, and more than twelve miles of well-marked trails that are open to the public for hiking, skiing, and snowshoeing throughout the year. Lake Myosotis, at the core of the preserve, is a reservoir for the town but is open to the public for canoeing and kayaking.

Any visit to the Huyck Preserve should begin at the visitor center, which has a small parking lot in the back of the old mill house at the foot of Rensselaerville Falls. Parking is limited, but the preserve has arranged for overflow parking at Hilltown Café and the post office, both within easy walking distance. The visitor center has educational displays, a restroom, free trail maps, and information on the preserve's seasonal activities. It is also the trailhead for the Falls Trail and the east and west trails around Lake Myosotis. There is an additional small parking area on the east side of the lake at the canoe launch on Pond Hill Road, but it is gated in winter and sometimes full in summer. A third small parking area is located at the south end of Lincoln Pond, on the south side of Pond Hill Road. This lot provides easy access to the trail around Lincoln Pond and to two connector trails, Wheeler-Watson and Ordway, which join up with the three Partridge Path loops in the northern twelve hundred acres of the property. These six miles of hiking trails are somewhat remote, and they were only opened to the public in 2012, so their birds are poorly known.

Most birders with only a day to visit the Huyck Preserve spend their time on the Falls Trail and the trails around Lake Myosotis and Lincoln Pond. Rensselaer Falls should not be missed. There is a short, steep climb on a

Golden-crowned Kinglet breeds at the Huyck Preserve. © Scott Stoner, Naturelogues.

well-tended trail and stairs to the falls overlook. Belted Kingfisher is common here even in winter, because the current in Ten-Mile Creek keeps the water open. The forests and pine plantations that border the Falls Trail support the usual forest birds, including Broad-winged Hawk.

Lake Myosotis offers productive birding year-round. Wood Duck and Hooded Merganser breed here, and a variety of waterfowl appear on the lake in late October and early November. All three scoters have been reported from the Huyck Preserve. Bald Eagle, Common Raven, and Great Blue Heron are common. Beginning in late August, the lake's water level starts to fall, exposing mudflats and shoreline, especially at the north end of the lake. The lake supports a variety of fall shorebirds, including Killdeer, Semipalmated Plover, Spotted Sandpiper, Solitary Sandpiper, Least Sandpiper, Pectoral Sandpiper, Semipalmated Sandpiper, both yellowlegs, and occasional rarities. The spillways below Lincoln Pond and at the south end of the lake sometimes have shorebirds as well. Peregrine Falcons regularly appear, to take advantage of the seasonal influx of easy prey.

The trails around the lake are good for warblers during migration, and both sides can be used to access Lincoln Pond. The west Lake Trail is cool and shady, passing through stands of hemlocks and boggy wet areas, while the east Lake Trail is flatter, more open, and shrubby, offering different varieties of birds. More than twenty species of warbler are reported from the area, including Tennessee Warbler, Cape May Warbler, and Bay-breasted Warbler, which are usually seen in the fall. Ruffed Grouse, Woodcock, Winter Wren, Blue-headed Vireo, Dark-eyed Junco, Purple Finch, and Golden-crowned Kinglet breed here.

Deer Mountain Nature Trail

GPS ADDRESS 175 Deer Mountain Village Road, Ravena

LATITUDE/LONGITUDE 42.49663 –73.85301

DIRECTIONS From I-87 Exit 22, take NY 144 south 0.5 mile to NY 369. Turn west (right) and go about 5.0 miles to CR 101/South Street. Turn south (left) and go 0.8 mile to Jarvis Road North, and follow Jarvis Road North 1.1 miles to Deer Mountain Village Road. Turn right onto Deer Mountain Village Road, and follow it 0.8 mile to the parking area.

Deer Mountain Nature Trail is owned and managed by Lafarge North America, a cement company that first operated as Atlantic Cement and later as Blue Circle Cement. The industry has mined limestone out of this part of the Helderberg Escarpment for more than fifty years. Never seen as a friend of the environment, the company purchased this property in 1995 and established the trail in an effort to give back to the community. It was designed to be an educational resource, and the forty-two interpretive signs along the trail are very well done, tackling topics that range from erosion to turtles to the role of wetlands in flood control. Unfortunately, this well-intentioned use failed to take into account that the preserve protects a magnificent wetland complex. As a result, parts of the trails are wet, muddy, and buggy. For birds, the site is a veritable Garden of Eden, but the area is rarely used by local school children. This is a place for hardy, well-prepared nature lovers—the kind who are willing to walk, wear boots, and use insect repellent. It is uncrowded, quiet, and a pretty great place to see birds.

The parking area on Deer Mountain Village Road has a mowed grassy area, picnic tables, a portable toilet, an information kiosk, and a small pond. Two trails, the East and West Trails, originate here, and the trailheads are clearly marked with wooden archways. The large wetland at the center of the preserve sits on limestone soil in a deep valley bordered by hemlock-northern hardwood forest and deciduous woods. The limey soil supports a rich and diverse wetland community, with a big deciduous swamp that grades into an extensive old beaver meadow and cattail marsh at the south end. The spring wildflowers here are especially beautiful. A large power line crosses the property at the south end, and provides an area of shrubby habitat for birds that prefer more open landscapes.

Both of the trails are out-and-back footpaths that run parallel to the wet-

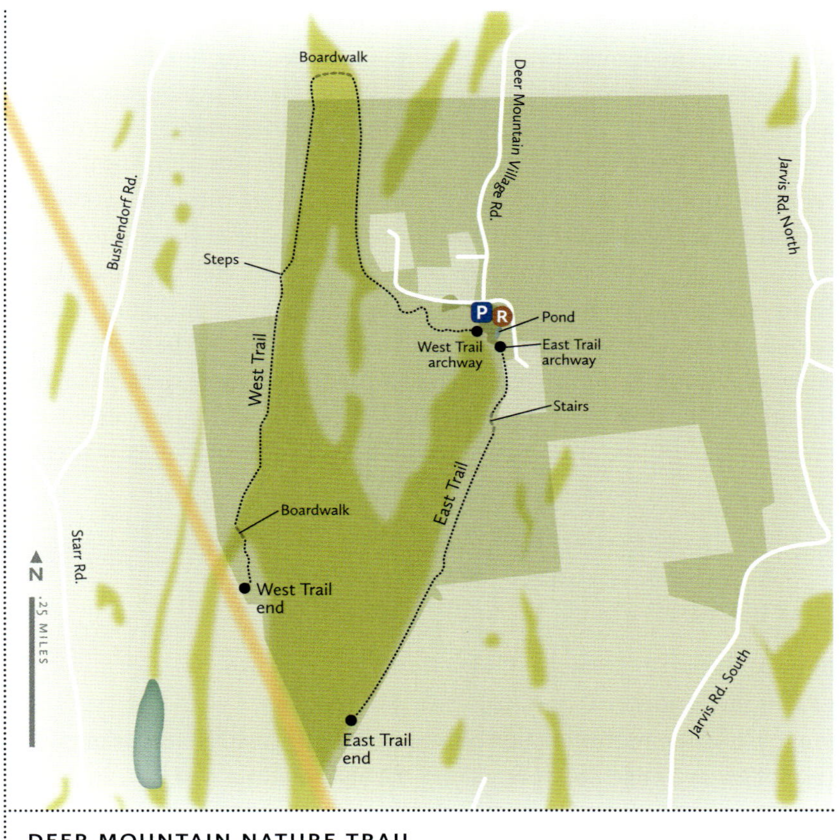

DEER MOUNTAIN NATURE TRAIL

land and do not form loops. The only trail markers are the interpretive signs. Probably because it is significantly shorter and a little drier, the 1.5-mile-long East Trail sees the most traffic. A set of stairs with a rope railing takes the trail up a steep slope that offers good views into the swamp. Worm-eating Warbler has been reported from areas along these steep slopes and may nest here. In places the trail moves into the surrounding woods, but then it ends abruptly at a barrier in a stand of common reed that blocks a clear view of the marsh. Marsh birds can be heard from this vantage point, including Virginia Rail and Swamp Sparrow; and Rusty Blackbird can be found during migration in the dead trees bordering its perimeter, along with an assortment of woodpeckers and other cavity nesters.

Though the West Trail is longer and wetter, birders who do not make the effort to explore it miss some of this site's most exciting bird habitats. The trail begins in deciduous woods, and then dips down to run along the swamp, with dense hemlocks on the other side. Blue-headed Vireo and Black-throated Green Warbler are regular visitors here. Though this part of the trail can be very wet, it soon comes to a long, elevated boardwalk through the swamp. After the boardwalk, the trail continues along the edge of the swamp, eventually moving up the hillside into the drier hemlock-northern hardwood forest, and harbors a good diversity of woodland species, including nesting Barred Owl. The trail ends at a bridge that crosses an old beaver meadow with open water in one direction and a magnificent, huge cattail marsh in the other. The rocky outcrop at the edge of the marsh and the cleared area under the power line provide shrubland habitat for a host of upland species.

RENSSELAER COUNTY

Lock 4 Canal Park

GPS ADDRESS 947 Stillwater Bridge Road, Schaghticoke
LATITUDE/LONGITUDE 42.93140 –73.65500
DIRECTIONS From the junction of US 4 and NY 125 in Stillwater, take CR 125/Stillwater Bridge Road east across the Hudson River and the canal. Immediately after crossing the canal, take the first right south through the gate onto the access road to Lock 4 Canal Park, and follow it to the parking lot on the left, just beyond the lock.

This small, scenic park at the confluence of the Hudson and Hoosic Rivers in the far northwestern corner of Rensselaer County is one of the few places on the Upper Hudson where shale ledges create shallows and rapids. Both the rapids and the hydroelectric dam at this site make it necessary for boats to lock around them. The New York State Canal Corporation, which administers the lock, owns and manages the surrounding property as a public day-use facility. Officially the park is open whenever the New York State Canal System is operative, usually May 1 to November 30, and the gates are open for cars to enter the parking lot from 7:00 a.m. until 8:30 p.m. Pedestrians, however, may use the park from dawn to dusk.

The area immediately around the lock and parking area includes picnic ta-

LOCK 4 CANAL PARK

bles and a walkway over the lock to Stillwater Island. This open area has good views of the river to the south and the shoreline of the Hudson River, where Belted Kingfisher, Great Blue Heron, and Bald Eagle are common. Northern Rough-winged Swallow sometimes nests on the locks. In addition, it is interesting to watch the lock operation up close. Canoeing the Upper Hudson is a good way to see birds, and since there is no fee for non-motorized vessels, canoeists can experience the fun of passing through the lock free of charge.

But there is more to see here than just the area around the lock. The construction of the lock was a massive undertaking that diverted streams, merged islands, and significantly altered the shorelines of both rivers, yet time has restored some of the unusually natural communities at this site. Two trailheads at the south end of the parking lot lead to a 1.5-mile loop nature trail through an oak-hickory forest on a peninsula of land between the Hoosic and Hudson Rivers. This unmarked but easy-to-follow trail parallels the edges of the two rivers with great views of the water, rapids, and shorelines from outcrops and bluffs on the main trail itself, or sometimes on spur trails that lead to the water. At the tip of the peninsula, the trail leads down to the water on a riverside sand and gravel bar with views of both waterways.

This part of the Hudson is beyond the influence of the tides, and the river level is regulated based on electrical demand and lock depths required for some kinds of boat traffic, such as those used in dredging operations. Unfortunately, that makes the water levels unpredictable, but if they are low during shorebird migration, the exposed mudflats and riverside sandbars can attract a remarkable diversity of birds, especially in the spring.

Before leaving the park, birders should also take the time to walk north on Canal Road, which runs west of the canal from CR 125. To the east, this lightly traveled road looks out on the lock canal and farm fields. To the west, there are good views of the dam at the hydroelectric plant, which has open water in winter. The power lines that cross this road attract a variety of aerial insectivores in summer, and this is the perfect place to study the field marks of many kinds of swallows, including juveniles, when they perch cooperatively over the water in late summer.

Tomhannock Reservoir

GPS ADDRESS 2 Lakeshore Road, Pittstown
LATITUDE/LONGITUDE 42.81889 −73.524648
DIRECTIONS From Troy, take NY 7 east about 8.0 miles to the hamlet of Raymertown. Just east of Raymertown, before NY 7 crosses the causeway across the reservoir, look for the NYSDEC sign for the fisherman's parking area on the left at its junction with Lakeshore Road.

Tomhannock Reservoir is the public water supply for the City of Troy and surrounding communities in northern Rensselaer County. Fed by Tomhannock, Otter, and Sunkauissia Creeks, this five-mile-long body of water is surrounded by a variety of undeveloped habitats including wooded hillsides, pine plantations, and farms. NYSDEC manages the reservoir as a fishing area in cooperation with the City of Troy, and special rules and regulations apply to protect water quality. Boating is prohibited, and the perimeter of the reservoir is plastered with signs that say "No trespassing except for fishing by permit only, activities other than fishing are unlawful." However, the superintendent of public works for the City of Troy has stated that birding from shore is allowed at fishing access sites. This is good news for birders, because Tomhannock is one of the most productive water-bird sites in the Capital Region.

The best and safest way to bird Tomhannock is to follow the roads around its perimeter (in a counterclockwise direction for favorable lighting), and stop at pull-offs that allow views of the water. This is a big body of water, so a spotting scope is helpful. NY 7 is a very busy road, with fast-moving vehicles; but there are two parking areas, one on each side of the causeway. Reservoir Lake Road (CR 115) is a quieter road. It skirts the east side of the reservoir, with parking at Nortonville Road near the inlet of Sunkauissia Creek, Croll Road, and Otter Creek inlet. Surrounded by shrubby vegetation used by migrating passerines, the inlets often stay open when other parts of the reservoir are frozen, and they concentrate waterfowl and waders. There is also access to the water at the spillway at the north end, as well as on Ford Hill Road on the north side of a small bridge just before the pump house. The pump house area is off-limits and is monitored by security cameras.

Tomhannock is famous for its water birds, which are slightly more diverse in fall and winter than in spring. Among the birds reported from this site are all three species of scoter and both scaup, Barrow's Goldeneye, Long-tailed Duck, Redhead, Northern Shoveler, Northern Pintail, American Wigeon,

Northern Pintail is seen annually at Tomhannock Reservoir. © Naomi Lloyd.

Blue-headed Vireo.
© Deborah Tracy-Kral.

Gadwall, and Greater White-fronted Goose. Bald Eagle, Common Raven, and Common Loon are often present; and Horned Grebe, Red-necked Grebe, and Pied-billed Grebe have all been reported. Fall usually sees an influx of waders, including Great Egret and rarely, Snowy Egret. The site also gets shorebirds in the fall, especially if water levels are low.

Dyken Pond Environmental Education Center

GPS ADDRESS 475 Dyken Pond Road, Cropseyvillle

LATITUDE/LONGITUDE 42.72302 −73.43509

DIRECTIONS From Troy, take NY 2 east about 7.0 miles to Cropseyville. At the wooden Dyken Pond sign on the right, turn right onto CR 79/Blue Factory Road and continue another 2.0 miles to CR 80/Madonna Lake Road on the left. Take CR 80/Madonna Lake Road 2.2 miles to a right fork for Dyken Pond Road, a single-lane dirt road marked with a sign for Dyken Pond. Continue 2.5 miles to the parking area on the right near buildings at the end of this road. Trail map at dykenpond.org.

Of all the public land in the Rensselaer Plateau, birders like Dyken Pond for its habitat diversity, uncommon species, and level terrain. Located in the sparsely settled northeast corner of Rensselaer County, the property is embedded in a high-elevation forest with Adirondack affinities that is the fifth-largest unfragmented forest in New York State. Fortunately for birders and hikers, the ascent to eighteen hundred feet occurs on roads on the way to the center, and most of the property itself is relatively level.

Dyken Pond was founded in 1973 when Manning Paper Company donated its holdings, including the dam on the lake and the headwaters of the Poesten Kill, to Rensselaer County. Today, publicly accessible land totals more than six hundred acres, with some owned and managed as an outdoor classroom by Rensselaer County, and other private "conservation lands" open to the public through conservation easements. The center is working to add new parcels that will connect existing tracts and add new trails.

Dyken Pond is first and foremost an outdoor education center, with full-time staff who live on the property year-round. The facility hosts a summer day camp during July and August, as well as a wide variety of nature-based activities, ranging from guided bird walks to moonlight canoe paddles, throughout the year. Dyken Pond is the largest lake in the Rensselaer Plateau. The property includes a launch for non-motorized boats, and the center rents canoes and encourages fishing.

The property has more than six miles of well-marked trails, ranging from 0.25-mile-long self-guided interpretive trails to the 4.0-mile Long Trail. Trail maps are available at the kiosk near the parking area. With the exception of the extension of gravel-covered Dyken Pond Road, which leads to the canoe launch, the trails are mostly easy woodland paths with occasional tree roots, rocks, wet spots, and boardwalks.

The property is a diverse mix of habitat patches, but there are a few spots that birders will not want to miss. Dustin Swamp is a large wetland with beaver activity. The four-hundred-foot boardwalk that once crossed the swamp is now partly underwater, but it is still possible to get good views into the wetland from dry parts of the boardwalk and Dyken Pond Road. This is a good place to see flycatchers, including Alder, as well as swallows, Swamp Sparrow, and woodpeckers. The Mary McFalls Trail includes a short boardwalk through a "demonstration bog" that has unusual plants such as pitcher plants, leatherleaf, bog rosemary, and a sphagnum mat that could attract uncommon birds. The lake sometimes has interesting ducks, especially in early spring. Occasional fruit trees and farm clearings along Dyken Pond Road can add a few shrub-loving species, but the woods are the main attraction, with stands of hemlock, spruce, balsam fir, and northern hardwoods. A tour of the Dyken Pond woods in May should turn up warblers including Blackburnian, Magnolia, Black-and-white, Yellow-rumped, Black-

Blackburnian Warbler is found near the summit of Berlin Mountain. © Alan W. Wells.

throated Green, and Black-throated Blue, as well as Winter Wren, Dark-eyed Junco, and White-throated Sparrow. Hermit Thrush, Blue-headed Vireo, and Common Raven are often seen, and Barred Owl and Broad-winged Hawk breed on the property. Birding Dyken Pond is like having a little piece of the Adirondacks right in the Hudson Valley.

TACONIC CREST TRAIL, PETERSBURG PASS TO BERLIN MOUNTAIN

GPS ADDRESS 651 NY 2/Taconic Trail, Petersburgh
LATITUDE/LONGITUDE 42.72313 −73.27750
DIRECTIONS From the junction of NY 22 and NY 2 in Petersburgh, take NY 2 east 5.5 miles to the Petersburg Pass hikers' parking area on the south side of the road.

Compared to the mighty Catskills on the west side of the Hudson, the Taconic Mountains are mere hills. Forming the border between New York and the western New England states of Vermont, Massachusetts, and Connecticut, the summits of the tallest peaks are all below timberline; they are not tall enough to support extensive stands of spruce-fir forest, the high-elevation habitat used by Bicknell's Thrush, Blackpoll Warbler, Yellow-bellied Fly-catcher, and other altitudinal specialists. However, a few of the peaks have

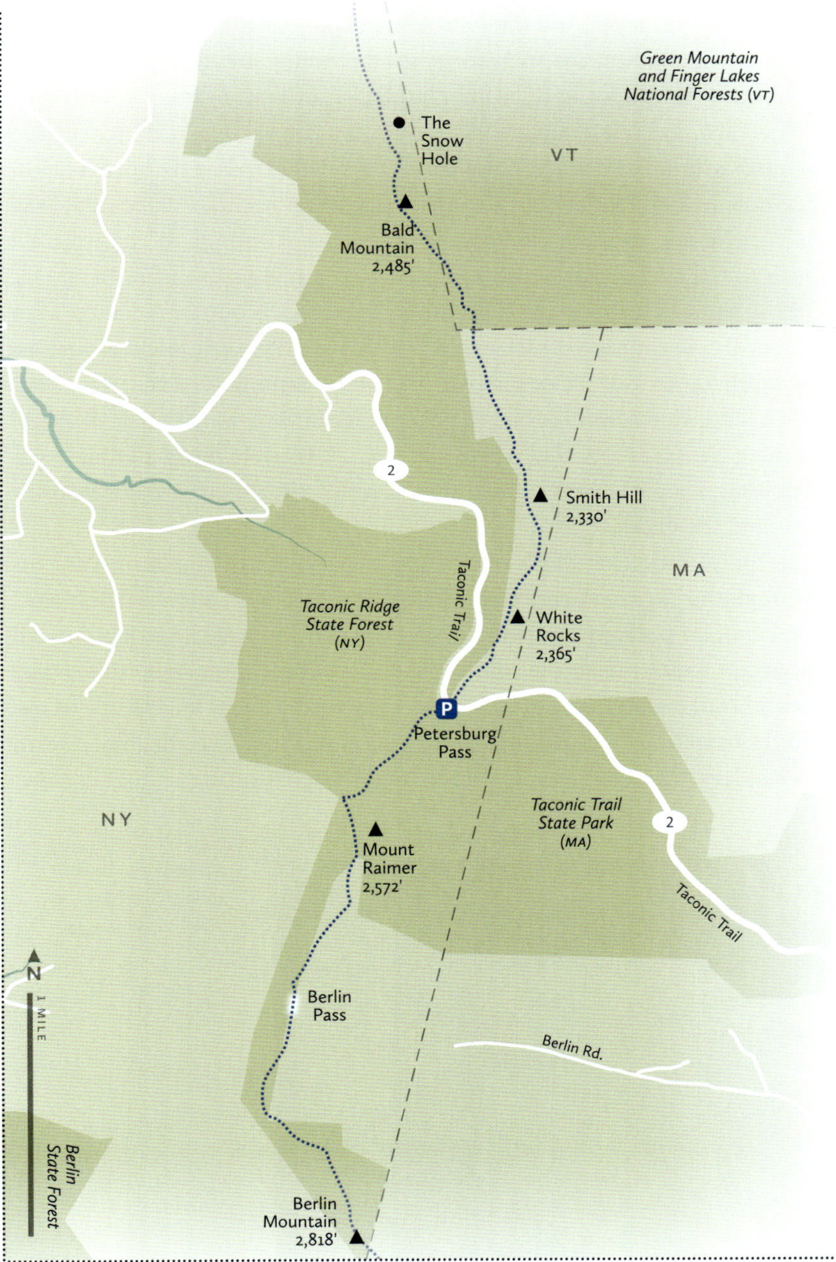

TACONIC CREST TRAIL, PETERSBURG PASS TO BERLIN MOUNTAIN

small stands of spruce, and the rolling slopes of continuous deciduous forest are excellent habitat for migrating and breeding songbirds. These "little mountains" have a lot to offer for a moderate amount of hiking effort.

The Taconic Crest Trail is a hiking trail that runs between Hancock, Massachusetts, and Petersburg, New York. It weaves across state borders along the Taconic Ridge for about thirty-five miles. Serious hikers love ridge trails for their moderate grades and continuous views. Although the 2.7-mile hike south to the summit of Berlin Mountain—the highest point in Rensselaer County at 2,818 feet—is not easy, most of the trail is quite moderate. Many birders are discouraged from exploring this area because the steepest and most difficult part of the entire hike is at the beginning. The trail does begin with a long, steep climb to the ridge, but this muscle-burner is manageable for most people, especially when taken at a "leisurely birdwatching pace." After that, it's a pretty easy hike that is well worth the effort for both the birds and the views.

Berlin Mountain is south of the hikers' parking at Petersburg Pass, and although the Taconic Crest Trail is clearly marked with blue trail markers, a number of unmarked paths and ATV roads lead from the area; so it is critically important to start from the southwest corner of the lot, where there is a kiosk and trail register. The area around the parking lot, at an altitude of over two thousand feet, actually has pretty good birding. The shrubby clearing has Killdeer, Chestnut-sided Warbler, and Indigo Bunting; and in fall, a va-

Trail markers for the Taconic Crest Trail. © Kathryn J. Schneider.

riety of raptors can be seen migrating through Petersburg Pass. South of the parking lot, the trail climbs through a deciduous forest dominated by beech and maple, with a well-developed understory and patches of birch woodland. The route to the summit is dotted with fern glades, small wetlands, patches of conifers, and low vegetation. Be careful to ignore all unmarked side roads and trails, and stay with the blue markers of the Taconic Crest Trail. Scrub oak and other stunted vegetation grow along the rocky ridge, keeping the birds visible even when the trees are fully leafed out. A rock cairn marks the summit of Berlin Mountain, which is clear, open, and grassy. The perimeter has a fringe of low-bush blueberries surrounded by spruce trees. Magnolia Warbler, Yellow-rumped Warbler, Blackburnian Warbler, Red-breasted Nuthatch, White-throated Sparrow, and Dark-eyed Junco breed here. The summit is always cool and breezy, and the vista from the top includes Mount Greylock and the Berkshires in Massachusetts, Jiminy Peak ski area, and a number of new wind turbines.

Papscanee Island Nature Preserve

GPS ADDRESS 100 American Oil Road, Rensselaer
LATITUDE/LONGITUDE 42.59535 −73.75297
DIRECTIONS There are two entrances, both accessible from NY 9J. For the north entrance, take NY 9J south 0.2 mile from its origin at the junction of US 9 and US 20, to a traffic light, and turn west (right) onto Irwin Stewart Port Expressway, which becomes American Oil Road as it winds 2.6 miles through an industrial park and tank farm. Park well off the road in the small dirt parking area at the end of the road. For the south entrance, take Staats Island Road west off NY 9J 2.9 miles north of the Village of Castleton. Continue 0.5 mile, crossing Papscanee Creek and the railroad tracks, to a small parking lot on the right surrounded by a split-rail fence.

Papscanee Island Nature Preserve is actually a peninsula of floodplain forest on the east side of the Hudson River. Located just south of the Port of Albany-Rensselaer, this piece of Hudson River shoreline was rescued from development by the Open Space Institute through purchases and easements in the early 1990s; and in 1997, the institute turned the area's management over to Rensselaer County. The 156-acre preserve is a long, linear strip of forest and agricultural land bounded by the river on the west and the rail-

PAPSCANEE ISLAND NATURE PRESERVE

road on the east. About thirty acres, mostly in the northeast corner of the property, are still actively farmed as a part of existing land-use agreements. The southern end of the property has more trails. The preserve also has two riverside picnic tables and occasional informational signage. More than 150 species have been reported from this site.

There are two entrances, one at either end of the preserve. The north entrance is also called the winter entrance, because it is plowed in winter and can be accessed year-round, but parking is very limited. Its access, through a depressing industrial development of parking lots, buildings, petroleum storage tanks, and truck traffic, with only distant and largely obstructed views of the river, is enough to discourage most birders. However, before the road ends at the preserve entrance, it passes through open fields and wet meadows that support an abundance of bird life, including winter flocks of sparrows, larks, buntings, and longspurs, Wilson's Snipe, Northern Harrier, and other raptors. An American Kestrel often perches on wires along the roadside.

From the north entrance, the white trail heads south as a wide dirt road passing through a swamp that attracts Rusty Blackbird, Wood Duck, Mallard, Canada Goose, and other waterfowl in early spring. The white trail is the longest footpath, running 1.6 miles though the eastern edge of the property away from the river. It passes through swampland, woods, shrubby areas along the railroad tracks, and agricultural fields before it joins the red trail near the south entrance. In late summer and fall, fruiting shrubs along the railroad edge attract Gray Catbird, Eastern Bluebird, Northern Cardinal, and sparrows.

Both the green and red trails branch off from the white trail and lead to the river. The green tail starts at a maintenance shed about halfway between the north and south entrances and leads to a picnic table and a good view of the river, which is quite narrow here. Waterfowl, cormorants, gulls, and Bald Eagle perched on the opposite shore are easy to study up close and personal. The red trail originates at the south entrance, and is only 0.2 mile long. It is the quickest route to the river if the south entrance is passable. At low tide during shorebird migration, Spotted Sandpiper and Solitary Sandpiper feed along the river's edge, and swallows, swifts, and nighthawks feed over the river. Common Raven and Fish Crow are often heard. Baltimore Oriole nests in the trees on the river's edge, and Orchard Oriole has been reported.

The blue and yellow trails pass through a floodplain forest that is dotted with small ponds and wet areas fed by the tides. Huge cottonwoods form the canopy, but the open understory is full of poison ivy vines with long-lasting fruits that are heavily used by migrating warblers, thrushes, and sparrows. More than twenty species of warbler have been reported from Papscanee, including both waterthrushes; Blue-winged Warbler, Mourning Warbler, Magnolia Warbler, Northern Parula, Cerulean Warbler, and Hooded Warbler in spring; and Wilson's Warbler, Orange-crowned Warbler, Pine Warbler, Black-throated Green Warbler, and Black-throated Blue Warbler in fall. Five species of vireo have been seen here. Green Heron, Great Blue Heron, and Belted Kingfisher sometimes hunt in the small tidal pond between the blue trail and the river.

The approach to the south preserve entrance on Staats Island Road, between NY 9J and the railroad tracks, often has interesting birds. In spring, the flooded agricultural fields have shorebirds, and the marshy edges of Papscanee Creek are good for waders, flycatchers, and swallows. In winter, these agricultural fields along with other open areas in the northeast part of the preserve provide good habitat for Horned Lark, Snow Bunting, Lapland Longspur, and American Pipit.

Schodack Island State Park

GPS ADDRESS 1 Schodack Island Way, Schodack Landing
LATITUDE/LONGITUDE 42.49960 −73.77584
DIRECTIONS From the junction of NY 150 and NY 9J in the Town
of Castleton, follow 9J south about 1.0 mile to the park entrance road
on the west side of NY 9J. Continue 1.8 miles to the parking area.
Trail map at parks.ny.gov/parks.

Schodack Island State Park is not an island at all, but a seven-mile-long peninsula jutting into the Hudson River from the eastern shore. Its location in the middle of the river makes it an important stopover site for migrating songbirds. The park is a reliable place to see Bald Eagle, Peregrine Falcon, and Great Blue Heron that nest in the area, but birders come to Schodack Island State Park because Cerulean Warbler breeds there. One of New York State's first Bird Conservation Areas, 864 of the park's 1,052 acres have been set aside for the protection of birds.

Despite the large amount of protected habitat, this area has a long history of human disturbance. The park's peninsula was created by joining three large

Cerulean Warbler breeds at Schodack Island State Park.
© Deborah Tracy-Kral.

islands and several smaller ones with dredge spoil taken from the bottom of the Hudson River. The ice industry thrived here, and during its heyday, at least eleven icehouses stood along the shoreline. The land was cultivated by Native Americans and the Dutch, and timbered for building and firewood. Ruins and remnants of all these activities are still evident. Today the park is managed as a day- and multiple-use area, which includes hunting in the fall to control the deer population. A modern cement quarry operates on the opposite shore, and the railroad and New York State Thruway bridges loom over the entrance road. Despite all this, Schodack Island remains a great place to see birds.

The entry road ends in a developed section of the park that includes a boat launch, a large parking lot, pavilions, a campground, a picnic area, and heated restrooms that are open year-round. This area tends to be busy and noisy, especially on weekends, but the boat launch is a good place to search the river for gulls, Osprey, eagles, waders, and waterfowl, and to look for Peregrine Falcon on the New York State Thruway bridge, where they have nested for many years.

All of the trails in the park's well-maintained trail system begin near this busy central area. The orange trail runs 3.5 miles down the west side of the peninsula, often close to the river, while the shorter yellow trail is more interior, with occasional forays east to the marshy edges of Schodack Creek.

Several red connector trails join the two, creating options for hikes of differing lengths. The trails are all flat and easy walking. The orange trail dead-ends before reaching the southern tip of the peninsula, where a restricted area owned by the federal government is still used for the deposition of dredge spoil.

Most of the upland habitat is occupied by a successional forest of varied ages that has grown up on the dredge spoils. Cerulean Warbler feeds and nests in the canopy of the large-diameter cottonwoods in the more mature parts of this forest. These birds seem to prefer sites with gaps in the canopy, such as the area near the wooden bridge on the yellow trail. They are always high up and difficult to see, but they are persistent singers. Find them in May and June by listening for their distinctive song with an ascending buzzy trill at the end.

The entire peninsula has small pockets of floodplain forest, vernal pools, and tidal swamps, especially along the east side. Schodack Creek and the freshwater tidal marsh are visible along northern parts of the yellow trail, especially from the canoe and kayak launch site; but the best way to see breeding Marsh Wren, shorebirds, and Great Egret that visit in the fall is to take a canoe or kayak into the marsh and explore the quiet waters on the east side of the peninsula.

Mud Pond Preserve

GPS ADDRESS 591 CR 16, Nassau
LATITUDE/LONGITUDE 42.55855 −73.54762
DIRECTIONS From the intersection of US 20, NY 203, and CR 15 in Nassau, travel north on CR 15 about 2.75 miles past Nassau Lake to its junction with CR 16. Turn east (right) onto CR 16/Central Nassau Road and continue another 2.5 miles to a parking lot with a kiosk on the north (left) side of the road, just past Mud Pond Road.

Mud Pond Preserve is a small but ecologically unusual site that was recently acquired by the Town of Nassau. It features a six-acre bog lake surrounded by a peatland and red maple swamp embedded in nearly seven hundred acres of unfragmented forest. Because the bog would be damaged by foot traffic, part of the trail system leads to an overlook that offers unobstructed views of the open water and surrounding wetland. The lighting is especially good

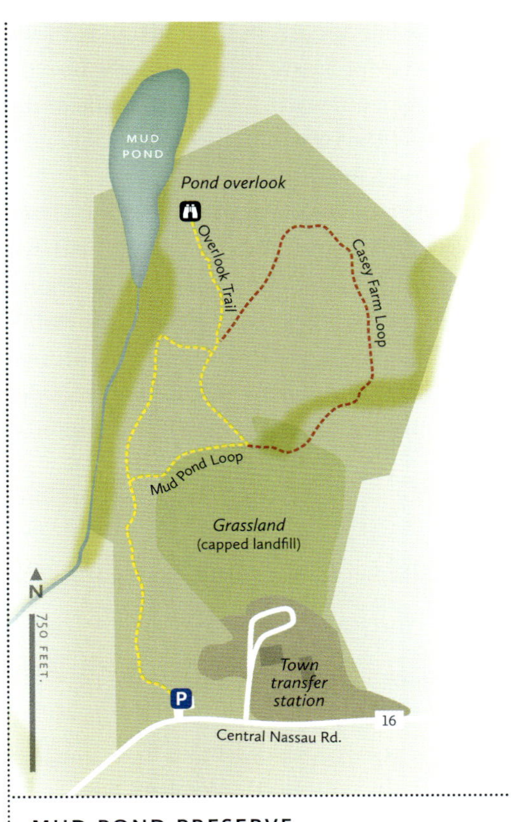

MUD POND PRESERVE

for viewing birds in the morning, when the sun shines on the opposite shore but the overlook remains shaded.

From the parking lot on CR 16, the yellow Mud Pond Loop runs through a wooded landscape along the marshy headwater stream that drains the lake. Eventually it turns east through a short, steep section of hemlock forest. Overlook Trail, also with yellow markers, branches off to the north through the forest, dead-ending at the pond overlook. The pond is big enough to support a variety of waterfowl. Wood Duck and Mallard breed here, and the fringe of marshy vegetation is good habitat for marsh birds and Swamp Sparrow. The overlook is a great spot to see cavity-nesting birds, because some of the larger trees growing on the sphagnum mat have punched through into the water below, drowning their roots. The resulting dead snags are riddled with nest holes that are used by Tree Swallow, Eastern Bluebird, and at least four species of woodpecker. Pileated Woodpecker breeds here. Scan the oaks on the opposite shore for Scarlet Tanager and warblers. The east side of the loop leads back to the parking lot along the edge of a capped landfill, now an open field big enough to support grassland birds.

Volunteers recently added a new 0.75-mile-long trail, named the Casey Farm Loop after the family whose ancestors farmed the area. Marked with red trail markers, this pathway intersects the Mud Pond Loop in two locations, one near the beginning of Overlook Trail and the other on the perimeter of the field at the edge of the landfill. The majority of the trail passes through hemlock-northern hardwood forest containing many mature old trees despite some evidence of past logging. Barred Owl is regularly encountered in this area.

GREENE COUNTY

Hannacroix Creek Preserve and Hudson River Interpretive Trail

GPS ADDRESS 12 NY 144, New Baltimore
LATITUDE/LONGITUDE 42.46217 −73.79176
DIRECTIONS From Ravena, take US 9W south about 3.0 miles to NY 144. Take NY 144 north 3.3 miles to a sign on the west (left) side of NY 144 marking the short entrance road to the preserve parking area. Trail map at newbaltimoreconservancy.org.

Based on the potholed entry road and battered farm gate across the main trail, one would never guess that this 141-acre preserve has so much interesting bird habitat and pretty scenery. Initial impressions aside, the Hannacroix Creek Preserve and the associated Hudson River Interpretive Trail, directly across the road on the west side of NY 144, are worth a visit. Located in the very northeastern corner of Greene County, the property is jointly owned by the Open Space Institute and the Town of New Baltimore, but is managed by the New Baltimore Conservancy, a private nonprofit. This relatively small area has good examples of Hudson River habitats and a variety of upland communities, including a pretty waterfall and some interesting local history.

There are two trailheads, one on NY 144 and another on Madison Avenue in New Baltimore, but only the trailhead on NY 144 has parking. The Laverne

Louisiana Waterthrush favors forested streams. © Alan W. Wells.

Irving Trail begins at the gate and follows an old farm road uphill from the parking area, and then continues about a mile to Hannacroix Falls. Though the trail passes through a scrubby area and is hilly at first, the grade becomes more moderate as it follows the creek through mixed woods and hemlocks. Blue-winged Warbler is found in the shrubs and vines close to the parking area, and both Lawrence's Warbler and Brewster's Warbler hybirds have been reported from this site. Because these birds often sing the Blue-winged Warbler's song, it is a good idea to check out each Blue-winged Warbler carefully with binoculars. Louisiana Waterthrush breeds along the creek and is seen and heard from the trail. There is a nice view of the falls from the trail, along with views of the foundation of an old mill.

The Paper Mill Trail, which originates on Madison Avenue in New Baltimore, once brought workers to the mill site and bathers to the swimming hole at the falls. This path goes through mixed forest with some sections of older woods. Close to Madison Avenue, it enters a wet area among the foundations of old farm buildings. Barred Owl lives in the ravine and is sometimes heard calling in the middle of the day. The red loop and the north trail both lead to drier elevated sites with viewpoints.

Not to be missed is the Hudson River Interpretive Trail, which begins on the east side of the parking area and after a short section through woods, crosses NY 144 to a boardwalk through a small cattail marsh. This trail continues to the river and includes a side spur to an observation deck overlooking a tidal pond that features extensive mudflats at low tide. The trail dead-ends in an area of tall cottonwoods on a sandy dredge spoil beach, with a bench and a good view of the creek inlet. Bald Eagle and waders are common here, and the riverfront features interpretive signage as well as one of the old spur dikes that were built to divert silt out of the river's main channel. This quiet, shallow cove is a pleasant place to sit and view the river and wait for good birds.

Coxsackie Creek Grassland Preserve

GPS ADDRESS 16 Houghtaling Road, West Coxsackie
LATITUDE/LONGITUDE 42.37801 −73.82643
DIRECTIONS The Coxsackie Creek Grassland Preserve is north of NY 385, east of US 9W, and west of CR 61. There are access points with limited parking at Houghtaling Road, along CR 61, and at the end of Vermilyen Lane. To get to the Houghtaling Road entrance from the junction of US 9W and NY 385 in Coxsackie, go north about 1.0 mile to Houghtaling Road on the right, and enter Kalkberg Commerce Park. Follow this road to the end, and park behind the Serta facility near the kiosk.

The Coxsackie Creek Grassland Preserve is still very much a work in progress. Greene County has always had well-protected natural areas in the Catskills and along the river, but sadly, most of its grasslands are found on active farmlands that are mowed three times a year. The grassland birds set up territories in May, but rarely breed successfully. In 2004 it was this knowledge of the scarcity of protected grasslands that drove a small group of local citizens to protest the creation of an industrial commerce park on the grasslands surrounding Coxsackie Creek, a tributary of the Hudson River.

Today, the Greene Land Trust owns and manages about three hundred acres that are surrounded by commercial industries. The land is protected from further development and identified as a Habitat Conservation Area with goals and objectives that clearly put the protection of wildlife first. For this small, cash-strapped conservation organization, this means that creating trails and user-friendly public access has taken a back seat to buying land, setting policy, and mitigating the development of warehouses and parking lots. There are currently no formal trails, so birders can either use binoculars

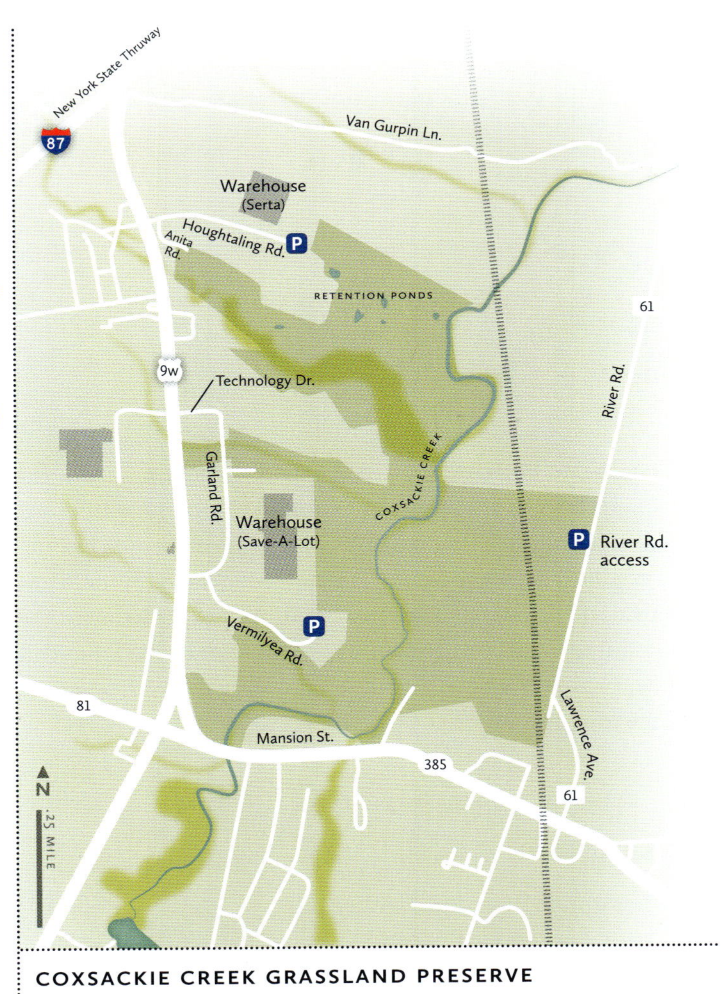

COXSACKIE CREEK GRASSLAND PRESERVE

to scan from accepted "viewing points" around the perimeter, or strike out through deep grass to explore the landscape. In winter, when snow is on the ground, cross-country skis or snowshoes are a good option.

Despite these barriers, the undeveloped fields and wetlands that remain at this site represent Greene County's most diverse grassland, with eBird records for more than 180 species. The natural and engineered wetlands support a good variety of waterfowl, waders, shorebirds, and wetland songbirds. The "hills" created from grading the industrial park have long views

Savannah Sparrow,
a grassland bird.
© Carena M. Pooth.

in all directions. Grassland birds are seen in the fields along CR 61, and the brush-hogged fields at the end of Vermilyen Lane add habitat for shrubland species. This site is especially exciting in winter, when Short-eared Owl and Northern Harrier regularly hunt the wetlands for meadow voles. Some years, Rough-legged Hawk and Snowy Owl are reported. A new bridge over the creek and the long-anticipated recreational trails that many hope for at this site will provide easier access and make the Coxsackie Creek Grasslands a more pleasant place to visit.

Four-Mile Point Preserve and Vosburgh Swamp Wildlife Management Area

GPS ADDRESS 169 Four-Mile Point Road, Athens
LATITUDE/LONGITUDE 42.31761 −73.790574
DIRECTIONS From the junction of NY 23 and NY 385, just west of the Rip Van Winkle Bridge in Catskill, take NY 385 north 7.6 miles to Four-Mile Point Road, a dead-end road on the east (right) side. The parking lot for Four-Mile Point Preserve is 0.3 mile down the road on the left, marked with a sign and kiosk. Parking for Vosburgh Swamp Wildlife Management Area is another 0.7 mile farther on the left by the kiosk after a big curve in the road, or along the roadside.

These two properties are both on the same dead-end road that runs along the west shore of the Hudson River. Conservation-minded organizations have struggled to get ahead of development pressure here, and have purchased

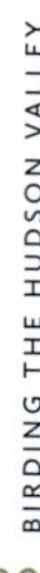

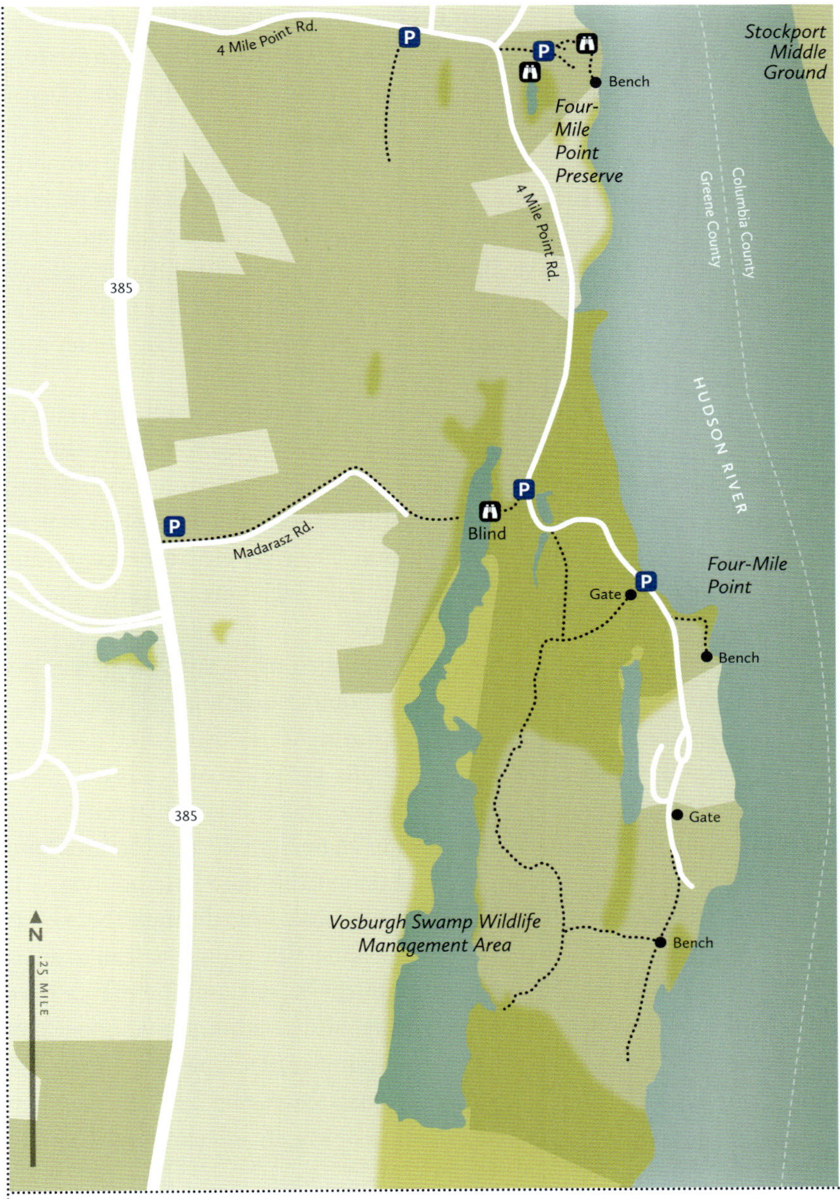

FOUR-MILE POINT PRESERVE AND VOSBURGH SWAMP WILDLIFE MANAGEMENT AREA

parcels as they became available in an effort to buffer ecologically important wetlands and preserve access to the river. As a result, the land here is a mixture of private residences along with public and private conservation land. Please do not trespass on private property.

Scenic Hudson owns Four-Mile Point Preserve, a small, 7.6-acre property on the northern tip of the point. The short trail to the right from the parking area leads to a handicapped-accessible viewing platform for a pond and cattail marsh. Though the pond is small, this is a lovely place to sit and wait for birds to vocalize or emerge from the shoreline vegetation. Green Heron and Great Blue Heron hunt the edges, and Mallard and Wood Duck are sometimes present. Rusty Blackbird has been seen here in the spring.

The 0.25-mile-long red trail leads to the river. Both the uphill spur trails to the right end at river overlooks, but the first is so overgrown that it is difficult to see the river. However, the overlooks provide an opportunity to look into the tops of cedar trees where owls sometimes roost, and warblers, kinglets, and other passerines feed during migration. The river view is best from the riverside picnic area at the end of the trail. Bald Eagles breed nearby and are common on this part of the river year-round.

Vosburgh Swamp WMA, owned and managed by NYSDEC, is 0.75 miles farther down Four-Mile Point Road. This popular hunting and fishing area has limited parking and tends to be busy during waterfowl and striped bass season. Despite its name, the wetland at this site is actually a marsh, since grasses, sedges, cattails, and rushes dominate, and it is largely treeless. The blue trail begins at the gate by the kiosk in an overgrown shrubby area, and dead-ends near the south end of the marsh at the state land boundary. It forks in the woods, and the left path continues south through the woods along the east side of the marsh, with occasional side trails that lead to areas with good views of this big wetland. Both the woods and the marsh have good bird diversity. Birders have recorded all the common woodpeckers and flycatchers, along with an impressive number of warblers and sparrows during migration. Swamp Sparrow and Marsh Wren sing from the marsh in the spring, ducks use the open water areas in March and early April, and in fall Great Egret is sometimes present.

The WMA also offers access to about half a mile of Hudson River shoreline, with good visibility from the lightly traveled dead-end road. The pond in the bend of the road has a nest box that is used by Wood Duck during the breeding season and by roosting Eastern Screech-Owl in winter. Waterfowl, gulls, Bald Eagle, and Osprey are often seen here. Across the river are the sandy bluffs of Stockport Middle Ground Island, which has nesting Bank and Northern Rough-winged Swallow and Belted Kingfisher. There is also a well-worn fisherman's footpath that runs through the poison ivy along the river and ends at a rock outcrop, and an impressive homemade bench with a nice view of the river.

Hunter Mountain

GPS ADDRESS 2620 Spruceton Road, Lexington
LATITUDE/LONGITUDE 42.18409 −74.271694
DIRECTIONS From the junction of NY 23A and NY 42 in the Town of Lexington, turn south (left) on NY 42 and continue 3.0 miles to its intersection with CR 6/Spruceton Road in West Kill. Turn east (left) onto CR 6 and continue 6.7 miles, crossing the West Kill on five bridges. There are three parking areas on this road. The Spruceton trailhead begins at the second parking lot, marked with blue trail markers. Trail map at www.catskillmountaineer.com.

Because one of the goals of this book is to identify a suite of sites for each county that presents the full range of bird habitats and birds that each county has to offer, it is obvious that the counties that have high peaks like the Catskill Mountains need at least one site at elevation. The boreal birds in these high peaks are among the rarest in the Hudson Valley and are thrilling to see, but the sites where they occur are not easily accessible or truly "birder friendly" because they are found near the tops of mountains. This site, Hunter Mountain, is not an easy hike, but it is probably the most accessible of the high-elevation candidates in Greene County. It has a restored fire tower and a lovely 360-degree view, and because it is only the second-highest Catskill peak, it does not get the crowds that flock to Slide Mountain.

There are several different routes to get to the boreal habitat near the summit of Hunter Mountain. The Becker Hollow Trail originates on NY 214 and at 2.2 miles is the shortest way up Hunter, but it is very steep. Another alternative is to pay to take the Sky Ride from Hunter Mountain Ski Center, which operates on weekends and some weekdays during the summer (hunter mtn.com). The ride typically begins operations around 10:00 a.m. and ends at the Colonel's Chair trailhead. The best boreal habitat is 2.0 miles from the

Bicknell's Thrush, a bird of high-elevation mountain spruce–fir forest. © Joan Collins.

drop-off point, which puts birders on the summit in the middle of the day, not the best time to see or hear Bicknell's Thrush.

For those willing to do a moderately challenging hike that is suitable for kids and reasonably fit adults, the Spruceton Trail, at 3.4 miles and a little under two thousand feet of elevation gain, is a feasible, rewarding trek. The trail is an old jeep road that was used to access the fire tower, so it is relatively easy walking, though still steep in places, especially beyond the 1.7-mile mileage marker. Horses are allowed on the Spruceton Trail, and both the trailhead parking lot and the fire tower clearing have mounting platforms for handicapped riders.

From the trailhead on CR 6, the route follows blue trail markers along Hunter Brook, a pretty mountain stream through mixed but mostly deciduous woods. This forest is productive habitat at any time of year, but in spring, Black-throated Blue Warbler and thrushes are especially abundant. A sign at 1.7 miles marks the halfway point. The John Rabb lean-to is just below thirty-five hundred feet on a spur trail with a nice overlook. Camping is not allowed above thirty-five hundred feet, so this is the place to camp to be at the summit at dawn.

From here, the forest begins to include stunted spruce, birches, and mountain ash. High-elevation breeders such as Blackpoll Warbler, Yellow-bellied Flycatcher, Ruby-crowned Kinglet, White-throated Sparrow, Dark-eyed

Junco, Swainson's Thrush, and Bicknell's Thrush are expected here. Bicknell's Thrush is a habitat specialist that prefers areas dominated by dense, stunted balsam fir. The trail emerges from the woods into an open area around the fire tower, with picnic tables, a cabin, and an outhouse. The habitat with the most balsam fir is on the blue trail in the quarter mile beyond the fire tower and before a four-way intersection. Taking the yellow spur trail southwest at this intersection leads to a spectacular overlook as well as an opportunity to look for Ruby-crowned Kinglet, which is known to breed here.

Mountain Top Arboretum

GPS ADDRESS 379 Maude Adams Road, Tannersville
LATITUDE/LONGITUDE 42.22216 −74.13465
DIRECTIONS From US 9W in Catskill, travel south to NY 23A. Continue west on 23A through Palenville to Tannersville. Turn north (right) at the traffic light onto NY 23C and continue 2.0 miles to Maude Adams Road, a dirt road on the right that leads to the arboretum parking lot. Trail map at www.mtarboretum.org.

The seasons are later at the Mountain Top Arboretum because it stands at an elevation of twenty-four hundred feet. Birds are still easy to find at this site in late spring, when birds in the valleys have stopped singing and started to nest. This privately owned preserve is open to the public from dawn to dusk free of charge, and there are restrooms in a small building next to the parking lot. The arboretum is basically a botanical garden that displays species native to the Catskills alongside exotic specimens from around the world that are capable of surviving the rigorous climate. This eclectic mix creates a nice variety of habitats in a relatively small area of less than two hundred acres. The trails are clearly marked and meticulously maintained.

West Meadow, directly across Maude Adams Road from the parking area, has a rain garden, pond, rock outcrops, and an interesting collection of conifers. The grasses around the perimeter are unmowed, and though the open area is too small and shrubby for many grassland birds, there are nest boxes for House Wren, Eastern Bluebird, and Tree Swallow. Chipping Sparrow, Song Sparrow, Purple Finch, and Eastern Towhee frequent this area, and other sparrows and finches should be expected, especially during migration. Listen for Cedar Waxwing and flycatchers here—Least Flycatcher, Great Crested

Yellow-bellied Sapsucker drills holes for sap that also attract insects. © Bruce Dudek.

Flycatcher, and Eastern Phoebe are known from this site. The meadow also offers the best opportunity to scan the sky for raptors and vultures.

East of the parking lot lies the Woodland Walk, a small area of native Catskill plantings. Here, mountain laurel, ferns, and wildflowers are protected from browsing with a tall, effective deer exclosure. A stream flows through the woodland, eventually feeding a wetland on another part of the property. Hermit Thrush nests in this woodland.

The entrance to the East Meadow is a quarter mile east down Maude Adams Road, through a gate that leads into a grove of tall pines with an open understory of ferns. Woodpeckers, including Yellow-bellied Sapsucker, Northern Flicker, and Red-bellied Woodpecker, are easy to see in this area. Outside the gated area to the east is an extensive boardwalk through a shrub-dominated wetland full of native grasses, sedges, and wildflowers. Swamp Sparrow nests here.

The green trail though Black Spruce Glen begins another quarter mile down Maude Adams Road to the south. The glen's habitat diversity makes it great for spring migrants, especially warblers. The boggy black spruce forest with lichen-covered trunks transitions into hemlocks on the drier ridges. A spur off the loop trail leads to a short boardwalk into a large, open graminoid-dominated wetland or fen. The eastern side of the green trail loop includes stone walls and an old road. Winter Wren is often heard along this part of the trail.

RamsHorn-Livingston Sanctuary

GPS ADDRESS 84 Dubois Road, Catskill

LATITUDE/LONGITUDE 42.20869 –73.86597

DIRECTIONS From the junction of US 9W and Grandview Avenue in Catskill, just south of the junction of 9W and NY 385, take Grandview Avenue 0.8 mile to a traffic circle. Take the second right onto DuBois Road. Follow DuBois Road 0.2 mile to the parking area, kiosk, and sanctuary entrance. Trail map at www.scenichudson.org.

RamsHorn-Livingston Sanctuary sits in the freshwater tidal portion of the Hudson River on the river's western shore. Henry Livingston, who donated the first parcel of land for this preserve, was a direct descendent of the Livingston family that settled in the Hudson Valley in the 1700s. Scenic Hudson and Audubon New York share ownership of the sanctuary, where protected land now totals over four hundred acres, including the largest freshwater tidal swamp on the Hudson River. RamsHorn Creek, the twisted tidal creek in the center of the preserve, is the dominant landscape feature, and while it is the estuary habitats that make this site special, the sanctuary has other natural communities as well. A small section of upland deciduous woods rises above the marsh just south of the creek and contains many of the trails.

A kiosk in the parking lot has free trail maps. From this entry point, Old

Virginia Rail, a secretive marsh bird that is more often heard than seen. © Alan W. Wells.

Farm Road leads south through an area bordered by small trees, dogwood, nonnative honeysuckle, and the remnants of an old orchard. After about a half mile, there is a twenty-eight-foot observation tower with spectacular views of the marsh and surrounding woods. Bald Eagle is often seen from here. Old Farm Road continues across the open tidal marsh, ending where it crosses RamsHorn Creek. Virginia Rail, which breed in the marsh, sometimes cross Old Farm Road.

The sanctuary maintains a dock and canoe launch here on the creek, and guided canoe trips through the swamp and marsh are scheduled during the summer. Exploring the sanctuary by canoe or kayak at high tide is one of the best ways to see marsh birds, especially in the tidal flats along the main stem of the river—home to Least Bittern and Marsh Wren. It is possible to put in at Dutchman's Landing Park, just upriver from the preserve, and paddle down the creek to the preserve. Just remember, this is a tidal creek, so timing is everything. Parts of the creek become unnavigable mudflats at low tide.

South of the dock, three short, well-marked and nicely maintained loop trails offer an opportunity to explore the woods for birds that prefer forested habitat. On its southern side, the white trail skirts the edge of a hayfield, with views of the Catskills in the distance. Great Horned Owl nests in these woods. On its eastern side, the blue trail crosses a small field and runs along the edge of the marsh. The red trail has an observation platform that looks west down the creek and into the marsh. The best deciduous forest habitat is found along the ridge on the red and blue trails.

COLUMBIA COUNTY

Lewis A. Swyer Preserve at Mill Creek

GPS ADDRESS 1599 NY 9J, Stuyvesant
LATITUDE/LONGITUDE 42.41800 −73.76914
DIRECTIONS From the blinking light at the intersection of CR 26A and NY 9J in Stuyvesant, continue north on 9J for about 2.0 miles to a small parking lot on the west (left) shoulder of the road. The boardwalk begins about five hundred feet south of the parking lot. Trail map at www.nature.org.

The Swyer Preserve is an unusual place, both for the birds and for its rare natural communities. Located at the northern end of the estuary, this part

Wood Ducks (male and females). © Bruce Dudek.

of the river has low salinity but remains tidal, so twice a day the floodplain forest, marsh, and mudflats are inundated with roughly four feet of fresh-water. Only certain kinds of plants can survive this twice-daily disturbance, so the resulting natural communities contain some plants that are globally rare, and many others that are rare in New York State. To protect the rare plants from trampling, The Nature Conservancy (TNC) has constructed a half-mile-long boardwalk through the swamp that ends in a tower overlooking the railroad to the river. Though TNC owns only ninety-five acres, it holds an additional five hundred acres of easements to protect the surrounding land from future development.

The boardwalk runs along the north side of Mill Creek, crossing several small tributaries on bridges along the way. Low tide exposes extensive mud-flats in the creek and on the shores of the Hudson River, which are used by shorebirds in season. Walk quietly down the boardwalk to avoid flushing waterfowl on the creek. Wood Duck is especially common, thanks in large part to the nest boxes scattered throughout the preserve.

The floodplain forest has an open understory dominated by herbs and vines that make it easy to see birds that live on the forest floor. Good views of Ovenbird, Wood Thrush, Veery, and Northern Waterthrush are common. Poison ivy wraps itself around trees along the boardwalk, and its fruit is an important high-energy food for fall migrants. Ruby-throated Hummingbirds collect nectar from jewelweed in the understory that is usually in full bloom by August. In winter, Brown Creepers forage on the tree trunks right next to the boardwalk.

In several places, the boardwalk veers south to the creek edge for views of the edge of the swamp, where Swamp Sparrow nests, and the marsh. The protected floodplain forest features an abundance of standing dead trees, so it is a good site for woodpeckers, especially Hairy Woodpecker, which likes the tall ones. Dead snags that hang out over the water provide prominent perches for flycatchers and nest sites for Baltimore Oriole. Rusty Blackbird and Acadian Flycatcher have been reported from this site during spring migration.

From the tower at the end of the boardwalk, there is a view of the shallows where Mill Creek enters the Hudson. Because the river is a migration corridor, the tower is a great place to sit up high and watch what passes by. The power lines along the railroad serve as convenient perches for Belted Kingfisher, Eastern Bluebird, and swallows, especially young of the year later in the fall. Osprey and Bald Eagle are regulars, and a spotting scope can sometimes pick out waders and waterfowl lurking in the marsh.

At one time, TNC had plans to build more trails at this preserve, but to date there is only the boardwalk. It is possible to access TNC-owned property south of the boardwalk by parking on the shoulder near the junction of 9J and Gibbons Road, about 0.6 mile south of the boardwalk entrance. On the other side of the guardrail, an unmarked and overgrown path leads west to an abandoned railroad bed that parallels the state highway. The railroad ties are gone, but the stone of the railbed is still evident. Though severely overgrown, the raised bed is a good route for viewing spring warblers.

Wilson M. Powell Wildlife Sanctuary

GPS ADDRESS 75 Hunt Club Road, Old Chatham
LATITUDE/LONGITUDE 42.43125 −73.56397
DIRECTIONS From the junction of CR 13 and Albany Turnpike in the hamlet of Old Chatham, travel southwest on CR 13 for 0.9 mile to Pitt Hall Road on the left, where two signs mark the road to Powell House and the sanctuary. Follow Pitt Hall Road 0.25 mile, then bear left (east) onto Hunt Club Road, and continue 0.25 mile to the main parking lot. A second, two-car parking lot 0.3 mile beyond the main lot provides wheelchair access to Reilly Pond.

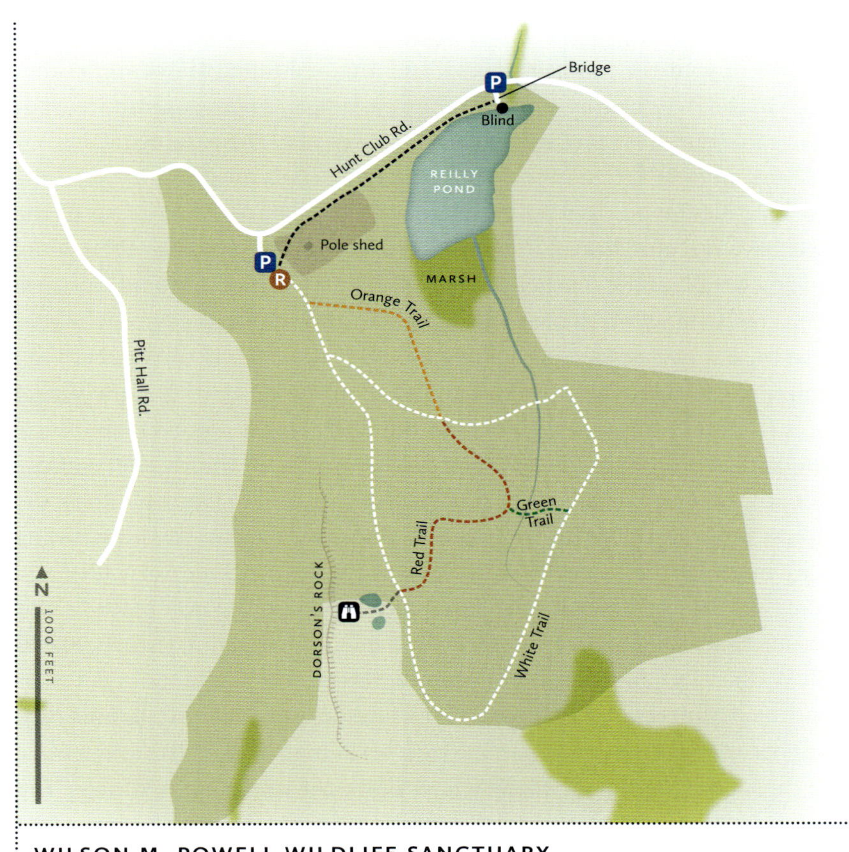

WILSON M. POWELL WILDLIFE SANCTUARY

The Wilson M. Powell Wildlife Sanctuary has been owned, managed, and maintained by the Alan Devoe Bird Club since 1959. Acquired through a series of donations and protected by conservation easements, the preserve now totals about 145 acres. Horses are occasionally ridden through the property because equestrian access was part of the original donation agreement. In the early 1900s, the owner of what was then farmland planted some parts of the property with nonnative evergreens, but today much of the land supports mature hardwood forest. Scientists and naturalists have studied this preserve for more than fifty years, and the club includes more than two hundred species on the sanctuary's bird list.

The group maintains a number of bird feeders in the main parking lot area. In winter, at least fifteen common species frequent the feeders, and if you park appropriately, you can study these birds at very close range from the warmth of your car. Cooper's Hawk and Sharp-shinned Hawk sometimes perch in the trees nearby, looking for an easy meal. There is a primitive but serviceable outhouse on the edge of the woods near the parking lot.

Three miles of interconnected, color-coded trails take visitors to all the best bird habitats in the Wilson M. Powell Wildlife Sanctuary. All of the trails have ups and downs, but with the exception of sections of the white and green trails at the southern edge of the preserve, most are gentle grades. From the parking lot, the white trail parallels the western edge of the preserve on a rocky, eroded path along an old rock wall where Winter Wren sometimes forages among the rocks. One of the property's many vernal pools is located in a low area behind the wall. This is a good place to see Wood Duck and Mallard. Less than half a mile down the west side of the white trail, an arrow nailed to a tree marks a side trail to Dorson's Rock, the highest point in the preserve at 924 feet. On a clear day, this west-facing rocky outcrop offers spectacular views of the distant Hudson Valley and serves as a decent hawkwatch. This overlook is also the best place to find the sanctuary's high-elevation specialists including Hermit Thrush, Black-poll Warbler in migration, and Common Raven. The white trail continues near the perimeter of the property for a total length of about 1.0 mile, running between vernal pools, passing by a small marsh, and climbing a steep hill through mature hardwoods where Black-throated Green Warbler and American Redstart are common and easily seen. The trail forms a loop and rejoins the path back to the main parking lot.

The red trail branches off from the white trail loop and passes through the interior of the property. At the top of a hill is a memorial bench dedicated to Elsie K. Powell Jr., who donated the property to the bird club. This is a good place to sit and watch birds on the steep slope directly across the ravine. Brown Creeper, thrushes, Ovenbird, Yellow-rumped Warbler, Blackburnian Warbler, and Scarlet Tanager are often present in this area of the preserve.

The northern path from the parking lot leads through a hedgerow to a four-acre field with a pole shed and hand pump. The trees and shrubs on the edge of the field attract Indigo Bunting, Chestnut-sided Warbler, Yellow Warbler, Song Sparrow, and American Goldfinch. Eastern Bluebird and Tree Swallow sometimes occupy the nest boxes here. The path through the field leads to Reilly Pond, which is diked at one end to create a shallow pond and wetland; here, the dead trees provide nest holes for Tree Swallows and woodpeckers and water for waders and waterfowl. There is a blind at the south end of the pond, and the shoreline attracts many warblers during migration.

Hand Hollow Conservation Area

GPS ADDRESS 4079 CR 9, New Lebanon
LATITUDE/LONGITUDE 42.47242 −73.47551
DIRECTIONS From the junction of NY 22 and US 20 in New Lebanon, take US 20 4.5 miles to CR 9. Take CR 9 south 1.2 miles and turn west (right) into a parking lot at the farmhouse just past the pond. There is a second parking area on the west side near Meizinger Lake, at 387 Gale Hill Road. Trail map at clctrust.org.

Pieced together over the years from family properties, Columbia Land Conservancy (CLC) now owns and manages 433 acres at Hand Hollow Conservation Area for the protection of wildlife and open space. The property has an active beaver pond and two lakes, as well as a variety of upland habitats that reflect past land use. Most of the woods are successional, but some impressive old pines remain, and the forests are a patchwork of young woods and older stands with a well-developed understory. Hand Hollow is CLC's oldest public conservation area, and over the years, donations have allowed the construction of benches and shelters at well-placed viewing areas throughout the property. These typically overlook streams, lakes, or food sources that are used by birds and other wildlife.

The 1.7-mile-long green trail is the main pathway through the preserve, and connects the two parking lots. All the other trails are relatively short loop circuits that branch off and rejoin the green trail. Starting at the east end of the preserve, the green trail passes near a beaver pond and wet meadow, before entering the woods. Green and Great Blue Heron are almost always present, and Belted Kingfisher is hard to miss. Willow Flycatcher is found along the edges, along with Yellow Warbler, Chestnut-sided Warbler, and Common Yellowthroat. Beyond the wetland, the trail follows a stream and then descends into a hemlock ravine. Black-throated Green Warbler breeds in the ravine, and many other warblers are reported from the woodlands along this trail, especially during spring migration. At the west end, the green trail skirts the edge of Meizinger Lake, where shorebirds, waders, and waterfowl are likely. Fluctuating water levels and beaver have killed some trees along the

Cedar Waxwing.
© Alan W. Wells.

perimeter of the lake, thereby creating good perches for flycatchers, swallows, Cedar Waxwing, and other insect-hawking species. A grove of white birch along this trail is good habitat for winter finches.

Though short, the yellow trail is the most interesting loop that branches off the green trail. It passes through a grove of mature white pines, and a section of meadow that has swallows, raptors, and grasslands birds. Tree Swallow, House Wren, and Eastern Bluebird occupy nest boxes on this part of the property. The red trail passes through an open woods and leads to a gazebo, while the blue trail near the Gale Hill Road parking lot provides another vantage point from which to view that lake.

Stockport Flats

GPS ADDRESS 200 Station Road, Hudson
LATITUDE/LONGITUDE 42.31023 −73.77190
DIRECTIONS From Hudson, take US 9 north to the bridge crossing
Stockport Creek, and then turn immediately west (left) onto CR 22/
Station Road. Follow Station Road about 1.0 mile to the parking area at
the end. To get to the Ferry Road parking area, continue north on US 9
another 2.0 miles to its junction with NY 9J. Take the left fork onto NY
9J and continue another 2.5 miles to Ferry Road. Turn west (left) onto
Ferry Road and continue 0.2 mile past the private residences to a small
parking area. The third and most northern parking area is at the end of
Ice House Road, which turns west off NY 9J 0.3 mile farther north.
Map at www.dec.ny.gov.

One of the most beautiful sections of the freshwater tidal Hudson River is
protected in these five miles of state-owned shoreline collectively referred
to as Stockport Flats. Located in the towns of Stuyvesant and Stockport,
Stockport Flats is the northernmost site in the Hudson River National Estuarine Research Reserve. A canoe or kayak—by far the best way to explore
this site—allows access to beautiful marshes, bays, coves, and islands that
cannot be reached from the mainland. For those without a boat, trails and
overlooks accessible from the main shoreline provide an adequate opportunity to take in much of the rich bird diversity the reserve has to offer. Cartop
boats can be launched at all three entrances, but the boat launch at Station
Road, which can also accommodate small motorboats, provides the best
route to the most interesting bird habitats. Because many parts of Stockport
Flats are very shallow at low tide, canoe exploration is best on a rising tide.

The parking area and boat launch on Station Road are located at the mouth
of Stockport Creek. Upstream from here, there are channels through the
marsh that lead to sheltered areas on the backsides of islands inhabited by
rails and grebes. Bald Eagle nests here and is easily seen year-round. At high
tide, small boats can travel all the way up to the rapids just below the US 9
highway bridge.

Downstream from the boat launch, Stockport Creek passes under the railroad bridge and south of Stockport Middle Ground island. Both this island
and the shores of the peninsula to the north, Gay's Point, have boat access but

Bank Swallow nests in the sandy bluffs of Stockport Middle Ground.
© Denise Hackert-Stoner, Naturelogues.

only primitive campsites. Bank Swallow, Northern Rough-winged Swallow, and Belted Kingfisher nest in the sandy bluff on the southwest corner of Stockport Middle Ground. The larger emergent marshes in the coves north of Priming Hook, behind Gay's Point and south of Nutten Hook, support good populations of Least Bittern, Virginia Rail, Swamp Sparrow, and Marsh Wren during the spring and summer. Landing on Gay's Point provides access to 1.75 miles of trails on the peninsula and a chance to explore the woods that border the river. Baltimore Oriole, Willow Flycatcher, Warbling Vireo, and other passerines commonly nest here, and these woods are filled with warblers during spring migration.

Birding the Flats without a boat is also rewarding, but access is more limited. The parking area on Station Road has a wonderful view of the river and parts of the marsh. In addition to eagles, this area is good for Osprey, cormorants, waterfowl, swallows, gulls and sometimes terns, as well as waders, including Great Egret in the fall. High-speed trains travel on the tracks between the parking area and the river, so all observation of the river must be done from behind the barrier.

The only marked hiking trails at Stockport Flats are found at Nutten Hook, a bedrock outcrop at the north end of the property. Bounded by Ice House Road on the north and Ferry Road on the south, Nutten Hook was once a thriving community where seasonal workers cut ice from the river and a ferry took passengers and goods to Coxsackie. The preserved remains of the old icehouse still stand along the river on Ice House Road. The hiking trail is a 0.6-mile-long loop, marked with yellow nature trail markers, which can be accessed from either parking lot. It follows the river on the west and the old Federal Footpath inland, a trail that workers historically used to reach industrial sites on the river's edge.

Just north of the icehouse is a sheltered cove and sandy beach that sometimes has interesting ducks and shorebirds. From the icehouse, the trail follows the top of the rocky outcrop along the edge of the river, with good views of the water and the Coxsackie boat launch on the opposite shore. In spring, white flowering shad trees reach out over the water along this rocky cliff, and Belted Kingfishers perch just above the water, waiting to ambush the fish below. Spotted Sandpipers forage on the rocks at the base of the cliff. The oak woods near Ferry Road are reliable for Scarlet Tanager and Pileated Woodpecker in summer, and the old ferry landing provides a 270-degree view of the river. Great Cormorants occasionally perch on channel markers in this reach of the Hudson in winter. A short path from the landing, south through the woods, leads to a sheltered sandy cove with a large mudflat at low tide. The return path north along the eastern side of the loop begins just east of the Ferry Road parking area at the foot of a large, rocky knoll, and runs between a steep wooded hillside and the freshwater tidal marsh. Winter Wren is seen among the rocks and ledges of the rocky outcrop, and American Woodcock has been flushed from the woods near the edge of the

Great Cormorants perched on a channel marker in the Hudson River. © Deborah Tracy-Kral.

marsh. Before reaching Ice House Road, the trail descends into a low area full of blackberries and vines that supports large numbers of sparrows, especially in winter. Half-hardy birds, such as Gray Catbird, Hermit Thrush, and Carolina Wren, are often present in this low spot well into winter.

There is also good foot birding along both Ice House and Ferry Roads, where they pass through the wetlands between the railroad tracks and the parking areas. Used only by local residents, these roads are lightly traveled, and the neighbors are accustomed to sharing their backyards with birders. Swamp Sparrow and Song Sparrow are often heard in the marsh; and blackbirds, including Red-winged Blackbird, Common Grackle, and Brown-headed Cowbird, roost among the common reeds during migration and winter. Rusty Blackbird regularly visits the swampy area on the south side of Ferry Road during spring migration. Cedar Waxwing and Eastern Bluebird, as well as Downy Woodpecker, Hairy Woodpecker, Red-bellied Woodpecker, and Pileated Woodpecker, use the fruits and tall dead snags that line Ferry Road.

Ooms Conservation Area at Sutherland Pond

GPS ADDRESS 480 Rock City Road, Chatham
LATITUDE/LONGITUDE 42.40373 −73.569262
DIRECTIONS From Chatham, take NY 295 north 2.4 miles to Hartigan Road near the southbound entrance ramp to the Taconic Parkway. Turn north (left) onto Hartigan Road and continue 1.1 miles to Rock City Road. Turn left onto Rock City Road, and go 0.3 mile to the main parking area on the left. There are two smaller parking areas along Rock City Road before the main lot, which is fenced. The boat launch is near the parking lot opposite George Road. Trail map at clctrust.org.

This 180-acre preserve on the outskirts of Chatham is one of the best sites for grassland birds in the Upper Hudson Valley. The property was once part of a local dairy farm, and for many years the land was hayed to feed the cows, but today it is owned and managed by Columbia Land Conservancy, a private land trust. In 2016 CLC agreed to use mowing only to maintain the trails and to manage the fields as grasslands. Now safe from destructive mowing practices, the grassland birds at Ooms should be able to breed successfully every year.

Even non-birders are struck by the pastoral beauty of the rolling grasslands that surround Sutherland Pond, a thirty-five-acre impoundment that has

Male Bobolink on its territory. © Naomi Lloyd.

been a community gathering site for decades. Fishing and non-motorized boating are allowed on the pond, and there is a shady picnic area on the north side near the parking area. The site includes three miles of easy-to-moderate trails. The green trail loops around the pond; it runs close to the pond along the road and on the east side, but on the south side it ascends through open fields to viewpoints and a gazebo on the top of one hill. The hike around the pond can be lengthened by taking the red trail spur that follows a hedgerow and adds another 0.75 mile.

Ooms is a reliable site to see breeding grassland birds. In May and June, displaying Bobolinks are easily viewed and photographed in most of the fields, along with Eastern Bluebird, Tree Swallow, Red-winged Blackbird, Eastern Meadowlark, Savannah Sparrow, Field Sparrow, and American Kestrel. Grasshopper Sparrow has been observed during summer but is not yet known to breed, though there is a good chance that more of the grassland birds will become breeders now that the site has a bird-friendly mowing regime. Northern Harrier is regularly present in winter and during migration, and Osprey are seen often enough that CLC has put up a nesting platform for them.

Sutherland Pond receives a nice diversity of ducks in April and November during waterfowl migration. Ring-necked Duck, Hooded Merganser, Common Merganser, Ruddy Duck, Green-winged Teal, and Pied-billed Grebe stopover, and Mallard and Wood Duck stay to breed. The pond edges are good for Belted Kingfisher, Eastern Towhee, Swamp Sparrow, Brown Thrasher, Willow Flycatcher, Yellow Warbler, and Blue-winged Warbler. Both Baltimore and Orchard Oriole are reported as well. On cool mornings in early fall, large mixed flocks of swallows gather to perch and feed on insects along the shore.

Beebe Hill and Harvey Mountain State Forests

GPS ADDRESS 1 Beebe Forest Road, Chatham

LATITUDE/LONGITUDE 42.33894 −73.473699

DIRECTIONS To get to the main parking area for Beebe Hill, take New York State Thruway Exit B3 to NY 22, and continue south for 2.0 miles to Middle Road. Turn west (right) onto Middle Road, and follow it 1.5 miles until it intersects Fog Hill Road. Bear left onto Fog Hill, and follow it to CR 5/Osmer Road. Turn south (left) onto CR 5, and make a quick right onto Beebe Forest Road into the Barrett Pond parking area.

Beebe Hill and Harvey Mountain State Forests adjoin each other and together encompass over three thousand acres of public land in the Town of Austerlitz in the northeast corner of Columbia County. Harvey Mountain was acquired in 1999, while Beebe Hill has been in state ownership since the 1960s. These properties include the highest elevations in the county. Harvey Mountain, at 2,065 feet, is Columbia County's highest point. These state forests feature a fire tower, a big blueberry patch that is visited by both bears and humans, a boundary marker between New York and Massachusetts, ponds, an interesting old cemetery, unusual wetlands, and splendid views of the Taconics, Catskills, and Berkshires. In short, this place has something for everyone.

The best birding habitats in this large area are scattered, and there are multiple trails to the same destinations with varying degrees of difficulty. Some trails are well marked, but others are not. Barrett Pond, which has an information kiosk and easy access, is a good place to start. The pond has a well-vegetated edge of emergent plants that should be good for waterfowl and marsh birds. The dead trees and wires near the road attract a variety of swallows during the breeding season. This parking area is also one of the

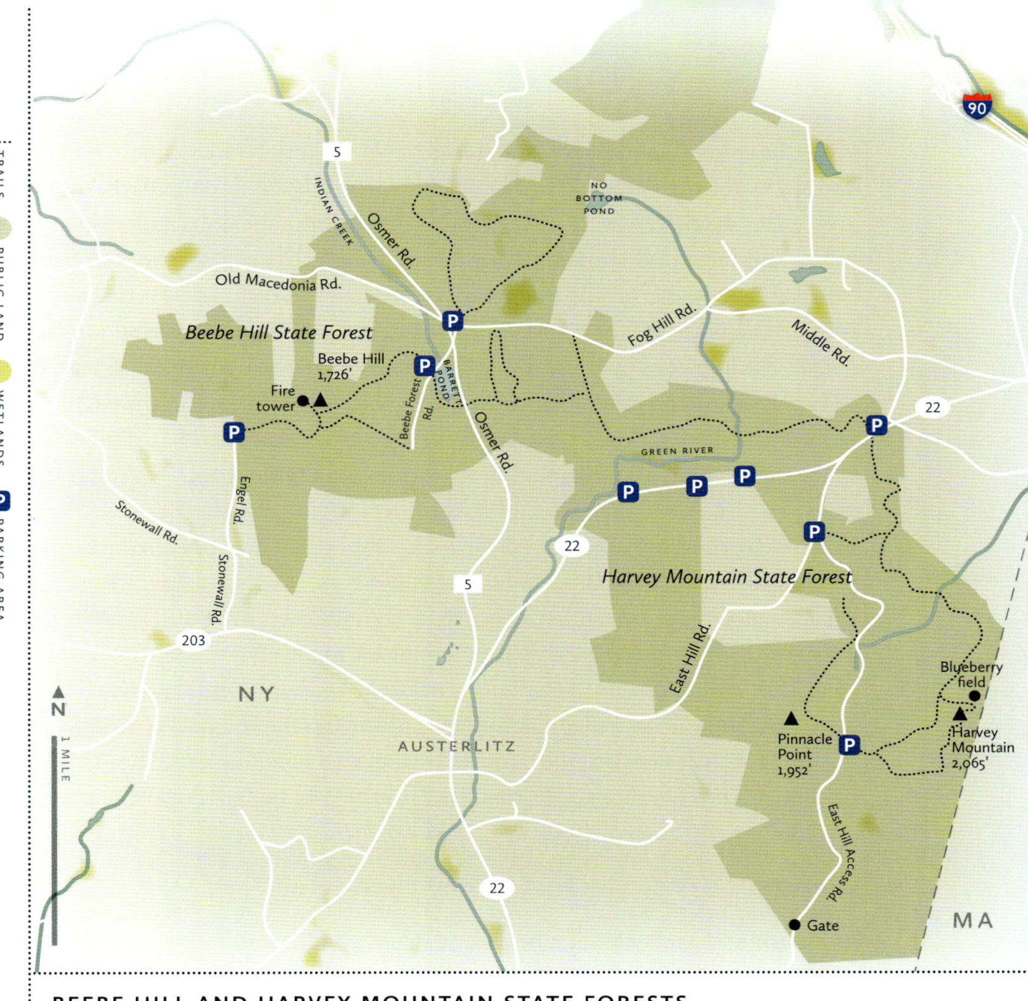

BEEBE HILL AND HARVEY MOUNTAIN STATE FORESTS

trailheads for the Beebe Hill summit and fire tower. The foot trail with blue trail markers is a pleasant, easy hike. From this parking area there is also a steeper, longer horse trail to the summit. Another easy trail begins on the west side from a parking area on Engle Road. All of these trails travel through mid-elevation deciduous woods and end at the observer's cabin and sixty-foot fire tower, which offers treetop views of birds and long views of the surrounding landscape. These woods are perhaps the most reliable site in Columbia County for breeding Black-throated Blue Warbler, Black-and-white Warbler, Chestnut-sided Warbler, Dark-eyed Junco, and Hermit Thrush.

From the parking area on Fog Hill Road, the north edge of Beebe Hill State

Forest has poorly marked trails that lead to No Bottom Pond, a small, shallow body of water with unusual hydrology that probably connects to caves in the area. In dry years, the pond is reported to shrink dramatically, a situation that might support good shorebird habitat. Be aware that part of the shoreline is privately owned, so it is important to stay on the trail. Even if the water is high, the pond is worth a visit. The easternmost and easiest trail crosses a stream and passes by several small marshes with good birding potential.

The shortest and easiest route up Harvey Mountain begins on the east side of East Hill Access Road, 1.2 miles south of its junction with East Hill Road at the parking lot. The trail begins at a gate as an ATV road and continues 0.7 mile to a large blueberry bald on the summit. In fall, blueberries, bear scat, Eastern Towhee, and Dark-eyed Junco are abundant. The open habitat and 360-degree view makes this a good place to see raptors during migration, and Broad-winged Hawk nests in the nearby forest. Following the trail another 0.1 mile east brings you to a small concrete block marking the border between New York and Massachusetts. This quick hike to the summit can be turned into a longer loop hike through forest by following the red trail north where the blue trail leads back to the parking area on East Hill Road, and then hiking the lightly traveled dirt access road back to the parking area near the gate.

Greenport Conservation Area and Harrier Hill Park

GPS ADDRESS 319 Joslen Boulevard, Hudson
LATITUDE/LONGITUDE 42.26908 −73.768469
DIRECTIONS From Hudson, take US 9 north to its intersection with Joslen Boulevard at a traffic light. Turn north (left) and continue 1.0 mile to a parking area on the left. There are additional entrances and parking areas for this large site. Map with details at clctrust.org.

This large preserve on the east shore of the Hudson River offers spectacular views of North Bay, the main stem of the river, and the Catskill Mountains on the opposite shore. Pieced together by conservation groups and government agencies over many years, the public land still has multiple landowners. Columbia Land Conservancy owns most of the land and manages much of it, but Scenic Hudson has retained ownership of six acres at Harrier Hill on the north end of the property, and NYSDEC protects some of the uplands. The open habitats are maintained through rotational mowing, and each fall

CLC issues permits to a few hunters to keep the deer population in check. Most of the area remains open during this time.

The natural communities and bird habitats at this site reflect the fact that most of the land was once actively farmed for corn, hay, and dairy production. Open fields and meadows dominate the uplands. Their substantial acreage makes good habitat for grassland birds. The hedgerows that border the fields support shrubland-nesting songbirds and migrants. The most extensive forest communities are on the steep western edge of the property, bordering small streams that descend to the Hudson River. These steep slopes block trail access to the river and marshes, but it is easy to see and hear birds in the marshes below from the overlooks, and even better with the aid of a spotting scope.

With more than five miles of clearly marked trails and many access points, it is difficult to see the entire site in one visit. The two-mile-long Stockport-Greenport Trail joins the northern Harrier Hill property to CLC land to the south, but it does not form a loop trail, so returning to the same parking lot requires retracing your steps over a long distance. Leaving a second car at the Greenport Town Park entrance is another option. However, no one should visit this site without at least witnessing the breathtaking view of the Hudson River and Catskills from Harrier Hill. From the parking lot, a 0.13-mile-long wheelchair-accessible trail leads up a gentle grade past a small pond to benches and a pavilion overlooking fields and shrublands. Bobolink, Eastern Bluebird, Eastern Meadowlark, and American Kestrel are often seen in this area. American Kestrel, Tree Swallow, and Eastern Bluebird breed in the nest boxes here, and young of the year often perch on wires near the road in late summer.

The Stockport-Greenport Trail begins across the road from the Harrier Hill parking lot and passes through fields, along edges, and through small woodlots, skirting private inholdings. The trail enters the woods and crosses a stream on a steep slope, before joining the Town Park (red) Trail. Because songbirds use the river as a migration corridor, these woods collect warblers in the spring. Spur trails to the west lead to overlooks into the marsh on North Bay, while the loop trail connects to a trail leading to the Town Park entrance.

The land between the Greenport Town Park and the main entrance on Joslen Boulevard has more trails and more opportunities for hikes that let you avoid retracing your steps. Another handicapped-accessible pathway, the 1.5-mile Access for All Trail, leads from the southern parking lot through a beautiful wet meadow to a gazebo overlooking the Hudson River. The beginning of this pathway passes through shrubs and mature cedars. Indigo Bunting nests here, and sometimes perches on power lines along the edge of the property. This trail includes a wet meadow with shaded benches strategically placed to view nest boxes, stands of dogwoods, and other fruiting plants that attract birds. Sit a few minutes, and the birds will come to you. The gazebo has a good view of the freshwater tidal marsh in North Bay, but the next overlook to the north on the blue trail gives a less obstructed view of the same area. Great Blue Heron often perch on duck blinds in the bay, using them to peer into the water for prey. Bald Eagle, Osprey, gulls, and ducks on the river are most easily seen with a spotting scope.

South of the Access for All Trail, there are dry fields and sections of woods with old cedars. A spur trail to the river follows a ridge that allows treetop views of warblers and runs between seasonal streams where Louisiana Waterthrush is seen in the spring. The overlook on the orange trail from a high cliff far from the river is spectacular. CLC and local municipalities have plans to increase access to the area around North Bay, so the southern part of the preserve may soon have new trails and connectors to nearby conservation areas.

Olana

GPS ADDRESS 5720 NY 9G, Hudson
LATITUDE/LONGITUDE 42.21714 −73.829278
DIRECTIONS From Hudson, take NY 9G south past its junction with NY 23 and past where NY 23 turns west across the Rip Van Winkle Bridge. Continue south on 9G another 0.9 mile to the sign on the east side of the road that marks the entrance road to Olana. Park only in designated parking areas.

Olana, the historic home of Hudson River School artist Frederic Edwin Church, sits atop a rocky drumlin on the east side of the Hudson River. Church was an accomplished artist, but when arthritis made it difficult for him to paint, he put his creative energy into landscaping his estate, which, in Church's time, also functioned as a working farm. With meticulous attention to detail, he planned and built carriage roads that were designed to showcase the breathtaking scenery surrounding his Hudson Valley home. He managed the landscape for both beauty and function, removing muck from a swamp to create a lake, planting gardens, orchards, and woodlands, and

TRAILS
CARRIAGE ROAD
PUBLIC LAND
VIEWPOINT
PARKING AREA
23
23
North Meadow
Ridge Rd.
North Rd.
North Rd.
Visitor Center
Olana (main house)
Lawn and terrace
Flower garden
Bethune Rd.
Farm Rd.
Orchard
Cosy Cottage
9G
South Rd.
South Rd.
Wagon House Education Center
Contact Station
LAKE
Kitchen garden
Farm
Lake Rd.
N
.25 MILE
Crown Hill Rd.
Crown Hill
Entrance

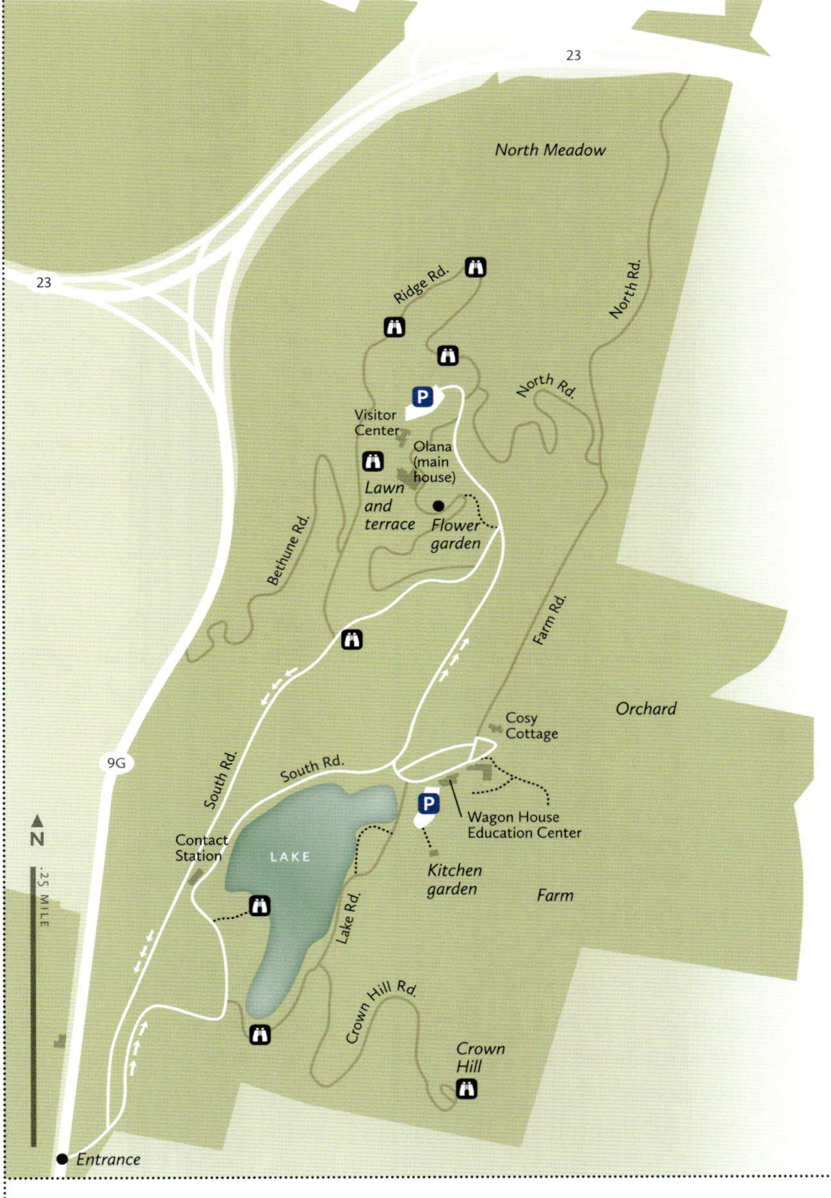

OLANA

grazing livestock in the North Meadow. New York State acquired Olana in 1967, and OPRHP has been working ever since to restore the 250-acre property to Church's original plan.

Because of its close proximity to the Hudson River, Olana attracts a good variety of spring and fall migrants, but the estate's diversity of habitats makes it a great place to see birds year-round. The carriage roads that wind around the long hill are perfect trails for birdwatching because they pass through all the natural and cultural communities on the property. From the parking area by the Wagon House Education Center and Kitchen Garden one can walk around the lake and explore the barns and open fields where American Kestral, Eastern Bluebird, Tree Swallow, Eastern Phoebe, and Barn Swallow nest. During migration, many warblers and thrushes can be found in the forested habitat around the lake. A short, easy hike south on the carriage road through the woods passes by a swamp where Wood Duck are common. Beyond the woods, a switchback leads to the top of Crown Hill, which looks down on the barn, fields, and Olana in the distance. This view to the north is a good place to scan the skies for soaring raptors.

Farm Road runs north of the lake past Cosy Cottage, where the Churches lived while Olana was being built. This route looks down on the orchard where Eastern Kingbird and orioles are likely, and the shrubby road edge and fencerows are a good place to look for Brown Thrasher and Indigo Bunting. Farm Road connects to North Road, which Church built to be the dramatic front entrance to Olana. After the junction, the road winds up the hill through woods to the house, but walking north at the junction with Ridge Road leads to the North Meadow restoration area and a view of Mount Merino. With time, this meadow should provide enough grassland habitat to support grassland birds. Northern Harrier is seen here from time to time. A grove of planted pines on the edge of the meadow is also good for conifer-loving species.

Though it tends to be busy with visitors during the summer, the area around the main house may also produce some interesting birds, especially in the gardens where Ruby-throated Hummingbirds forage on flowers. On the west side of the property, Ridge Road faces the river at the bottom of a steep hillside below the house. This is a good place to look for sparrows, especially in the fall. One of the reasons that people come to Olana is to take in the spectacular views. Though the scenery is wonderful, birders will want to use the view from around the house to look for Peregrine Falcon, Bald Eagle, and Osprey.

Lake Taghkanic State Park

GPS ADDRESS 1582 NY 82, Ancram

LATITUDE/LONGITUDE 42.09110 –73.69958

DIRECTIONS From the Taconic State Parkway, take the exit for
NY 82/Hudson/Ancram and go south on NY 82 about 2.4 miles to the
park entrance. This entrance is closest to the best birding sites, but
there is another entrance directly off the Taconic State Parkway 1.0
mile south of the exit for NY 82/Hudson/Ancram. Trail map at
parks.ny.gov/parks.

Lake Taghkanic State Park in south central Columbia County is listed in eBird
as the county's number-one birding hotspot, with more than 160 species recorded. Its fifteen-hundred-plus acres include a mix of habitats surrounding
a large lake at the center. Because the park has a beach, campground, playgrounds, and picnic facilities, it tends to be busy during the peak summer
months; but many of the best birding areas are on the east edge of the lake,
well separated from the crowds. The entrance from NY 82 provides the easiest
access to these places.

The lake itself attracts aerial insectivores, Belted Kingfisher, the typical
waders, and occasional interesting waterfowl in the early spring, but its most
noteworthy feature is the marsh and shrub swamp at its east end. American
Bittern and Virginia Rail are reported from this area, and Swamp Sparrow
is common. A trail around the south
side of the lake offers good views of
the water and skirts a wooded hillside,
which, because of its proximity to the
water, is especially good for spring warblers. Worm-eating Warbler, rare in the
county, is known from this area. The
walk along the south side of the lake
also crosses two streams, good habitat
for Louisiana Waterthrush.

Brown Thrasher is common in the shrubby
fields of the Fitness Trail at Lake Taghkanic
State Park. © Alan W. Wells.

The area around the park's Fitness Trail is mostly overgrown old fields, where Wild Turkey, Brown Thrasher, Eastern Towhee, Blue-winged Warbler, and Prairie Warbler are common during the breeding season. The nearby pine plantations have Barred Owl and Pine Warbler. The species list for this site also includes an impressive ten raptor species, with breeding season records for Northern Harrier, Sharp-shinned Hawk, Cooper's Hawk, Red-shouldered Hawk, Broad-winged Hawk, and Red-tailed Hawk.

Harlem Valley Rail Trail, Copake Falls to Under Mountain Road

GPS ADDRESS 214 NY 344, Copake
LATITUDE/LONGITUDE 42.12042 −73.52300
DIRECTIONS Copake Falls trailhead. From the junction of NY 23 and NY 22 at the traffic light in Hillsdale, take NY 22 south 4.0 miles to NY 344. Take NY 344 west 0.4 mile to a triangular green, and bear left at the stop sign. Continue east on NY 344 0.2 mile to the designated Rail Trail Parking area across from the Depot Deli. At the south end of this site, there is another small parking area on the north side of Under Mountain Road. Map at parks.ny.gov/parks.

This four-mile section of the Harlem Valley Rail Trail passes through a particularly scenic part of Columbia County known as the Harlem Valley. The trail derives its name from the New York and Harlem Railroad, which operated on 131 miles of track between Manhattan and Chatham from the mid-1800s until the 1970s. In 1873 it merged with the New York Central Railroad and became known as the Harlem Division or Harlem Line. When service between Dover Plains and Chatham was discontinued in 1976, the state bought twenty-two miles of the forty-six-mile right-of-way, laying the groundwork for the future Harlem Valley Rail Trail.

Today, the completed rail trail includes fourteen miles in two locations, but there are plans to improve and open additional segments when funding becomes available. Eventually, OPRHP hopes to purchase additional parcels to create a forty-six-mile-long linear park through some of the most beautiful rural landscapes of the Hudson Valley. The northern section, described here, runs between Copake Falls and Under Mountain Road, but an additional 10.7-mile section links the towns of Millerton and Wassaic in Dutchess County.

Rail trails are not specifically designed for birding. They are paved bicycle/

One of the old concrete markers from the railroad showing the distance to New York City.
© Kathryn J. Schneider.

pedestrian pathways that are used by hikers, runners, cyclists, rollerbladers, and cross-country skiers. You should expect to encounter almost any type of non-motorized transportation, along with plenty of children and leashed dogs. However, several factors make rail trails desirable birding destinations. First, they are mostly flat. The Harlem Valley grade is typically 0.8 percent. To achieve this evenness, the railbed is filled and raised in places, thus creating excellent views of treetop bird habitat. Second, rail trails often pass through villages and public parks that provide conveniences such as public restrooms, shops, and restaurants. Finally, rail trails provide pedestrian access to undeveloped rural landscapes and wonderful opportunities to observe plants and animals in an undisturbed setting.

Because the trail is a through hike and not a loop, many birders like to leave a second car at the destination trailhead, in order to cover more ground and avoid retracing their steps. The Copake Falls trailhead is across the road from the parking lot, near the former railroad station, which is now a convenience store called the Depot Deli. The trail crosses Cedar Brook on a footbridge that offers outstanding views of the stream below and the trees above. From here, the trail continues south, along shrubby hillsides covered with fruit-bearing plants that attract a nice variety of thrushes and sparrows in the fall and winter, and then enters a forest dominated by sugar maples. For a short distance, the trail merges with Valley View Road, passing through a stand of very tall walnut trees where Hairy Woodpecker and Pileated Woodpecker are typically present.

The trail continues south for a total distance of 4.0 miles, passing by farmland that includes goats, llamas, horse pastures, open fields, and row crops. In winter, Horned Lark, Snow Bunting, blackbirds, and Brown-headed Cowbird are attracted to manure from the farm animals that contains grass seed. The farm ponds sometimes have interesting waterfowl, and during spring and summer, shorebirds such as Killdeer and Spotted Sandpiper may be present if water levels are low enough to create exposed mudflats. Some of the larger, unmowed grasslands support Bobolink, Savannah Sparrow, and Eastern Meadowlark. Eastern Bluebirds and Tree Swallows use the nest boxes along the trail. It is worth taking the time to sit on the benches that are strategically placed to take in panoramic views of the Harlem Valley and the Catskills beyond, and to watch for soaring raptors. Just north of the Under Mountain Road trailhead, the trail passes through a rock cut with a dripping seep where birds come to bathe, and then later skirts a stream and ravine. A concrete marker indicates that you are precisely 101 miles from New York City.

7 The Mid–Hudson Valley

Best place to....	Site
SEE WATERFOWL	Falling Waters Preserve
FIND GRASSLAND BIRDS	Shawangunk Grasslands NWR
FIND SHOREBIRDS	Wallkill River NWR
SEE MIGRATING WARBLERS	Peach Hill Park
FIND HIGH-ELEVATION BIRDS	Balsam Lake Mountain
WATCH MIGRATING RAPTORS	Mount Peter
FIND A RARE BIRD	Sterling Forest State Park, Ironwood Drive
GO BIRDING IN LATE SUMMER	Kenneth L. Wilson Campground
GO BIRDING IN WINTER	Dennings Point State Park
BIRD FROM A BOAT	Tivoli Bays WMA
HIKE AND BIRDWATCH	Minnewaska State Park Preserve
TAKE THE KIDS	Hudson Highlands Nature Museum
EXPERIENCE BIRDS AND CULTURE	Mills Norrie State Park
TAKE THE GRANDPARENTS	Cary Institute of Ecosystem Studies

The Mid–Hudson Valley counties of Ulster, Orange, and Dutchess are part of a region characterized by transitions. Anywhere south of Albany, the tides serve as a reminder that the Hudson is connected to the sea, and in this stretch the river's water becomes salty enough to be considered brackish. This change in salinity diversifies the river's natural communities, which now include species that tolerate both freshwater and salt water.

Several important tributaries bring freshwater into this part of the river. Wappinger and Fishkill Creeks drain Dutchess County, entering the river at Wappingers Falls and Beacon. To the west, Esopus Creek collects water from the Catskills to be impounded at Ashokan Reservoir, before joining the Hudson in northern Ulster County. Also on the west side, the Wallkill River flows northeast through a wide agricultural valley that runs from New Jersey through the center of Orange County. The Wallkill joins Rondout Creek to form the Hudson's largest tributary, before emptying into the river at Kingston.

The topography of the Mid–Hudson Valley features the Catskills, the Sha-

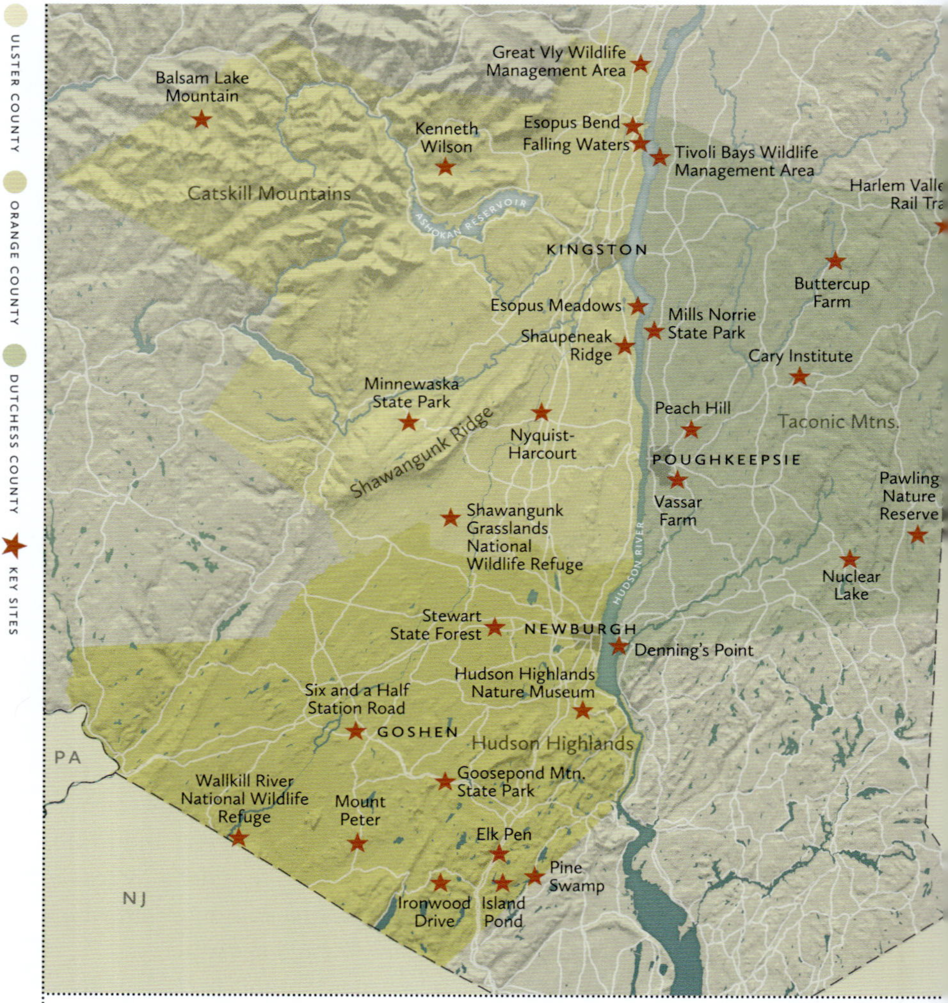

THE MID–HUDSON VALLEY

wangunks, the Hudson Highlands, and the Taconics. The Catskill Forest Preserve protects Slide Mountain and a cluster of other peaks over four thousand feet in the mountainous western part of Ulster County. The Hudson Highlands, that hard band of ancient rock that forms the spectacular and rugged scenery of West Point, marks the border between Orange and Rockland Counties and continues east across the river into Putnam. The Taconics lie on the border between northeastern Dutchess County and Connecticut.

The population of the Mid–Hudson Valley is growing, especially in Orange County, which is less than an hour from New York City. The majority of the people still live near the river in the cities of Kingston, Poughkeepsie, and Newburgh, but now there are major population centers away from the river on interstates such as I-84. In the face of ongoing change, both government and private conservation organizations are actively working to protect important natural areas from development.

ULSTER COUNTY

Great Vly Wildlife Management Area

GPS ADDRESS 200 West Camp Road, Saugerties
LATITUDE/LONGITUDE 42.13578 −73.94509
DIRECTIONS From I-87, take Exit 20/Saugerties and follow NY 32 north 1.8 miles to Old Kings Highway. Bear right onto Old Kings Highway, and drive about 2.5 miles to West Camp Road. Turn east (right) onto West Camp Road and continue about 2.5 miles. Turn left onto a dirt road at the NYSDEC sign and continue to a dirt parking area, or drive 0.1 mile farther on West Camp and park on the shoulder where the road crosses the wetland.

The Great Vly is a difficult site to bird, but it is included here because it is an amazing birding hotspot. Just a mile inland from the Hudson River, on the border between Greene and Ulster counties, the Vly has the misfortune of being located west of a limestone ridge that is owned by a cement company. The company takes trespassing very seriously, and as a result, most of the land surrounding this diverse 184-acre marsh is off-limits to birdwatchers. Public access is restricted to a small area of less than ten acres, which is owned by NYSDEC, and West Camp Road, which crosses the marsh at its north end. Given these restrictions, the best option for a serious birdwatcher who wants to see rare marsh birds, along with some of the other 185 species that have been recorded from this place, is to explore this site by canoe or kayak. Common Gallinule, American Bittern, Least Bittern, and Pied-billed Grebe are reported every year, and rarities such as King Rail and Clapper Rail are also seen. The Vly is a great site for ducks, and one of the main reasons NYSDEC owns land at this site is to provide access for fishermen and duck hunters. The DEC parking area off West Camp Road has a place to put in a boat on the Sawyer Kill, which drains into Great Vly. The marsh is quite shallow and most navigable when water levels are high.

Without a boat, seeing birds at this site is more of a challenge, but lightly traveled West Camp Road cuts right through a very nice part of the marsh. Many people have seen great birds by parking on the shoulder of the road and using their vehicle as a blind. With binoculars, or better yet, with a spotting scope, it is often possible to spot waterfowl, waders, Swamp Sparrow, and

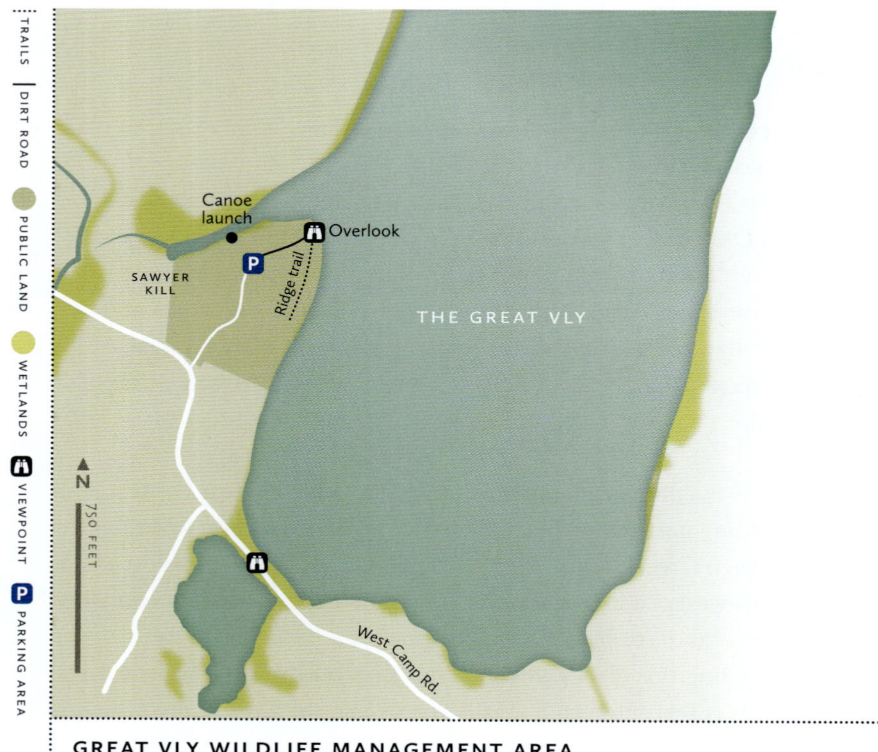

GREAT VLY WILDLIFE MANAGEMENT AREA

Common Gallinule is frequently reported from Great Vly. © Alan W. Wells.

Marsh Wren without getting out of your car. Sometimes ducks or rails and their young cross the road right in front of you. The dead trees that poke out of the water and power lines along the road also provide perches for an amazing assortment of swallows, flycatchers, warblers, and raptors that pass through during migration.

A third alternative is to take advantage of the topography of the Vly, which is bordered by rock cliffs. From the DEC parking area, there is a well-worn trail east up a steep hill. Especially when the leaves are down, this ridge is a good vantage point for viewing the marsh with a spotting scope, particularly for larger birds such as waterfowl, waders, and raptors.

Esopus Bend Nature Preserve

GPS ADDRESS 21 Kalina Drive, Saugerties
LATITUDE/LONGITUDE 42.06573 −73.95662
DIRECTIONS From I-87 Exit 20, take NY 32 north 5.4 miles through Saugerties to US 9W. Turn north onto US 9W and go 1.0 mile to Overbaugh Street (sign for Esopus Bend Nature Preserve). Turn west onto Overbaugh, and then bear right onto Kalina. The "birders'

entrance" with the most direct access to the marsh but very limited
parking is on Kalina Drive near its junction with Edgewood. Park on
the side of the road and walk through the gate on the right-of-way
between the two houses. There is more parking at the main entrance
at 10 Shady Lane and the south entrance at 50 Sterley Avenue. Map
at www.esopuscreekconservancy.org.

Esopus Creek starts on the east side of the Catskills and drains into the
Hudson River at Saugerties. As it enters the town, the creek makes a sharp
turn east to form an elbow of land known as the Esopus Bend. In low areas
along the shore and east of the elbow, the creek deposited rich soil that was
used for farmland before 1970. Today this ecologically sensitive part of the
preserve includes a restored meadow, vernal pools, and an impressive marsh.
Upstream on the western side of the preserve, the land is higher and more
forested. Inland, the preserve is surrounded by the housing development
of Barclay Heights, which was built in the 1950s. All the preserve trailheads
enter the property through local neighborhoods, and therefore it is especially
important for visitors to park legally and respect private property. Fortunately,
the Esopus Creek Conservancy, a private conservation organization, arranged
to protect this historic and ecologically significant site in 2003. Since then,
the group has worked tirelessly to maintain the preserve and to educate the
local community about the importance of protecting natural habitats like
this hidden gem.

While Esopus Bend hosts great birds year-round, its habitats are especially
valuable to half-hardy species that attempt to overwinter in the Hudson
Valley. Perhaps because of the tributary stream that usually does not freeze
and also because of open drainages and swales, individuals of species that
typically migrate find winter refuge here. For many years, the Esopus Creek
Conservancy has conducted a winter bird count in mid-January, finding birds
such as Cedar Waxwing, Hermit Thrush, Eastern Bluebird, Golden-crowned
Kinglet, Gray Catbird, Field Sparrow, and large numbers of Red-winged
Blackbirds.

There are four marked trails with connectors, and a maze of deliberately
unmarked paths in the meadow area that allows for flexible mowing. On the
west side of the elbow, some of the trails follow the old farm roads. The main
Schroeder Trail from Shady Lane follows the creek to the big bend, where
farm goods were once ferried across the creek to Stony Point on the opposite

Belted Kingfisher (male) is sometimes present even in winter
at Esopus Bend. © Deborah Tracy-Kral.

shore in Saugerties. This easy 1.2-mile loop through deciduous woods has a canoe and kayak landing, spur trails to views of the creek, and a stream crossing. The South Trail has a trailhead on the Sterley Avenue entrance, but also connects to the Schroeder Trail via a bridge across a stream entering Esopus Creek. This trail is short and steep in places. It passes through a hemlock stand that could be good for owls, and includes a ravine with a stream that stays open in winter and features a small cave. There is also a side trail that leads to the highest point in the preserve.

The north side of the bend holds the ecologically sensitive wetland and meadow habitats, and though there is a connector from the Schroeder Trail, the most direct access is from Kalina Drive. The Wetlands Trail loop leads down the hill north to the meadow, and east to a boardwalk with a view of the creek and the marsh as well as the East Trail. The meadow has edge and old field habitat where American Woodcock display in early spring, a remnant floodplain forest, and a natural sandbar area at the edge of the creek. The Wetlands Trail has Wood Duck boxes, beaver, a vernal pool, and at its junction with the East Trail, an excellent boardwalk overlooking the marsh. This cove is a good place to see swallows, woodpeckers, Osprey, Bald Eagle, herons, Belted Kingfisher, and waterfowl.

Esopus Meadows Preserve and Lighthouse Park

GPS ADDRESS 257 River Road, Ulster Park

LATITUDE/LONGITUDE 41.86822 −73.95119

DIRECTIONS From I-87, take Exit 19 toward Kingston and enter the roundabout, taking the exit for I-587S/NY 28/Colonel George F. Chandler Drive, which becomes Broadway. Make a slight left onto Delaware Avenue, and merge onto 9W south/Broadway on the left. Go 2.2 miles to CR 24/ River Road on the left, and follow it 2.6 miles to the parking area on the left for Esopus Meadows Preserve. Map at www.scenichudson.org.

These two Hudson River sites are immediately adjacent to each other on the west bank of the river. Lighthouse Park is owned by the Town of Esopus and occupies a few acres at the north end. It has a number of marble memorial benches for people who just want to sit by the river and take in the view or watch the Bald Eagles that frequent this site. A short trail south along the river connects the park to Scenic Hudson's ninety-six-acre Esopus Meadows Preserve. Both parcels look out on the Esopus lighthouse, the only remaining wooden lighthouse on the Hudson, which was built in 1871 to aid navigation around the shallows here. Historically, this shoreline supported large beds of native aquatic plants where farmers grazed their livestock at low tide. Today the cows are gone, and exotic plants such as water chestnut and Eurasian watermilfoil fill parts of the "meadow," but the shallows are still ecologically productive habitat for plants, invertebrates, and an abundance of young fish. Esopus Meadows is a critically important spawning and nursery area for striped bass and shad, and birds come to feed on this bounty. The area near the parking lot includes the Esopus Meadows Environmental Center, an outdoor classroom and pavilion that were built for resiliency, meaning that they were designed to stand up to flooding. This investment in environmentally friendly infrastructure speaks to the importance of the area for wildlife and its observers.

Esopus Meadows is a great place to see birds on the river. Bald Eagle, Great Blue Heron, Double-crested Cormorant, Belted Kingfisher, and gulls are common at this site. Unusual waders, waterfowl, and rare gulls appear unexpectedly. At low tide there are mudflats, which are good for shorebirds during migration. Terrestrial songbirds frequent the trees and shrubbery on the river's edge as well as the inland forests.

Esopus Meadows is in the heart of the Hudson Valley. © Kathryn J. Schneider.

Two miles of well-marked trails form loops throughout the property. The blue trail runs south along the river, where eagles often perch. This route offers magnificent views of the river and the east shore mansions, before turning inland through the woods. The red trail is an easy, well-done forest ecology interpretive trail along the Klyne Esopus Kill, a small creek that drains into the river at the "meadow." At 0.7 mile, the yellow trail is the longest and most remote pathway on the preserve. It can be accessed only from the red and blue trails. Habitats include forests of differing composition and ages; a variety of wetlands including vernal pools, red maple swamps, and a small cattail marsh; views into the valley of the Klyne Esopus Kill; and hills with rock outcrops. A spur trail (white) that comes off the east side leads to the river and a stop on the Hudson River Greenway Water Trail where canoeists and kayakers come ashore. The landing area features a picnic shelter with great river views, interpretive signs, and a composting toilet.

Balsam Lake Mountain

GPS ADDRESS 7350 Mill Brook Road, Hardenburgh

LATITUDE/LONGITUDE 42.07850 −74.56926

DIRECTIONS From NY 28 in Highmount in the northwest corner of
Ulster County, take CR 49A (Galli-Curci and Todd Mountain Roads)
about 6.0 miles past Belleayre Ski Area to its junction with NY 49/Dry
Brook Road. Turn south (left) and go about 1.5 miles to Mill Brook Road.
Turn west (right) onto Mill Brook Road and continue about 2.0 miles to
the trailhead parking lot and kiosk on the north side of the road. Trail
map at www.dec.ny.gov.

There are three routes to the summit of Balsam Lake Mountain, with trailheads on Beaverkill Road, Alder Lake, and Mill Brook Road. The most popular
and moderate hiking route is the Dry Brook Ridge Trail from the NYSDEC
kiosk and trailhead on Mill Brook Road in Hardenburgh. This trail begins
with blue trail markers across the road from the parking area. It follows an old
jeep trail for 2.25 miles, eventually joining the red trail for a slightly steeper
0.75-mile hike to the top. The total elevation gain over this three-mile route
is only 1,120 feet, making it one of the easier routes to the high-elevation
spruce-fir habitat, with its unique assemblage of uncommon species. It is also

Swainson's Thrush, a high-elevation specialist. © Alan W. Wells.

possible to be on the summit early in the morning by camping in a lean-to less than half a mile from the top on the Balsam Lake Mountain Trail (red).

At 3,723 feet, the summit of Balsam Lake Mountain has an extensive stand of red spruce, balsam fir, and mountain ash forest that provides good habitat for birds such as Blackpoll Warbler, Blackburnian Warbler, Swainson's Thrush, Red-breasted Nuthatch, and Dark-eyed Junco. Bicknell's Thrush may breed here sporadically, but Swainson's Thrush and Hermit Thrush are reliable, and the 360-degree view of the central Catskills from the fire tower is spectacular. A cleared area around the fire tower has a picnic table, an observer's cabin that is sometimes occupied by volunteers on summer weekends, and a very nice outhouse. Mourning Warbler has been reported from lower elevations of this peak.

Kenneth L. Wilson Campground

GPS ADDRESS 859 Wittenberg Road, Mt. Tremper
LATITUDE/LONGITUDE 42.02436 –74.22160
DIRECTIONS From I-87, take Exit 20 to NY 32 and then go 0.1 mile to NY 212 west. Follow NY 212 west about 11.0 miles, passing through the villages of Woodstock and Bearsville, to its junction with CR 45/Wittenberg Road. Turn left and continue 3.8 miles on Wittenberg Road, bearing right where it joins CR 40 and continuing to the campground entrance on the south (left) side of the road.

A state campground may seem like a strange place to go birdwatching, but this facility, just five miles from Woodstock, is small, immaculately maintained, and packed with exciting, easily accessible bird habitats. During the season, there may be a small day-use fee (Empire Pass accepted, however), and on weekends and holidays, the campground is sometimes packed with families picnicking and kayaking at the Upper Pond; but the facility is small and there is no swimming, so this beautiful site, nestled in the Slide Mountain Wilderness Area, is definitely worth a visit. Ruffed Grouse and Alder Flycatcher are reliable here, and in irruption years, it is a good place for winter finches.

The entry road leads to the parking and picnic area on Upper Pond, which is formed by an impoundment on the Little Beaver Kill. The pond is ringed with alders and other natural vegetation, and a handicapped-accessible trail with benches borders the pond all the way to the spillway at the west end.

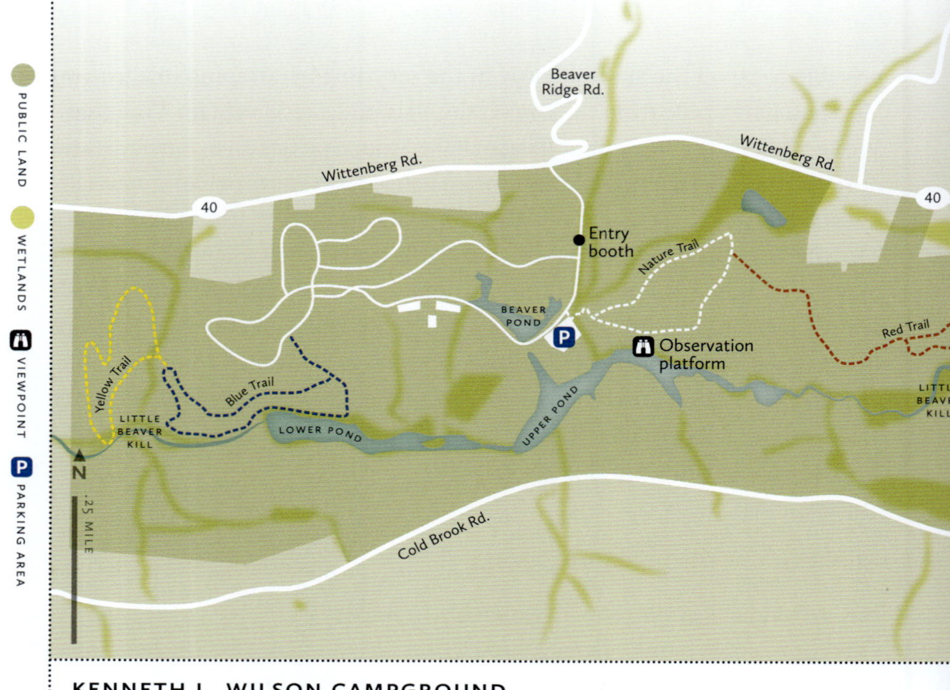

KENNETH L. WILSON CAMPGROUND

West of the picnic area on the road to the showers, there is a spectacular beaver pond. Birding in this area can be especially exciting in spring, when hungry migrants gather to gorge on emerging aquatic insects. The small, wet meadows nearby have courting American Woodcock in early spring.

East of the parking lot, a kiosk and trail register indicate the entrance to a series of very well-marked trails, including the mile-long nature trail, a handicapped-accessible pathway to an observation platform that extends out over the marsh. The Nature Trail itself is a nicely designed hike through hemlock-northern hardwood forest to a pond fringed with cattails, and a return through the boggy headwaters of the Lower Beaver Kill. Extending the hike, the red trail adds another 1.25 miles and a chance to explore slightly higher elevations, an old pine plantation, and a section of mature floodplain forest where Wood Duck breed.

There is a second area of nice trails in the western part of the campground, originating near campsite number 72 on the C loop of the camping area. The blue trail is a 1.25-mile loop along Lower Pond, where the beaver have raised the water level of the Little Beaver Kill. Picking up the yellow trail from the west end of the blue trail leads up a rocky ridge into drier forest and an area of dead pines, where Winter Wren and Blackburnian Warbler have been reported. Before rejoining the blue trail, the path descends to a viewpoint along a rocky section of the Little Beaver Kill.

Falling Waters Preserve

GPS ADDRESS 996 Dominican Lane, Glasco

LATITUDE/LONGITUDE 42.04863 –73.94062

DIRECTIONS From I-87 Exit 20, drive south on US 9W and bear left on NY 32 south through the Village of Saugerties. Cross Esopus Creek and continue 1.5 miles to Josephs Drive on the east (left). Follow Josephs Drive to a T intersection, turn right onto York Street and go 0.1 mile, and then take the first left onto Dominican Lane to the parking area. Map at www.scenichudson.org.

In 2012, *Hudson Valley Magazine* called Falling Waters Preserve the best new park in the Hudson Valley. Before 2011, this beautiful stretch of Hudson River shoreline was a private summer vacation retreat owned by the Dominican Sisters of Sparkill. Seeing themselves as caretakers of God's land and believing that it should be conserved, restored, and shared, they formed a partnership with Scenic Hudson and the Esopus Creek Conservancy to work together to make the property accessible to the public. In addition to providing access, this collaboration also protects the land from development; this is especially important because this section of the Hudson is directly across from Tivoli Bays Wildlife Management Area, a unique and ecologically sensitive wetland.

At 168 acres, Falling Waters Preserve is not very big, but it is scenic and historic, and it includes several interesting bird habitats. The preserve gets its name from two unnamed tributaries that enter the river via pretty waterfalls at the north and south ends of the property. There are a little over two miles of well-marked trails, with a number of comfortable benches strategically placed at scenic viewpoints. The quarter-mile-long Entry Drive Trail is actually Dominican Lane, the lightly traveled paved road to the preserve that passes through old fields and shrubby habitat. All the other trails begin north of the information kiosk in the parking area.

The most direct path to the river is the Father C. Jorn Trail, which switch-

Falling water at Falling Waters Preserve.
© Kathryn J. Schneider.

backs through the woods for 0.33 mile past the southern waterfall and skirts the remains of an old icehouse on the edge of the river.

The red-blazed Upland Trail follows an old gravel road along the highest ground on the property. Near the parking lot, it runs along the edge of a field with distant views of the Catskills. These grasslands are mowed annually to exclude woody plants and to provide habitat for field-nesting birds. This trail connects to the Riverside Trail (white) near the northern waterfall and dead-ends on a rocky ledge where the stream enters the river. There are good but distant views of the river and marsh from this vantage point. A spotting scope, which is helpful, is most easily carried to this point along the relatively level Upland Trail. As might be expected, this part of the river near the marshes of Tivoli Bays has exceptional waterfowl diversity. April visits have produced sightings of American Wigeon, Ring-necked Duck, Surf Scoter, White-winged Scoter, Long-tailed Duck, Ruddy Duck, Horned Grebe, and Red-necked Grebe, as well as many more common species.

The Riverside Trail is a footpath along the river's edge that follows the bluffs through a hardwood forest for most of its length, but descends to the shore periodically. The scenic overlooks offer good views of the river but also collect migrating warblers, especially in the fall, when more than twenty species have been reported, including Wilson's Warbler, Bay-breasted Warbler, Tennessee Warbler, and Nashville Warbler.

Shaupeneak Ridge

GPS ADDRESS 1169 CR 16/Old Post Road, Ulster Park

LATITUDE/LONGITUDE 41.82673 −73.97020

DIRECTIONS There are two parking areas, one on the top of the ridge by Louisa Pond and another at the base. To get to the lower lot, take CR 16/Old Post Road from its junction with US 9W by the Esopus Fire Department in the Town of Esopus 0.2 mile to the gated lower parking lot on the right. To get to the upper lot, continue another 1.8 miles on CR 16/Old Post Road to Poppletown Road, on the right. Turn right onto Poppletown Road and continue another 0.7 mile to the gated parking area on the left. Map at www.scenichudson.org.

The Marlboro Mountains rise steeply on the west side of the Hudson River, forming a twenty-five-mile-long broken ridgeline from Kingston to New-

Rose-breasted Grosbeak (male).
© Alan W. Wells.

burgh. Even though these low mountains never attain even two thousand feet in elevation, they form a steep, forested barrier on the west side of the Hudson River. Shaupeneak Mountain is a hogback peak near the northern end of this range, and Scenic Hudson's Shaupeneak Ridge preserve includes its slopes and ridgeline. The two parking areas provide access at different elevations. The Old Post Road parking area is only a few hundred feet above sea level, but the upper lot on Poppletown Road sits on the ridgeline. Passerines migrate along the ridge, and this area has trailheads to an extensive network of footpaths and bike trails as well as Louisa Pond, one of this conservation area's main attractions.

Louisa Pond is a kettle-hole pond created when a retreating glacier dropped a chunk of ice, leaving behind a water-filled depression. Later, beaver moved in and dammed the outlet, so today this pond includes a large, open bog with a floating peat mat at the north end. Although the pond occupies ten acres, less than half of it is open water. An easy loop trail just over a mile long circles the pond, and the first quarter mile is handicapped accessible. The bog and surrounding wetlands have habitat for marsh birds, though few have been reported from this lightly birded area. The trail around the pond passes through intermittent clearings, rock outcrops, and second-growth woods of varying ages and composition. In winter, Saw-whet Owl has been heard calling from conifer stands in this area.

The green, aqua, and orange trails to the west of Louisa Pond have more mixed-wood habitat, and because of the terrain, these areas are sometimes used by mountain bikers. The red trail, to the east, leads to the edge of the ridge and has an impressive Hudson River overlook. In addition, winds hitting the ridge create updrafts that provide lift for soaring eagles, hawks, and vultures, which can sometimes be seen at eye level from this prominent vantage point.

Finally, the white trail runs along the east side of the preserve between the two parking lots. It is purported to be the most challenging trail in the park, and although it does have one steep section, the path passes by a small waterfall, clusters of maidenhair fern, and a pretty babbling brook where Louisiana Waterthrush breeds. Worm-eating Warbler and other uncommon species favor these eastern slopes, and the trail cut into the hillside offers terrific looks at Scarlet Tanager and Rose-breasted Grosbeak. The trail's terminus at the south end includes an open field and the opportunity to add a few open-country birds to the list. The elevational change alone should not be a deterrent, especially if you start at the upper parking lot and walk at a leisurely birdwatching pace to a waiting car in the lower lot.

Minnewaska State Park Preserve

GPS ADDRESS 5281 US 44/NY 55, Kerhonkson
LATITUDE/LONGITUDE 41.73040 −74.23441
DIRECTIONS From New Paltz, take NY 299 west to a T intersection with US 44/55. Turn right and continue 4.0 miles to the main park entrance on the south (left) side of the road. Once past the entry booth, continue straight to the Awosting Falls (lower) parking lot or turn uphill to the Windmere/Lake Minnewaska (upper) lot. If the park is not yet open, continue another 1.1 miles on US 44/55 to a small parking area on the right for the Jenny Lane footpath. Maps at parks.ny.gov/parks.

Minnewaska State Park Preserve is famous for its rocky cliffs, white ledges, scenic waterfalls, and rainwater-fed sky lakes. Located two thousand feet above sea level high atop the Shawangunk Ridge, the area is well known as a rock-climbing destination. The breathtaking beauty of the region prompted twin brothers Albert and Alfred Smiley to purchase property near Lake Minnewaska in the mid-1800s. Their mountain house hotels soon became major tourist destinations, where travelers enjoyed boating and swimming on the lakes and touring the countryside via carriage roads and footpaths. Sadly, both of the mountain houses on park property burned in the late twentieth century, and only the privately owned Mohonk Mountain House at the adjoining Mohonk Preserve remains.

The state began acquiring land for Minnewaska State Park in the early 1970s, and today's park preserve protects about twenty-three thousand acres of ecologically unique forest. Glaciers crushed and scraped the bedrock of the northern Shawangunks, leaving exposed rock outcrops and thin, acidic soils. Where the soils are especially dry and poor, pitch pine-oak barrens dominate, while other forested sites range from deciduous woods to hemlock and northern hardwoods with a mountain laurel understory. Not surprisingly, this huge expanse of diverse forest landscape supports an unusually rich bird community, especially during spring migration.

Fortunately for birders, the "Big M" is still a relatively undeveloped facility that emphasizes passive recreation. Being fairly new, Minnewaska still lacks many amenities, though there are small swimming areas on both lakes and many picnic sites. There are plans for better facilities, including a visitor center, another parking lot, and better restrooms. In the meantime, the park's eighty-five-mile trail network of well-marked carriage roads and footpaths is a hiker's dream. The carriage roads are wide, covered with crushed stone, and generally less steep than the single-track footpaths. Each carriage road trailhead has signage with detailed information about distances, trail markers, and elevation changes.

Minnewaska is a day-use facility that does not open until 9:00 a.m., a distressingly late hour for birders. Those looking for an earlier start have two choices: (1) The Jenny Lane footpath is accessible from a small parking area on US 44/55 about a mile west of the park entrance. This trail features oak woodland and crosses the Sanders Kill, with connections to the Lower Awosting Carriage Road. (2) A second alternative is to join the weekly public bird walks that leave from the main park entrance every Tuesday morning from mid-April through October (see the calendar of events at parks.ny.gov/parks).

Inside the park, there are currently two parking lots: the Awosting Falls (lower) lot and the Wildmere/Lake Minnewaska (upper) lot at the top of the entrance road. The lower lot provides the best access to the Lower Awosting Carriage Road, but many routes originate from the upper lot.

Although Minnewaska has great birding from April to October, it is most

Magnolia Warbler, common at the Big M. © Bruce Dudek.

exciting in early May, when the trees are not fully leafed out and the wood warblers are abundant, vocal, and easy to see. On a good day in May, fifteen species of warbler can be seen along the Upper Awosting Carriage Road, including Canada Warbler and Bay-breasted Warbler. Local birders have called this route "the birdiest of all carriage roads," perhaps because its habitats include an old orchard and small meadow as well as forest.

There are many other potentially great birding hikes at Minnewaska. The eight-mile loop from the south end of Lake Minnewaska on the Hamilton Point Carriage Road via Echo Rock and Hamilton and Castle Point, and back along the Castle Point Carriage Road, runs along the edge of the ridge with great birding and fantastic views. Alternatively, take the Lake Minnewaska and Millbrook Carriage Roads to Patterson's Pellet for views of soaring Common Raven, Black Vulture, and Turkey Vulture. In mid-September, the summit of Millbrook Mountain is a good place to view Broad-winged Hawk kettles and other raptors migrating along the Shawangunk Ridge. Millbrook Mountain has nesting Peregrine Falcons that can be viewed from the ridge between the summit and Gertrude's Nose. Winter Wren, Hermit Thrush, Dark-eyed Junco, Black-throated Green Warbler, and other species of higher elevations breed in the park, and charismatic vertebrates such as porcupine and bear are sometimes seen. The Big M never disappoints.

Nyquist-Harcourt Wildlife Sanctuary

GPS ADDRESS 85 Huguenot Street, New Paltz
LATITUDE/LONGITUDE 41.75189 −74.09012
DIRECTIONS From I-87 Exit 18, take NY 299 (Main Street) west through the Village of New Paltz 1.4 miles to Huguenot Street, on the right just before the bridge over the Wallkill River. Turn right onto Huguenot Street, then take the first left toward the sewage treatment plant, and park in the parking lot. Walk north along the river past the Gardens for Nutrition to the sign marking the property boundary for the wildlife sanctuary.

Owned and managed by the Thomas and Corrine Nyquist Foundation, the sanctuary property is only fifty-six acres, but it is surrounded by a number of large, undeveloped parcels that include farmland and gardens. The main entrance from the south is through lands owned by the Village of New Paltz and set aside as a large community garden called the Gardens for Nutrition.

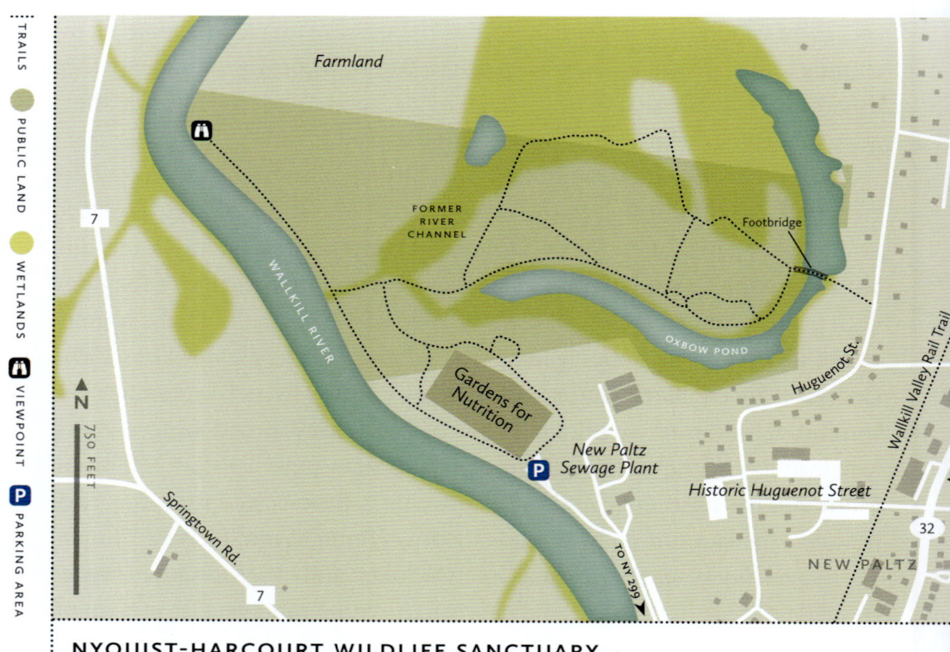

NYQUIST-HARCOURT WILDLIFE SANCTUARY

The western border consists of nearly a quarter mile of shoreline on the main stem of the Wallkill River. On the north, two historic farms occupy 180 acres, and a bridge east across a pond leads to Huguenot Street, a historic part of New Paltz that was settled by French Protestants in the late 1600s.

Before humans began to tame rivers with dams and channelization, streams wandered through the landscape a lot more than they do today. Every spring, they overtopped their banks, leaving behind nutrients for rich floodplain forests of silver maple, pin oak, box elder, and walnut. Occasionally, streams formed great bends or oxbows, which were sometimes cut off from the main stem when the river straightened itself again, leaving behind wetlands and rich alluvial soils. These bottomlands were highly desirable farmland for both Native Americans and early Hudson Valley settlers like the Huguenots. Nyquist-Harcourt Wildlife Sanctuary includes impressive remnants of both these uncommon natural communities.

All the trails at this preserve are unmarked, but they are generally obvious, flat, mowed grass pathways with interpretive signs about the natural history of the preserve wherever a trail crosses a preserve boundary. The official preserve property boundary is marked at the edge of the Gardens for Nutrition, but these garden plots are good habitat for some birds, especially in fall and winter, when sparrows feed among the untended crops. From the community gardens, a footpath continues along the edge of the river, with frequent clear views of the water used by waterfowl and waders, and the muddy shores that attract shorebirds during migration. This trail fades away into the adjacent hayfield to the north.

Just south of a metal bridge, the river trail intersects a pathway that leads east away from the water, along the edge of the old oxbow into a beautiful marsh and a series of interconnected shallow ponds. Sora, American Bittern, Marsh Wren, Sedge Wren, Wilson's Snipe, Green Heron, Swamp Sparrow, Willow Flycatcher, Wood Duck, and many other more common marsh birds have been recorded from these wetlands. A bridge over the pond exits the preserve to Huguenot Street, but following the perimeter trail around to the west leads into an open floodplain forest with huge trees. These woods host a variety of warblers during migration, breeding Baltimore Oriole, and owls and woodpeckers year-round. Eventually, the perimeter trail loops around beside additional wetlands formed where the historic main channel of the Wallkill once ran. Alternatively, there are shortcuts south that lead back to the oxbow.

Shawangunk Grasslands National Wildlife Refuge

GPS ADDRESS 883 Hoagerburgh Road, Wallkill

LATITUDE/LONGITUDE 41.63682 –74.21917

DIRECTIONS From the junction of NY 299 and US 44/NY 55 west of
New Paltz, turn onto US 44/55 east (left) toward Gardiner, and continue
2.0 miles to CR 7/Bruynswick Road. Turn right onto Bruynswick Road,
and continue 4.0 miles to its intersection with CR 18/Hoagerburgh
Road just after the Shawangunk town line and the Shawangunk Valley
firehouse. Turn left and go 2.0 miles on Hoagerburgh Road to the refuge
entrance on the east (left) side of the road. If the gate is open, the
refuge is open. Drive past the kiosk and through the gate on the access
road to the parking and observation area. Map at www.fws.gov/refuge
/shawangunk_grasslands.

The Shawangunk Grasslands National Wildlife Refuge may be the best place
in the Hudson Valley to see grassland birds. This flat, wet valley was drained
and filled, and then used as an army airfield and training facility. The property
was excessed to the US Fish and Wildlife Service in the early 1990s; the service
removed the runways, planted native forbs and grasses, and has continued
to invest significant resources to maintain suitable wintering and nesting
habitat for grassland birds. The refuge is a satellite parcel managed by the
Wallkill River National Wildlife Refuge with offices in Sussex, New Jersey.

Grassland birds need large, unfragmented fields dominated by grasses,
with little or no woody vegetation. Forest succession and development have
reduced the number of big fields in the Northeast, and those that remain
are typically on farms, where early haying destroys nests before the young
are fledged. These factors have contributed to the decline of grassland bird
populations in New York. But here, where the government manages nearly
six hundred acres of contiguous and diverse grassland habitat, both the
common and declining grassland species do well. Adding to the refuge's
attraction is the fact that it is surrounded by horse farms, which augment
the open habitat and provide a buffer that attracts birds of its own. Bobolink, Eastern Meadowlark, and American Kestrel, as well as Field, Savannah,
and Grasshopper Sparrow breed at the refuge. Upland Sandpiper, Northern
Harrier, and Henslow's Sparrow are seen and may soon breed.

Wintering birds include a different assortment of sparrows, but most ex-

Upland Sandpiper is seen at the Shawangunk Grasslands NWR and neighboring Blue Chip Farm. © Alan W. Wells.

Short-eared Owl hunting. © Deborah Tracy-Kral.

citing is the regular appearance of wintering raptors including endangered Short-eared Owl, Rough-legged Hawk, Red-tailed Hawk, and large numbers of Northern Harrier. Harrier young of the year begin to move into the area in late August as a part of post-breeding dispersal, but the numbers build and include more adults as the season progresses. The Short-eared Owls usually arrive after the end of October, and although they are occasionally active during the day, they usually roost on the ground at the grasslands and begin to perch and feed just before dusk. For the winter-weary birder, there is nothing quite like a winter afternoon trip to the grasslands that begins with diurnal viewing of Northern Harrier, rare winter hawks, and perhaps a Northern Shrike, and ends with a dozen Short-eared Owls swooping, soaring, hunting, vocalizing, and perching at close range while they hunt voles as night closes in.

This refuge is designed for wildlife viewing and photography. In such open habitat, you can sit in the car or set up a spotting scope in the parking area and see lots of birds. However, walking some of the mowed trails that originate on opposite sides of the parking lot, or spending time in one of the observation blinds in the middle of the grasslands offers a special opportunity to experience the birds, hear vocalizations, and watch bird behavior up close and personal. The recently completed Hunters Trails around the perimeter delineate safety zones for archery season and are closed to the public at that time, but during the spring and summer, they provide good access to the wooded edge of the property. In summer, the meadows also have a nice assortment of butterflies, and birders are especially grateful for the new composting toilet.

DUTCHESS COUNTY

Tivoli Bays Wildlife Management Area

GPS ADDRESS 177 Cruger Island Road, Tivoli
LATITUDE/LONGITUDE 42.03187 −73.92560
DIRECTIONS From the junction of NY 9G and CR 78 just east of the hamlet of Tivoli, follow 9G south about 2.2 miles to CR 103/Annadale Road. Turn west (right) onto CR 103/Annadale Road toward the Bard College Performing Arts Center. When the road curves, continue straight onto the dirt road (Cruger Island Road) 1.3 miles, past a large red

building on the right, and through a yellow gate to a small parking area on the right with NYSDEC signage. Map at www.dec.ny.gov.

The railroads changed the shoreline of the Hudson River, and nowhere is this change more evident than at Tivoli Bays. Tivoli North and South Bays were once two large deepwater coves, but the construction of the railroad bridge across their mouths in 1850 restricted the tidal flow to the amount of water that could pass through the bridge openings. Low flows increased the accumulation of sediments in the bays, so that today, the bays have evolved to become large freshwater tidal wetlands.

Together, Tivoli North and South Bays occupy about two miles of shoreline south of the hamlet of Tivoli. The seventeen-hundred-plus-acre property is managed by NYSDEC as part of the Hudson River National Estuarine Research Reserve, which uses the land as a field laboratory for research and education about the estuary. Tivoli North Bay is buffered to the east by hundreds of acres of upland woods and meadows, and Bard College stands immediately east of Tivoli South Bay.

The two bays, the focal points of the property, have very different characters. North Bay is fed by Stony Creek and dominated by cattail. Its network of tidal creeks, pools, and passageways is an adventure to explore by canoe or kayak, and an extended paddle through the railroad bridge provides access to the river and islands. Despite the challenges of steep bluffs and twice-daily tides, the DEC has constructed an impressive boat launch on North Bay that is accessed via a 15-mph dirt road from Kidd Lane at the north end of the property. There is a drop-off area for boats and equipment, but the real parking area is a short walk uphill. A canoe trip through the marsh in the late summer, when young are dispersing, is one of the best ways to see secretive marsh birds such as Least Bittern, Sora, and Virginia Rail, which are all known to breed here.

South Bay, on the other hand, is shallow. At low tide, there are extensive near-shore shallows and tidal mudflats. In summer, the bay fills with Eurasian water chestnut, effectively excluding small boats. Once the water chestnut clogs the cove, birds in Tivoli South Bay are best viewed from the South Bay Trail, which runs along the steep bluffs of Bard College. The Saw Kill, which drains into Tivoli South Bay by the Bard College field station, is accessible via hiking trails.

For birders on foot, the Cruger Island causeway, a 0.5-mile deteriorating

Least Bittern, most easily
seen from a canoe or kayak
in late summer at Tivoli Bays.
© Alan W. Wells.

trail through the freshwater tidal marsh, is usually the main attraction. This trail begins at the end of Cruger Island Road and dead-ends at the railroad. It floods at high tide, so rubber boots are highly recommended. The causeway offers spectacular views into the marsh and bay, which teem with waterfowl, Bald Eagle, Osprey, and marsh birds. It is almost as if the birds see the causeway as part of the marsh, because Virginia Rail have been known to cross the trail right in front of hikers.

The main trails at Tivoli are well maintained and well marked with color-coded trail markers. The North and South Bay Trails (Bard College Trails on some maps), as their names imply, skirt the edges of the two bays. At its north end, the North Bay Trail joins to a connector into the hamlet of Tivoli, which includes the Tivoli Bays Visitor Center. Going south, the trail follows Stony Creek, where it joins the Hudson and then runs through the woods along the shore of North Bay, with good views into the tidal creek and marsh. The trail continues past the canoe launch and, after 1.2 miles, terminates at the North Bay Overlook, with views of the marsh on Cruger Lane. From here, it connects to other trails in the uplands.

Birders should be sure to explore the trails in the uplands. The Overlook Trail passes through shrublands, woods, and fields to a view of Tivoli North Bay and the Catskills. These habitats have good diversity, and in spring the pristine forest floors are carpeted with native wildflowers.

Buttercup Farm Sanctuary

GPS ADDRESS 6862 NY 82, Stanfordville

LATITUDE/LONGITUDE 41.91640 −73.66934

DIRECTIONS From the Taconic State Parkway exit for NY 199/Red Hook/ Pine Plains, go south on NY 199 about 7.0 miles to Pine Plains. In Pine Plains, turn right onto NY 82 south and go 4.8 miles, just past CR 88/ Attlebury Mountain Road, to a dirt parking lot on the left marked with a sign for Buttercup Farm Audubon Sanctuary. For parking for Buttercup Farm West, continue another 0.8 mile south on NY 82 to the next right, Stissing Lane. Turn right at the stop sign onto Mountain Road, a dead-end road. After 0.2 mile, turn right at the Audubon sign into a dirt parking area.

Tucked at the base of Stissing Mountain in the northeastern corner of Dutchess County, Buttercup Farm Audubon Sanctuary is a favored destination for local birders because of its habitat diversity, accessibility, and

BUTTERCUP FARM SANCTUARY

Wappinger Creek floodplain at Buttercup Farm in autumn. © Carena M. Pooth.

beautiful scenery. Back when NY 82 was a sleepy rural road, it bisected the farm property, which was donated to Audubon in pieces during the 1970s and 1980s. Today, this much busier highway divides the 642-acre preserve into two pieces, with separate parking lots and very different characters. Most of Buttercup West is flatland in the floodplain of Wappinger Creek, while Buttercup East is dominated by rolling hills of open fields and second growth.

Buttercup West is primarily a wetland site. Beaver have built dams along the creek, creating ponds, backwaters, and an extensive red maple swamp that is attractive to a large variety of water birds, from waterfowl to water-thrushes. The two wide main trails at Buttercup West follow an old railroad grade, which, though raised, is often wet because of its proximity to the creek. These trails split at a fork near the trailhead and run more or less from south to north for a little less than a mile, with the eastern fork close to the more open main stem of the creek. The western fork passes through woods and a red maple swamp. The northernmost connector can be very wet and even impassable if the level water is high. The eastern railroad bed has spectacular views of the swamp and marshland to the east and woodland species along the trail. The trail ends at a large beaver pond that attracts a great diversity of waterfowl. A spotting scope is helpful here.

If not flooded out by the beaver, two footbridges cross the creek to trails on the east side. This area includes a pond ringed with common reed, a stone tower, and a gazebo on the top of a hill that overlooks the adjacent fields. Virginia Rail breeds near the pond, and the area around the tower has a stand of evergreens that attracts conifer-loving species such as kinglets, Black-throated Green Warbler, and Magnolia Warbler. Though narrow and wet, the trail north on the east side of the creek along the edge of the swamp rises high above the water on a hill, before descending to the railbed. It has nice views into the wetland and the tops of trees. Brown Creepers frequent the shagbark hickories in this area. The mowed trails across the hayfields connect to Buttercup East on the other side of NY 82. Except for the road, these fields are contiguous with the grasslands in the eastern part of the preserve and large enough to support an impressive suite of grassland birds, including Red-winged Blackbird, Eastern Meadowlark, Savannah Sparrow, Field Sparrow, Bobolink, and Northern Harrier.

Buttercup Farm East has a scenic open field with nest boxes, a hilltop bench with a panoramic view of the pastoral farmland below, and shrublands. The land between the grasslands and CR 88/Attlebury Mountain Road was once farmland, and today the property is a mosaic of old fields, abandoned orchards, shrublands, woodlands, and forest stands of mixed age classes. There are patches of mature forest along the stream that parallels Attlebury Mountain Road and drains into Wappinger Creek. The bird list for this side of the preserve is extensive, including uncommon vireos, flycatchers, and warblers. Blue-winged Warbler breeds in the shrublands, and Lawrence's Warbler (a Golden-winged X Blue-winged hybrid) has been reported, so Audubon is trying to manage parts of this area to maintain the early stages of old field succession preferred by Golden-winged Warbler.

Harlem Valley Rail Trail, Millerton Station to Sharon Station Road

GPS ADDRESSES 60 Main Street, Millerton

LATITUDE/LONGITUDE 41.95306, −73.51120

DIRECTIONS From the junction of NY 199, NY 22, and US 44 west of Millerton, follow US 44 into Millerton, where it becomes Main Street, and continue to the parking area for the Harlem Valley Rail Trail near the junction of Main and Center Streets. There are additional parking areas and trailheads for the rail trail at Coleman Station Road and the southern crossing of Sharon Station Road, both accessible from NY 22 south of Millerton. Map at parks.ny.gov/parks.

This section of the Harlem Valley Rail Trail is a continuation of the rail trail described in Columbia County. The entire completed section between Millerton and Wassaic covers 10.7 miles, but the 5.5-mile segment between Millerton and the southern crossing of Sharon Station Road is especially scenic and rich with bird life. The Harlem Valley Line once carried New York Central Railroad passengers between Chatham and Manhattan, but when service was discontinued in 1976, OPRHP began acquiring the old railbed for public recreation. Today, people bike, walk, jog, rollerblade, cross-county ski, and of course, birdwatch on this scenic byway. The raised railbed offers spectacular views of the rural countryside and excellent visual access to nearby wetlands and Webatuck Creek. The picturesque town of Millerton, located at the north end of the segment, sits on the border between New York and Connecticut. This end tends to be busier, especially in summer, so birders generally prefer to start south of Millerton and walk north into town, where there are not only more people, but also restaurants and shops and interesting places to explore.

The area between the two Sharon Station Road crossings borders a very large wetland that is a mix of cattail and open water. Over the years, birders have reported an impressive array of waterfowl from this marsh as well as other interesting wetland species such as Virginia Rail, the uncommon Common Gallinule, American Bittern, and Least Bittern. Bald Eagles nest on private property not far from this location and are sometimes observed in the area. Sharon Station Road is lightly traveled, and walking the triangle formed by the rail trail and the two Sharon Station Road crossings offers many

White-crowned Sparrow.
© Carena M. Pooth.

opportunities to search the marsh. The 1870 Sharon railroad station has been restored as a private residence and still stands near the northern crossing.

North of the Sharon Station Road north crossing, the trail passes by flooded old beaver ponds with standing dead trees, and other pocket wetlands with nesting swallows and occasional Wilson's Snipe. Northern Harriers use this wetland complex, and they are sometimes seen flying over the fields to the east. There is a large parking area and picnic tables where the trail crosses Coleman Station/Sheffield Road, and residences in this area sometimes have active bird feeders that have hosted White-crowned Sparrows in winter.

Just north of Coleman station, the trail passes by a capped landfill with good grassland habitat and the possibility for flyovers of both species of vulture, and then it enters a wet area with beaver activity in the floodplain of Webatuck Creek. Continuing north, the trail goes through farmland, near a slow-moving stream and a shrub swamp, and finally through an impressive rock cut, until it begins to parallel Webatuck Creek in a hemlock ravine. This leg includes an exciting variety of bird habitats from which Winter Wren, Golden-crowned Kinglet, Ruby-crowned Kinglet, Ruby-throated Hummingbird, and a variety of sparrows and warblers have all been recorded.

Approaching Millerton behind residences and businesses, this segment ends in the rail trail parking lot next to Millerton station, which now houses local businesses.

Yellow-breasted Chat, a southern species expanding its range north that has been seen at Hopeland. © Bruce Dudek.

Mills Norrie State Park

GPS ADDRESS 14 Old Post Road, Staatsburg

LATITUDE/LONGITUDE 41.84022 −73.93068

DIRECTIONS This park has three different sections—Hopeland, Mills, and Norrie—each with a separate entrance off Old Post Road. Old Post turns west off US 9 about 4.5 miles south of the intersection of NY 308 and Mill Street in Rhinebeck. The entrance to Hopeland is about 0.25 mile south of the junction of US 9 and Old Post Road, just south of the Columbia/Dutchess County line. The entrance to Mills State Park is another 0.6 mile south across the road from the Dinsmore Golf Course. The Norrie entrance is off Old Post Road 1.2 miles farther south, close to where Old Post rejoins US 9. Map at parks.ny.gov/parks.

The northwestern corner of Dutchess County has large areas of public land along the river that are owned and managed by OPRHP. Working from north to south, they include the Hopeland Area, 107 acres of state park land that was once the site of a large estate. The mansion is gone, but the property includes two short, easy trails through diverse habitats. The Huntington Trail to the east passes through a shrubby field of dogwood and small trees, where Yellow-breasted Chat has been seen and may have nested. Nest boxes here have Eastern Bluebird, Tree Swallow, and House Wren. Field Sparrow, Indigo Bunting, and Brown Thrasher also nest here during the breeding season.

There is also a pond with a small cattail marsh. The Hopeland Trail passes through a variety of woodlands with small streams, and a spur tail leads to a splendid stone chair that sits on a hill in the midst of a grove of white pines. There is currently no trail access to the river at Hopeland.

Further south on Old Post Road is the Ogden and Ruth Livingston Mills State Park and the Staatsburg State Historic Site, better known as the Mills Mansion. This opulently decorated, seventy-nine-room house from the Gilded Age is the focal point of the 192-acre estate that includes English-style gardens, carriage roads, support buildings, sweeping mowed lawns, woods, and riverfront. Most of the walking is easy because the trails follow old roads. The riverfront trail is readily accessible and very close to the water, and it continues south along the shore all the way to Norrie Point. The shoreline varies with the tide and includes mudflats as well as sandy and rocky beaches that are attractive to shorebirds and waders, while the cove is especially good for waterfowl in winter and early spring. Bald Eagle nests nearby and is common year-round.

The most exciting part of Margaret Lewis Norrie State Park at the south end of this area is the tidal marsh that borders the Indian Kill where it enters the Hudson River. The yellow trail, which is on the park entrance road, provides good access and decent views into the wetland. The mouth of the Indian Kill is occupied by a marina and campground, but there are quiet places to view the river near the Norrie Point Environmental Center southwest of the parking lot.

Cary Institute of Ecosystem Studies

GPS ADDRESS 2931 US 44/Sharon Turnpike, Millbrook
LATITUDE/LONGITUDE 41.78959 −73.72396
DIRECTIONS From the Taconic State Parkway exit for US 44/Millbrook, take US 44/NY 82 east toward Millbrook for 2.0 miles to where US 44 splits from NY 82 and forks left. Continue about 1.0 mile on US 44 to Gifford House and its parking lot on the south side of the road. The Lowlands area is accessed from entrances on Fowler Road and NY 82. Map at www.caryinstitute.org.

The Cary Institute of Ecosystem Studies (CIES) is a private, nonprofit environmental research and education center that has conducted ecosystem research on its two-thousand-acre campus for more than thirty years. Fortunately for birders, the institute allows the public to use some parts of the campus for passive recreation from April 1 to October 31. The grounds, complete with well-marked trails, information kiosks, self-guided science tours, maps, and brochures, are open from sunrise to sunset.

The trail system occupies two different parts of the campus. The Lowlands, accessed from either NY 82 or Fowler Road, includes a paved wildlife observation road that can be walked, biked, or driven, with a 10-mph speed limit. This is one of Cary's internal roads that are gated between 7:00 p.m. and 8:30 a.m., but there are two parking areas on Fowler Road where early birders can park and walk the Lowlands if the gates are closed.

More than 126 species have been reported from the Cary Lowlands. The flooded fields support a diversity of waterfowl in early April, and Wilson's Snipe and other water birds inhabit the flooded fields between the wildlife loop and Fowler Road. The two bridge crossings with nearby parking are good vantage points to look up and down Wappinger Creek for birds including Louisiana Waterthrush and Rusty Blackbird in early spring. This area is attractive to swallows and flycatchers in summer. The successional old fields hold an assortment of sparrows in all seasons. Prairie Warbler and Blue-winged Warbler are likely, and nest boxes house Tree Swallows and Eastern Bluebirds. American Kestrels have raised young in a hole in the red barn along Fowler Road and regularly hunt in the nearby Lowlands.

The second public area of hiking trails is easily accessed from the parking area next to Gifford House on US 44. The Wappinger Creek and Cary Pines Trails, both a little

American Kestrel (male), a small falcon that nests in tree cavities, nest boxes, and openings in buildings. © Alan W. Wells.

over a mile, pass through a variety of habitats and connect to each other as well as to shorter trails in the area. Named for the stream that drains into the Hudson River, the Wappinger Creek Trail is the most diverse, starting out through an old hayfield with open-country birds, and descending via steps to the edge of a wetland. The old pasture, now overgrown with huge old oaks, cedars, and shrubs, has good habitat for early successional species such as Brown Thrasher and American Woodcock. The trail runs along a ridge that parallels the creek for some distance, with great views of the water. The mudflats on exposed areas of shoreline and mid-channel gravel bars are good places to look for shorebirds and waterthrushes. This high area of the trail also offers opportunities to see birds in the foliage on the trees below. Winter Wren forages among the stone walls where the trail descends down to the stream.

The Cary Pines Trail intersects the Wappinger Creek Trail and can be used to extend the hike into a section of the property that is especially good for evergreen-loving species. Pine Warbler uses the white-pine stand near the trail junction, and Red-breasted Nuthatch breeds in the hemlock ravine adjacent to the creek. Barred Owl is reported from the planted stand of Norway Spruce. The south side of this trail borders an open area with the potential for raptor sightings.

Other public spaces on the cies campus can produce interesting birds simply because they are part of a large, lightly developed area. For example, uncommon birds are often seen along Fowler Road, which is a lightly traveled dirt road, suitable for walking and roadside birding. The Fern Glen on Lovelace Drive is designed to showcase plants that are native to Dutchess County, and it is a lovely and relaxing place to go birding.

Peach Hill Park

GPS ADDRESS 32 Edgewood Drive, Poughkeepsie
LATITUDE/LONGITUDE 41.73121 −73.88049
DIRECTIONS From the Taconic State Parkway, take the exit for NY 115/ Salt Point Turnpike and go south on NY 115/Salt Point Turnpike 9.4 miles to Edgewood Drive. Turn left onto Edgewood Drive and continue 0.25 mile to Peach Hill Park on the right. Map at peach-hill-park.org.

In 1999, when the Hudson Valley was about to lose yet another orchard to development, friends and neighbors in the Town of Poughkeepsie came together, and with the help of Scenic Hudson, managed to preserve Peach Hill. The park opened in 2006, and today this property is owned by the town and managed by the Friends of Peach Hill, a private nonprofit organization. The "Friends" could not have protected a prettier place. Because unsprayed orchards tend to have insect pests, this preserve is a good feeding site for migrating songbirds.

Peach Hill was once a commercial fruit operation that grew a variety of fruits, including peaches. By the time the land was sold, the fruit was mostly apples, but the name stuck despite the change in crops. The dedicated volunteers of the Friends have recently planted a few new peach trees, but most of their hard work has gone into mowing and marking trails, fundraising, adding picnic tables and benches, and reestablishing a model orchard. At 485 feet, the summit of Peach Hill is the highest point in the Town of Poughkeepsie, offering visitors long, beautiful views of the Hudson Valley in all four directions.

There are a little less than four miles of trails through and around the old orchard at Peach Hill. Because the site is on a hill, all these paths involve at least a bit of a climb, but the trails vary in length and steepness, so there are options for the less physically inclined. The easiest route is the blue-marked 0.4-mile gravel trail. This route is designed to be an introduction to the preserve. It loops through open fields with nest boxes, picnic tables, and parts of the orchard.

All the other trails are longer, typically a mile or more, and take different routes to the summit of Peach Hill. They intersect and run together in many places, so they can be combined to take in various habitats and create longer or shorter hikes. While the primary habitat at this site is orchards, the orchards vary. Some are overgrown, and others have been mowed and rescued from invasive shrubs and vines. The unkempt orchards on the Orchard Trail (white) are a good place to look for White-eyed Vireo and Mourning Warbler. Warbler diversity hits its peak during migration in May, but Baltimore Oriole and Orchard Oriole breed in the orchards. There is a nice patch of maple-dominated forest on the Habitat Trail (green). The main water feature is a small pond, also along the Orchard Trail, but other wet areas are visible from paths that run along the east edge of the property. The woods that buffer the orchard to the southeast are easily viewed from the trails and can produce some interesting birds. But equally important, visitors to Peach Hill Park should be sure to pause a moment at the overlooks and take in the Hudson Valley vistas as well as the soaring raptors that are visible from this orchard on a hill.

Male Orchard Oriole. © Bruce Dudek.

Vassar Farm and Ecological Preserve

GPS ADDRESS 50 Vassar Farm Lane, Poughkeepsie

LATITUDE/LONGITUDE 41.67783 −73.89677

DIRECTIONS From the traffic light at the junction of US 44 and NY 376/ Raymond Avenue in Poughkeepsie, take NY 376 south about 1.5 miles through several traffic circles to an intersection where NY 376 becomes Hooker Avenue. Turn left, staying on NY 376 (now Hooker Avenue), and make an immediate right into the entrance for Vassar Farm and Ecological Preserve. Follow Vassar Farm Road about 0.2 mile over a stream and past the barns to the parking lot next to the gardens and athletic fields. Map at farm.vassar.edu.

Most of the land that is now Vassar Farm and Ecological Preserve was once farmland, but since 1976, the majority of the acreage in this mixed-use property has been actively managed as a preserve. Conveniently located adjacent to the Vassar College campus, the farm property is used by the school's cross-country and rugby teams. Some land is leased to the Poughkeepsie Farm Project for community-supported agriculture (CSA), and another portion is used as a community garden. The 1.6-mile-long Farm Road leads to

Palm Warbler, one of the earliest warblers to migrate north in spring. © Deborah Tracy-Kral.

the Vassar College Field Station on the east side. Three-quarters of the more than five hundred acres are used for ecological research and recreation. This urban oasis on the edge of Poughkeepsie is birdy and accessible in all seasons.

The farm has an extensive color-coded trail system that is generally well marked, and a diversity of natural habitats including a floodplain forest, upland deciduous woods, shrublands, old fields, meadows, streams, and a beaver pond. Even the cultural communities, like the athletic fields and gardens, support some interesting birds. Killdeer can be found on the rugby fields during migration, and in fall, the fallow, unkempt community gardens, compost piles, and the brush and tree dump are good spots to look for sparrows. Visitors with only a short time to spend usually walk to the south end of the property on the Farm Road and take the short Davis Trail (brown) to the beaver pond and its associated wetlands. Waterfowl can be viewed from the boardwalk, which continues into a shrubland and a swamp. Swamp Sparrow is abundant here and Green Heron occurs regularly. Farther east, the Wright Trail (black) passes through a floodplain forest, a good place to sit on a log for a few minutes and watch for Wood Duck and Rusty Blackbird. Continuing east on this trail takes you away from Casper Creek and into drier deciduous woods.

The old fields at the farm area are concentrated on the east side of the property along the branch of the Farm Road that forks east, and between the gardens and the Collins Field Station on the Collins Trail (blue). The fields vary in age and cover type. Some are dominated by grasses and goldenrod, while others have succeeded to shrubs and red cedars. A field with Field Sparrow, Savannah Sparrow, Eastern Bluebird, and Bobolink also surrounds the Poughkeepsie Farm Project.

The trails on the western edge of the preserve are longer, and the college describes them as difficult because of wet areas, roots, and hills, but none are particularly strenuous. Once farmland, most of this ridge is now covered with young deciduous woods, but there are small areas of pine woods on the hillside where the red and yellow trails come together. Barred Owl is sometimes heard calling in the middle of the day from this part of the property.

North of the barns beside Casper Creek, the Swain (blue) and North (orange) Trails loop though a small patch of deciduous woods. About half of this route is within sight of the creek, which broadens into a small cattail marsh in places. This section of the preserve is not visited regularly by birders, and though small, the marshy area looks like it might provide habitat for wetland species.

Nuclear Lake

GPS ADDRESS 150 Old Route 55, Pawling
LATITUDE/LONGITUDE 41.58608 –73.65231
DIRECTIONS From the Taconic State Parkway exit for NY 55 East/ Pawling, take NY 55 east 9.8 miles through a number of traffic lights and the Town of Poughquag to its intersection with Old NY 55 on the north (left) side of the road. Take Old NY 55 0.1 mile to an unmarked gravel parking area on the left with a kiosk.

Some people will be put off by Nuclear Lake's unfortunate name, but hikers have called this site the most beautiful lake on the Appalachian Trail (AT). From 1958 to 1973, United Nuclear Corporation, a private, government-

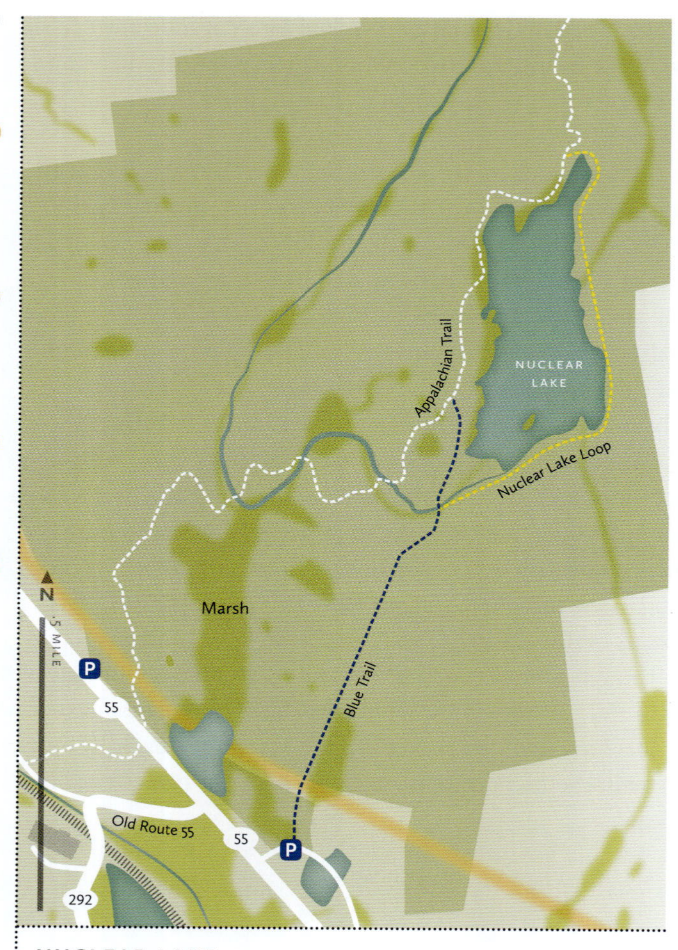

NUCLEAR LAKE

licensed research facility, conducted experiments with bomb-grade uranium and plutonium in a small lab located here. After an explosion in 1972 contaminated the area, the plant was closed and decommissioned. The cleanup that followed involved the removal of tons of contaminated debris and soil. Subsequent testing, scrutinized by watchdog groups and the us Forest Service, has shown radiation levels no higher than normal background levels. However regrettable the circumstances, protecting the lake from people and development for the last forty years has produced a wonderfully scenic area for hiking and birding.

The trails around Nuclear Lake are well marked with white, blue, and yellow blazes—white for the Appalachian Trail, which skirts the northwest side of the lake, blue for a spur trail from the parking lot that joins the AT, and yellow for the Nuclear Lake loop on the east side that is not part of the AT.

From the parking lot, the old access road is wide and level, passing along a marshy area and under a power line to enter some nice deciduous woods. This short, level hike to the lake has an impressive diversity of warblers in May (twenty-six species recorded), and Acadian Flycatcher has been seen near the stream, where it passes through a culvert under the road. The lake trail loop joins the road near this culvert.

At the lake, the trail emerges from the woods on a grassy berm that overlooks the water. Though the lake does not attract large numbers of waterfowl, waders and shorebirds forage along the shoreline and Spotted Sandpiper breeds on the island. Bald Eagles sometimes hunt on the lake. The southwest shore has several clearings overgrown with honeysuckle that attracts Ruby-throated Hummingbird. There is also a vernal pool near the junction with the AT that should be good for Wood Duck.

Black-and-white Warbler, one of twenty-six warbler species reported at Nuclear Lake. © Alan W. Wells.

The hiking trail around the lake is mostly level, but rocky, uneven, and wetter than the access road. The entire circuit is less than 2.0 miles through beautiful oak-dominated woods with an understory of mountain laurel, azaleas, witch hazel, and blueberry. It passes by secluded coves as well as two small marshes, one on the lake and another along a small stream. The pathway crosses the stream on stepping-stones and ascends to lichen-covered rock outcrops. There are side spurs to lake overlooks and idyllic picnic spots before the trail dips through a small area of hemlocks and rejoins the access road.

Worm-eating Warbler nests in the wooded understory
on steep slopes at Pawling. © Alan W. Wells.

Pawling Nature Reserve

GPS ADDRESS 125 Quaker Lake Road, Pawling

LATITUDE/LONGITUDE 41.60719 −73.55811

DIRECTIONS From the junction of NY 55 and NY 22 just south of Pawling, turn north onto NY 22 and go 2.8 miles to CR 68/North Quaker Hill Road. Take CR 68/North Quaker Hill Road 0.3 mile to Quaker Lake Road. Turn left onto Quaker Lake Road and continue 1.2 miles to a parking area with a sign on the left. Map at www.nature.org.

Pawling Nature Reserve is a 1,060-acre preserve in southeastern Dutchess County that is owned by The Nature Conservancy as a sanctuary for rare species and important natural communities found at this site. Located in the foothills of the Berkshire Mountains, Hammersley Ridge runs from north to south at 1,530 feet above sea level, forming the backbone of the preserve. The property's well-marked and carefully maintained ten-mile trail network includes about 2.5 miles of the Appalachian Trail and connects to other trail systems in the eastern part of the county.

Despite the size of the preserve and the abundance of trails and trailheads, there are only two parking areas, both on the east side of the property. The main entrance on Quaker Lake Road provides easy access to some of the most scenic areas, including the picturesque gorge of Duell Hollow Brook, a lovely waterfall, and a scenic footbridge. Acadian Flycatcher, Winter Wren, and Louisiana Waterthrush are reliably found in this ravine every summer.

The preserve is a big place, but the loop formed by the red, white (Appalachian), and yellow trails from the main entrance gives a good introduction to some of the ecological communities and bird habitats. The red trail starts in deep, dark hemlock forest around the ravine. Moving up the slopes below the ridge, the hemlocks begin to mix with northern hardwoods such as beech, maple, and witch hazel. Worm-eating Warbler nests in the understory along steep slopes in these woodlands. Many other warblers and woodland birds use the rocky oak woods with scattered pines, mountain laurel, and blueberry understory that grow on the thinner, drier soils near the top of the ridge. Tucked in the forests on poorly drained sites are a number of vernal pools that provide breeding sites for the preserve's rare amphibians, but also attract Wood Duck and other birds.

The Nature Conservancy permits hunting in the fall, a practice that has allowed the understories of parts of these forests to recover from overbrowsing by deer. However, disturbed habitats still remain, and these areas typically have dense vegetation with young trees, vines, and thorny deer-resistant invasive species such as multiflora rose and barberry. This dense, low cover gives Hooded Warbler and other ground-nesting species protection from predators.

The second parking area, about a mile north of the main entrance, provides access to a small wetland and the yellow trail that connects steeply to the AT. The reserve also features an overlook along the orange trail in the northwest corner. The challenging trail to the top of the ridge passes through hemlock forests with pretty marble rock outcrops to a view of the Harlem Valley and the Great Swamp watershed. The ridge itself creates updrafts that power the raptor migration over these low mountains, so scanning the skies for soaring birds of prey, especially on clear days with favorable winds, is often productive.

Denning's Point State Park and Madam Brett Park

GPS ADDRESS 100 Dennings Avenue, Beacon

LATITUDE/LONGITUDE 41.49391 −73.98175

DIRECTIONS From I-84, take Exit 11 to NY 9D and go south toward Beacon. Continue 1.5 miles to South Avenue and turn right, then go 0.1 mile to Denning Avenue on the right and follow it to the end. Park near the kiosk and gate on the right, opposite the Beacon Recycling Center and Water Treatment Facility and a capped landfill. There is also a parking area for Madam Brett Park on South Avenue in Beacon.

These two ecologically important parks are on the east side of the Hudson, where Fishkill Creek enters the main stem of the river. Denning's Point is part of Hudson Highlands State Park, while Madam Brett Park is owned by Scenic Hudson. Though they are owned and managed separately, these two properties are right next to each other, joined by a connecting trail along the railroad. Denning's Point, a peninsula that juts out into the Hudson River, is best known as a Bald Eagle wintering area, but it is also strategically located to collect birds that use the Hudson as a migration corridor. Madam Brett Park includes the north shore of Fishkill Creek from its fall line to the Hudson as well as the tidal marshes at its mouth. Together, these two parks capture a nice collection of interconnected ecological communities and a diversity of bird habitats.

At Denning's Point, there is no public parking on the peninsula, so visitor access from the parking lot is via a trail that begins at the gate and parallels the railroad tracks. The trail passes by junctions with the Dave Miller Connector Trail, which leads to Madam Brett Park, and the Klara Sauer Trail, which goes north all the way to the Beacon Waterfront Park, before crossing over the railroad on a bridge. Once you're on the peninsula, there is a sort of reception area with signage. Going straight leads to a restored and renovated building with gardens that houses the Beacon Institute's Center for Environmental Innovation and Education and a public visitor center. Turning left leads past the old Denning's Point Brick Works, which operated from 1881 to 1939, an information kiosk, and the beginning of the Denning's Point Trail.

Despite past disturbance and a plethora of invasive species, the peninsula is heavily forested with impressive old cottonwoods and other deciduous species. The Denning's Point Trail is dry and flat, and follows the perimeter of

DENNING'S POINT STATE PARK
AND MADAM BRETT PARK

the peninsula for 1.2 miles. There are periodic side trails out to the water. The west side looks out on the river and the industrialized Newburgh shoreline. A side trail to the south leads to the point, while the east side looks out on the cove and passes through a disturbed wet, shrubby area near the trailhead. The Denning's Point Trail is a good place to see land migrants, wintering waterfowl, migrating Osprey, and waders. Black-crowned Night-Heron stalks fish in the vegetated shallows of the cove.

The Bald Eagles that occupy this site in winter are primarily fish eaters, and in cold weather they congregate here near areas of open water to feed and

Bald Eagle adult. In the Hudson Valley, trains kill many Bald Eagles when they feed on deer carcasses along the railroad tracks. © Scott Stoner, Naturelogues.

roost. Denning's Point and the mouth of Fishkill Creek have been identified as critical habitat for wintering Bald Eagles, and NYSDEC closes the trail around the perimeter of the peninsula from December 1 to March 31 in an effort to minimize disturbance to these birds. However, land managers at Denning's have recently constructed an eagle observation blind that is located on the cove east of the old brick factory and west of the railroad. It is accessed via an unmapped trail that starts at an opening in the fence and runs beside the old building east to a trail that comes out on the waterfront. The blind is open in winter, and its location provides an opportunity to see and photograph the Bald Eagles when they perch along the shoreline before the trees leaf out.

It is a short walk to Madam Brett Park via the David Miller Connector Trail. There are benches with views of the marsh, and the red side trail leads to an observation deck that looks out on an expansive stand of cattail, tidal mudflats, and areas of submerged aquatic vegetation. Marsh Wren, Belted Kingfisher, breeding waterfowl, and swallows frequent this area. As this trail approaches the old Tioronda Hat Works, it becomes an elevated boardwalk with views of Fishkill Creek. It ends at an observation deck by the factory's sluiceway that looks out on Tioronda Falls. It's hard to beat these two parks for their combination of history, scenery, habitat diversity, and bird life.

ORANGE COUNTY

Stewart State Forest

GPS ADDRESS 130 Ridge Road, Montgomery
LATITUDE/LONGITUDE 41.51461 –74.15728
DIRECTIONS From I-84 going toward Stewart International Airport, take the exit for NY 17K Montgomery/Newburgh and follow NY 17K west 2.3 miles to Ridge Road. Follow Ridge Road south about a mile, just past where it goes under I-84 to a parking area with a kiosk. There is another parking area on the north side of the property on Barron Road (about a mile farther west on NY 17K) and five parking areas along NY 208 and NY 207 on the south side. Map at www.dec.ny.gov.

Once known as the Stewart Airport buffer lands, Stewart State Forest covers about sixty-seven hundred acres west of Stewart International Airport, south of I-84 and north of Routes 208 and 207 in northeastern Orange County. Crisscrossed with eighteen miles of dirt and gravel roads and twenty-two miles of trails, the property includes a mixture of old fields, woods, and wetlands that are open for hiking, biking, horseback riding, hunting, dog training, skiing, snowmobiling, fishing, and of course, birdwatching. It is important for birders to remember that all these varied forms of recreation are allowed at this site. Fortunately, most of these activities are not incompatible with birding, and Stewart State Forest is a big place, so conflicts are easily avoided. During the regular big-game hunting season, Stewart State Forest is closed to everyone except hunters, and permits are issued for motorized access.

The trails diverge from the roads and are generally well marked with good signage and trail markers. Birders have only begun to explore what this vast property has to offer. There has been great interest in the new Great Swamp Boardwalk, which traverses the forest's largest wetland between Ridge Road and Maple Lane. The disabled can obtain a permit to drive to this ADA-compliant site, but able-bodied patrons must walk from Ridge Road or more

Green Heron. © Deborah Tracy-Kral.

distant access points. The loop from the parking lot, south on Maple Lane, across the boardwalk and back via the Scofield Trail, is a little under 3.0 miles. This wetland has extensive stands of cattail and standing dead trees that are perfect marsh bird habitat.

Another recommended birding route involves using two cars, and leaving one at each of the parking areas at both ends of Barron Road, which runs north/south on the west side of the property. This flat gravel road has side trails to Kelly's Pond, Stick Pond, and Wilkins Pond via the Pond Trail and Big Tree Trail. Barron Road itself passes through deciduous woods and fields, and beside ponds and wetlands. Wilkins Pond is an especially nice side trip to a three-acre beaver impoundment, with opportunities to see waterfowl, waders, and shorebirds in season. The NYSDEC website for this state forest lists a dozen trails, with habitat descriptions and mileages under two miles. The site seems to be lightly birded, but it has a large amount of habitat diversity and the potential to support many more species than those reported to date.

Six and a Half Station Road Wildlife Sanctuary

GPS ADDRESS 88 Six and a Half Station Road, Goshen
LATITUDE/LONGITUDE 41.40327 −74.35530
DIRECTIONS From I-84, take Exit 4E/NY 17 east toward New York City.
Follow NY 17 east 3.5 miles, and get off at Exit 122A/Fletcher Street toward
Goshen. Take Fletcher Street west 0.1 mile, and then turn right onto
Cheechunk Road. After 0.2 mile, turn left on Six and a Half Station Road.
The sanctuary parking area with a sign and a kiosk is 0.5 mile down this
road on the left. Additional access from US 6/NY 17M.

This small wildlife sanctuary is owned and managed by Orange County Audubon Society. Its unusual name dates back to when farmers left their milk at the railroad station for transport to New York City. The pick-up point on this road was 6.5 miles to the next stop, where the milk was then transferred to go to the city. In 1981, the Audubon Society acquired a loan to purchase the sixty-two-acre marsh, which is adjacent to the Orange County Heritage Trail. The wetlands at this site also provide tertiary sewage treatment for the area.

Six and a Half Station Road Wildlife Sanctuary was a good investment! While the Heritage Trail is a carefully manicured rail trail that is heavily used by joggers and bikers, the sanctuary is a beautiful wetland with terrific bird habitat. Moreover, because the marsh is a Class I wetland and an aquifer recharge area, its buffer is mostly natural and somewhat protected from future development. The sanctuary is convenient to NY 17, but that busy highway is far enough away that road noise is not a significant problem for hearing the birds.

The mowed trail network is very limited, and what trails exist are unmarked, but the sanctuary itself is small, and it is impossible to get lost. The trails are primarily designed to access observation platforms, benches, and viewing areas that look into the marsh from various angles. This site is the perfect place for a spotting scope, because the walk to the platforms is short and easy; and also because a scope, although not essential, greatly enhances the birds that can be seen and identified. One of the viewing platforms is on the very edge of the marsh among the cattails, which makes it easy to actually see Marsh Wren and Swamp Sparrow that breed here.

There are also short trails around the perimeter of the marsh that pass through woods, shrublands, and meadows. Though the actual acreage of

SIX AND A HALF STATION ROAD WILDLIFE SANCTUARY

each of these habitats is small and the trails dead-end, they are nicely laid out with benches placed near bird magnets like fruiting vegetation. When I sat on one of the trailside benches, an accipiter zoomed along the footpath in front of me at eye level. The trail through the meadow includes a group of nest boxes, and the entire network has well-done interpretive signs about the trees found on the property.

There are two other access points. The Orange Heritage Trail crosses Six and a Half Station Road 0.25 mile west of the main parking area. It offers glimpses into the wetlands and shrubby habitat. There is better birding from a pathway locally known as the "Citgo Trail," which begins on US 6/NY 17M, with parking at a nearby gas station. Citgo Pond is considered a local birding hotspot.

Orange County Audubon has recorded nearly two hundred species from the sanctuary and its environs, including rarities such as Glossy Ibis, Sandhill Crane, Sora, and Nelson's Sparrow. The site sees a good variety of waterfowl in early spring and shorebirds in spring and fall. This is not an especially good place for warblers, but most of the typical sparrows have been reported each fall. Waders, especially egrets, and maybe even another Glossy Ibis, are fall visitors.

Hudson Highlands Nature Museum and Outdoor Discovery Center

GPS ADDRESS 100 Muser Drive, Cornwall
LATITUDE/LONGITUDE 41.42217 −74.03400
DIRECTIONS From Exit 10 on I-84, follow US 9W south 6.8 miles to CR 9/Angola Road. Turn south (left) and follow Angola Road 0.1 mile west to the preserve entrance on Muser Drive, directly across from 174 Angola Road. Continue down Muser Drive 0.7 mile to the parking lot. Map at www.scenichudson.org.

The Hudson Highlands Nature Museum and Outdoor Discovery Center was once a famous dairy and horse operation known as Kenridge Farm. Today, 178 acres of open space surround the old farm buildings, which are used for offices and classrooms to support a thriving environmental education program. The Outdoor Discovery Center is an especially good place to take children. Four different Quest Trail booklets, available for a modest fee at the visitor center, provide guided walks along the trails through four different habitats. There is also a fenced-in area called Grasshopper Grove, where small children can participate in hands-on nature explorations. The undeveloped parts of the property, which feature a brook, ponds, wetlands, fields, meadows, shrublands, woods, and about five miles of well-marked trails, are managed as wildlife habitat and open to the public.

Muser Drive, the entrance road to the center, is a lightly traveled thoroughfare with a 15-mph speed limit and excellent opportunities to view open-country birds. Most of the open land is around the buildings, and Muser Drive takes vis-

A pair of Eastern Bluebirds at their nest box. © Denise Hackert-Stoner, Naturelogues.

itors away from this hub of activity to quieter viewing sites like the nearby fields with American Kestrel, Bobolink, Red-winged Blackbird, and sparrows.

Goose Pond and the smaller ponds and wetlands adjacent to the visitor center have resident Canada Geese, but they attract a wide variety of interesting ducks in April, as well as Great Blue Heron and Green Heron. Some of the trails run so close to the ponds that the birds tend to move into the vegetation. However, the observation platform on the ridge above the ponds is positioned to provide an unobstructed view of most of the area. Some of the ponds and marshes are also easy to see from Muser Drive.

Muskrat Pond, which should not be missed, is a short, easy walk from the visitor center. Removed from the main part of the farm, it contains a small island and a more natural shoreline with a few trees. The trail out to Muskrat Pond passes through a shrubby, wet field and a woodlot with a barberry understory. This thorny exotic was not eaten by the horses and cows pastured here, so it persists in many parts of the farm property.

The Woodland Trail on the east side of the land crosses Canterbury Creek first as a small headwater stream, and then again lower down as a good-sized brook. As its name implies, this trail winds through woods of oak and hickory, at one point emerging on a moss-covered rock outcrop. The trail is moderately steep in places, but it has good warbler habitat. The yellow Hiking Trail that traverses the perimeter of the property is mostly in the woods on steep terrain, rising to nearly seven hundred feet. The composition of the forest is similar to that found along the Woodland Trail.

Goosepond Mountain State Park

GPS ADDRESS 1198 NY 17M, Chester
LATITUDE/LONGITUDE 41.34566 –74.22614
DIRECTIONS From I-87, take Exit 16 Harriman/US 6/NY 17W. Follow NY 17 west to exit 128 CR 51/Oxford Depot. Continue 0.3 mile, and then turn south (right) onto CR 51/Craigville Road. In 0.25 mile, turn left onto NY 17M east, and go about fifty yards to a dirt parking lot with a sign for Access to Goosepond Mountain State Park. The trailhead for Lazy Hill Road is on the opposite side of the road. Alternatively, turn right (west) on NY 17A and go 0.3 mile to a parking area edged with boulders for the nature trail/ boardwalk. Map at parks.ny.gov/parks.

The boardwalk at Goosepond Mountain. © Kathryn J. Schneider.

Goosepond Mountain State Park is a 1,558-acre undeveloped park that was acquired by the state in pieces during the 1960s. Just six miles north of the Woodbury Commons shopping mecca, the park is a rural refuge with a lot to offer. Much of the property was once farmland, and Lazy Hill Road runs about three miles through the east side of the park between NY 17M and CR 45/Laroe Road. Though there are places to park at both ends, the Laroe Road end is not recommended because the lot is small and eroded, and has limited sight distance onto a busy highway. It is best to experience Goosepond Mountain as a linear out-and-back hike or with a prearranged pick-up or drop-off at the Laroe Road end that avoids the need to park there.

As the name implies, Lazy Hill Road is a lovely, easy hike. Once a paved road, it includes a 2.6-mile portion of the aqua-diamond-blazed Highlands Trail, which, when completed, will run between Storm King Mountain, New York, and Philipsburg, New Jersey. The land immediately adjacent to Lazy Hill Road was once farmland, so the path passes through a variety of habitats, including woods of varying ages, old fields and pastures, and small wetlands.

The road has good warbler diversity during spring migration. A bridge over Seely Brook, about 0.5 mile north of the Laroe Road trailhead, allows views into a floodplain with a fairly large cattail marsh. In addition to the main pathway, there are other unmarked trails created by horseback riders, mountain bikers, and deer. Most of these do not seem to go anywhere interesting, but the trail north to Board Family Cemetery leads across fields to a memorial bench with a lovely view of the mountain and open sky for viewing raptors.

Goosepond Mountain State Park also includes a small boardwalk and nature trail that is accessed from a parking lot on the south side of NY 17M. This marsh was constructed in the floodplain of Seely Brook to mitigate a wetland destroyed during the construction of I-86 and the Chester interchange. The quarter-mile boardwalk through this lovely emergent marsh in the shadow of Goosepond Mountain offers nice views into the wetland and is a good place to see Swamp Sparrow. Interpretive signs on the left (east) loop focus on wetland ecology.

Wallkill River National Wildlife Refuge

GPS ADDRESS 169 Oil City Road, Pine Island
LATITUDE/LONGITUDE 41.28358 −74.52606
DIRECTIONS From I-84, take Exit 3E for US 6 and NY 17M east toward Goshen. After about 1.0 mile, turn right onto Sly Place, and merge right onto CR 56. At the T intersection, turn right onto CR 12/Lower Road. Drive 7.8 miles and merge onto CR 1. Continue 1.0 mile farther and turn left onto Lower Road. Go about 2.5 miles on Lower Road, and then turn left onto State Line Road. Follow State Line Road 1.0 mile across the Wallkill River, and then merge onto Oil City Road and go a short distance to the parking area on the right side of the road.

The Wallkill River National Wildlife Refuge (NWR) sits along a ten-mile stretch of the Wallkill River, which runs north between the Kittatinny and Shawangunk Ridges on the west and the Hudson Highlands on the east. Before joining Rondout Creek and emptying into the Hudson at Kingston, the river passes through the former "drowned lands" of the Wallkill Valley. The extensive wetlands that once bordered this slow-moving river were drained and diverted to expose the deep organic muck that once formed the bottom of a glacial lake. Today, these modified wetlands support the region's black-dirt agriculture, and the US Fish and Wildlife Service is working to restore some of the wetlands, floodplain forests, and other natural habitats that sustain the river's natural processes and support migratory birds, wintering raptors, endangered species, and other wildlife.

Most of the Wallkill River NWR is actually in New Jersey, but the small portion that juts into New York is worth a visit even if you have no interest in seeing New Jersey birds. The refuge currently has five nature trails, and the two that are partly or entirely in New York have wonderful birds year-round. The 2.5-mile Liberty Loop Trail begins at a parking lot, kiosk, and observation platform on the south side of Oil City Road, and follows the

WALLKILL RIVER NATIONAL WILDLIFE REFUGE

Greater Yellowlegs showing its bright yellow legs and bill that is longer than its head. © Alan W. Wells.

Appalachian Trail for about a mile. The mowed path is on an elevated berm around the perimeter of several ponds with managed water levels built on a former sod farm. The Fish and Wildlife Service relies on rainwater to fill the ponds, and gradually lowers the water levels for shorebirds during migration. Because the service is also trying to reduce purple loosestrife (an invasive species) with water level manipulations, conditions may not always be ideal for shorebirds; but ducks, waders, and even Marsh Wrens use this area, so there are almost always birds of interest. There is a very nice pond that sometimes has extensive mudflats on the south side of the loop, technically in New Jersey. In winter, the platform is a fine place to set up a scope and view Northern Harrier and Short-eared Owl, which roost and hunt here. The surrounding fields and open landscape are good places to see uncommon wintering raptors such as Rough-legged Hawk.

The Winding Waters Trail, entirely in New York State, begins near the boat launch about a mile west of the viewing platform on Oil City Road on the east side of the Wallkill River. For most of its 2.6-mile distance, the trail follows an old farm road. Starting out through the floodplain forest, the river is initially slow, winding along with exposed mudflats on the edges. Spotted Sandpiper and Solitary Sandpiper are often seen here. Farther along, the river runs over exposed bedrock outcrops with riffles and pools and even a small waterfall. The trail eventually turns away from the river through open fields that support grassland birds. This trail is fairly new, but birders have already found a nice variety of birds in these habitats.

Like most national wildlife refuges, Wallkill allows some hunting with valid permits, but hunting is not allowed on Sundays and is prohibited on the Liberty Loop Trail at all times. Birders who venture outside this area during hunting season are encouraged to wear blaze orange. There are three additional nature trails in the New Jersey section of the refuge, other boat launches, and thousands of acres of wetlands. The refuge headquarters, just over the state line in Sussex, New Jersey, houses the refuge staff, informational exhibits, and restrooms.

Mount Peter

GPS ADDRESS 385 NY 17A, Warwick
LATITUDE/LONGITUDE 41.24450 –74.28893
DIRECTIONS From Greenwood Lake, take NY 17A north 2.7 miles up Bellvale Mountain. Look for a sign for Bellvale Creamery, and turn right here onto Kain Road. The potholed, dirt road to the parking area is about twenty yards down Kain Road on the right. The hawkwatch is a short uphill hike along the path from the parking lot.

Mount Peter proudly claims to be one of the oldest continually run all-volunteer fall hawkwatches in the country. The watch is a testament to interstate cooperation. Members of the Fyke Nature Association of Bergen County, New Jersey, founded the hawkwatch in 1958; and over the years, Audubon Societies in both New York and New Jersey have worked to manage, staff, and support the operation. When the site was threatened by development in 1990, NYSDEC stepped in and purchased the five-acre summit.

Like their counters, the raptors that fly over Mount Peter cross state boundaries. The lookout is on the highest point of Bellvale Mountain, at the northern end of New Jersey's Bearfort Range, which forms a narrow northeast/southwest ridge across the state line. The northwest winds from fall cold fronts hit the ridge and create the updrafts that raptors use to power their migration south along the Appalachians. From here, most of the birds continue southwest toward the Kittatinny Ridge. On a clear day, High Point, the highest peak in the Kittatinny Mountains in New Jersey, is visible from Mount Peter. In the spring, favorable winds for migration do not concentrate birds over this site, so Mount Peter is staffed only in the fall from September 1 to November 15.

Mount Peter typically counts around ten thousand raptors a season, including large numbers of Broad-winged Hawk, Red-tailed Hawk, and Sharp-shinned Hawk. Black Vulture numbers are increasing, and Common Ravens are prevalent. The 1,253-foot lookout has a wooden observation platform with limited seating and spectacular views to the north, west, and south. There is a connector trail from the summit to the nearby Appalachian Trail that offers the opportunity to pursue woodland birds if the hawks are few and far between. Whether the birding is good or bad, every trip to Mount Peter should include a stop at the nearby Bellvale Creamery on 17A, which is open April 1 through October 30 and features over fifty flavors of homemade ice cream.

Sterling Forest State Park, Ironwood Drive

GPS ADDRESS 299 Ironwood Drive, Tuxedo Park
LATITUDE/LONGITUDE 41.23281 −74.23732
DIRECTIONS From I-87, take Exit 16 NY 17/US 6/Harriman. Follow NY 17 south about 7.0 miles to NY 17A. Take 17A toward Sterling Forest and continue 1.4 miles to CR 84/Long Meadow Road. Turn left onto CR 84/Long Meadow Road and follow it 1.3 miles to Ironwood Drive. Turn right onto Ironwood Drive and continue 1.1 miles to the parking area at the end of the cul-de-sac.

Unlike most of the sites in this book, this area is not ecologically unique, pristine, historic, birder friendly, or unusual in any way except for the fact that it has been one of the most reliable sites for breeding Golden-winged Warbler for at least twenty years. Ironwood Drive is a large power line right-of-way that crosses the cul-de-sac and the end of this lightly traveled residential street within the boundaries of the twenty-thousand-acre Sterling Forest State Park. Though Golden-winged Warbler is found in a variety of habitats throughout its range, in the Hudson Valley this species usually occupies successional sites that become unsuitable over time. For reasons that are probably clear only to Golden-winged Warblers, this large power line right-of-way currently constitutes acceptable breeding habitat.

As power lines go, this one is somewhat unusual in that it runs through a protected landscape that is rocky, mountainous, and heavily forested. The large transmission line cuts a swath through an otherwise relatively pristine landscape, and probably because of that, there seem to be fewer exotic species and more native plants in the vegetation along the older parts of the

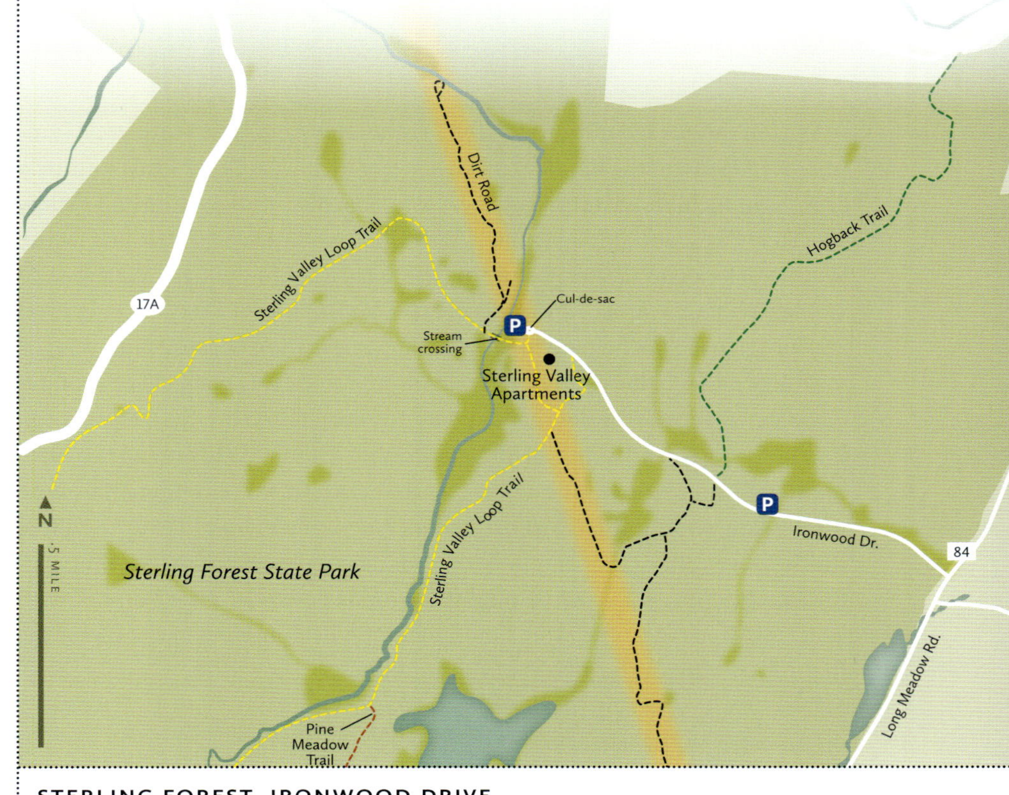

STERLING FOREST, IRONWOOD DRIVE

right-of-way. The habitat includes flowering dogwoods, willows, viburnums, blueberries, mountain laurel, azaleas, sumac, and saplings of trees from the surrounding forest, as well as the usual alien species of honeysuckle and multiflora rose.

To get to the northern part of the transmission line, step over the chain and follow the dirt road from the cul-de-sac, which is also the Sterling Valley Loop Trail (yellow) that leads to Sterling Lake. The combined road and trail pass beside a beaver pond and cross a small stream. After the stream crossing, the trail heads left, but the dirt road to the northern side of the transmission line continues straight and emerges from the woods on an uphill dirt path among boulders, shrubland, and the huge steel towers that support the power lines. This open habitat is a great place to see birds, especially early in the season before the vegetation is fully leafed out. Edge and woodland species such as Baltimore Oriole, both cuckoos, flycatchers, woodpeckers, and vireos are heard and seen hanging out near the edge of the woods. The high, open hillside is also an excellent place to view soaring raptors and Common Raven.

Within the cut area, Prairie Warbler is abundant and Ruby-throated Hummingbird feeds on the honeysuckle when it is in flower. Other birds routinely seen here include Eastern Towhee, Field Sparrow, Indigo Bunting, Yellow Warbler, Chestnut-sided Warbler, Worm-eating Warbler, Black-and-white Warbler, Hooded Warbler, Common Yellowthroat, Blue-winged Warbler and Golden-winged Warbler, and their hybrids. It's important to try to get eyes on any bird that sings a buzzy winged-warbler vocalization because Blue-winged Warblers and Golden-winged Warblers sometimes sing each other's songs.

Golden-winged Warblers have apparently been found on this transmission line both north and south of the cul-de-sac. Though it is possible to walk up the hill along the transmission line to the south, it is easier and far more interesting birding to go a short distance down Ironwood Drive to where the Sterling Valley Loop enters the woods again just east of the Sterling Valley Apartments. This trail through the woods passes by a vernal pool with standing dead trees, and after a moderate uphill, it emerges at the top of the first hill on the southern part of the cut line.

Golden-winged Warbler, one of the rarest warblers in New York State. © Alan W. Wells.

Harriman State Park, Island Pond

GPS ADDRESS 1369 CR 106/Kanawauke Road, Southfields
LATITUDE/LONGITUDE 41.23442 −74.14889
DIRECTIONS From I-87, take Exit 16 NY 17/US 6/Harriman and follow
NY 17 south about 7.0 miles to the junction with CR 106/Kanawauke
Road on the right. Go east (left) on CR 106/Kanawauke Road about 2.3
miles to an unsigned dirt parking area on the south side of the road.

Island Pond is a lovely, pristine glacial kettle hole in one of the less visited parts of Harriman State Park. Though hikers and boaters use this area, boat access is by permit only through a locked gated at the north end. This restriction and the fact that seeing the pond requires a short hike have helped protect this special place from the crowds that visit Harriman State Park. The simplest route in from the south along Island Pond Road is an easy walk of just over a mile that begins across the road from the parking lot. Island Pond Road, which is gated, actually joins CR 106 0.1 mile west of the parking lot, but rather than walk the road, it is safer and more scenic to cross the road and follow the rocky white bar trail west along the stream through the forest until it crosses the old road.

Like most of the hemlock forests in the Hudson Highlands and Catskills, the hemlock trees in the ravine at the start of the trail have been damaged by the hemlock woolly adelgid. The standing dead trees that remain support a diverse community of woodpeckers and other birds that use dead snags and eat wood-boring insects. The long, gentle uphill out of the ravine leads to woods dominated by oaks with an understory of blueberries and mountain laurel, spectacularly beautiful when flowering in June. These woods have good warbler diversity, especially during spring migration. The road soon becomes sufficiently grass covered that it can be used by Chipping Sparrow.

The trail descends into some low areas with seasonal wetlands just before crossing the Dunning Trail marked with yellow. Tiny Green Pond, which has very little open water, makes an interesting side trip and lies less than half a mile west of the road. A few meters east on the Dunning Trail is the old Boston Mine, one of Harriman's abandoned iron mines that operated in the mid-1800s. A pile of old tailings marks its entrance, and Eastern Phoebe often nests within the overhang. By flooding these mines, the park discourages their exploration.

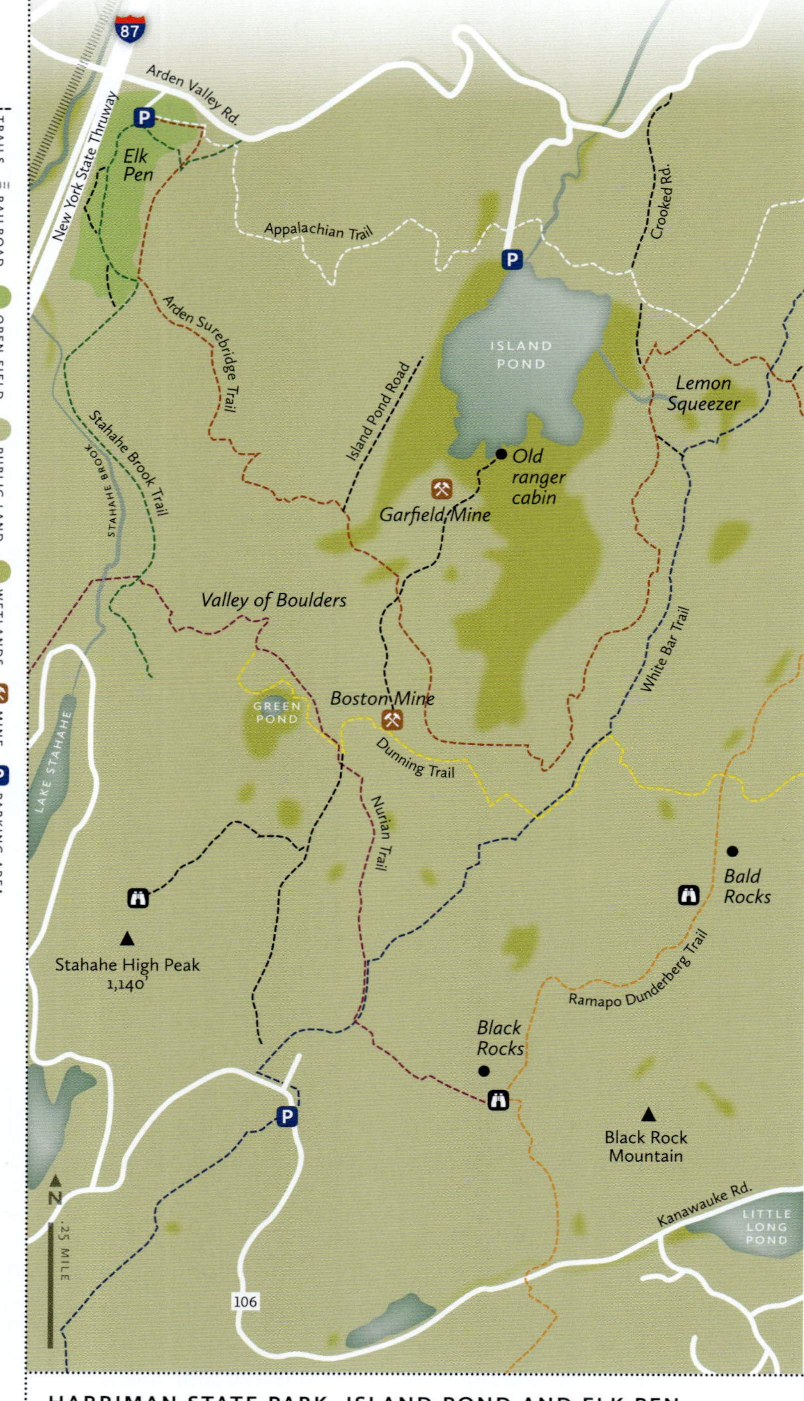

HARRIMAN STATE PARK, ISLAND POND AND ELK PEN

Just before reaching Island Pond, the road passes through an area dominated by large hemlocks where Blue-headed Vireo is seen in migration. The trail runs very close to some coves and the boggy shrub swamp that surrounds Island Pond. Accipiters and Red-shouldered Hawk live in these woods.

At Island Pond, the road breaks out of the woods near the rock foundation of the old park ranger cabin, strategically placed on the shore with a breathtaking view of the water and its island. Because the lake is deep, there are relatively few dabbling ducks; but the lake supports a healthy fish population, so waders, Belted Kingfisher, Osprey, and Bald Eagle are regularly reported. In the uplands beside the cabin, tall pines replace the hemlocks and create good habitat for kinglets and Pine Warbler.

Island Pond does not have a lengthy bird list because relatively few birders take the time to do this easy hike, but given the fine condition of the ecological community and the unspoiled landscape, this area has great potential for seeing exciting birds. The beautiful setting alone makes it worth the trip.

Harriman State Park, Elk Pen

GPS ADDRESS 1004 Arden Valley Road, Southfields
LATITUDE/LONGITUDE 41.26468 –74.15426
DIRECTIONS From I-87, take Exit 16 to NY 17/US 6/Harriman. Follow NY 17 south about 4.0 miles to Arden Valley Road. Follow Arden Valley Road east about 0.3 mile over I-87 to an unmarked gravel road and parking area on the right. Because this space is also a hikers' parking lot, it sometimes fills on weekends.

The Elk Pen in Harriman State Park is a stretch of open fields near the parking area and trailhead for the Arden-Surebridge and Appalachian Trails. In the early 1900s, this property was a meadow used for grazing elk that were imported from Yellowstone National Park. Remnants of the fence are still visible on the perimeter of the fields. Today the elk are gone, but the old fields and meadows provide habitat for grassland and shrubland birds not found in this naturally forested part of the Hudson Valley.

A dirt track leads east across the northern field and into the edge of the woods, where there are signs for the AT and other hiking destinations, but at this point, the red-marked "birders trail" heads south in the woods along the edge of the fields. This path takes in the edge habitat between the forest

Field Sparrow with nesting material. © Alan W. Wells.

and fields. Despite the noise from I-87, it is possible to hear many birds that live in the fields. The disturbed woods along the edge are part of a large area of unfragmented forest that rises steeply from the valley floor to the summit of Green Pond Mountain. As a result, this short mile or so of trail has the potential for field, edge, and deep-forest species, including such goodies as Worm-eating Warbler, Hooded Warbler, Blue-winged Warbler, Chestnut-sided Warbler, and Prairie Warbler. The trail continues south to Stahahe Brook, where many birds come to drink and bathe in summer, and where Louisiana Waterthrush is often seen.

Energetic hikers can follow the rocky trail uphill though the forest to explore the brook, but most birders opt to turn west and return to the parking area through the fields. There are at least four fields at the Elk Pen, separated by fencerows with magnificent old oaks. Some have shrubs while others are more herbaceous, but they usually have breeding Field Sparrow and Indigo Bunting, as well as Eastern Bluebird and Tree Swallow in the nest boxes that are maintained and monitored by volunteers from the local Audubon Society. If the birds are unexciting, there are several large stands of milkweed that attract an array of butterflies in summer. In fall, these fields should be explored for interesting sparrows.

Harriman State Park, Lake Skannatati Pine Swamp Loop

GPS ADDRESS Seven Lakes Drive, Tuxedo
LATITUDE/LONGITUDE 41.24179 −74.10229
DIRECTIONS From I-87, take Exit 16 to NY 17/US 6/Harriman. Go east 5.75 miles on US 6 to the Long Mountain traffic circle, and take the exit for Seven Lakes Drive. Follow Seven Lakes Drive to Tiorati Circle, taking the exit toward Lake Kanawauke, and then continue 2.5 more miles on Seven Lakes Drive to the parking area for Lake Skannatati on the west side of the road.

Despite the fact that Harriman State Park is the second-largest state park in New York State and covers nearly fifty thousand acres, it is sometimes a very busy place. Only thirty miles north of New York City, the park's thirty-one lakes and reservoirs and two hundred miles of hiking trails draw millions of visitors each year. Fortunately, most of this activity remains close to the park's picnic areas and beaches at Lake Tiorati and Lake Welch. For birdwatchers and others willing to hike just a little, there are still lovely, quiet corners of the park with a variety of habitats and wildlife.

This easy-to-moderate loop trail begins at Lake Skannatati, where waterfowl, gulls, and Osprey are possible. The hike totals a little less than four miles and combines parts of three different pathways. From the parking lot, the path uses the Arden-Surebridge Trail, marked with red triangles on a white background. The old trail involved a steep scramble to a scenic overlook, but a recent rerouting now takes the path over the shoulder of Pine Swamp Mountain. This short, steep section at the beginning is the only strenuous part of walk. The trail soon descends through an area with mossy vernal pools, a mountain laurel understory, and good habitat for both waterthrushes. From here, one can also begin to see into parts of Pine Swamp and soon, the flooded pits of an old iron mine.

The trail passes through an area of blowdown and dead trees on a hillside, a good place to look for some of the five species of woodpecker that have been reported from this trail. After crossing a stream, take an immediate left onto the more road-like Dunning Trail, marked with yellow blazes. This trail follows along the edge of the marsh for about 0.7 mile, with good views of the wetland. This wetland is one of the few sites in the Hudson Highlands where Acadian Flycatchers have nested.

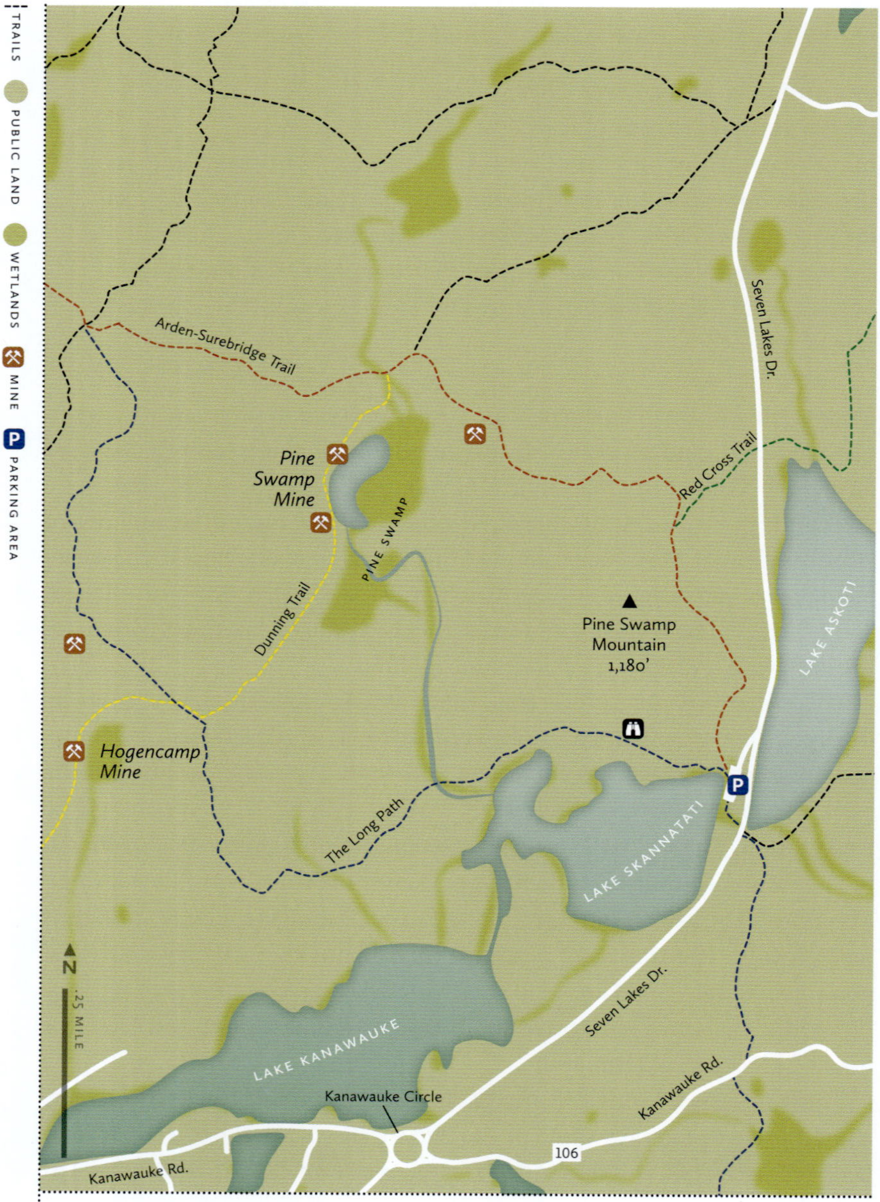

HARRIMAN STATE PARK,
LAKE SKANNATATI PINE SWAMP LOOP

The Dunning Trail intersects the Long Path (aqua) and passes through woods with an open understory and beside a magnificent rock outcrop. Worm-eating Warbler and Yellow-billed Cuckoo, also reported from this loop, are likely along this section before the trail returns to the shore of Lake Skannatati.

Because this site is not an eBird hotspot, there is no comprehensive bird list for the Pine Swamp loop, but the mix of habitats and the uncommon species reported to date suggest that this area has much to offer birders who are willing to venture just a few miles off the beaten path. On top of that, it is also a very pretty walk in the woods.

8 The Lower Hudson Valley

Best place to....	Site
SEE WATERFOWL	Rockland Lake State Park
FIND GRASSLAND BIRDS	Croton Point Park
FIND SHOREBIRDS	Marshlands Conservancy
SEE MIGRATING WARBLERS	Bear Mountain State Park, Doodletown
FIND HIGH-ELEVATION BIRDS	Clarence Fahnestock State Park
WATCH MIGRATING RAPTORS	Hook Mountain
FIND A RARE BIRD	Croton Point Park
GO BIRDING IN LATE SUMMER	Piermont Pier
GO BIRDING IN WINTER	Edith G. Read Wildlife Sanctuary
BIRD FROM A BOAT	Constitution Marsh Audubon Center & Sanctuary
HIKE AND BIRDWATCH	Teatown Lake Reservation
TAKE THE KIDS	Muscoot Farm
EXPERIENCE BIRDS AND CULTURE	Rockefeller State Park Preserve
TAKE THE GRANDPARENTS	Little Stony Point State Park

To an upstater, the Lower Hudson counties of Rockland, Putnam, and Westchester seem congested and developed, and in fact, the population density of these three counties is much greater than that of the two regions to the north; but despite the proximity to New York City, this region has nice places to see birds. Early in the twentieth century, as development marched north from the city, far-sighted conservationists banded together to protect private farms, estates, and scenic vistas by setting them aside as parks and nature sanctuaries. Today, these sites exist as havens for wildlife in a heavily populated and developed landscape.

This southern part of the Hudson Valley, with its brackish river water and warmer winters, is suitable overwintering habitat for some bird species that leave the valley's northern counties. Water remains open longer, spring comes earlier, and this region's avifauna includes marine birds from the coastal lowlands that border Long Island Sound. After it cuts through the Hudson Highlands, the river widens at the Tappan Zee for a distance of about ten

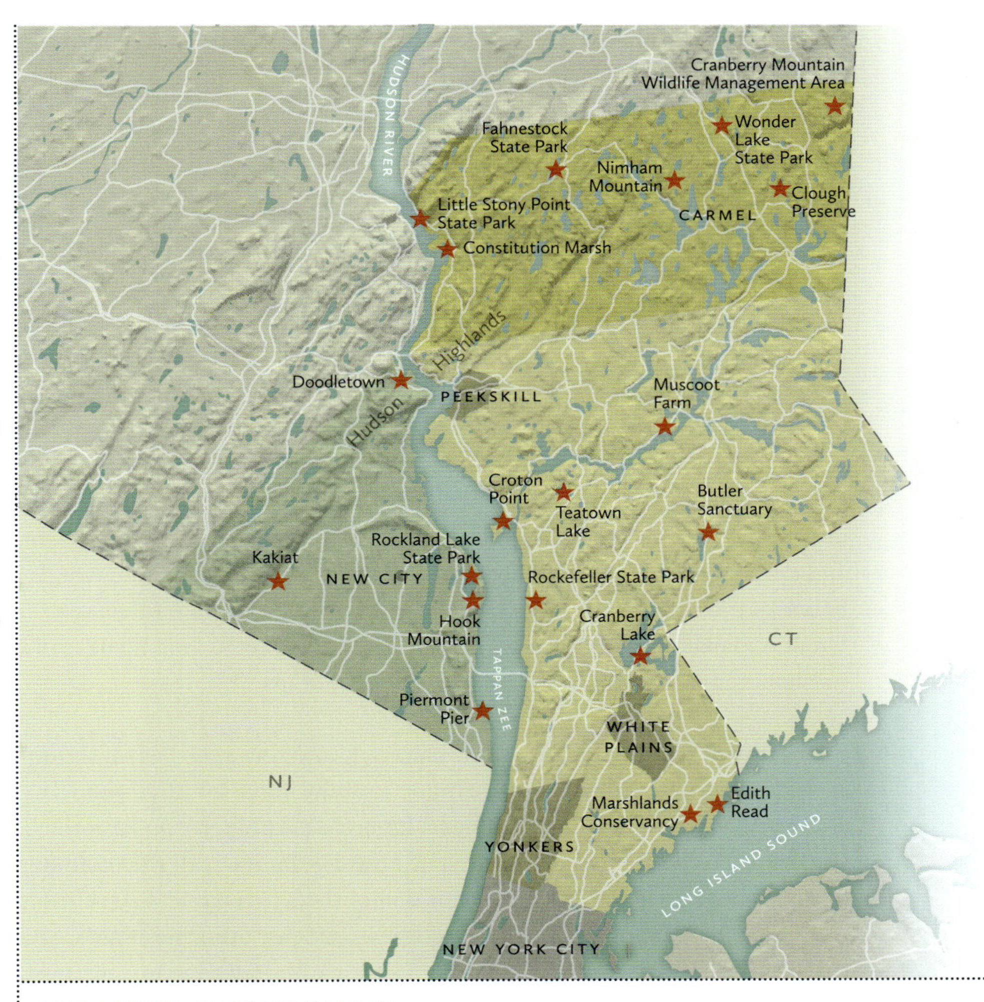

THE LOWER HUDSON VALLEY

miles, reaching a maximum width of three miles at Haverstraw Bay. On the east side, the Croton River, the only major tributary on this part of the river, enters the Hudson after leaving the reservoir.

The topography of the region is dominated by the Hudson Highlands. These low, rocky, thin-soiled mountains form the northwest border of Rockland County and extend diagonally across the Hudson River to cover most of Putnam County. The coastal areas of Westchester County that border

Long Island Sound have the only marine habitats in this book's ten-county study area.

Bear Mountain State Park—Doodletown and Iona Island

GPS ADDRESS US 9W/US 202, Tomkins Cove
LATITUDE/LONGITUDE 41.30033 –73.98600
DIRECTIONS From the north on Palisades Interstate Parkway, take US 6 north to the Bear Mountain traffic circle at the intersection of US 6, 202, and 9W. Take the Bear Mountain State Park exit from the circle and go south on US 9W. At the traffic light, follow the left fork and continue south on 9W for about a mile to several small parking areas along the east side of 9W near two white concrete abutments over Doodletown Brook. Park here, and cross 9W to the trailhead for Doodletown Road, which is in the woods between the bridge abutments and the entry road to the Bear Mountain Inn. It is marked with a historical marker. The causeway to Iona Island is five hundred feet farther south on the east side of 9W.

Doodletown is the name of a historic hamlet, located between Bear and Dunderberg Mountains, that was once home to about three hundred residents. As Bear Mountain State Park expanded, it purchased property on its borders, sometimes using the buildings for staff housing. By 1966, all the buildings had been purchased or condemned and demolished, so today all that remains of Doodletown is foundations, cemeteries, gardens, other remnants, and ruins of a once-thriving Hudson River settlement. Posted maps, pictures, and interpretive signs are on-site to lead visitors on a self-guided walking tour of the historic "ghost town" whose history is thoroughly documented in a book by Elizabeth Stalter (1996).

When the people moved out of Doodletown, nature began to take over what was left of the town. Today barberry, wisteria, trumpet vine, and other exotic plants that may have originated in residents' gardens have invaded the clearings, foundations, and much of the understory. The birds don't seem to mind, because in May and June especially, Doodletown is famous for its unusual abundance and diversity of warblers and other Neotropical migrants. Some uncommon species, including Hooded Warbler, Cerulean

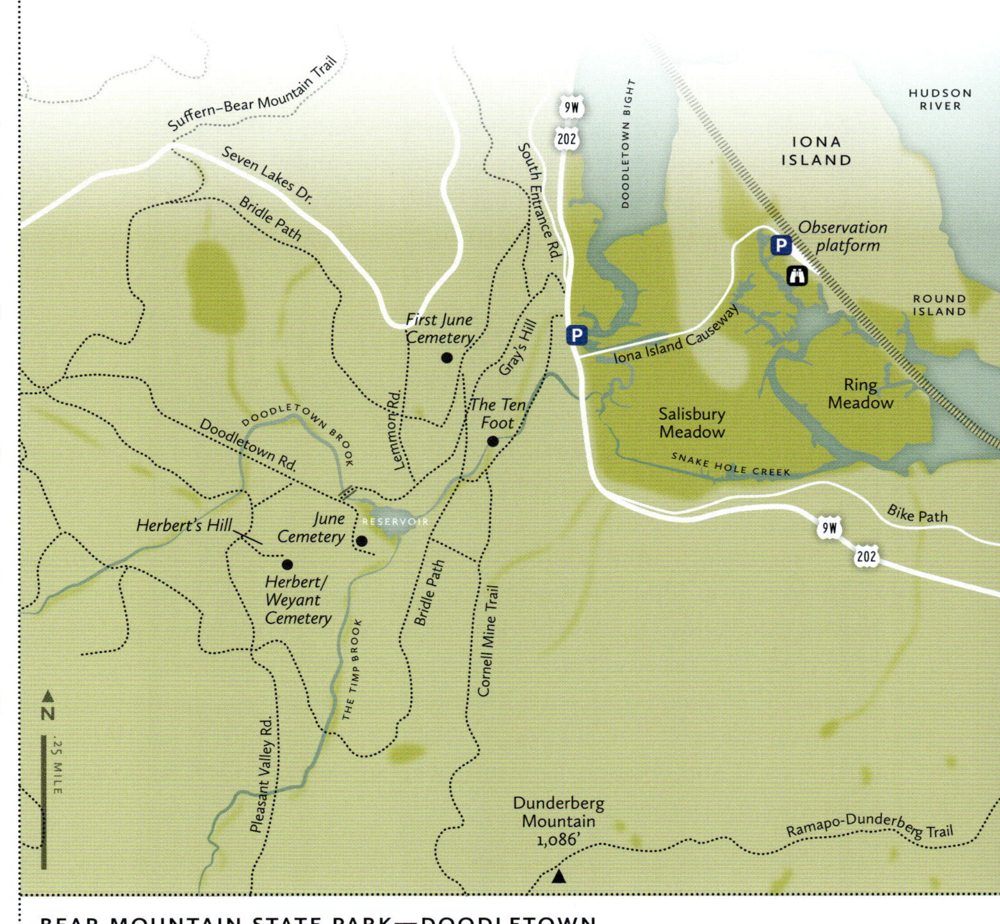

BEAR MOUNTAIN STATE PARK—DOODLETOWN AND IONA ISLAND

Warbler, Worm-eating Warbler, and both cuckoos, are especially abundant, and rare species are often reported. The disturbed hillside setting with old power lines, overgrown gardens, and dead snags occasionally offers great looks at species that are usually hard to see.

The trail to Doodletown begins on the west side of US 9W and continues up Gray's Hill on an old blacktopped road that is cut into the hillside and runs parallel to the highway and an old power line for some distance. Though it is steep for the first quarter mile, it soon levels out. From this vantage point, there are good views of the vegetation and birds below. A short side trail leads to "the Ten Foot," a pretty waterfall and plunge pool that served as the town's swimming hole. Lemmon Road leads to a clearing and the location of the town's first cemetery, as well as to an area where a former park superinten-dent experimented with raising local and ornamental trees. Farther down Gray's Hill is a small reservoir fed by two streams, Doodletown Brook and Timp Brook. The reservoir has a fringing cattail marsh and attracts many birds. A faint path to the right leads to some sitting stones with a good view of the water.

Shortly after the reservoir, the road forks at a sign showing a map of Doo-dletown in 1957 and the location of sites on the self-guided walking tour. Doodletown Road continues west (right), while Pleasant Valley Road is south (left). Either route is a fascinating trip back into history and a unique op-portunity for great birdwatching among the rapidly disappearing ruins of a Hudson Valley hamlet.

Iona Island, another well-known Bird Conservation Area and part of the Hudson River Estuarine Research Reserve, is usually visited in conjunction with Doodletown because it is just across us 9w and easily accessed via the Iona Island causeway. This extensive, brackish tidal marsh was once domi-nated by common reed, but a habitat restoration project has improved the area for marsh birds such as Virginia Rail, Swamp Sparrow, Marsh Wren, and Osprey. The observation platform just before the railroad tracks is the main viewing area at this site.

Hooded Warbler breeds in the briars at Doodletown. © Deborah Tracy-Kral.

Yellow-billed Cuckoo is easily seen during spring migration
at Doodletown. © Carena M. Pooth.

Hook Mountain

GPS ADDRESS 271 Rockland Lake Road, Valley Cottage
LATITUDE/LONGITUDE 41.12282 −73.91807
DIRECTIONS Take Exit 11, US 9W/Nyack, off I-87 and follow US 9W north
2.7 miles past Christian Herald Road to the south entrance for Rockland
Lake State Park on the right. Follow the signs to the Executive Golf
Course and park away from the clubhouse. There is also a small pull-
off on the east side of 9W with parking for five cars between Christian
Herald Road and the entrance to Rockland Lake State Park.

Established as a hawkwatch site in 1971, Hook Mountain is one of the premier
raptor observation areas in the Hudson Valley. "The Hook" is state park land
in the Palisades Interstate Park system, just north of the Nyacks. Positioned
on the west side of the Hudson, the park juts out into the river between
the Tappan Zee Bridge and Haverstraw Bay. Most important for the hawks,

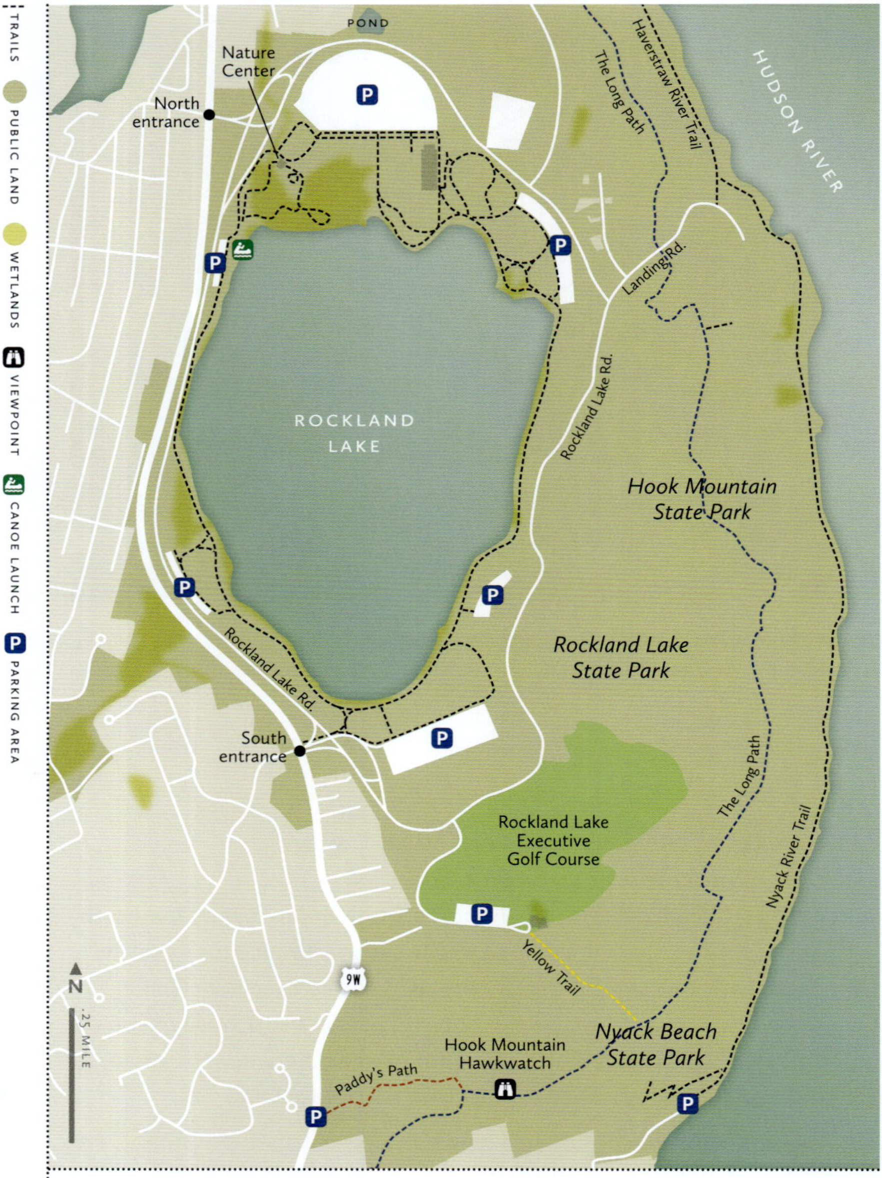

HOOK MOUNTAIN AND ROCKLAND LAKE STATE PARKS

Black Vultures, distinguished from Turkey Vultures by their silvery wingtips and short, square tails. © Deborah Tracy-Kral.

however, is the fact that the steep cliffs of New Jersey's Palisades Ridge border the river here. In spring and fall, migrating raptors take advantage of strong winds from weather fronts that are deflected upward by the cliffs. These updrafts allow the birds to cover long distances with energetic economy, and the concentrations of raptors create a thrilling spectacle for birdwatchers.

There are two routes to the hawkwatch on the summit. The one from the golf course is a little longer but not as steep, and has the advantage of ample parking. At the flagpole in the turnaround, look south (right) into the woods and find a yellow blaze on a tree marking the trail. Follow the yellow trail uphill for about a quarter mile until it intersects with the Long Path (aqua) at the river, then turn right and follow this trail along the escarpment for another 0.25 mile to the clearing at the summit. The alternative route is Paddy's Path from US 9W, named after hawk counter Padraic French. Parking at the trailhead is very limited, and a steeper, 0.25-mile, yellow-blazed trail through the woods leads to the summit.

Hook Mountain is part of a 676-acre undeveloped park that stretches nearly seven miles along the Hudson River. The Long Path crosses the summit, and offers spectacular views of Rockland Lake, long views of the Hudson in both directions, and Croton Point on the opposite shore. The observation area, at an elevation of 730 feet, puts the migrating raptors very close, often at eye level, and some are drawn in to the mounted owl at the site. On average, more than twelve thousand raptors pass over the Hook each fall, including thousands of Broad-winged Hawks that peak in mid-September and increasing numbers of Black Vulture and Osprey. Unlike at some other hawkwatches, there is no seating on the summit, so if you plan to spend the day, consider bringing a folding chair.

Observers have been counting hawks at the Hook since 1971. Trained counters are present during both spring and fall migration, and they submit data to the Hawk Migration Association of North America, where the information is combined with data from other hawkwatches across the country to track the status of raptor populations. Hook Mountain was designated a New York State Important Bird Area in 1997, primarily based on its importance to raptor migration. Though the focus at the summit is migrating hawks, the surrounding hardwood forest of oak, maple, and beech has good bird diversity, and migrating raptors and songbirds are known to use the meadows and wetlands at the base of the south face of Hook Mountain for resting and feeding. This area can be accessed via the bike path that follows the river's edge at Nyack Beach State Park.

Rockland Lake State Park

GPS ADDRESS 299 Rockland Lake Road, Valley Cottage
LATITUDE/LONGITUDE 41.14764 −73.92226
DIRECTIONS From I-87/287, take Exit 11 US 9W/Nyack and turn onto US 9W north. Go about 5.0 miles to the second (north) entrance into the park, Rockland Lake Road, the county road that circles the lake. Do not take the south entrance to the Executive Golf Course. Follow Rockland Lake Road north about 0.5 mile to Parking Field 1.

Rockland Lake State Park is a very busy, highly developed recreation center only twenty-four miles north of New York City that is embedded in the spectacular rocky landscape of the west shore of the Hudson River. Because of its recreational facilities, which include a fitness/bike trail, two Olympic-sized swimming pools, picnic areas, boating, fishing, tennis courts, and two golf courses, and because of its proximity to the city, this park teems with humanity, especially during the summer, weekends, and holidays. Nevertheless, this site is a wonderful place to see birds, and the lake is part of a New York State Bird Conservation Area that includes neighboring Nyack Beach, Hook

Mountain, and Haverstraw Beach State Parks. A positive birding experience depends on avoiding the crowds.

The centerpiece of the park is 256-acre spring-fed Rockland Lake, which attracts both birds and people. From 1831 to 1924, it supported a thriving industry centered on ice that was harvested in winter and shipped on barges downriver to New York City. The remnants of the Knickerbocker Ice Company icehouses are still evident on the northeast corner of the lake, but today, the 3.2-mile paved fitness/bike trail around the lake dominates the scene.

Birders come to Rockland Lake to see waterfowl especially in spring and fall, and all winter if the lake does not freeze. Although the trail can be accessed from any of six large parking areas around the lake, there is a small pond just before the entrance to Parking Field 1 that should not be missed, because it sometimes hosts a nice collection of ducks. A path downhill leads from Parking Field 1 to the trail around the lake, and a clockwise route takes advantage of the morning sun on the west shore. Unlike at many waterfowl sites, one rarely needs a scope to see the waterfowl at Rockland Lake. Many of the birds seem accustomed to people, and the lake is small enough for easy viewing. Bufflehead, Common Merganser, Ring-necked Duck, Wood

Hooded Merganser pair. © Alan W. Wells.

Duck, Gadwall, Green-winged Teal, Northern Shoveler, and Ruddy Duck are reported annually.

The bike trail is also excellent for other species because it passes near athletic fields with nest boxes, shrubby areas, small wetlands, and other birdy habitats. During migration, warblers and Rusty Blackbird forage along the shoreline. The park has a nature center west of Parking Field 1 that is staffed by volunteers. Though the building may not be open, the habitats around the center include a small swamp, a stream inlet, and scrubby fields with a nice mix of sparrows. White-crowned Sparrow, Fox Sparrow, and Swamp Sparrow have all been reported.

Hiking trails away from the lake itself provide access to the forest and rocky ridgeline along the west shore of the Hudson River. These can be accessed from Landing Road, which intersects Rockland Lake Road on the east side of the park. The Haverstraw River Trail follows the river to Haverstraw about 3.5 miles to the north, while the Nyack River Trail runs 1.5 miles south to Nyack Beach State Park. Bald Eagles are seen on these river trails, and Peregrine Falcon and Common Raven nest on the rocky cliffs that border the river. Landing Road also has a trailhead for the Long Path, the famous hiking trail between the George Washington Bridge and John Boyd Thacher State Park in Albany County. Marked with aqua, the trail passes through Rockland Lake State Park just east of the lake and can be followed north to adjacent Hook Mountain.

Kakiat County Park

GPS ADDRESS 592 US 202/Haverstraw Road, Montebello
LATITUDE/LONGITUDE 41.14394 −74.11238
DIRECTIONS From I-87/287, take Exit 15A to NY 17N. Follow 17 north 0.3 mile to NY 59/Orange Turnpike. Take NY 59 east and go 1.4 miles to US 202/Wayne Avenue. Turn left and take US 202 east about 3.0 miles to the entrance for Kakiat County Park on the south side of the road opposite the Viola School. Map at rocklandgov.com.

Kakiat County Park borders Harriman State Park and buffers the state-protected land on its southeast side. Most of the 376 acres now owned and managed by Rockland County were once part of the Blauvelt family farm, which included an orchard and power mill on the Mahwah River. The park

Barred Owl. © Alan W. Wells.

is transected by a gas pipeline and power line right-of-way and hosts a gas compressor station, but these easements actually add some habitat diversity to the forested landscape of the surrounding Hudson Highlands.

Some of the most interesting habitat here centers on the Mahwah River, which flows southwest through the park on its way to the Ramapo River in New Jersey. An area of floodplain forest is visible both upstream and downstream from the bridge near the parking area. The Old Mill Trail (blue) also follows the river, and although it connects to the Kakiat Trail, there is also an unmarked informal trail that leads farther up the river to the service road. The foundation of the old mill is interesting enough, but its position on the shore is the perfect vantage point for viewing the water in both directions as well as the open wet meadow on the opposite shore. This reach of the river is used by a variety of waterfowl, Veery, Rusty Blackbird, Baltimore Oriole, Yellow-throated Vireo, Louisiana Waterthrush, Yellow-bellied Sapsucker, Carolina Wren, Belted Kingfisher, and assorted waders.

The trails to the south of the bridge lead to a meadow with nest boxes where Eastern Bluebird breeds, and also to shrubby habitat where American Woodcock, Brown Thrasher, and Lawrence's Warbler have been reported. The property includes a few pine stands where Barred Owl is known to roost.

The Kakiat Trail leads away from the river along a small brook, eventually crossing the gas pipeline and service road that run the length of the park. Beyond the gas line, the hike continues up a very difficult, steep trail with intimidating backcountry signage into Harriman State Park. The public is permitted to use the wide, level service road and the gas pipeline as a hiking trail, but users need to watch for timber rattlesnakes and copperheads that sometimes leave the ridges to the west and warm themselves in the sunny right-of-way. The utility corridor has wide, open field, shrubland, and edge habitats where Indigo Bunting, Field Sparrow, and Blue-winged Warbler are common. Northeast of the compressor station, the service road leaves the gas pipeline right-of-way and enters a fairly pristine, open, deciduous hardwood forest that is excellent habitat for woodland birds.

The Ramapo Escarpment rises sharply through the woods west of the service road and pipeline. Both the Mountain (orange) and Kakiat (white) Trails ascend this ridge after leaving the lowlands around the river. These trails are steep, rocky, difficult, and not for the faint of heart, but the Mountain Trail is especially scenic. It passes through open oak woods dotted with immense boulders. In two places this trail breaks out of the trees on rock outcrops with magnificent views of the valley below.

Piermont Pier and Marsh

GPS ADDRESS 31 Ferry Road, Piermont
LATITUDE/LONGITUDE 41.04001 −73.91037
DIRECTIONS From I-87/287, take Exit 10 or 11 to Nyack/South Nyack/ US 9W. Go south on 9W under the New York State Thruway for 3.5 to 4.0 miles, and then turn left after crossing the bridge over Sparkill Creek onto Ferdon Avenue. Follow Ferdon Avenue 0.9 mile to a traffic light. Turn right at the light onto Paradise Avenue for 0.2 mile, then right onto Ferry Road. Follow Ferry Road 0.3 mile to the ball fields, and park in the parking lot. Map at www.dec.ny.gov.

Most people would not think of a pier as a good place to go birding, and in fact, Piermont Pier wouldn't be anything special if not for its location. The mile-long pier juts out about half a mile into one of the wider reaches of the brackish tidal portion of the Hudson River. When the pier was built in 1841, it was known as the Erie Pier because it was at the eastern end of the Erie Railroad, but in 1981 it was given to the people of Piermont. Cars can drive

Ring-billed Gull.
The most common gull
on the Hudson River.
© Alan W. Wells.

Dunlin in nonbreeding
plumage on the rocks
at Piermont Pier. ©
Carena M. Pooth.

down the pier at 15 mph, but free legal parking on the pier itself is extremely limited, and violations carry hefty fines. Although permits can be purchased from the Piermont village clerk's office, most birders park in the free lot across from the ball field and walk a short distance down Ferry Road to the pier.

The pier sits just south of the Tappan Zee Bridge at the north end of Piermont Marsh, a large brackish tidal marsh that occupies two miles of the Hudson River shoreline. Piermont is one of four sites on the Hudson that are managed by NYSDEC as part of the National Estuarine Research Reserve. Visibility in the marsh is limited because it is dominated by common reed, but just south of the pier, Sparkill Creek cuts through the ridge that forms the famous New Jersey Palisades and empties into the Hudson, creating extensive tidal shallows and intertidal mudflats. The forests on the rocky slopes of Tallman Mountain border the marsh south of the pier.

With condos, power lines, roads, and sidewalks, the access to the pier feels like suburbia, but the tree-lined pier is more like an urban park in an unusual landscape setting. It has benches and clear views of both the water and the shoreline in many different directions. Gulls and cormorants perch on old dock and pier supports that stick up out of the water, offering opportunities to study subtle plumage characters at close range. At low tide, the pier offers especially good views of the shoreline. To the north, the shoreline is rocky, but the south side has exposed mudflats near the mouth of Sparkill Creek. In winter and early spring, this is a great place to see waterfowl. Rockland Audubon, which often leads field trips to the pier, has compiled an impressive list of nearly two hundred species for this site. Perhaps because of its location in the middle of the river, the pier seems to attract vagrants, including uncommon migrants, exotic escapees, and other odd species. Ivory Gull, Snowy Owl, King Eider, White Ibis, Monk Parakeet, and American Avocet are just of few of the unexpected rarities confirmed over the years.

In addition to visiting the pier, one can walk south along a trail on the edge of the marsh by following the road along the creek to a kiosk. This short, wide dirt road has some good views of the creek and peaks east into Piermont Marsh. A canoe launch into Sparkill Creek near the road offers the opportunity to venture deeper into the marsh by boat. On the west side, the trail follows the steep, wooded side of Tallman Mountain, which is good for warblers and other woodland passerines during migration.

PUTNAM COUNTY

Clarence Fahnestock State Park

GPS ADDRESS 1087 NY 301, Hopewell Junction
LATITUDE/LONGITUDE 41.46214 −73.82984
DIRECTIONS From the Taconic State Parkway, take the exit for NY 301/Carmel/Cold Spring and go west about 0.5 mile to the park office headquarters on the north side of 301. Map at parks.ny.gov/parks.

Clarence Fahnestock State Park encompasses roughly fourteen thousand acres of the Hudson Highlands that extend east into Putnam County. Large, forested ridges running southwest to northeast dominate the landscape, with wetlands and streams in the valleys below. Early in its history, much of the park was mined for iron or farmed, but the state began acquiring land here in the 1920s; during the 1930s, the Civilian Conservation Corps built impoundments to create lakes and ponds, and also established many of the park's picnic and camping facilities. Today, New York State recognizes large portions of the park as a valuable Bird Conservation Area, thus protecting a large area of contiguous, unfragmented forest that provides breeding and migratory stopover habitat for forest-dependent birds.

Ironically, many birders have never explored Fahnestock. The best opportunities to see the forest interior species that live here generally require leaving the heavily traveled main roads and doing some walking. The park is huge, and some of the terrain is challenging; while it isn't necessary to climb mountains to see great birds here, it is important to get out of the car and walk a little. The trails in the park are meticulously groomed and well marked by volunteers from the New York–New Jersey Trail Conference. Dozens of routes can be combined to create pleasant hiking loops. The conference's trail maps, available for purchase at the park office and online, are a useful supplement to the simplified maps that OPRHP offers for free. Few birders have even scratched the surface of the park's more than fifty miles of trails, and the suggestions that follow are just a few places to begin exploring this publicly protected gem.

Hidden Lake can be accessed from the blue trail off NY 301 at the south end of Canopus Lake and combined with a section of the Appalachian Trail to make a circuit hike. The lake is ringed with mountain laurel and covered with water lilies, and the view from the dam on the yellow trail is a great place to sit and watch birds. These trails are part of a long Three Lakes hike described on the OPRHP simplified trail map, and the hike can be extended to include John Allen Pond, but the loop to Hidden Lake is only about three miles and fairly easy.

Steeper, but definitely worth the effort, is a hike north on the blue trail from the parking area at the south end of Canopus Lake to Beaver Pond. The trail begins with a short ascent up a rocky hill through deciduous woods and mountain laurel that is spectacularly beautiful when flowering in June. The path breaks out into the open on a rocky oak outcrop covered with blueberries. The blue trail descends through woods and continues east at the junction with the red trail to pretty, laurel-ringed Beaver Pond. Returning to the red trail brings you back to NY 301 about two miles south of the other trailhead, so it is good to leave a second car here. During the breeding season, birders find more than ten species of warbler along this trail, including Worm-eating

Warbler, Chestnut-sided Warbler, Black-and-white Warbler, Prairie Warbler, Louisiana Waterthrush, and even Cerulean Warbler. Beaver Pond has breeding Wood Duck and other water birds. One way to extend this hike and add some additional diversity is to take a side trip west on the yellow trail, before the red trail reaches NY 301, to the property owned by Glynwood Therapeutic Equestrian Center. This is a working horse farm, but OPRHP has a trail easement through the open landscape where birders find swallows, including Purple Martin, and Blue-winged Warbler.

Another outstanding birding area is a patch of hemlock-northern hardwood forest that can be accessed from the white trail, which is really an old road, starting at a kiosk near sites 69 to 71 in the campground. The park has dedicated seventeen acres of forest to the memory of a talented young birder, Martin Hugh McGuire, who died tragically in an auto accident at age twenty-five. Locally known as Marty's Woods, this habitat is more typical of sites farther north, and it was here that McGuire was able to confirm breeding of northern species such as Canada Warbler, Winter Wren, Red-breasted Nuthatch, and Blue-headed Vireo. The gentle road/trail continues through a swamp, ending at a lovely marsh on the north end of Stillwater Pond.

Finally, there are good bird habitats in the vicinity of Hubbard Lodge, which is owned by the park and located on Campbell Road, a dead-end street east of US 9 just north of the junction with NY 301 in Cold Spring on the western perimeter of the park. The fields behind the lodge are kept open to provide nectar sources for the Ann Odell Butterfly Garden. The white trail (School Mountain Road) that begins near the lodge leads up to a beautiful beaver meadow with great viewing from a bridge where it crosses the wetland.

Red-breasted Nuthatch nests in Marty's Woods at Clarence Fahnestock State Park. © John Hershey.

234

Blue-gray Gnatcatcher. © Alan W. Wells.

Wonder Lake State Park

GPS ADDRESS 380 Luddingtonville Road, Holmes
LATITUDE/LONGITUDE 41.49475 −73.66289
DIRECTIONS From I-84, take Exit 18 Lake Carmel/Patterson. Turn right onto NY 311 north and continue 0.2 mile to Luddingtonville Road. Turn left onto Luddingtonville Road and continue 1.8 miles to a parking lot on the right with a kiosk. Map at parks.ny.gov/parks.

Wonder Lake State Park is a lightly used, little-known, largely undeveloped preserve close to I-84 in eastern Putnam County. Set aside for hiking, snow-shoeing, horseback riding, and hunting, the property has more than eight miles of well-marked and beautifully maintained trails. When completed, the park's Highland Trail will connect two hundred miles of footpaths through the highlands in Pennsylvania, New Jersey, New York, and Connecticut.

Like many parks in the Hudson Highlands, Wonder Lake was once part of a large estate, so its historical land use included agriculture and timber cutting. Rock walls, old orchards, second-growth woods, weedy edges, and dammed streams come with the territory, but these diverse disturbed habitats support abundant bird life. The terrain is hilly, but the trails have been thoughtfully laid out so that they are only moderately difficult. Unfortunately, the trail from the parking lot is somewhat steep, and this probably discourages many birders from hiking into the quieter, more remote and scenic areas of this park's more than one thousand acres of undeveloped forest.

The park features two artificial lakes. At thirty acres, Wonder Lake is large enough to support nesting waterfowl and waders that come to feed in the shallows near the shoreline. The lake is covered with lily pads in summer. Laurel Lake is much smaller. One pleasant way to access most of the habitats at this site is to follow the well-marked Highland Trail. This footpath starts out in a dense, overgrown area of multiflora rose, blackberry, and grapevines. After an easy stream crossing, the path enters a rocky, disturbed woods with a barberry understory, where Hooded Warbler breed. Worm-eating Warbler is reported from this area in June, which suggests that it breeds here. The Heritage Trail then descends to the edge of rock-rimmed Wonder Lake. Here the woods are less disturbed, and the trail around the lake is close to the water much of the time. There are multiple opportunities to approach the water quietly and view birds. On the east side, the trail moves away from the lake into an area of hemlocks and mountain laurel, inhabited by conifer-loving birds. The trail network offers birders many trip options, including longer hikes into Laurel Lake and forays to Bare Hill, which features old fruit trees, a pine plantation, and dry oak and blueberry outcrops. Getting away from the road noise of I-84 and visiting the best parts of this preserve requires hiking a bit, but this site has the habitat and potential to produce surprises.

Cranberry Mountain Wildlife Management Area

GPS ADDRESS 136 Stage Coach Road, Patterson
LATITUDE/LONGITUDE 41.50865 −73.54980
DIRECTIONS From the junction of NY 22/55 and NY 311 in Patterson, continue south another 0.3 mile to a fork on the left to Birch Hill Road. Take Birch Hill Road 2.6 miles to a T intersection. Turn right onto dead-end Stage Coach Road, and follow it 0.6 mile to a small parking area on

the right. There is a second parking lot another 0.2 mile farther south on Stage Coach Road, also on the right. Map at www.dec.ny.gov.

Cranberry Mountain Wildlife Management Area in the northeast corner of Putnam County has been managed as wildlife habitat for more than fifty years. NYSDEC began acquiring land at this site in 1964, and recent additions have brought the total protected land to more than one thousand acres. The property's extensive network of loop trails uses mainly old woods roads; and because the area is on top of a mountain, the topography is mostly gentle ups and downs, and the hiking is fairly easy. Beyond the gate at the northernmost parking area, an old road marked with blue trail markers leads into open successional habitat with trees, shrubs, and fields full of grasses and forbs. These fields are large enough to support grassland birds besides the Field Sparrow that breeds here; but grassland birds have not yet been reported from this under-studied area, and it is possible that poorly timed mowing has eliminated some grassland species.

The blue trail enters the woods and continues past several small artificial ponds that are too small for most waterfowl, but the one on the property boundary has a small, marshy perimeter. The biggest pond is ringed with common reed and seems to attract mostly Red-winged Blackbirds.

At the trail junction, just beyond the largest pond, the yellow trail loops through upland forest that is dominated by oaks. Worm-eating Warbler

Common Yellowthroat (male). © Alan W. Wells.

and Scarlet Tanager breed here, along with other common forest-nesting species. The east side of the yellow trail follows a stream and passes through woods that have more maple and beech and somewhat different birds. This section of the yellow trail connects with the blue trail, which leads to the second parking lot on Stage Coach Road; it also passes through a portion of the property that is being managed as young forest to provide habitat for New England cottontail, a rare species of rabbit that has a small population on Cranberry Mountain. The dense habitat that this species prefers will also be attractive to shrubland birds such as Eastern Towhee, Brown Thrasher, Chestnut-sided Warbler, Blue-winged Warbler, Golden-winged Warbler, Mourning Warbler, and Ruffed Grouse.

Little Stony Point State Park

GPS ADDRESS 3011 NY 9D, Cold Spring
LATITUDE/LONGITUDE 41.42612 −73.96541
DIRECTIONS From the Taconic State Parkway, take the exit for NY 301W/Cold Spring and travel west 8.5 miles to NY 9D. Turn north onto 9D/Morris Avenue and go 0.7 mile to the sign for Little Stony Point State Park. There is parking on both the sides of NY 9D.

Little Stony Point is a tiny, twenty-five-acre state park that is part of about six thousand acres of disjunct parcels between Beacon and Peekskill that OPRHP has set aside for public use and grouped into the Hudson Highlands State Park Preserve. It is neither pristine nor remarkably birdy, but it packs lots of habitat into a very small area. Located on busy NY 9D on the east shore of the Hudson River, Little Stony Point is one of the easiest places to access the Hudson River shoreline. A short, level walk of a quarter mile will put you on a sandy beach with awesome views of Storm King, Breakneck Ridge, Mount Taurus, and Bannerman Island. You can walk all the trails in thirty minutes, but most people will want to stay longer.

If there is one unfortunate thing about Little Stony Point, it is the fact that an area that was once a local picnic site has been discovered and is in danger of being "loved to death." The Little Stony Point Citizens Association does an amazing job of managing the site with limited resources, but hot summer weekends attract sunbathers and boaters to the sandy beach, including some people who ignore the regulations, block the highway, leave litter, and destroy

Peregrine Falcons nest on the cliffs across the river from Little Stony Point.
© Carena M. Pooth.

the quiet beauty of this special place. There are plans in place to improve facilities to deal with the crowds, but the best advice is to try to visit Stony Point "off peak," especially if you want to see more birds than people.

There are no marked trails here, but all access begins on the west side of a pedestrian bridge that crosses the railroad tracks west of NY 9D. The cleared areas along the railroad grade have Indigo Bunting, Northern Cardinal, and other birds that use early successional habitats. The forest between the railroad and the Hudson River is disturbed, but it still attracts a diversity of Neotropical species during migration, including many warblers, vireos, and flycatchers. The path south is a loop trail along the edge of the river, with access to the popular sandy beach and several side trails to the shore of the river. The river is deep and narrow here, so waterfowl tend not to linger in this area, but cormorants and gulls fly by often. This trail passes through a cleared area with gravel piles and small trees that was once part of a mining operation. The rocky outcrop of Little Stony Point is visible from this area. A side trail around the back and uphill leads to the top of these cliffs and out onto a dry, open, rocky summit with a panoramic view of West Point to the south, the river, and the mountains of the Hudson Highlands to the north and west. This outcrop is a good raptor viewing site during migration and a great place to see both vultures and the Peregrine Falcons and Common Ravens that nest nearby.

The parking lot at Little Stony Point connects to some of the most popular, scenic, and challenging hiking trails in the Hudson Highlands. The park's small size and easy Hudson River access make it simple to do a quick stop to check out the birds on the way home, or maybe just take in the sunset.

Nimham Mountain Multiple Use Area

GPS ADDRESS 392 CR 41/Gypsy Trail Road, Carmel
LATITUDE/LONGITUDE 41.45448 −73.71106
DIRECTIONS From the Taconic State Parkway, take the exit for NY 301. Follow NY 301 south about 9.0 miles to its junction with CR 14/Gypsy Trail Road on the left. Do not cross the reservoir. Turn left onto Gypsy Trail Road and go north 2.0 miles to a dirt parking area on the right with a NYSDEC sign. Parking for the fire tower is at the end of Mount Nimham Court, a left turn 0.3 mile farther north on Gypsy Trail Road. There is also parking 0.2 mile east on Nichols Street, 1.1 miles south of here off Gypsy Trail Road. Map at www.dec.ny.gov.

To those unfamiliar with this site, everything about Nimham Mountain seems a little confusing. The mountain was named to honor Daniel Nimham, the last sachem of the Wappingers, who died fighting with revolutionary forces in 1778, yet the DEC signage calls the property "Ninham" Mountain Multiple Use Area. Once classified as a state forest that was managed for sustainable timber, its current classification as a multiple-use area supports forestry along with other forms of public recreation ranging from mountain biking to hunting. With mostly unmarked trails, it is not surprising that birders have sought more user-friendly places to see birds. Nevertheless, Nimham Mountain's 1,023 acres of public land in the Taconic hills of Putnam County have a lot to offer in the way of bird habitats and uncrowded, undeveloped landscapes.

The property has both dirt roads (Rinaldi Trail, Tower Road, and Coles Mills Road), which are opened to motorized vehicles by permit, and footpaths. For purposes of discussion, it is useful to divide the area into two sections, one west and the other east of Gypsy Trail Road. The western part is hilly and includes 1,220-foot Nimham Mountain with its ninety-foot fire tower. A gate at the end of Mount Nimham Court marks the parking area. From this lot, Tower Road leads uphill to the summit and the fire tower that was built in 1940 by the Civilian Conservation Corps. It is open to the public for a panoramic view of New York City to the south, the Catskills to the west, the Berkshires to the east, and soaring raptors in all directions.

On its way to the summit, Tower Road passes by two of Putnam County's mysterious stone chambers, curious structures built into hillsides; they have

Indigo Bunting (male),
a bird that breeds in shrublands.
© Deborah Tracy-Kral.

been described as root cellars built by early settlers, or even Neolithic stone monuments of Celtic visitors who arrived before Columbus (Kilgannon 2001). Eastern Phoebe nest inside these structures. Near the parking area, a brook crossing forms a small wetland beside the road. Tower Road passes by an old foundation and through young woods dominated by oaks, before emerging into a more open summit, where Prairie Warbler and Eastern Towhee breed.

East of Gypsy Trail Road is land that has been managed for timber production, which has resulted in a diversity of forest types in a relatively small area. Mountain biking is the primary recreational use on this part of the property, and the trail network consists of a series of loop trails off the main Rinaldi Trail. If these loop trails are marked at all, they are marked with blue trail markers. The Rinaldi Trail, however, is a quiet, flat, needle-covered road that runs between the parking lot on Gypsy Trail Road and Nichols Street. From the Gypsy Trail Road parking lot, it descends to the north end of the pond. Before crossing to the east side of the pond, the biker's Blue Loop 2 heads south along the west edge of the impoundment, and provides excellent views into a quiet backwater and good waterfowl habitat. After passing the north edge of the pond, the Rinaldi Trail goes through hardwood forest with an understory of invasive species, a spruce plantation, stands of tamarack and pine, and areas of older, more mature hardwoods; the trail finally emerges into a large old field near Nichols Road. The cottontail rabbit populations in this area of second growth are the focus of an ongoing research project, but these "young forests" also support a diversity of shrubland birds.

William Clough Preserve

GPS ADDRESS 166 Farm to Market Road, Brewster
LATITUDE/LONGITUDE 41.44500 −73.60574
DIRECTIONS From I-84, take Exit 19 to NY 312. Follow NY 312 east 1.6 miles to CR 62/Farm to Market Road. At the light, turn north onto CR 62/Farm to Market Road and continue 0.7 mile to the preserve entrance on the left, just after Brewster High School. The parking area is small, and there is a sharp drop-off from the pavement. There is easier parking a short distance from the preserve entrance by the high school athletic fields.

The Nature Conservancy donated the fifty-eight-acre William Clough Preserve to the Town of Patterson in 1978 after owning it for sixteen years. With a lovely marsh as its centerpiece, this small preserve is part of the Great

Yellow Warbler.
© Deborah Tracy-Kral.

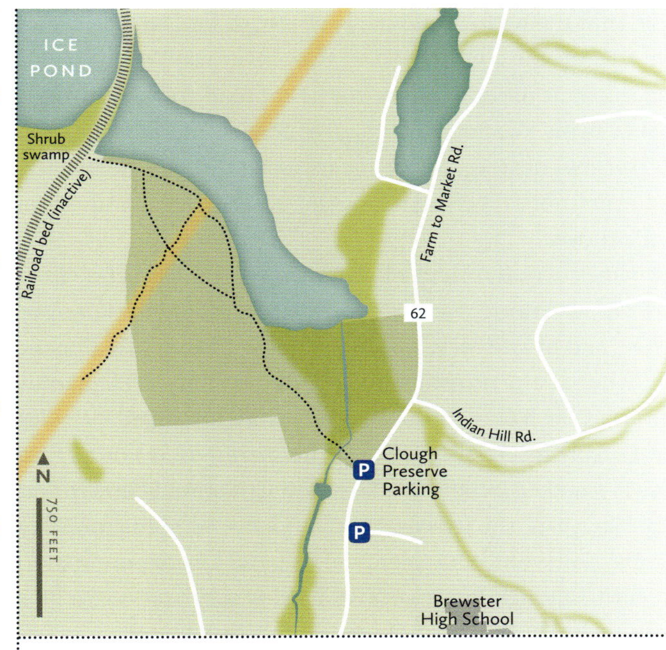

WILLIAM CLOUGH PRESERVE

Swamp. Other nearby properties in conservation ownership, to the northeast (Twin Hill Preserve) and west (Ice Pond Preserve), also protect this valuable watershed. The wetland is surrounded by a forest buffer of hemlocks and northern hardwoods, and cut through by a large transmission line that adds some shrubland to the suite of bird habitats. At the northwest border, an inactive and abandoned railroad bed provides a raised pathway to look into the shrub swamp and Ice Pond on the other side of the tracks. The active railroad line now travels on the other side of Ice Pond. There is only one trail at this small preserve, and it is obvious and well marked with yellow trail markers. About 0.25 mile after crossing a small stream on stepping-stones, the trail splits, and one side of the loop stays close to the edge of the marsh while the other travels farther inland through the woods.

Birders rarely visit this preserve. Fewer than ten checklists were submitted to eBird in the last three years, attributed to only a few people who stopped by briefly in fall and winter. In spring, Veery, Wood Thrush, and Ovenbird sing nonstop. The adjacent cattail marsh is in fine condition, and the shoreline trail has great views into the wetland, which begins with fairly dense cattail and standing dead trees at the south end, but then gives way to large areas of open water and muskrat mounds closer to the railroad tracks. During a May visit, there were many swallows, swifts, flycatchers, Wood Duck, and other common waterfowl nesting, but it seems likely that a visit in early March would find even more diversity when the water is open and ducks and geese are on the move.

The transmission line cut that runs through the preserve is wide enough to have Blue-winged Warbler, Prairie Warbler, Field Sparrow, Chipping Sparrow, and Eastern Towhee, and in late May, a pretty stand of pink lady's slippers. Experience has shown that any transmission line in the Hudson Highlands with Blue-winged Warbler has the potential for Golden-winged Warbler and their hybrids. Equally interesting is the shrub swamp that borders Ice Pond, with Willow Flycatcher, Yellow Warbler, and Common Yellowthroat present. As its name suggests, the Ice Pond at the north end of the property probably freezes most years, but it has plenty of fish and lots of potential to attract fish-eating birds. Clough Preserve gives birders easy access to a nice assortment of high-quality bird habitats packed into a small area.

Constitution Marsh Audubon Center and Sanctuary

GPS ADDRESS 127 Warren Landing Road, Garrison
LATITUDE/LONGITUDE 41.40422 −73.93432
DIRECTIONS From the junction of NY 301 and NY 9D in Cold Spring, take 9D south 1.3 miles past Boscobel Restoration to Indian Brook Road, a single-lane dirt road on the right. Drive 0.4 mile on Indian Brook Road to a sign on the right for Constitution Marsh Audubon Center and a parking area for eight cars. Walk down the hill on the old dirt road 0.25 mile to the center. Map at constitutionmarsh.audubon.org.

Constitution Marsh is a brackish tidal marsh. The twice-daily tides that inundate the vegetation contain more of the ocean's salt than do tides farther north, and the resulting natural community includes a mixture of saltwater and freshwater marsh species. Surrounded by the Hudson Highlands and across the river from West Point, this is an incredibly diverse and productive environment that is home to rare plants, fish nurseries, muskrats, and great birds.

Osprey with nesting material. © Denise Hackert-Stoner, Naturelogues.

Once owned by members of the Rockefeller family, the marsh was donated to OPRHP in 1969, with the provision that the property be managed by Audubon as a bird sanctuary. Today, Audubon New York maintains two buildings on the site, including offices and the James P. Rod Education Center. Audubon also monitors bird populations, maintains trails and a seven-hundred-foot boardwalk, offers educational programs, and leads guided canoe trips by reservation for a fee. Despite signage to the contrary, the trails are open from dawn to dusk, although the buildings are open only from Memorial Day to Columbus Day.

It is the character of the site that it is moderately difficult to access Constitution Marsh either by foot or canoe. Getting from the parking lot to the marsh involves walking down a quarter-mile-long hill on Warren Landing Road to the edge of the river. From the reception area by the buildings, a well-marked half-mile-long footpath climbs up and over a beautiful, steep, rocky ledge with spectacular views of the marsh and the Hudson River below. The boardwalk begins at the end of this trail. It extends out into the cattail marsh and includes benches and interpretive signs. From the open boardwalk on the river, it is easy to spot Bald Eagle, Osprey, and a variety of other raptors, ducks, geese, and gulls that travel up and down the river, and to scan the trees and shoreline for other birds. Occasionally, patient, early, lucky birders catch glimpses of secretive marsh birds from the boardwalk.

However, the best way to see the Least Bittern, Marsh Wren, herons, Swamp Sparrow, and Virginia Rail that this site is known for is to take a boat out into the marsh. The only boats that are allowed to launch directly into the marsh at the Audubon center are the ones used during its guided canoe programs. Private individuals have to access Constitution Marsh from the river. The closest boat launch is 1.5 miles north in Cold Spring at Scenic Hudson's Foundry Dock Park, located in the train station parking lot at the end of Market Street. Parking is free on weekends, but there is a fee on weekdays. Taking a canoe or kayak into the marsh this way requires checking the tides, because the marsh is impassable at low tide. From the river, the only access into the marsh is under the north railroad trestle, which must also be timed to the tide. Boaters are asked to stay in the main channels of the marked water trail and not attempt to land or walk on the fragile marsh vegetation. Finally, the marsh is closed to boaters during waterfowl hunting season to provide the birds with undisturbed shelter. These closures are posted seasonally. If all these logistics seem like too much of a hassle, consider joining an Audubon-led trip so you can leave the planning to the professionals.

Though the 270-acre marsh with its uncommon birds is the main attraction at this site, the protected uplands also have a variety of birds. A short path marked with yellow trail markers branches off the blue trail to the boardwalk into the woods and leads to a rock shelter. Woodland passerines, including Worm-eating Warbler and Scarlet Tanager, nest here. Warren Landing Road follows Indian Brook, where Louisiana Waterthrush breeds. Whether you bird Constitution Marsh by land or by boat, it is one of the most scenic marshes on the Hudson, and fortunately, it has been set aside as a sanctuary for birds.

Muscoot Farm

GPS ADDRESS 51 NY 100, Katonah
LATITUDE/LONGITUDE 41.26137 −73.72507
DIRECTIONS From I-684, take Exit 6, NY 35/Cross River/ Katonah. Turn right onto NY 35 west and continue 1.6 miles to NY 100. Turn left onto NY 100 south, and go 1.2 miles to the parking area for the farm on the right. Trail map available on-site.

Muscoot Farm is maintained by the Westchester County Department of Parks, Recreation, and Conservation (Westchester County Parks) as a turn-of-the-century demonstration dairy farm. The historic property was home to three generations of the Hopkins family. The family patriarch made his money in pharmaceuticals, and used the farm as a summer retreat at first; but in 1924, the family moved to Westchester County permanently, and ran the dairy farm until 1967. Today, this award-winning living museum is open to the public year-round. The summer camps and weekend programs, which run the gamut from farmers' markets to fairy walks, draw crowds to the area around the farm buildings; but with 777 acres, it is easy to find quiet, birdy areas away from people. The farm borders the Muscoot River and Reservoir to the north and east, and the New Croton Reservoir to the south, so it is embedded in the protected landscape of New York City Watershed property. In addition, the western part of the farm property has been set aside as a bio-diversity reserve, so only about seventy acres are actually used for agriculture, and the farmland creates habitat diversity in the otherwise wooded landscape.

The entrance road brings visitors to the farm buildings, where there are trail maps, restrooms, and exhibits. This area is often quite busy, but the property has more than seven miles of well-marked trails through a variety of habitats. The Woodland Trail (red) is only 0.5 mile long, but it passes through a small hardwood forest that has had Red-headed Woodpecker. This trail also passes by an arm of the New Croton Reservoir, a good place to look for waterfowl and shorebirds.

The yellow trail, which branches off the farm road, makes a long loop of more than 3.5 miles through the perimeter of the property, but there are many options for shorter walks. A gazebo at the top of a hill looks down on fields and shrublands, and although many of the hayfields are mowed too often to allow breeding, some grassland birds stop in during migration. The farm is investigating the feasibility of creating and maintaining breeding habitat for grassland birds on some parts of the property. Field edges on the yellow trail near the biodiversity reserve support Indigo Bunting, Prairie Warbler, and Blue-winged Warbler. The manure piles, which move around a bit, can also have interesting sparrows, especially in winter, and should not be overlooked. The ice pond on the yellow trail near the center of the property has a small observation platform, a good place to see Spotted Sandpiper and Solitary Sandpiper along the edges and Yellow-throated Vireo in the trees. The white trail south of the ice pond passes through a south-facing forest that is especially good for warblers during spring migration.

Red-headed Woodpecker (male).
© Alan W. Wells.

Croton Point Park

GPS ADDRESS 7 Croton Point Avenue, Croton-on-Hudson

LATITUDE/LONGITUDE 41.18833 −73.88681

DIRECTIONS From the Taconic State Parkway, take the exit for NY 134 w/Ossining. Drive about 3.0 miles to its junction with NY 9A, and take 9A north (right) 2.1 miles toward Croton-on-Hudson. Take the Croton Point Avenue exit, and turn left onto Croton Point Avenue toward the Croton Harmon train station. Cross over the bridge, and enter the park at the sign. There is free parking on the entrance road near the baseball fields. From here, it is a short walk to the most productive birding areas. Map at parks.westchestergov.com.

Croton Point is a large, five-hundred-acre peninsula that juts out from the eastern shore of the Lower Hudson River, with Haverstraw Bay to the north and the Croton River and Bay to the south and east. The property is rich in natural and cultural history, and is owned and managed by Westchester County. Because the park includes a beach, pool, playgrounds, and a campground, this area is a sea of humanity in summer; but during the rest of the year, it is a birding paradise.

Croton Point is a natural stopover site for birds migrating along the Hudson. Moreover, the park is a large area of relatively undeveloped land in a semi-urban landscape, so birds settle here to feed and rest. One of the main attractions for birders is a large, capped landfill that has been planted with grasses and, with input from a coalition of local bird clubs, is being managed as much as possible as habitat for grassland birds. Mowing is limited to pathways that are needed to monitor the landfill's wells. Conveniently for birders, these wells are marked with stakes that some birds use as perches. The landfill "hill" has a trail around the perimeter and another that runs over the top. With a spotting scope, this elevated vantage point offers great views of birds on the rivers and Croton Bay.

During the spring migration and the breeding season, Bobolink, Savannah Sparrow, Vesper Sparrow, Field Sparrow, Grasshopper Sparrow, and Eastern Meadowlark are seen. This same habitat supports an interesting assortment of sparrows during fall migration, including White-crowned Sparrow and Fox Sparrow. Short-eared Owl winters here most years, along with Northern Harrier, American Kestrel, and Rough-legged Hawk. Bald Eagles congregate along this section of the river in winter, especially when it freezes farther north, and perch on ice floes and trees along the edge. In winter, the

Vesper Sparrow, one of the uncommon sparrows seen in migration at Croton Point.
© Carena M. Pooth.

Snow Bunting and Horned Larks feeding on weed seeds in winter.
© Bruce Dudek.

landfill is also good for Horned Lark, Snow Bunting, Lapland Longspur, and American Pipit. Upland Sandpiper has been seen during migration. Waterfowl on the river and in Croton Bay are most diverse in winter and early spring.

Many visitors to Croton Park go to the top of the landfill and miss other parts of the park. Wilson's Snipe and Woodcock can be found along the landfill perimeter trail in spring. This same trail has had a Yellow-breasted Chat and other rare warblers. A road to the right outside the entry gate leads to the Airfield 1 picnic area, an area used by model-airplane clubs. This wooded part of the park has tall trees and impressive warbler numbers each spring, and Red-headed Woodpecker has been seen in this area. The park also has a nature center with some shoreline woods and access to an area of seminatural Hudson River shoreline that can be good for shorebirds at low tide. Great Horned Owl nests in the campground, and half-hardy species overwinter along the lower trail to Teller's Point. Croton Point may be the best birding site in Westchester County. It never disappoints, and sometimes it produces wonderful surprises.

Teatown Lake Reservation

GPS ADDRESS 1600 Spring Valley Road, Ossining

LATITUDE/LONGITUDE 41.21110 −73.82694

DIRECTIONS From the Taconic State Parkway, take the exit for NY 134/Ossining. Take 134 west about 0.25 mile and turn right onto Spring Valley Road. Continue about 1.0 mile, bearing left at the fork. The nature center parking lot is on the right immediately after the building. Map at www.teatown.org and on-site.

This privately owned, nonprofit nature preserve and education center is one of the best-known environmental organizations in the Lower Hudson Valley. Founded in 1963 by a donation of land from the heirs of Gerald Swopes, the preserve has grown to about one thousand acres through acquisitions and hard work by its board of directors, staff, and dedicated volunteers. In keeping with its Westchester County surroundings, Teatown Lake Reservation is an elegant preserve. The nature center, adjacent to the paved parking lot, is housed in a Tudor-style building that was once a stable and carriage house. As a part of its educational mission and fund-raising, the preserve hosts many programs for school groups, weekend events such as its famous Eagle Fest, a maple syrup festival, a plant sale, and summer camps. The nature center includes classrooms, live animal exhibits, a gift shop, and offices. At Teatown Lake, individual trees are fenced to protect them from the beaver.

The preserve has fifteen miles of meticulously maintained trails with markers, boardwalks, and signage; trails are open to the public from dawn to dusk year-round without charge. The preserve includes lakes, streams, swamps, vernal pools, meadows, conifer stands, and mixed and deciduous forests. A power line right-of-way through the property adds shrubland habitat that is not usually found at sites in Westchester County, which is naturally wooded.

The large gated and fenced area between the nature center and the lake is known as Wildflower Woods. It is the site of an ambitious restoration project to create sustainable forest by excluding deer and reintroducing native plants. The restored area makes it possible to imagine what the woods of Westchester County might have looked like when deer populations were under the control of natural predators.

Teatown Lake is a shallow and marshy, so it attracts many dabbling ducks and other birds that feed in low water. The Lakeside Trail, around its perime-

Female Baltimore Oriole gathering nesting material.
© Deborah Tracy-Kral.

ter, is the most popular hike in the preserve. The easy 1.5-mile circuit includes a six-hundred-foot boardwalk and an observation blind. The lake is always in view, waterfowl and herons are abundant, and Baltimore Oriole and many other riparian-loving passerines breed along the shoreline. Shorebirds use the edges and shallows during migration.

Birders also love the Hidden Valley hike, which begins behind the nature center parking lot. Slightly more challenging, this trail has a variety of bird habitats in a 1.8-mile loop, including a short boardwalk through a sedge wetland, a meadow, several vernal pools, laurel groves, a babbling brook, and rock outcrops in deciduous woods. The newly created Twin Lakes Trail, with its trailhead across the road from the visitor center, is sure to become a favorite as well. This 2.3-mile loop passes by two lakes that are deeper than Teatown and therefore attract different waterfowl. The trail crosses the power line twice, and runs through several wet areas. Griffin Swamp, accessible off the Cliffdale/Teatown Trail from Teatown Lake, hosts a nice variety of low-woods birds and winter finches.

Rockefeller State Park Preserve

GPS ADDRESS 1 Tower Hill Road, Pleasantville
LATITUDE/LONGITUDE 41.11157 –73.83650
DIRECTIONS From Pleasantville, take NY 117/Phelps Way south 2.75 miles to the entrance to Rockefeller State Park Preserve at Tower Hill Road on the south (left) side of the road. Map at parks.ny.gov/parks.

In 1983, the Rockefeller family donated fourteen hundred acres of its Pocantico Hills estate to OPRHP, to create the Rockefeller State Park Preserve in western/central Westchester County. The use of the term "preserve" in the name is unusual and deliberate. It acknowledges the outstanding ecological value of the property, an oasis of natural and seminatural habitats set aside for passive recreation in a landscape of dense suburban development. The land encompasses the forested hills and valley streams of the Pocantico River watershed, but the public is also allowed to use the adjacent Rockefeller Family Trails, which provide access to many acres of beautiful farmland. The disjunct Rockwood Hall area in the northwest corner of the park includes the property that once surrounded the 220-room home of William Rockefeller. Though only the foundations remain, this area has large tracts of open habitat and panoramic views of the Hudson River.

One of the features of this park that makes it particularly attractive to birders is its extensive forty-five-mile network of carriage paths. Because these were originally designed for horses instead of hikers or cars, the grades are gentle and the paths are wide. Visitors enter the park from the parking lot on NY 117, where the path leads past the visitor center, a bird-feeding area, and an art gallery with rotating exhibits to twenty-two-acre Swan Lake. Because this preserve is located less than an hour's drive from New York City, it sees many visitors. Foot traffic is especially heavy near the entrance, and for this reason, it is best to visit Swan Lake early in the day before the park gets too busy. In season, the lake attracts cormorants, a diversity of waterfowl and waders, and even shorebirds at the southern outlet, but these birds retreat into the vegetation around the edges when there are too many people.

Rockefeller is best known for the amazing mixed warbler flocks that pass through the property in spring and fall. The migrants love the wet, buggy edges of Swan Lake, but many of the thirty-four species reported from the park are equally abundant and sometimes more easily seen in other, less

Blue-winged Warbler, one of the more common warblers at Rockefeller State Park Preserve. © Bruce Dudek.

visited parts of the preserve. Eagle Hill makes for a fine hawkwatch, and the nearby Pocantico River Trail is good for vireos, Worm-eating Warbler, and rarely, Kentucky Warbler. The mature forests and hemlock stands along the 13 Bridges Loop and Witch's Spring Trails attract conifer-loving warbler species, as well as migrating Gray-cheeked Thrush and Swainson's Thrush. The trail up Buttermilk Hill and Lucy's Loop in the far northeast corner is highly recommended. With woods, swamps, streams, adjacent fields, and a nearby power line, this area has impressive bird diversity. Orchard Oriole is reliable at the bottom of Buttermilk Hill. The Rockwood Hall part of the preserve, west of NY 9 on the Hudson River, offers an entirely different birding experience, with open fields, estate-like habitat, and river views of gulls and eagles. On a good day in May, the variety of birds tallied on the Rockefeller property can easily approach a hundred species.

Cranberry Lake Preserve

GPS ADDRESS 1615 Old Orchard Street, West Harrison
LATITUDE/LONGITUDE 41.08195 −73.75577
DIRECTIONS From I-684, take Exit 3 and turn onto NY 22 south.
Continue 4.2 miles to a traffic light, and turn left onto Quarry Heights/
Old Orchard Street. In less the 0.1 mile, turn right at the sign for
Cranberry Lake Preserve. If the gate is closed, park here. Otherwise,
proceed on the entry road to the parking area by the nature lodge.
Map at parks.westchestergov.com.

Cranberry Lake Preserve is a lightly birded "biodiversity reserve area" that
is part of the protected watershed for the Kensico Reservoir. The 190-acre
property has been managed by Westchester County Parks since 1967, and the
county runs ecology camps here in July and August; but most of the time,
this park is a relatively quiet place. Because the land is ecologically sensitive, pets, swimming, fishing, and biking are prohibited, thereby creating a
welcome respite from the crowded conditions at many public lands in this
densely populated part of the Hudson Valley. Given the site's rich habitats,
well-maintained trails, interesting history, and easy access, it is a mystery why
Cranberry Lake Preserve has received so little attention from skilled birders.

The centerpiece of the preserve is a four-acre, spring-fed glacial kettle
hole called Cranberry Lake. The wetland area to the south of the lake includes a shrub swamp, marsh, and two smaller bodies of water, South Pond
and Hush Pond. Beaver are active here, so bridges and trails are sometimes
flooded. The deciduous woods around the wetland are mostly very mature
hardwoods with a full and intact understory; this is unusual for Westchester
County because of its large deer population. There are also impressive bedrock outcrops throughout the area. Past land use in the southern part of the
preserve is linked to this bedrock, which was quarried to build the Kensico
dam that stands less than a mile to the west. The remnants of quarry operation, including parts of the stonecutting shed, the crushing plant foundation,
the quarry ponds, an old railroad bed, and trestle remains, are visible on the
preserve's History Trail (purple).

There is an extensive trail network, and although it is well marked with
colored trail markers, it can be confusing because many of the trails overlap

Northern Flicker nestlings almost ready to fledge. © Scott Stoner, Naturelogues.

and run together in places. There are actually four loop trails that vary in length from 1.0 to 2.4 miles. Birders can use the white and orange connector trails to combine paths and see the diversity of bird habitats the preserve has to offer. The blue trail goes around Cranberry Lake and South Pond, but it connects to the History Trail, which can be used to climb to the top of the quarry to scan for raptors and explore the quarry ponds and surrounding shrubby habitat. The quarry is near a small waterfall with a nice bench, and the southeast corner of South Pond has a bird observation tower that looks out on an extensive alder swamp. From the tower, the red Perimeter Trail leads south to Hush Pond, a quiet, boggy area where Northern Waterthrush breeds and Barred Owl has been heard calling during the day. The Bent Bridge on a connector trail along the west side of the marsh, between Cranberry Lake and South Pond, is a boardwalk with great views into the wetland. The combined purple and red trails north of the Bent Bridge on the edge of the preserve pass through a beautiful, mature woods with huge bedrock outcrops and spectacular stone walls that were built to delineate watershed property boundaries. This trail ends near a vernal pool with an observation deck close to the nature lodge parking area.

Arthur W. Butler Memorial Sanctuary and Chestnut Ridge Hawkwatch

GPS ADDRESS 265 Chestnut Ridge Road, Bedford

LATITUDE/LONGITUDE 41.18159 −73.68632

DIRECTIONS From I-684, take Exit 4 Bedford/Mount Kisco/NY 172 and follow 172 west toward Mount Kisco about 0.25 mile to Chestnut Ridge Road on the left. Follow Chestnut Ridge Road about 1.5 miles to The Nature Conservancy's Butler Sanctuary entrance on the right, and cross the bridge to the parking lot. Map at www.nature.org.

Large areas of natural habitat are few and far between in highly developed Westchester County, but the Arthur W. Butler Memorial Sanctuary is The Nature Conservancy's oldest preserve, and it has been protected and managed as conservation land since 1954. Although some of its rocky woods were farmed long ago, the sanctuary's forests are typical of what parts of the Lower Hudson Valley must have been like when the land was more gently used. Butler Sanctuary is right next to I-684, and in the parking lot, the road noise from the nearby highway is distressing. However, the preserve is 363 acres, and the hilly terrain and wooded landscape quickly muffle the noise as you move away from the highway. Walking west soon leads into a lovely forest where it is easier to hear the birds.

The preserve has more than five miles of trails and a variety of habitats, including red maple swamps and several kinds of forest. Stone walls from its agricultural past are found throughout the property. The Nature Conservancy and its volunteers are working to remove invasive exotic species such as barberry, and a limited bow-hunting season is permitted in an effort to manage the deer population.

Some of the interesting bird habitats include a wetland edge and moist deciduous forest on the northeast corner of the property, and a red maple swamp on the northwest side. A white spur trail off the northern part of the red trail leads to an overlook called Sunset Ledge. The yellow trail has spectacular glacial erratics, and the southern part includes a steep section of switchbacks through rocky outcrops with ancient dying hemlocks. These woods are full of warblers in spring, and Worm-eating Warbler is common.

In the fall, Butler Sanctuary is home to Bedford Audubon's Chestnut Ridge

Hawkwatch, purportedly the best place to watch migrating raptors in Westchester County. The watch is located on the Butler Sanctuary property on a rock outcrop above I-684 at the southern terminus of the orange trail. The path begins on the left side of the parking lot, and continues a short distance uphill to an observation platform with bleacher seating and a panoramic view north to the foothills of the Taconics, east into Connecticut, and south all the way to Long Island Sound. Migrating raptors make their way south in the fall on broad fronts and tend to avoid water, so the sight of Long Island Sound steers the birds inland over the hawkwatch. Chestnut Ridge is staffed by trained raptor counters from August 15 to December 1; they contribute data to the Hawk Migration Association of North America that is used to monitor populations of hawks, falcons, ospreys, vultures, and eagles. A cool, crisp, fall day in mid-September with a northwest or sometimes northeast wind can bring a thousand Broad-winged Hawks over the hawkwatch.

Marshlands Conservancy

GPS ADDRESS 220 US 1/Boston Post Road, Rye
LATITUDE/LONGITUDE 40.95778 –73.70428
DIRECTIONS From I-95, take Exit 19 for the Playland Parkway/Rye/Harrison. Once on the parkway, take an immediate right toward Rye/Harrison. Turn left and continue to a T intersection. Turn right and go 0.3 mile toward Mamaroneck, and continue straight where the road joins US 1. Go 0.8 mile to the entrance for Marshlands Conservancy, marked by a sign on the east (left) side of the road, just after the Rye Country Club.

Westchester County is the only county in the Hudson Valley that touches on the salt waters of Long Island Sound, and that makes Marshlands Conservancy a very special place for birds. This preserve has salt marsh, tidal creeks, mudflats, and other uncommon habitats that are rarely found in good condition in New York State, except perhaps on Long Island. Fortunately, the 150 acres at Marshlands Conservancy are owned and managed by Westchester County Parks, which provides public access to about a half mile of shoreline along Milton Harbor, an inlet of Long Island Sound. The land was once part of the estate owned by the family of John Jay, the country's first chief justice. The house is adjacent to the preserve, and the family cemetery is fenced off within the property.

MARSHLANDS CONSERVANCY

Westchester County Parks runs summer ecology camps on the property in July and early August, and the preserve includes a very small nature/visitor center next to the parking lot. Trail maps are available when this center is open. There are three miles of unmarked but obvious trails on the property. With the exception of two short trails that dead-end to the west on the north and south sides of the meadow, all of the trails are mostly level, easy walking loops through varied habitats.

The Marshlands property runs from the north near US 1 to the salt marsh and Long Island Sound to the south. The trails immediately south of the nature/visitor center, which is at the north end of the property, lead into a forest with seasonal streams, occasional patches of underbrush, small wet-lands, and near the shore, some huge trees that were uprooted during Super Storm Sandy. For the most part, these woods have very little understory, but they still support Wild Turkey, nesting Great Horned Owl, flycatchers, and woodpeckers, as well as a good variety of warblers during migration. Just west of the nature/visitor center, a mowed trail follows the edge of the woods along a large, beautiful, managed meadow that is a good place for grassland birds and American Woodcock in early spring. This path is also the most direct route to the shore.

Although the forest and meadow contribute diversity to the Marshlands Conservancy bird list, which stands at about three hundred species, most

Northern Harrier hunting over a salt marsh. © Deborah Tracy-Kral.

Common Tern foraging over Long Island Sound at Marshlands Conservancy. © Alan W. Wells.

birders come here to see the species that use the salt marsh and sound. The loop trail around Marie's Neck passes through a variety of shoreline habitats, including scrub and high and low salt marsh. There are several benches along the way that offer delightful views of mudflats, open water, marsh, and rocky shores. An Osprey nest is visible from shore; and egrets, herons, and an occasional ibis hunt in the marsh. This stretch of shoreline is also the place to see gulls and terns and salt marsh passerines like Saltmarsh, Nelson's, and Seaside Sparrow. Waterfowl, for which Long Island Sound is famous, reach their peak diversity in early spring but are often interesting throughout the winter. Shorebirds are abundant. Vagrants and rarities such as Wood Sandpiper, American Avocet, Ruff, Red-necked Phalarope, and King Rail are just a few of the unusual species that have been recorded at Marshlands. The trail out to Parson's Point on the east part of the property should not be missed. It features rock outcrops and views of the tidal creek, and offers the opportunity to scan the water to the east. It is best to visit this area at low tide, when the shallows and mudflats are exposed and shorebirds are most abundant.

Edith G. Read Wildlife Sanctuary

GPS ADDRESS 1 Playland Parkway, Rye
LATITUDE/LONGITUDE 40.96532 −73.67966
DIRECTIONS From I-95, take Exit 19, Playland Parkway, and go east on Playland Parkway about 1.6 miles around a traffic circle. Continue to the far northeast (right) corner of the large parking lot near the lake.

Edith G. Read Wildlife Sanctuary is an unusual place in many ways. Immediately adjacent to Playland, a historic amusement park and recreation area, the sanctuary is strategically located on Long Island Sound, offering birders

EDITH G. READ WILDLIFE SANCTUARY

a chance to see many species that are rare or absent in other parts of the Hudson Valley. This preserve is a great place to see birds, but the logistics of gaining entry are challenging for those who do not know the area.

Both Playland and the 179-acre wildlife sanctuary are owned and operated by Westchester County Parks. The amusement area includes rides, a game room, an indoor ice rink that stays open in winter for youth hockey, food vendors, boating on the lake, a marina, and a restaurant. The entrance to Edith Read is marked by a sign at the far end of the parking lot near the last roller-coaster and Manursing Lake, a.k.a. Playland Lake. Whenever Playland is open, usually from May to October (except on Mondays), there is a parking fee; but for six months of the year, parking is free. The driveway from the parking lot into the nature center is also gated, and automobile access is limited to Friends of Read Wildlife Sanctuary. For a nominal fee, regular visitors may want to join this organization and obtain a bar-coded access card for the gate. However, nonmembers are welcome to walk the flat, quarter-mile driveway to the nature center and trailheads.

While these gates and restrictions may seem like a hassle, they are a small price to pay for the opportunity to visit one of the premier Important Bird Areas in New York State. Just to the left of the entry road, eighty-five-acre Manursing (Playland) Lake sports a reliably diverse collection of waterfowl for most of the winter and early spring. Open to Long Island Sound and unlikely to freeze, this area is a good place to see both Lesser and Greater Scaup, Red-breasted Merganser, Hooded Merganser, Canvasback, American Wigeon, and Bufflehead. The deck at the boathouse offers shelter from the elements and a convenient place to set up a spotting scope to take in every bird the lake has to offer, from ducks to waders to kingfishers and gulls.

Just across the road from the lake are the beach and Long Island Sound, where wintering scoters, Brant, Northern Gannet, Long-tailed Duck, Common Goldeneye, Red-throated Loon, Red-necked Grebe, and Horned Grebe are regularly reported. Most of these birds are seen at a distance, and a spotting scope is needed to identify many of them. Seawatching—standing in

Purple Sandpiper is seen in winter on the rocky shoreline at Playland Amusement Park next door to Edith G. Read Sanctuary. © Deborah Tracy-Kral.

one place and watching birds on water at great distance—frustrates many beginners. Like hawkwatching, identifying birds at sea takes practice and depends on using less traditional characteristics such as size, flight style, posture, and flock structure. For anyone still cultivating these skills, it is helpful to visit this site as a part of an organized field trip, where more experienced birders can help with IDs and share their insights. Closer to shore, the jetties and rocks are good places to find wintering Purple Sandpiper, American Oystercatcher, and other shorebirds.

In addition to waterfront viewing, the sanctuary has three miles of trails that are open from dawn to dusk. In winter, Horned Lark, Snow Bunting, and occasionally American Pipit are found in the open areas along the driveway. The bird feeders at the nature center are usually stocked, and an Osprey platform is visible from the trails leading west from the center. While all of the trails at Edith Read are level and well maintained, they vary from mowed paths (on the eastern perimeter) to boardwalks (near the center) to woodsy foot trails (along the lake). The trail along the lake has several nice vantage points for viewing the islands and backwaters, and the far north end near Manursing Way leads to views of the marsh. Though disturbed and heavily used, Edith Read Sanctuary's unique combination of location on Long Island Sound and good public access makes it a required birding stop for any serious Hudson Valley birder. The site provides an unprecedented opportunity to diversify your bird list.

Beyond the Ten Counties
NEARBY SITES TOO GREAT TO BE MISSED

I chose to limit the geographic coverage of this book to the ten Hudson Valley counties that border the Hudson River between the Troy dam and New York City because I wanted to define a manageable piece of real estate for the birdwatching sites. This area matches a region that is widely used to market Hudson Valley tourism, and destinations within it are generally suitable for day trips. This practical decision and limited space forced me to exclude many wonderful birding spots, but a few unique sites stood out from all the rest. The following much-loved birding destinations are just outside the ten-county region, but each is truly exceptional and definitely worth a visit.

Vischer Ferry Nature and Historic Preserve

GPS ADDRESS 15 Riverview Road, Clifton Park

LATITUDE/LONGITUDE 42.79299 −73.79585

DIRECTIONS From I-87, take Exit 8, turn west onto Crescent Road, and continue 2.0 miles to Van Vranken Road. Follow Van Vranken Road 1.0 mile to a T intersection with Riverview Road. Cross Riverview Road into the main parking lot next to the historic Whipple bridge over the old Erie Canal. Parking is also available at the end of Ferry Drive about 2.0 miles farther west on Riverview Road just past the firehouse, and at Clute's Dry Dock about 1.5 miles east.

Located on the north shore of the Mohawk River in southern Saratoga County, Vischer Ferry Nature and Historic Preserve is one of the premier birding sites in the Capital Region. In 1727, Clifton Park's first settlement, Forts Ferry, grew up around the ferry crossing at this narrow point in the river. The Erie Canal was built here in the early 1800s using laborers from the town, and it finally opened between Albany and Buffalo in 1825. The restored

Whipple Truss Bridge at Vischer Ferry actually crossed the canal at another location and was relocated here, while Clute's Dry Dock serviced the packet boats. This section of the Erie Canal was eventually abandoned when the Barge Canal opened in 1917. As a part of the canal's construction, the Mohawk River was dammed, which made it navigable but raised water levels so that the towns along the river suffered intolerable seasonal flooding. Eventually the communities were abandoned, but what remains today is a preserve with easy access to the Mohawk River, wonderful freshwater wetlands, and fascinating historic remnants of the canals, locks, and towpaths.

The trails at Vischer Ferry are generally unmarked, with only occasional signage, but it is difficult to get seriously lost because the preserve boundary is Riverview Road to the north and the Mohawk River to the south. From the Whipple bridge at the main parking area, a wide north/south trail follows a power line directly to the river, with wetlands on either side. Trails also follow the old canal's towpath, running both east and west from the bridge, and the towpath trail continues mostly along the river into the Town of Halfmoon.

More than two hundred species have been seen at Vischer Ferry. Water levels fluctuate both annually and seasonally at this site, making the appearance of shorebirds, waders, and waterfowl somewhat unpredictable. Most birders favor the trails west of the entrance because they offer a variety of habitats, but there is hardly any part of the preserve that has not, at one time or another, turned up something unexpected.

The marshes west of the parking area can be viewed most easily from the

Ring-necked Ducks. © Deborah Tracy-Kral.

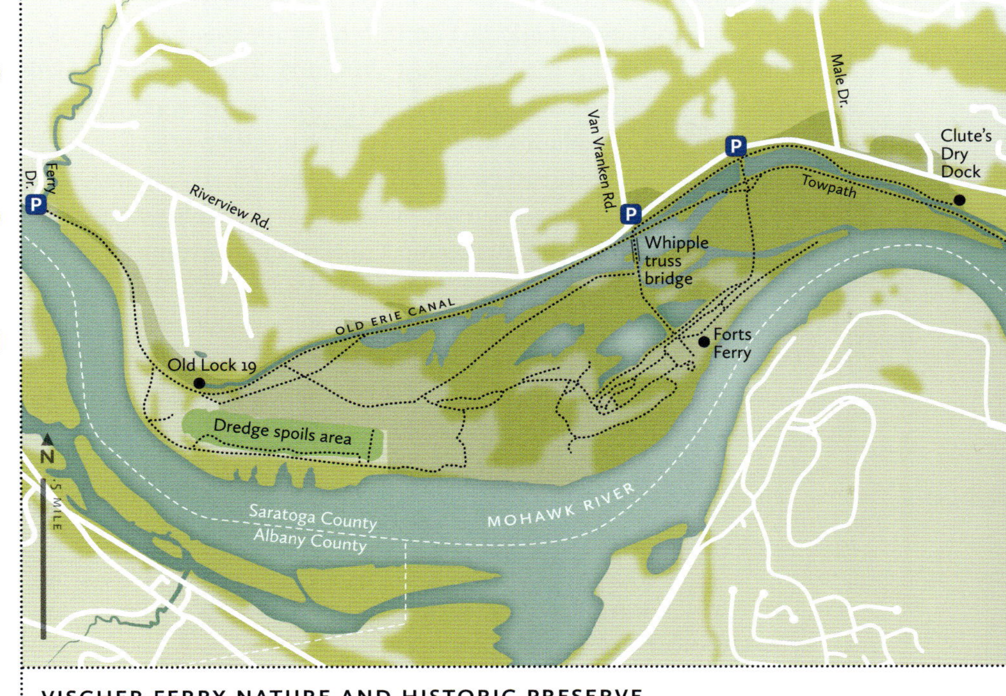

VISCHER FERRY NATURE AND HISTORIC PRESERVE

towpath, which has regular observation points that jut out into the wetland. The waterfowl, for which Vischer Ferry is famous, often congregate in greatest densities in the ponds along the towpath, especially in early April and then again in the fall. Ring-necked Duck and Hooded Merganser are sometimes common, along with larger numbers of Mallard and Canada Goose. American Wigeon, Northern Shoveler, Northern Pintail, Wood Duck, Gadwall, Green-winged and Blue-winged Teal, Common Gallinule, and Pied-billed Grebe occur annually. During migration, shorebirds use exposed mudflats along the wetland edge, and Rusty Blackbirds call from trees along the towpath. From the cover of the towpath trail, one can scan the edge of the marsh for secretive marsh birds such as Virginia Rail, American Bittern, and Sora. Least Bittern breeds in the marsh close to the parking area. Great Blue Herons are present whenever there is open water, but other waders, such as Great Egret, Green Heron, and occasionally, Black-crowned Night-Heron, are most common in the fall as a part of post-breeding dispersal.

A hike down the west towpath can be extended into a three-mile loop through mixed habitats by taking a trail to the south about 1.0 mile from the Whipple bridge. This path leads past a prohibited-access dredge spoils area and into woods with areas of tall dead trees (good for woodpeckers), a small spruce grove, deciduous woods, and pines bordering fields. Migrating songbirds, especially thrushes, warblers, and flycatchers, are likely in all these habitats. The trail emerges from the woods at the Mohawk River and continues east along the river for about 0.8 mile, with opportunities to view gulls, waterfowl, Belted Kingfisher, Osprey, and Bald Eagle. The birds on the river can be especially interesting in winter if the water remains free of ice. The shrubby woodland along the eastern part of the river-edge trail has had American Woodcock in early spring. From the river, there are two trails north back to the towpath. Both routes offer good views of the wetlands, and a variety of sparrows feed in the grassy edges along the trail.

Bashakill Wildlife Management Area

GPS LOCATION (Haven Road parking lot): 30 Haven Road, Wurtsboro
LATITUDE/LONGITUDE 41.53775 −74.51964
DIRECTIONS From NY 17, take Exit 113 and follow US 209 south about 2.0 miles toward Port Jervis to Haven Road. Turn east and continue about 0.25 mile to the NYSDEC parking lot on the left.

A birding destination for nearly half a century, the Bashakill sits in the valley between the Catskill Mountains and the Shawangunk Ridge at the southeastern edge of Sullivan County. Here, Bashakill Creek flows south on its way to the Neversink River and later the Delaware, spreading out across the basin to form the largest freshwater wetland in southeastern New York. Historically, much of the area was drained and farmed by settlers hoping to market crops via the Delaware and Hudson canal that ran though the Bashakill Valley in the nineteenth century (sections of the old towpath and an abandoned railbed have been incorporated into trails around the wetland). In 1972, NYSDEC established the Bashakill Wildlife Management Area and built a permanent dam at the south end to stabilize water levels and create habitat for waterfowl and other wetland species. The DEC improved public access by building parking areas, boat launches, trails, and observation towers. Today, the Bashakill is a magnificent three-thousand-acre natural area that is loved

BASHAKILL WILDLIFE MANAGEMENT AREA

and protected by birdwatchers and outdoor enthusiasts from all over New York State. This site is probably at its best from March to early June, and it is wise to avoid the fall hunting season.

The Bashakill is best known for its waterfowl, waders, Bald Eagle, and Osprey, but it also attracts large numbers of migrants, including warblers. The cumulative list for this Bird Conservation Area has more than two hundred species, including many rarities. The wetland is about six miles long, with access points off US 209 on the northwest and South Road on the south-

American Bittern in its concealment pose, with its bill pointed skyward.
© Deborah Tracy-Kral.

east. Lightly traveled Haven Road, which runs between 209 and South Road through the middle of the Bashakill, is the mostly frequently visited site. A large parking area on the north side provides easy access to a one-lane bridge and causeway with great views of the marsh in both directions. One of several waterfowl viewing sites, this road is also a good place to study swallows, because in spring, as many as five species may gather on the power lines to feed over the marsh.

Local birders at the Bashakill have given their favorite birding areas local names that do not appear on maps. A dirt road to the north along the wetland on the southeast side of Haven Road leads to an area known as "the Orchard." The parking area is just past the orchard itself. The Orchard is known for its warblers, vireos, sparrows, and thrushes. The road is gated to the north, but the Stop Sign foot trail leads through a brushy area along the marsh where American Bittern has been heard in spring. There is an observation tower over Moosehead Cove.

Along South Road south of Haven Road, the main boat launch offers a good view of the islands and dead trees favored by Bald Eagle and Osprey. It also provides access to the Birch Trail, which follows the old railroad bed northeast to an observation tower. During spring migration, Rusty Blackbird and secretive marsh birds such as American Bittern, Virginia Rail, and Sora are reported from this area. A mile south of the main boat launch is the parking area for the Nature Trail, another excellent birding area known for its warblers and thrushes. The trail features areas of brushy second growth with grasses and fruiting shrubs, a boardwalk through a dry streambed, and an observation tower that looks north and west into the southern part of the marsh.

Finally, Deli Fields is the local name for the Bashakill's best meadow. The dirt road to this area leaves US 209 opposite a deli and post office, and ends at a boat launch. This area is wonderful habitat for sparrows and Eastern Bluebirds, and grassland nesters visit this site during spring migration. On sunny days, an Eastern Screech-Owl can sometimes be seen sitting in a hole in a tree on the edge of these fields.

Franklin Mountain Hawkwatch

GPS ADDRESS 52 Grange Hall Road Spur, Oneonta
LATITUDE/LONGITUDE 42.42697 −75.04866
DIRECTIONS From I-88, take Exit 15 NY 23/NY 28 south toward Oneonta and Davenport. Turn left at the bottom of the ramp and then right by the light at the MacDonald's onto NY 23/28 south. Go 0.7 mile to the fourth traffic light, and turn left. At the T intersection, turn left again onto Southside Drive. Go 0.8 mile on Southside Drive, then turn right onto Swart Hollow Road, and follow it 1.5 miles to Grange Hall Road. Take a sharp right turn onto Grange Hall Road and go 0.2 mile. Then take a sharp left turn onto Grange Hall Road Spur, park on the right, and walk up the hill to the hawkwatch.

Whereas Bald Eagle is now fairly common in the Hudson Valley, Golden Eagle is a bird of open habitats, and is rare in the forested landscape of the Northeast. However, a small population breeds in the tundra of eastern Canada, and these birds migrate through New York. A small number also spend the winter here. If you want to see a Golden Eagle, Franklin Mountain Hawkwatch at

FRANKLIN MOUNTAIN HAWKWATCH

the Delaware-Otsego Audubon Society Sanctuary in Oneonta is the place to go. Research using Golden Eagles outfitted with GPS technology has shown that most of the eagle population that breeds in eastern Canada migrates through New York, and many of the eagles travel down the Susquehanna River Valley, right over this site.

Franklin Mountain is part of the hundred-acre wildlife sanctuary owned and managed by the Delaware-Otsego Audubon Society. The property has mowed fields, old pastures and second-growth forest, and three loop trails, all less than a mile long. The hawkwatch observation platform at the top of the hill is a wooden structure with a few benches, hay bales, a bird feeder, and educational displays. It has a spectacular 180-degree view of the valley below. Dedicated observers from the Delaware-Otsego Audubon Society count raptors at this site from August 15 to January 1. Their data can then be used by the Hawk Migration Association of North America to monitor raptor populations.

In the course of the fall season, Franklin Mountain usually sees about

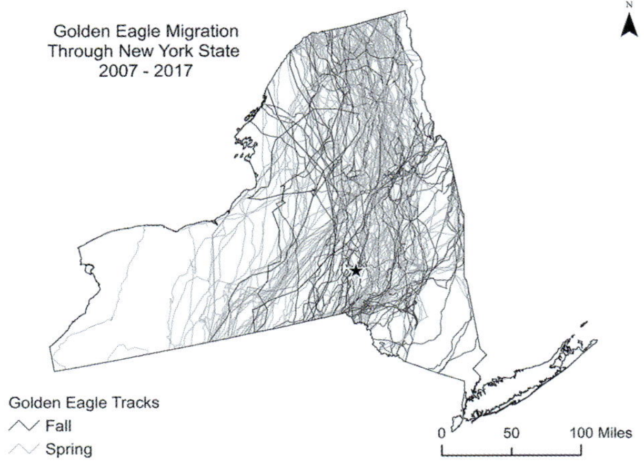

Golden Eagle migratory tracks through New York State. The star
shows the location of Franklin Mountain Hawkwatch. Cartographer:
Tricia A. Miller. Golden Eagle data: Conservation Science Global, Inc.
West Virginia University and Eastern Golden Eagle Working Group.
Background data: ESRI.

Golden Eagle, a late fall migrant at Franklin Mountain.
© Deborah Tracy-Kral.

fifteen different raptor species, but Red-tailed Hawk, Broad-winged Hawk, and Sharp-shinned Hawk are most abundant. The best flights take place on cool, crisp days with favorable winds from the northwest. The Broad-wings peak during the third week in September, while Red-tails and Sharpies come through in October. Golden Eagles, on the other hand, are late fall migrants whose numbers peak in mid-November. Therefore, the great Golden days at Franklin Mountain, with double-digit counts, are often very cold and windy, but nothing beats the thrill of satisfying long looks at New York's rarest eagle.

10 Species Accounts

10   Species Accounts

This chapter is a guide to the seasonal abundance of birds in the Hudson Valley. To a large degree, seeing birds involves being in the right place at the right time. While more than 400 species have been recorded in our area, this section focuses on just 284 that occur here regularly—meaning that most of them can be found somewhere in the valley almost every year. The exceptions are irruptive species, which normally reside farther north but periodically respond to local food shortages by moving south in great numbers, and coastal species that wander inland somewhat unpredictably. These birds may not be present every year, but they could be, and these tendencies are indicated at the top of each chart, along with the species' breeding status in the Hudson Valley and any special legal protection in New York State (McGowan and Corwin 2008).

The bar charts illustrate relative abundance by date throughout the year, based largely on data from eBird, but also from other state and regional sources (eBird 2017; DeOrsey and Butler 2014; Levine 1998; Bochnik 2013). Migratory species typically arrive in the Lower Hudson a week or even two weeks earlier than they do in the most northern parts of the valley. The arrival weeks shown here are averages. Departure dates have a similar north/south variability, with migrants leaving one or two weeks later in the Lower Hudson. Birders are encouraged to check eBird for a more precise indication of the period of occurrence and abundance at specific locations.

The charts show the times of peak abundance and the best time of year to find each species. They also illustrate some common patterns of migratory behavior. For example, the abundance of permanent residents, such as Downy Woodpecker, does not change appreciably throughout the year. Populations of true long-distance migrants, such as swallows, vireos, and warblers, decline over a period of several weeks each fall and increase in spring when the birds return to breed. Their charts show peak abundance in summer and absence in winter. Transients, such as Gray-cheeked Thrush and many shorebirds, breed outside the valley. Their numbers peak in spring and fall when the birds pass through our region. Winter residents, which include many waterfowl, migrate into the Hudson Valley in the fall and are most common in winter, but their numbers decline in spring when they head north to breed. The text that accompanies some of the bar charts is designed to provide additional guidance about where, when, and how certain birds can be found in this region.

The birds are listed in taxonomic order, according to the American Ornithological Society's *Checklist of North and Middle American Birds* through its fifty-eighth supplement. Following are definitions for the four levels of abundance shown in the graphs.

COMMON TO ABUNDANT—Widespread and easily found in appropriate habitat. Almost always seen in a day of birding.

UNCOMMON TO FAIRLY COMMON—Widespread in small numbers or common in restricted habitat, but present in good numbers. Seen on about half of all visits to appropriate habitat.

UNCOMMON—Present in small numbers, but seen on less than half of all visits to appropriate habitat.

RARE—Present in the Hudson Valley in very small numbers and unlikely to be encountered in a day of birding.

Snow Goose · *Anser caerulescens*

JAN	FEB	MAR	APR	MAY	JUN	JUL	AUG	SEP	OCT	NOV	DEC

Migrates through the Hudson Valley to wintering areas on the Atlantic Coast. Sometimes seen in huge flocks in late fall. Two color morphs, light (snow) and dark (blue).

Ross's Goose · *Anser rossii*

JAN	FEB	MAR	APR	MAY	JUN	JUL	AUG	SEP	OCT	NOV	DEC

Rare vagrant with an increasing population, now seen almost annually in the Hudson Valley, most often among Snow Geese in spring.

Greater White-fronted Goose · *Anser albifrons*

JAN	FEB	MAR	APR	MAY	JUN	JUL	AUG	SEP	OCT	NOV	DEC

Rare but regular visitor. Typically found among flocks of Canada Geese. Most likely in spring. Shawangunk Grasslands NWR.

Brant · *Branta bernicla*

JAN	FEB	MAR	APR	MAY	JUN	JUL	AUG	SEP	OCT	NOV	DEC

Passes through the Hudson Valley as a late migrant. Winters on the Atlantic Coast. Uncommon away from large bodies of water. Late summer and fall on the Hudson River.

Cackling Goose · *Branta hutchinsii*

JAN	FEB	MAR	APR	MAY	JUN	JUL	AUG	SEP	OCT	NOV	DEC

Rare migrant and winter visitor. Duck-sized version of the Canada Goose with a very short bill. Recently elevated to species status.

Canada Goose · *Branta canadensis*

JAN	FEB	MAR	APR	MAY	JUN	JUL	AUG	SEP	OCT	NOV	DEC

Canada Geese in our area include a mix of migratory subspecies and nonmigratory residents.

Mute Swan · *Cygnus olor*

JAN	FEB	MAR	APR	MAY	JUN	JUL	AUG	SEP	OCT	NOV	DEC

Introduced from Eurasia and now resident. More common in the southern part of the Hudson Valley, but expanding northward.

Tundra Swan · *Cygnus columbianus*

JAN	FEB	MAR	APR	MAY	JUN	JUL	AUG	SEP	OCT	NOV	DEC

Very rare migrant in spring on lakes, rivers, and reservoirs, and rare winter visitor. Lower Hudson River or Wallkill NWR in early spring.

Wood Duck · *Aix sponsa*

JAN	FEB	MAR	APR	MAY	JUN	JUL	AUG	SEP	OCT	NOV	DEC

Sometimes abundant during migration. Nests in tree holes and nest boxes.

Blue-winged Teal · *Spatula discors*

JAN	FEB	MAR	APR	MAY	JUN	JUL	AUG	SEP	OCT	NOV	DEC

Rare, local breeder. Usually seen in freshwater marshes in small numbers, in mixed flocks of dabblers. Wallkill River NWR or Bashakill WMA.

Northern Shoveler · *Spatula clypeata*

JAN	FEB	MAR	APR	MAY	JUN	JUL	AUG	SEP	OCT	NOV	DEC

More common in the southern Hudson Valley.

Gadwall · *Mareca strepera*

JAN	FEB	MAR	APR	MAY	JUN	JUL	AUG	SEP	OCT	NOV	DEC

Very rare breeder in the Hudson Valley.

Eurasian Wigeon · *Mareca penelope*

JAN	FEB	MAR	APR	MAY	JUN	JUL	AUG	SEP	OCT	NOV	DEC

Associates with American Wigeon. Wallkill River NWR.

American Wigeon · *Mareca americana*

JAN	FEB	MAR	APR	MAY	JUN	JUL	AUG	SEP	OCT	NOV	DEC

Very rare breeder.

Mallard · *Anas platyrhynchos*

JAN	FEB	MAR	APR	MAY	JUN	JUL	AUG	SEP	OCT	NOV	DEC

In all seasons, the most common duck in the Hudson Valley.

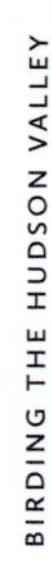

American Black Duck · *Anas rubripes*

JAN	FEB	MAR	APR	MAY	JUN	JUL	AUG	SEP	OCT	NOV	DEC

Second most common breeding duck in the Hudson Valley. Seasonal influx of migrants and winter visitors.

Northern Pintail · *Anas acuta*

JAN	FEB	MAR	APR	MAY	JUN	JUL	AUG	SEP	OCT	NOV	DEC

More likely in the southern Hudson Valley.

Green-winged Teal · *Anas crecca*

JAN	FEB	MAR	APR	MAY	JUN	JUL	AUG	SEP	OCT	NOV	DEC

Common during migration. Rare and local breeder in the Hudson Valley.

Canvasback · *Aythya valisineria*

JAN	FEB	MAR	APR	MAY	JUN	JUL	AUG	SEP	OCT	NOV	DEC

Often associates with Redhead and scaup on the Lower Hudson.

Redhead · *Aythya americana*

JAN	FEB	MAR	APR	MAY	JUN	JUL	AUG	SEP	OCT	NOV	DEC

More likely in the southern Hudson Valley. Rarest inland. Piermont Pier in winter.

Ring-necked Duck · *Aythya collaris*

JAN	FEB	MAR	APR	MAY	JUN	JUL	AUG	SEP	OCT	NOV	DEC

Often found on small ponds.

Greater Scaup · *Aythya marila*

JAN	FEB	MAR	APR	MAY	JUN	JUL	AUG	SEP	OCT	NOV	DEC

More common in the southern Hudson Valley, and more coastal than Lesser Scaup.

Lesser Scaup · *Aythya affinis*

JAN	FEB	MAR	APR	MAY	JUN	JUL	AUG	SEP	OCT	NOV	DEC

Migrant and winter visitor. Most likely scaup inland, and more common in the southern Hudson Valley.

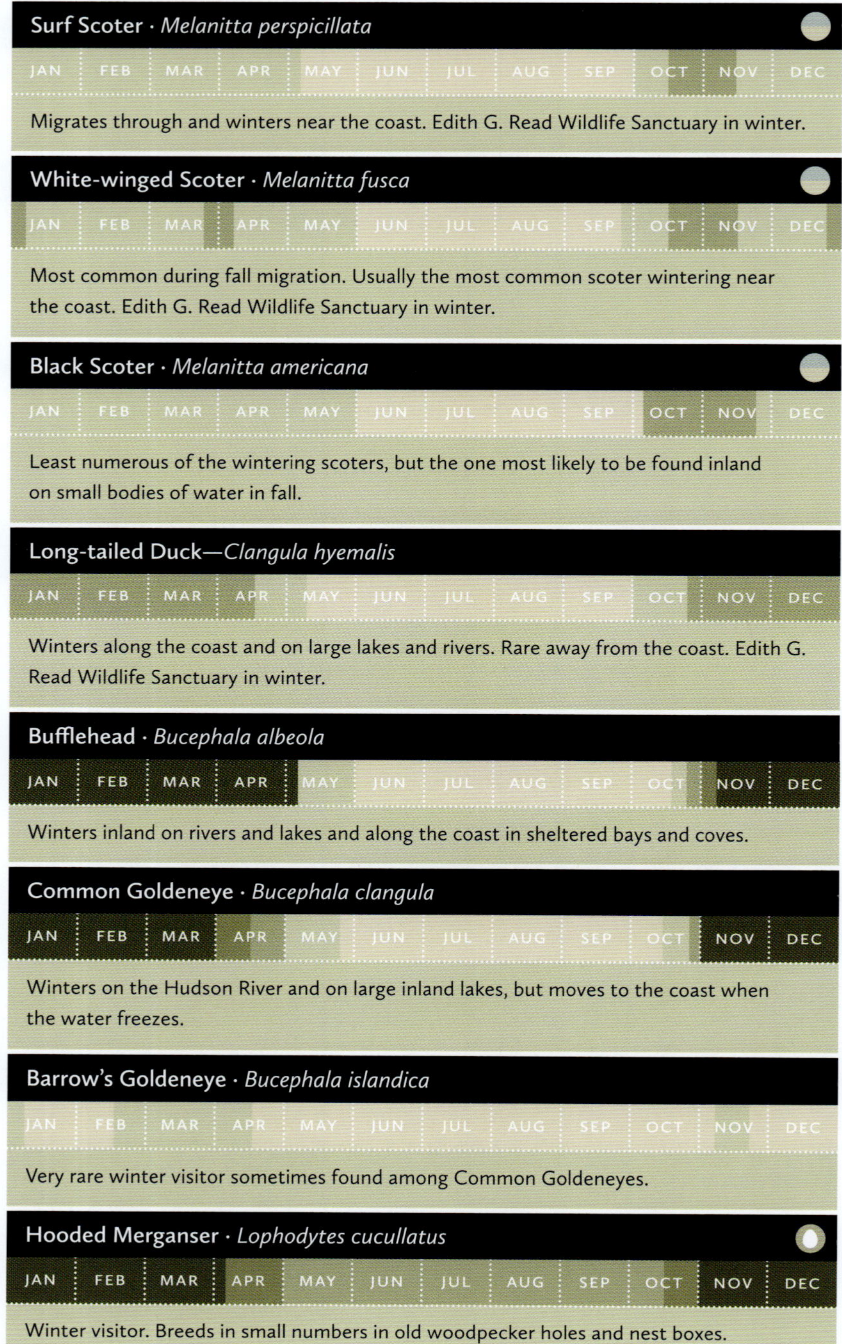

Surf Scoter · *Melanitta perspicillata*

Migrates through and winters near the coast. Edith G. Read Wildlife Sanctuary in winter.

White-winged Scoter · *Melanitta fusca*

Most common during fall migration. Usually the most common scoter wintering near the coast. Edith G. Read Wildlife Sanctuary in winter.

Black Scoter · *Melanitta americana*

Least numerous of the wintering scoters, but the one most likely to be found inland on small bodies of water in fall.

Long-tailed Duck—*Clangula hyemalis*

Winters along the coast and on large lakes and rivers. Rare away from the coast. Edith G. Read Wildlife Sanctuary in winter.

Bufflehead · *Bucephala albeola*

Winters inland on rivers and lakes and along the coast in sheltered bays and coves.

Common Goldeneye · *Bucephala clangula*

Winters on the Hudson River and on large inland lakes, but moves to the coast when the water freezes.

Barrow's Goldeneye · *Bucephala islandica*

Very rare winter visitor sometimes found among Common Goldeneyes.

Hooded Merganser · *Lophodytes cucullatus*

Winter visitor. Breeds in small numbers in old woodpecker holes and nest boxes.

Common Merganser · *Mergus merganser*

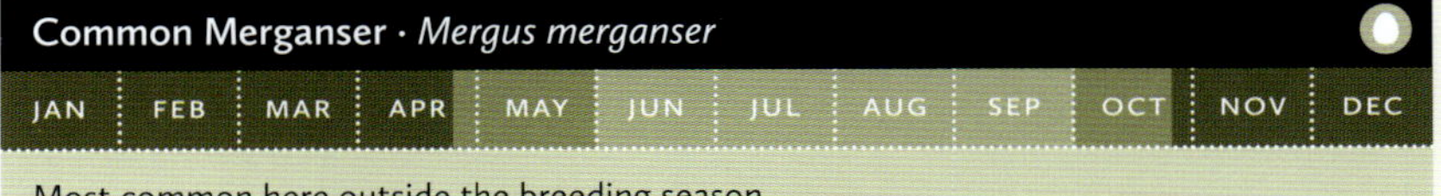

JAN	FEB	MAR	APR	MAY	JUN	JUL	AUG	SEP	OCT	NOV	DEC

Most common here outside the breeding season.

Red-breasted Merganser · *Mergus serrator*

JAN	FEB	MAR	APR	MAY	JUN	JUL	AUG	SEP	OCT	NOV	DEC

Rare away from the coast. Edith G. Read Wildlife Sanctuary in winter.

Ruddy Duck · *Oxyura jamaicensis*

JAN	FEB	MAR	APR	MAY	JUN	JUL	AUG	SEP	OCT	NOV	DEC

More common in the southern Hudson Valley in winter.

QUAIL, GROUSE, AND TURKEYS

Northern Bobwhite · *Colinus virginianus*

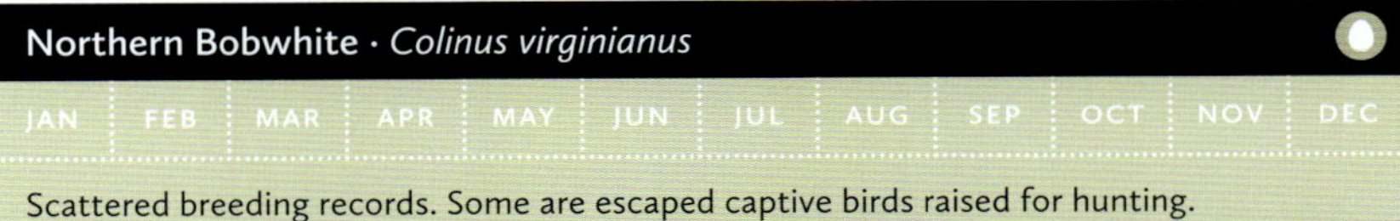

JAN	FEB	MAR	APR	MAY	JUN	JUL	AUG	SEP	OCT	NOV	DEC

Scattered breeding records. Some are escaped captive birds raised for hunting.

Ring-necked Pheasant · *Phasianus colchicus*

JAN	FEB	MAR	APR	MAY	JUN	JUL	AUG	SEP	OCT	NOV	DEC

Introduced from Asia as a game bird. Many sightings are captive-reared birds.

Ruffed Grouse · *Bonasa umbellus*

JAN	FEB	MAR	APR	MAY	JUN	JUL	AUG	SEP	OCT	NOV	DEC

Heard drumming in young woods and shrubland. Increasingly rare in the southern Hudson Valley. Edmund Niles Huyck Preserve or Kenneth L. Wilson Campground in spring.

Wild Turkey · *Meleagris gallopavo*

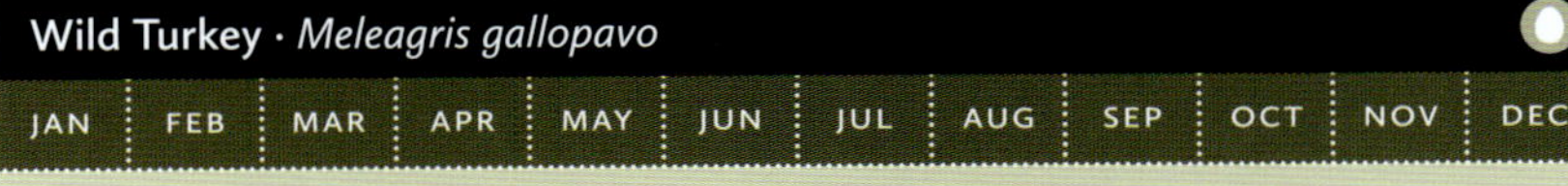

JAN	FEB	MAR	APR	MAY	JUN	JUL	AUG	SEP	OCT	NOV	DEC

Most easily seen in winter, when large flocks feed in open fields and pastures.

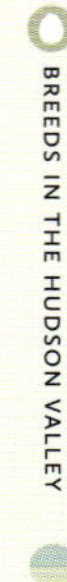

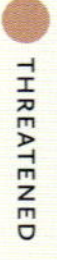
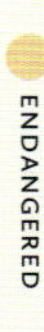

Pied-billed Grebe · *Podilymbus podiceps*

JAN	FEB	MAR	APR	MAY	JUN	JUL	AUG	SEP	OCT	NOV	DEC

Breeds in freshwater lakes and ponds with abundant emergent vegetation. In winter, most common along the coast. Rockland Lake State Park in winter.

Horned Grebe · *Podiceps auritus*

JAN	FEB	MAR	APR	MAY	JUN	JUL	AUG	SEP	OCT	NOV	DEC

Found on large rivers, lakes, and reservoirs during migration, and in winter along the coast. Edith G. Read Wildlife Sanctuary in winter.

Red-necked Grebe · *Podiceps grisegena*

JAN	FEB	MAR	APR	MAY	JUN	JUL	AUG	SEP	OCT	NOV	DEC

Most common during severe winters when the Great Lakes freeze. Typically seen as single birds on large bodies of water and in coastal areas. Edith G. Read Wildlife Sanctuary in winter.

PIGEONS, DOVES, AND CUCKOOS

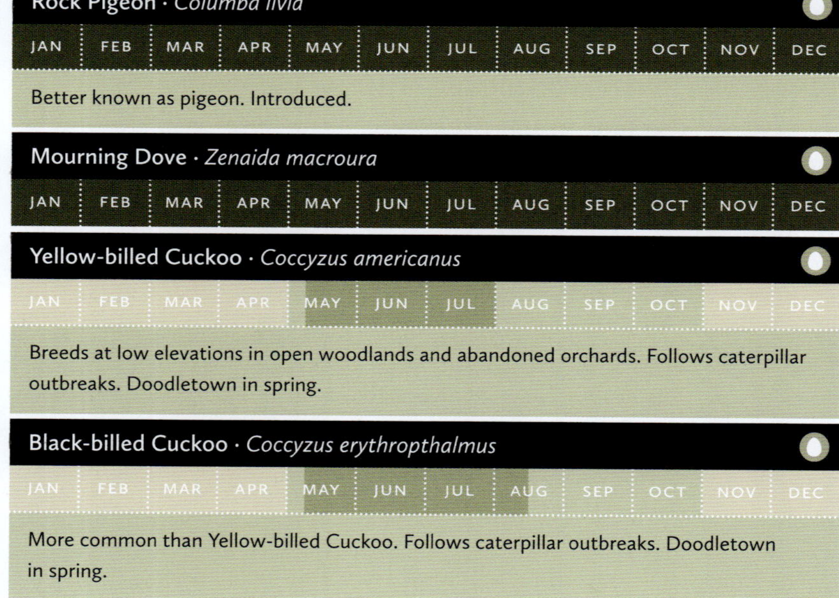

Rock Pigeon · *Columba livia*

JAN	FEB	MAR	APR	MAY	JUN	JUL	AUG	SEP	OCT	NOV	DEC

Better known as pigeon. Introduced.

Mourning Dove · *Zenaida macroura*

JAN	FEB	MAR	APR	MAY	JUN	JUL	AUG	SEP	OCT	NOV	DEC

Yellow-billed Cuckoo · *Coccyzus americanus*

JAN	FEB	MAR	APR	MAY	JUN	JUL	AUG	SEP	OCT	NOV	DEC

Breeds at low elevations in open woodlands and abandoned orchards. Follows caterpillar outbreaks. Doodletown in spring.

Black-billed Cuckoo · *Coccyzus erythropthalmus*

JAN	FEB	MAR	APR	MAY	JUN	JUL	AUG	SEP	OCT	NOV	DEC

More common than Yellow-billed Cuckoo. Follows caterpillar outbreaks. Doodletown in spring.

NIGHTJARS

Common Nighthawk · *Chordeiles minor*

| JAN | FEB | MAR | APR | MAY | JUN | JUL | AUG | SEP | OCT | NOV | DEC |

Most often seen at dusk over water during migration. Hudson River in late May.

Eastern Whip-poor-will · *Antrostomus vociferus*

| JAN | FEB | MAR | APR | MAY | JUN | JUL | AUG | SEP | OCT | NOV | DEC |

Nocturnal. Calls on moonlit nights in spring in open woodlands. Clarence Fahnestock State Park.

SWIFTS AND HUMMINGBIRDS

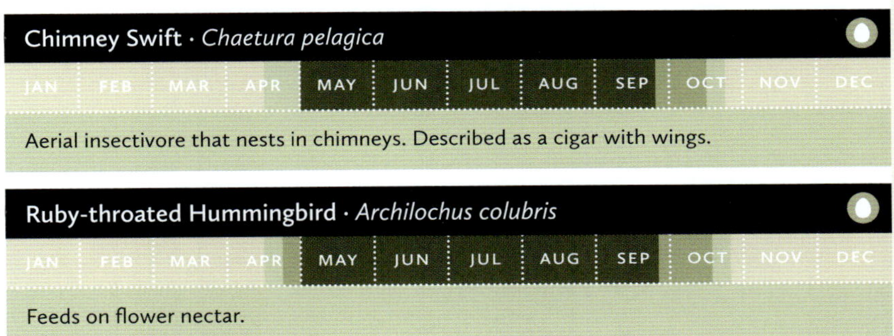

Chimney Swift · *Chaetura pelagica*

| JAN | FEB | MAR | APR | MAY | JUN | JUL | AUG | SEP | OCT | NOV | DEC |

Aerial insectivore that nests in chimneys. Described as a cigar with wings.

Ruby-throated Hummingbird · *Archilochus colubris*

| JAN | FEB | MAR | APR | MAY | JUN | JUL | AUG | SEP | OCT | NOV | DEC |

Feeds on flower nectar.

RAILS, GALLINULES, COOTS, AND CRANES

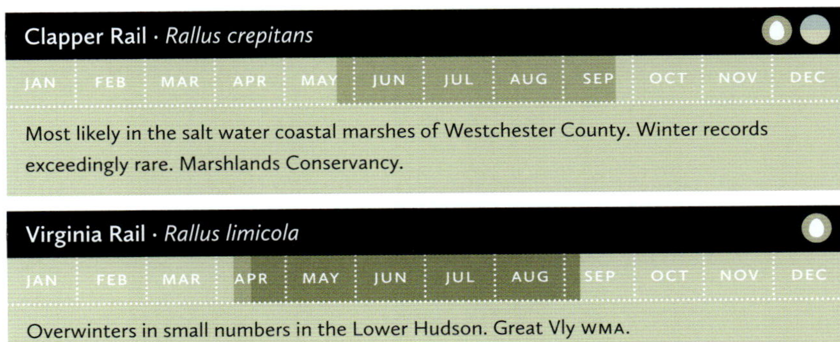

Clapper Rail · *Rallus crepitans*

| JAN | FEB | MAR | APR | MAY | JUN | JUL | AUG | SEP | OCT | NOV | DEC |

Most likely in the salt water coastal marshes of Westchester County. Winter records exceedingly rare. Marshlands Conservancy.

Virginia Rail · *Rallus limicola*

| JAN | FEB | MAR | APR | MAY | JUN | JUL | AUG | SEP | OCT | NOV | DEC |

Overwinters in small numbers in the Lower Hudson. Great Vly WMA.

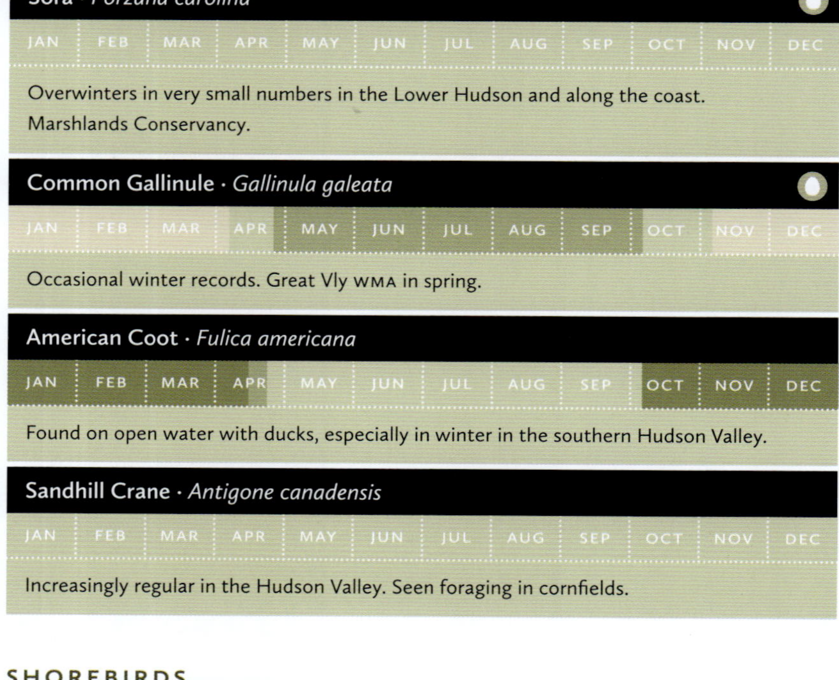

Sora · *Porzana carolina*

JAN	FEB	MAR	APR	MAY	JUN	JUL	AUG	SEP	OCT	NOV	DEC

Overwinters in very small numbers in the Lower Hudson and along the coast. Marshlands Conservancy.

Common Gallinule · *Gallinula galeata*

JAN	FEB	MAR	APR	MAY	JUN	JUL	AUG	SEP	OCT	NOV	DEC

Occasional winter records. Great Vly WMA in spring.

American Coot · *Fulica americana*

JAN	FEB	MAR	APR	MAY	JUN	JUL	AUG	SEP	OCT	NOV	DEC

Found on open water with ducks, especially in winter in the southern Hudson Valley.

Sandhill Crane · *Antigone canadensis*

JAN	FEB	MAR	APR	MAY	JUN	JUL	AUG	SEP	OCT	NOV	DEC

Increasingly regular in the Hudson Valley. Seen foraging in cornfields.

SHOREBIRDS

American Oystercatcher · *Haematopus palliatus*

JAN	FEB	MAR	APR	MAY	JUN	JUL	AUG	SEP	OCT	NOV	DEC

Fairly easily found on the coast. Edith G. Read Wildlife Sanctuary.

Black-bellied Plover · *Pluvialis squatarola*

JAN	FEB	MAR	APR	MAY	JUN	JUL	AUG	SEP	OCT	NOV	DEC

Most likely in fall on mudflats. Wallkill River NWR.

American Golden-Plover · *Pluvialis dominica*

JAN	FEB	MAR	APR	MAY	JUN	JUL	AUG	SEP	OCT	NOV	DEC

Most likely in short grass areas in fall.

Semipalmated Plover · *Charadrius semipalmatus*

JAN	FEB	MAR	APR	MAY	JUN	JUL	AUG	SEP	OCT	NOV	DEC

Found in muddy fields and on mudflats.

Killdeer · *Charadrius vociferus*

JAN | FEB | MAR | APR | MAY | JUN | JUL | AUG | SEP | OCT | NOV | DEC

Sometimes breeds on athletic fields.

Upland Sandpiper · *Bartramia longicauda*

JAN | FEB | MAR | APR | MAY | JUN | JUL | AUG | SEP | OCT | NOV | DEC

Breeds in large grasslands with a mix of high and low vegetation and perches. Shawangunk Grasslands NWR.

Whimbrel · *Numenius phaeopus*

JAN | FEB | MAR | APR | MAY | JUN | JUL | AUG | SEP | OCT | NOV | DEC

Marshlands Conservancy.

Ruddy Turnstone · *Arenaria interpres*

JAN | FEB | MAR | APR | MAY | JUN | JUL | AUG | SEP | OCT | NOV | DEC

Rocky shores. Edith G. Read Wildlife Sanctuary.

Red Knot · *Calidris canutus*

JAN | FEB | MAR | APR | MAY | JUN | JUL | AUG | SEP | OCT | NOV | DEC

Stilt Sandpiper · *Calidris himantopus*

JAN | FEB | MAR | APR | MAY | JUN | JUL | AUG | SEP | OCT | NOV | DEC

Most likely in fall. Often found singly with yellowlegs and dowitchers in shallow pools.

Sanderling · *Calidris alba*

JAN | FEB | MAR | APR | MAY | JUN | JUL | AUG | SEP | OCT | NOV | DEC

At the water's edge on rocky flats along the Hudson. Most likely in fall.

Dunlin · *Calidris alpina*

JAN | FEB | MAR | APR | MAY | JUN | JUL | AUG | SEP | OCT | NOV | DEC

Probes mudflats and flooded areas. Occasional winter records in the Lower Hudson. Marshlands Conservancy.

Purple Sandpiper · *Calidris maritima*

JAN	FEB	MAR	APR	MAY	JUN	JUL	AUG	SEP	OCT	NOV	DEC

Winter visitor to rocky shores. Not reported from the Upper Hudson.
Edith G. Read Wildlife Sanctuary.

Least Sandpiper · *Calidris minutilla*

JAN	FEB	MAR	APR	MAY	JUN	JUL	AUG	SEP	OCT	NOV	DEC

Our smallest sandpiper. Muddy shores and flooded grassy areas.

White-rumped Sandpiper · *Calidris fuscicollis*

JAN	FEB	MAR	APR	MAY	JUN	JUL	AUG	SEP	OCT	NOV	DEC

Very rare in spring, when most migrate though the center of the continent.

Buff-breasted Sandpiper · *Calidris subruficollis*

JAN	FEB	MAR	APR	MAY	JUN	JUL	AUG	SEP	OCT	NOV	DEC

Migrates through our area only in the fall. Prefers short, dry grassland.

Pectoral Sandpiper · *Calidris melanotos*

JAN	FEB	MAR	APR	MAY	JUN	JUL	AUG	SEP	OCT	NOV	DEC

Favors grassy pools after heavy rains.

Semipalmated Sandpiper · *Calidris pusilla*

JAN	FEB	MAR	APR	MAY	JUN	JUL	AUG	SEP	OCT	NOV	DEC

Tidal mudflats.

Short-billed Dowitcher · *Limnodromus griseus*

JAN	FEB	MAR	APR	MAY	JUN	JUL	AUG	SEP	OCT	NOV	DEC

Most likely in the southern Hudson Valley in fall.

Long-billed Dowitcher · *Limnodromus scolopaceus*

JAN	FEB	MAR	APR	MAY	JUN	JUL	AUG	SEP	OCT	NOV	DEC

Exceedingly rare in spring.

American Woodcock · *Scolopax minor*

| JAN | FEB | MAR | APR | MAY | JUN | JUL | AUG | SEP | OCT | NOV | DEC |

Displays at dusk in early spring in semi-open fields. Cary Institute of Ecosystem Studies.

Wilson's Snipe · *Gallinago delicata*

| JAN | FEB | MAR | APR | MAY | JUN | JUL | AUG | SEP | OCT | NOV | DEC |

Wet meadows. Heard "winnowing" at dawn and dusk in spring.
Shawangunk Grasslands NWR.

Spotted Sandpiper · *Actitis macularius*

| JAN | FEB | MAR | APR | MAY | JUN | JUL | AUG | SEP | OCT | NOV | DEC |

Most common breeding shorebird after Killdeer.

Solitary Sandpiper · *Tringa solitaria*

| JAN | FEB | MAR | APR | MAY | JUN | JUL | AUG | SEP | OCT | NOV | DEC |

During migration, found on freshwater pools, woodland ponds, and streams.

Lesser Yellowlegs · *Tringa flavipes*

| JAN | FEB | MAR | APR | MAY | JUN | JUL | AUG | SEP | OCT | NOV | DEC |

In migration, found in grassy pools and ponds, flooded fields, and salt meadows
along the coast.

Willet · *Tringa semipalmata*

| JAN | FEB | MAR | APR | MAY | JUN | JUL | AUG | SEP | OCT | NOV | DEC |

Now established as a breeder in coastal salt marshes of Westchester County.

Greater Yellowlegs · *Tringa melanoleuca*

| JAN | FEB | MAR | APR | MAY | JUN | JUL | AUG | SEP | OCT | NOV | DEC |

Wilson's Phalarope · *Phalaropus tricolor*

| JAN | FEB | MAR | APR | MAY | JUN | JUL | AUG | SEP | OCT | NOV | DEC |

Very rare. Only a few records.

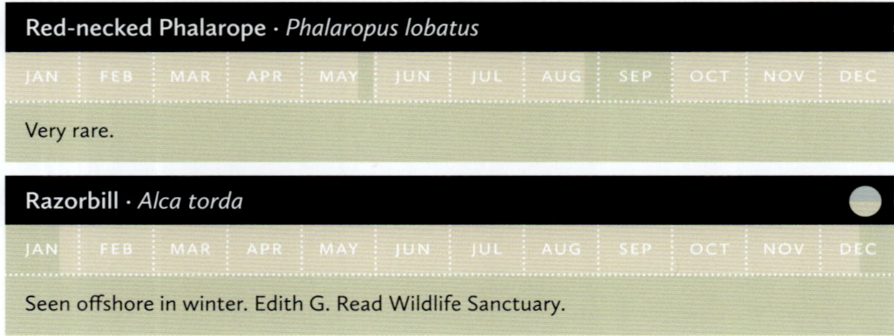

Red-necked Phalarope · *Phalaropus lobatus*

JAN	FEB	MAR	APR	MAY	JUN	JUL	AUG	SEP	OCT	NOV	DEC

Very rare.

Razorbill · *Alca torda*

JAN	FEB	MAR	APR	MAY	JUN	JUL	AUG	SEP	OCT	NOV	DEC

Seen offshore in winter. Edith G. Read Wildlife Sanctuary.

GULLS, TERNS, AND SKIMMERS

Bonaparte's Gull · *Chroicocephalus philadelphia*

JAN	FEB	MAR	APR	MAY	JUN	JUL	AUG	SEP	OCT	NOV	DEC

Seen as a migrant and wanderer on the Lower Hudson, and on large lakes and reservoirs.

Laughing Gull · *Leucophaeus atricilla*

JAN	FEB	MAR	APR	MAY	JUN	JUL	AUG	SEP	OCT	NOV	DEC

Post-breeding visitor. Rare inland. Much more common in the Lower Hudson.

Ring-billed Gull · *Larus delawarensis*

JAN	FEB	MAR	APR	MAY	JUN	JUL	AUG	SEP	OCT	NOV	DEC

The most common gull in the Hudson Valley.

Herring Gull · *Larus argentatus*

JAN	FEB	MAR	APR	MAY	JUN	JUL	AUG	SEP	OCT	NOV	DEC

Hudson River, large bodies of water, and landfills, especially in winter.

Iceland Gull · *Larus glaucoides*

JAN	FEB	MAR	APR	MAY	JUN	JUL	AUG	SEP	OCT	NOV	DEC

Most common in severe winters, when immature birds are usually seen. Cohoes Flats in winter with other gulls.

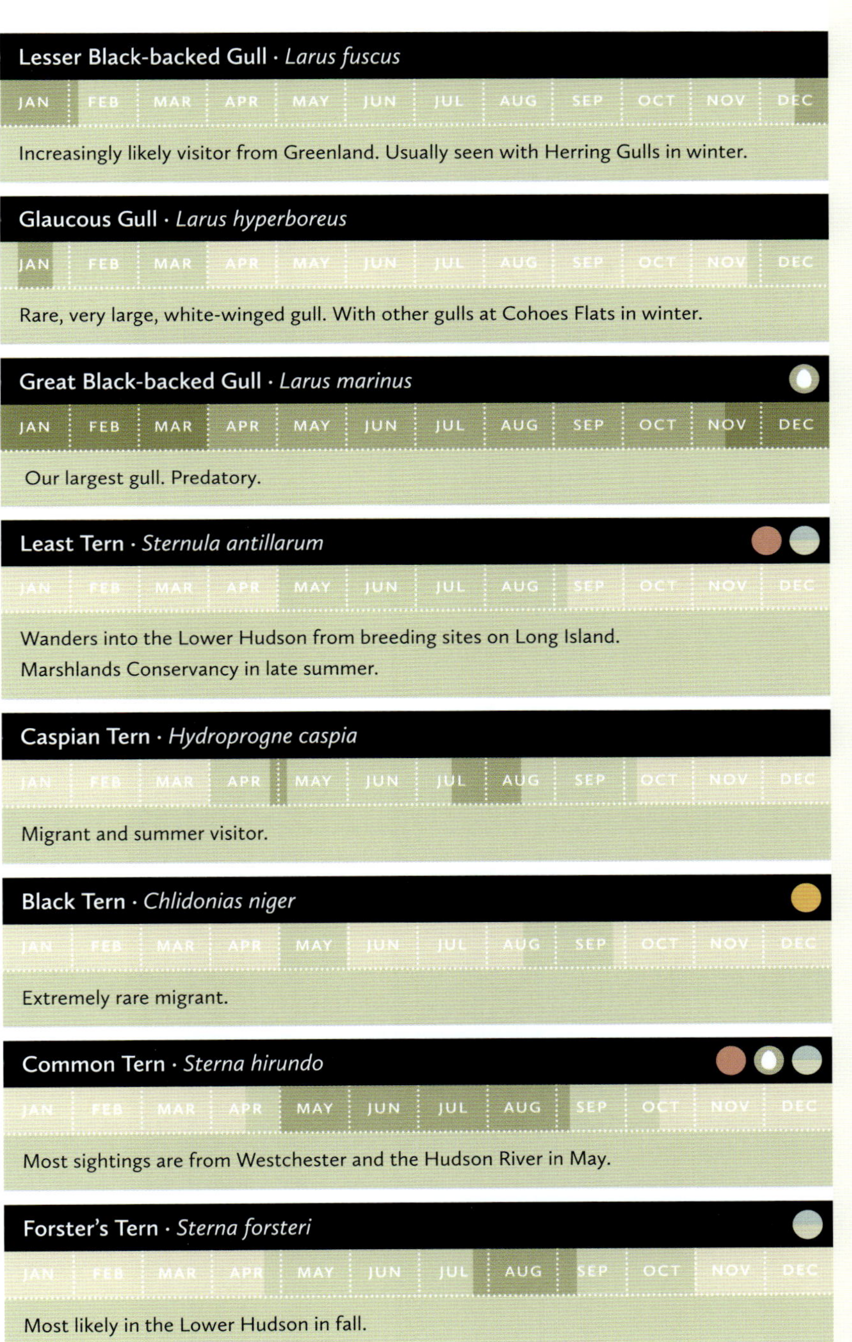

Lesser Black-backed Gull · *Larus fuscus*

JAN	FEB	MAR	APR	MAY	JUN	JUL	AUG	SEP	OCT	NOV	DEC

Increasingly likely visitor from Greenland. Usually seen with Herring Gulls in winter.

Glaucous Gull · *Larus hyperboreus*

JAN	FEB	MAR	APR	MAY	JUN	JUL	AUG	SEP	OCT	NOV	DEC

Rare, very large, white-winged gull. With other gulls at Cohoes Flats in winter.

Great Black-backed Gull · *Larus marinus*

JAN	FEB	MAR	APR	MAY	JUN	JUL	AUG	SEP	OCT	NOV	DEC

Our largest gull. Predatory.

Least Tern · *Sternula antillarum*

JAN	FEB	MAR	APR	MAY	JUN	JUL	AUG	SEP	OCT	NOV	DEC

Wanders into the Lower Hudson from breeding sites on Long Island.
Marshlands Conservancy in late summer.

Caspian Tern · *Hydroprogne caspia*

JAN	FEB	MAR	APR	MAY	JUN	JUL	AUG	SEP	OCT	NOV	DEC

Migrant and summer visitor.

Black Tern · *Chlidonias niger*

JAN	FEB	MAR	APR	MAY	JUN	JUL	AUG	SEP	OCT	NOV	DEC

Extremely rare migrant.

Common Tern · *Sterna hirundo*

JAN	FEB	MAR	APR	MAY	JUN	JUL	AUG	SEP	OCT	NOV	DEC

Most sightings are from Westchester and the Hudson River in May.

Forster's Tern · *Sterna forsteri*

JAN	FEB	MAR	APR	MAY	JUN	JUL	AUG	SEP	OCT	NOV	DEC

Most likely in the Lower Hudson in fall.

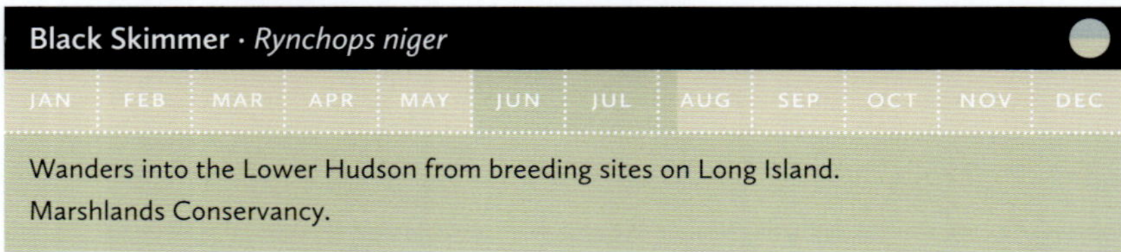

Black Skimmer · *Rynchops niger*

JAN	FEB	MAR	APR	MAY	JUN	JUL	AUG	SEP	OCT	NOV	DEC

Wanders into the Lower Hudson from breeding sites on Long Island. Marshlands Conservancy.

LOONS

Red-throated Loon · *Gavia stellata*

JAN	FEB	MAR	APR	MAY	JUN	JUL	AUG	SEP	OCT	NOV	DEC

Winters in numbers on the Great Lakes and the Atlantic. Seen inland in severe winters. Edith G. Read Wildlife Sanctuary in winter.

Common Loon · *Gavia immer*

JAN	FEB	MAR	APR	MAY	JUN	JUL	AUG	SEP	OCT	NOV	DEC

Most likely in winter on open water. A few nonbreeders summer on lakes and reservoirs.

GANNETS AND CORMORANTS

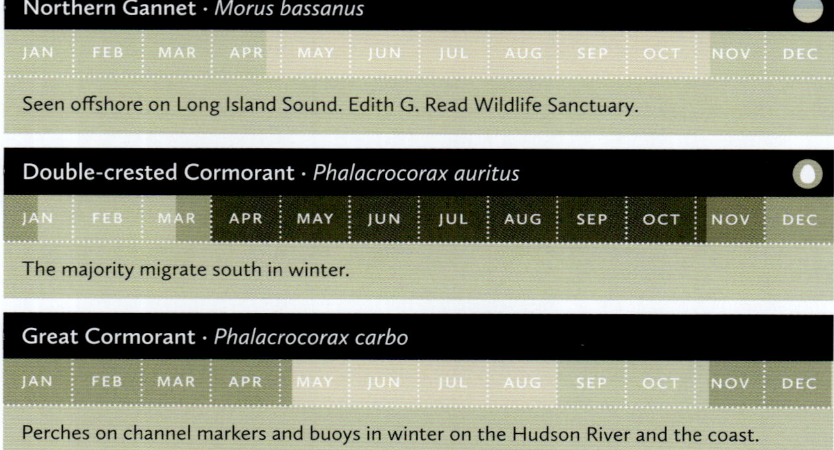

Northern Gannet · *Morus bassanus*

JAN	FEB	MAR	APR	MAY	JUN	JUL	AUG	SEP	OCT	NOV	DEC

Seen offshore on Long Island Sound. Edith G. Read Wildlife Sanctuary.

Double-crested Cormorant · *Phalacrocorax auritus*

JAN	FEB	MAR	APR	MAY	JUN	JUL	AUG	SEP	OCT	NOV	DEC

The majority migrate south in winter.

Great Cormorant · *Phalacrocorax carbo*

JAN	FEB	MAR	APR	MAY	JUN	JUL	AUG	SEP	OCT	NOV	DEC

Perches on channel markers and buoys in winter on the Hudson River and the coast.

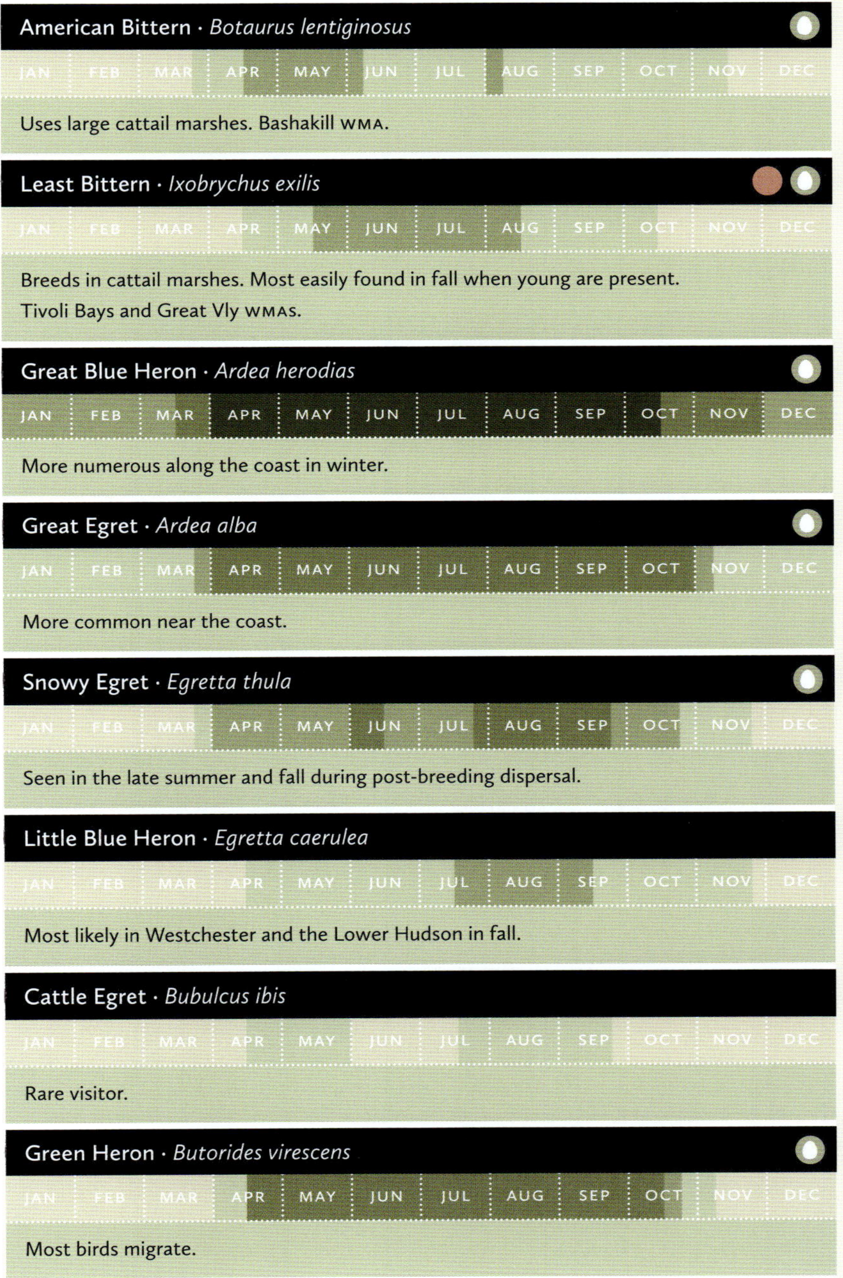

American Bittern · *Botaurus lentiginosus*

JAN · FEB · MAR · APR · MAY · JUN · JUL · AUG · SEP · OCT · NOV · DEC

Uses large cattail marshes. Bashakill WMA.

Least Bittern · *Ixobrychus exilis*

JAN · FEB · MAR · APR · MAY · JUN · JUL · AUG · SEP · OCT · NOV · DEC

Breeds in cattail marshes. Most easily found in fall when young are present. Tivoli Bays and Great Vly WMAS.

Great Blue Heron · *Ardea herodias*

JAN · FEB · MAR · APR · MAY · JUN · JUL · AUG · SEP · OCT · NOV · DEC

More numerous along the coast in winter.

Great Egret · *Ardea alba*

JAN · FEB · MAR · APR · MAY · JUN · JUL · AUG · SEP · OCT · NOV · DEC

More common near the coast.

Snowy Egret · *Egretta thula*

JAN · FEB · MAR · APR · MAY · JUN · JUL · AUG · SEP · OCT · NOV · DEC

Seen in the late summer and fall during post-breeding dispersal.

Little Blue Heron · *Egretta caerulea*

JAN · FEB · MAR · APR · MAY · JUN · JUL · AUG · SEP · OCT · NOV · DEC

Most likely in Westchester and the Lower Hudson in fall.

Cattle Egret · *Bubulcus ibis*

JAN · FEB · MAR · APR · MAY · JUN · JUL · AUG · SEP · OCT · NOV · DEC

Rare visitor.

Green Heron · *Butorides virescens*

JAN · FEB · MAR · APR · MAY · JUN · JUL · AUG · SEP · OCT · NOV · DEC

Most birds migrate.

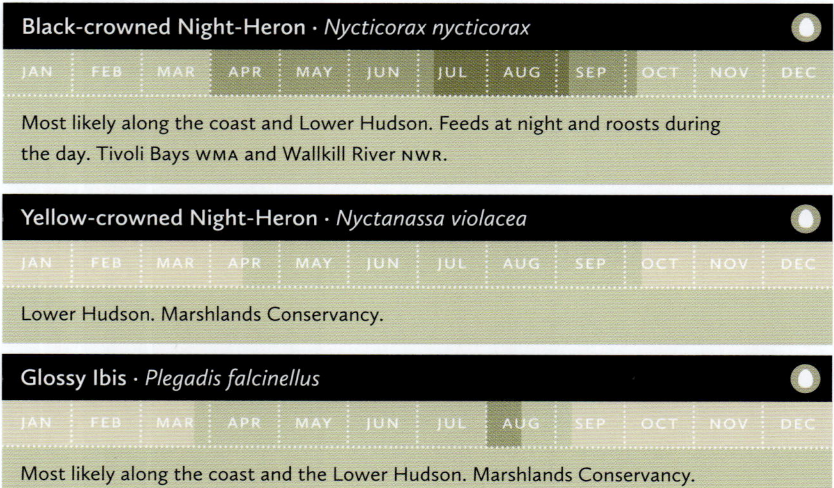

Black-crowned Night-Heron · *Nycticorax nycticorax*

JAN	FEB	MAR	APR	MAY	JUN	JUL	AUG	SEP	OCT	NOV	DEC

Most likely along the coast and Lower Hudson. Feeds at night and roosts during the day. Tivoli Bays WMA and Wallkill River NWR.

Yellow-crowned Night-Heron · *Nyctanassa violacea*

JAN	FEB	MAR	APR	MAY	JUN	JUL	AUG	SEP	OCT	NOV	DEC

Lower Hudson. Marshlands Conservancy.

Glossy Ibis · *Plegadis falcinellus*

JAN	FEB	MAR	APR	MAY	JUN	JUL	AUG	SEP	OCT	NOV	DEC

Most likely along the coast and the Lower Hudson. Marshlands Conservancy.

VULTURES

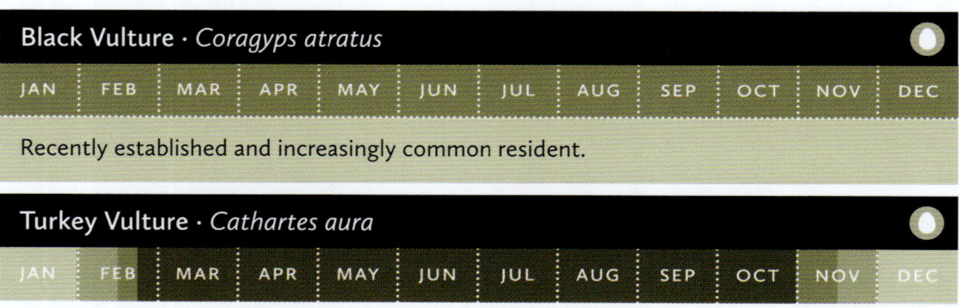

Black Vulture · *Coragyps atratus*

JAN	FEB	MAR	APR	MAY	JUN	JUL	AUG	SEP	OCT	NOV	DEC

Recently established and increasingly common resident.

Turkey Vulture · *Cathartes aura*

JAN	FEB	MAR	APR	MAY	JUN	JUL	AUG	SEP	OCT	NOV	DEC

OSPREY, KITES, HAWKS, AND EAGLES

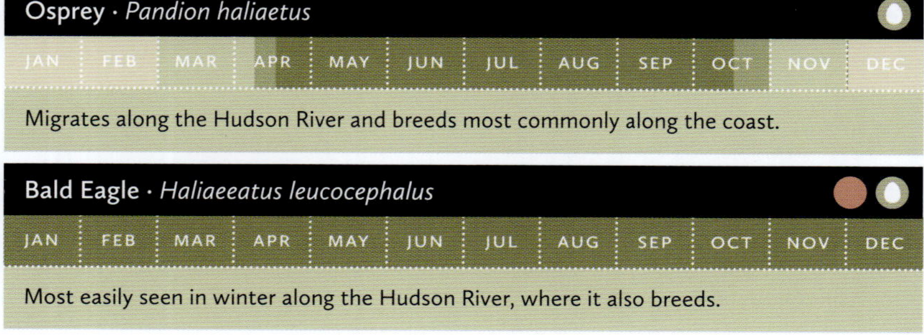

Osprey · *Pandion haliaetus*

JAN	FEB	MAR	APR	MAY	JUN	JUL	AUG	SEP	OCT	NOV	DEC

Migrates along the Hudson River and breeds most commonly along the coast.

Bald Eagle · *Haliaeeatus leucocephalus*

JAN	FEB	MAR	APR	MAY	JUN	JUL	AUG	SEP	OCT	NOV	DEC

Most easily seen in winter along the Hudson River, where it also breeds.

Northern Harrier · *Circus hudsonius*

JAN FEB MAR APR MAY JUN JUL AUG SEP OCT NOV DEC

Most likely to be seen in winter. Shawangunk Grasslands NWR.

Sharp-shinned Hawk · *Accipiter striatus*

JAN FEB MAR APR MAY JUN JUL AUG SEP OCT NOV DEC

Breeds secretively in forested areas.

Cooper's Hawk · *Accipiter cooperii*

JAN FEB MAR APR MAY JUN JUL AUG SEP OCT NOV DEC

Sometimes hunts birds at feeders in winter.

Northern Goshawk · *Accipiter gentilis*

JAN FEB MAR APR MAY JUN JUL AUG SEP OCT NOV DEC

Prefers higher elevations with large tracts of mature forest. Edmund Niles Huyck Preserve.

Red-shouldered Hawk · *Buteo lineatus*

JAN FEB MAR APR MAY JUN JUL AUG SEP OCT NOV DEC

Mature mixed forest, especially bottomlands.

Broad-winged Hawk · *Buteo platypterus*

JAN FEB MAR APR MAY JUN JUL AUG SEP OCT NOV DEC

Sometimes abundant during migration.

Red-tailed Hawk · *Buteo jamaicensis*

JAN FEB MAR APR MAY JUN JUL AUG SEP OCT NOV DEC

Most abundant hawk in the Hudson Valley.

Rough-legged Hawk · *Buteo lagopus*

JAN FEB MAR APR MAY JUN JUL AUG SEP OCT NOV DEC

Two color morphs.

BREEDS IN THE HUDSON VALLEY
COASTAL
IRRUPTIVE
THREATENED
ENDANGERED

NONE
RARE
UNCOMMON
UNCOMMON TO FAIRLY COMMON
COMMON TO ABUNDANT

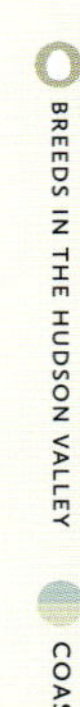

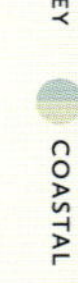

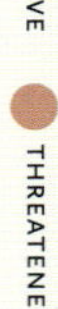

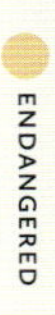

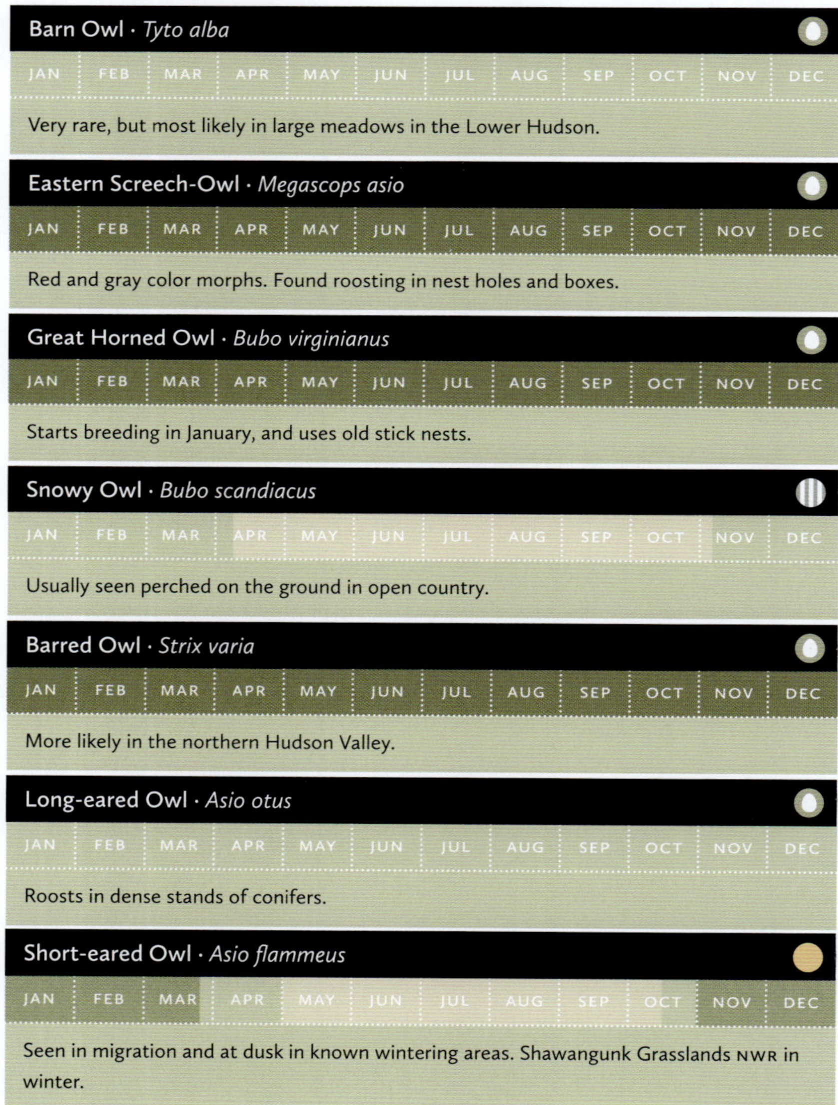

OWLS AND KINGFISHERS

Northern Saw-whet Owl · *Asio acadicus*

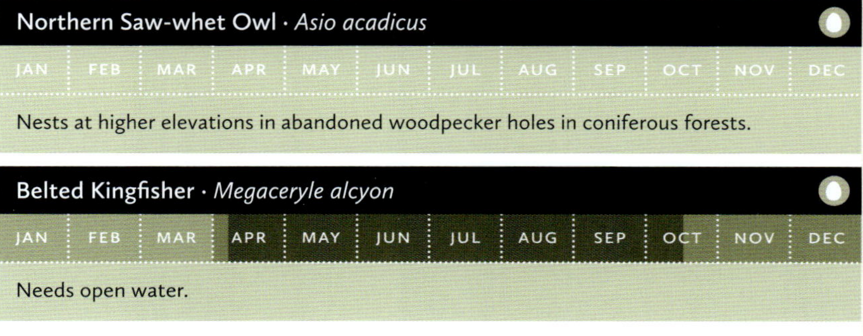

Nests at higher elevations in abandoned woodpecker holes in coniferous forests.

Belted Kingfisher · *Megaceryle alcyon*

JAN FEB MAR APR MAY JUN JUL AUG SEP OCT NOV DEC

Needs open water.

WOODPECKERS

Red-headed Woodpecker · *Melanerpes erythrocephalus*

JAN FEB MAR APR MAY JUN JUL AUG SEP OCT NOV DEC

Breeds in wetlands with dead trees or park-like, upland woods with scattered large trees. Muscoot Farm.

Red-bellied Woodpecker · *Melanerpes carolinus*

JAN FEB MAR APR MAY JUN JUL AUG SEP OCT NOV DEC

Yellow-bellied Sapsucker · *Sphyrapicus varius*

JAN FEB MAR APR MAY JUN JUL AUG SEP OCT NOV DEC

Nests in young forests at elevations over one thousand feet.

Downy Woodpecker · *Picoides pubescens*

JAN FEB MAR APR MAY JUN JUL AUG SEP OCT NOV DEC

Much more likely than its large look-alike, Hairy Woodpecker.

Hairy Woodpecker · *Picoides villosus*

JAN FEB MAR APR MAY JUN JUL AUG SEP OCT NOV DEC

Prefers mature forests with tall trees.

Northern Flicker · *Colaptes auratus*

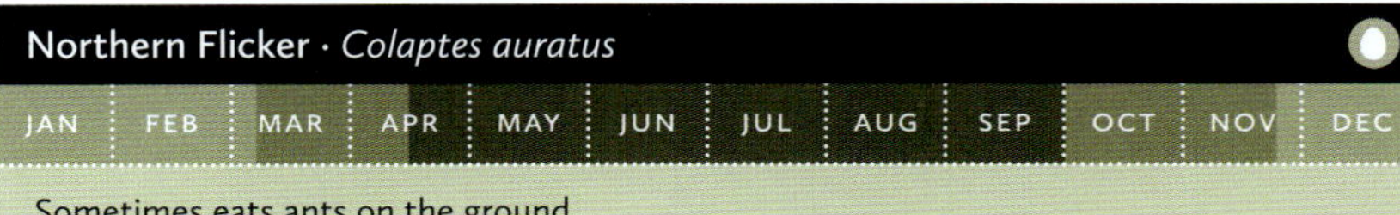

Sometimes eats ants on the ground.

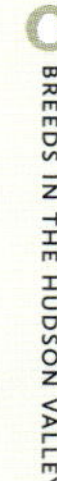

Pileated Woodpecker · *Dryocopus pileatus*

JAN	FEB	MAR	APR	MAY	JUN	JUL	AUG	SEP	OCT	NOV	DEC

Makes distinctive oblong holes.

FALCONS AND PARROTS

American Kestrel · *Falco sparverius*

JAN	FEB	MAR	APR	MAY	JUN	JUL	AUG	SEP	OCT	NOV	DEC

Prefers open country. Perches on telephone wires.

Merlin · *Falco columbarius*

JAN	FEB	MAR	APR	MAY	JUN	JUL	AUG	SEP	OCT	NOV	DEC

Winter visitors show site fidelity. Cohoes Flats in winter.

Peregrine Falcon · *Falco peregrinus*

JAN	FEB	MAR	APR	MAY	JUN	JUL	AUG	SEP	OCT	NOV	DEC

Nests on cliffs, tall buildings, and bridges with long views. Little Stony Point State Park.

Monk Parakeet · *Myiopsitta monachus*

JAN	FEB	MAR	APR	MAY	JUN	JUL	AUG	SEP	OCT	NOV	DEC

Introduced. Builds large, communal stick nests in urban habitats.

FLYCATCHERS

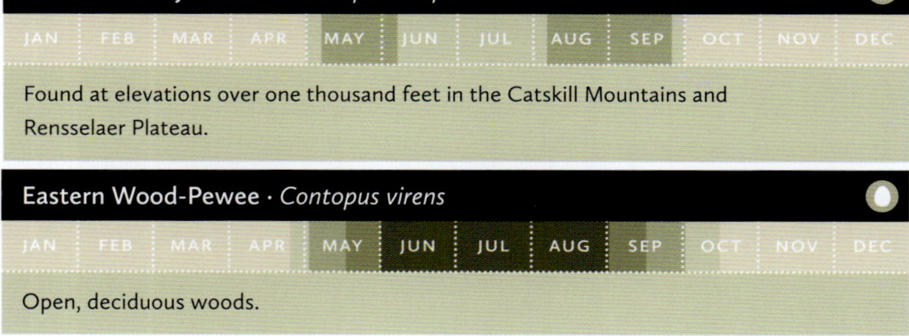

Olive-sided Flycatcher · *Contopus cooperi*

JAN	FEB	MAR	APR	MAY	JUN	JUL	AUG	SEP	OCT	NOV	DEC

Found at elevations over one thousand feet in the Catskill Mountains and Rensselaer Plateau.

Eastern Wood-Pewee · *Contopus virens*

JAN	FEB	MAR	APR	MAY	JUN	JUL	AUG	SEP	OCT	NOV	DEC

Open, deciduous woods.

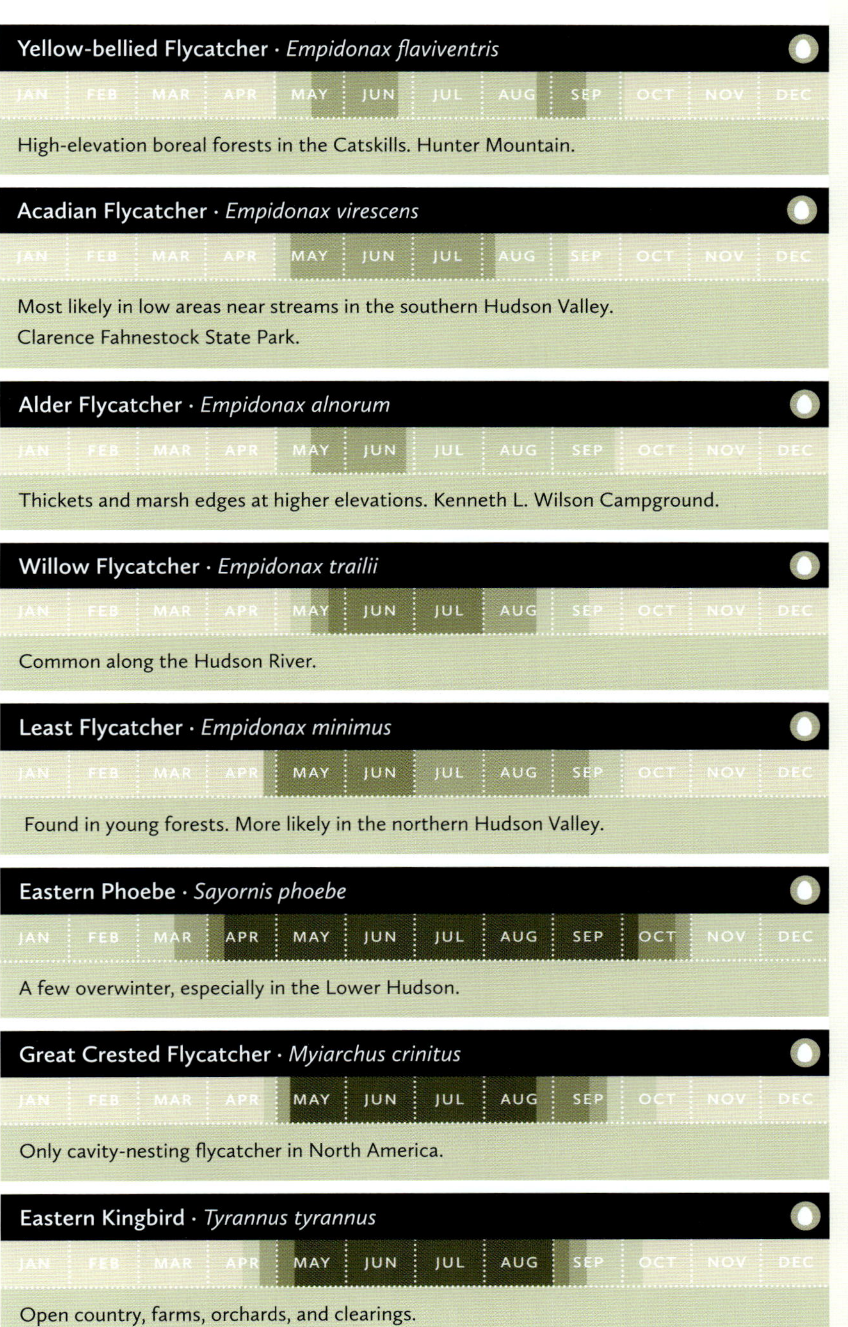

Yellow-bellied Flycatcher · *Empidonax flaviventris*

| JAN | FEB | MAR | APR | MAY | JUN | JUL | AUG | SEP | OCT | NOV | DEC |

High-elevation boreal forests in the Catskills. Hunter Mountain.

Acadian Flycatcher · *Empidonax virescens*

| JAN | FEB | MAR | APR | MAY | JUN | JUL | AUG | SEP | OCT | NOV | DEC |

Most likely in low areas near streams in the southern Hudson Valley. Clarence Fahnestock State Park.

Alder Flycatcher · *Empidonax alnorum*

| JAN | FEB | MAR | APR | MAY | JUN | JUL | AUG | SEP | OCT | NOV | DEC |

Thickets and marsh edges at higher elevations. Kenneth L. Wilson Campground.

Willow Flycatcher · *Empidonax trailii*

| JAN | FEB | MAR | APR | MAY | JUN | JUL | AUG | SEP | OCT | NOV | DEC |

Common along the Hudson River.

Least Flycatcher · *Empidonax minimus*

| JAN | FEB | MAR | APR | MAY | JUN | JUL | AUG | SEP | OCT | NOV | DEC |

Found in young forests. More likely in the northern Hudson Valley.

Eastern Phoebe · *Sayornis phoebe*

| JAN | FEB | MAR | APR | MAY | JUN | JUL | AUG | SEP | OCT | NOV | DEC |

A few overwinter, especially in the Lower Hudson.

Great Crested Flycatcher · *Myiarchus crinitus*

| JAN | FEB | MAR | APR | MAY | JUN | JUL | AUG | SEP | OCT | NOV | DEC |

Only cavity-nesting flycatcher in North America.

Eastern Kingbird · *Tyrannus tyrannus*

| JAN | FEB | MAR | APR | MAY | JUN | JUL | AUG | SEP | OCT | NOV | DEC |

Open country, farms, orchards, and clearings.

Northern Shrike · *Lanius borealis*

JAN	FEB	MAR	APR	MAY	JUN	JUL	AUG	SEP	OCT	NOV	DEC

Winter visitor. More likely in the northern Hudson Valley. Shawangunk Grasslands NWR.

White-eyed Vireo · *Vireo griseus*

JAN	FEB	MAR	APR	MAY	JUN	JUL	AUG	SEP	OCT	NOV	DEC

More likely in the southern Hudson Valley. Wet thickets and edges. Peach Hill in May.

Yellow-throated Vireo · *Vireo flavifrons*

JAN	FEB	MAR	APR	MAY	JUN	JUL	AUG	SEP	OCT	NOV	DEC

Found in the tops of mature stands of deciduous trees.

Blue-headed Vireo · *Vireo solitarius*

JAN	FEB	MAR	APR	MAY	JUN	JUL	AUG	SEP	OCT	NOV	DEC

Breeds in mixed evergreen-deciduous forests at higher elevations. Clarence Fahnestock State Park.

Philadelphia Vireo · *Vireo philadelphicus*

JAN	FEB	MAR	APR	MAY	JUN	JUL	AUG	SEP	OCT	NOV	DEC

Most likely in the Hudson Valley in fall.

Warbling Vireo · *Vireo gilvus*

JAN	FEB	MAR	APR	MAY	JUN	JUL	AUG	SEP	OCT	NOV	DEC

Avoids high elevations. Common along the Hudson River.

Red-eyed Vireo · *Vireo olivaceus*

JAN	FEB	MAR	APR	MAY	JUN	JUL	AUG	SEP	OCT	NOV	DEC

Most common vireo in the Hudson Valley.

JAYS, CROWS, AND RAVENS

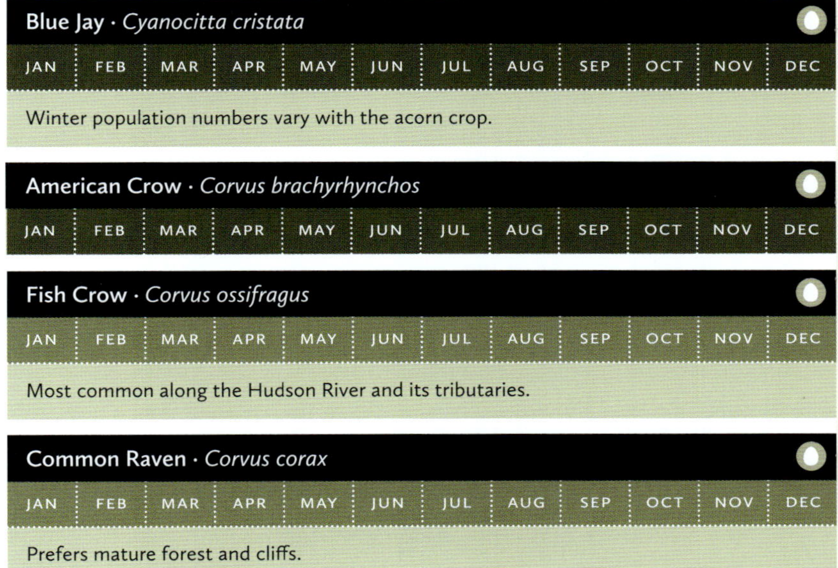

Blue Jay · *Cyanocitta cristata*

| JAN | FEB | MAR | APR | MAY | JUN | JUL | AUG | SEP | OCT | NOV | DEC |

Winter population numbers vary with the acorn crop.

American Crow · *Corvus brachyrhynchos*

| JAN | FEB | MAR | APR | MAY | JUN | JUL | AUG | SEP | OCT | NOV | DEC |

Fish Crow · *Corvus ossifragus*

| JAN | FEB | MAR | APR | MAY | JUN | JUL | AUG | SEP | OCT | NOV | DEC |

Most common along the Hudson River and its tributaries.

Common Raven · *Corvus corax*

| JAN | FEB | MAR | APR | MAY | JUN | JUL | AUG | SEP | OCT | NOV | DEC |

Prefers mature forest and cliffs.

LARKS, MARTINS, AND SWALLOWS

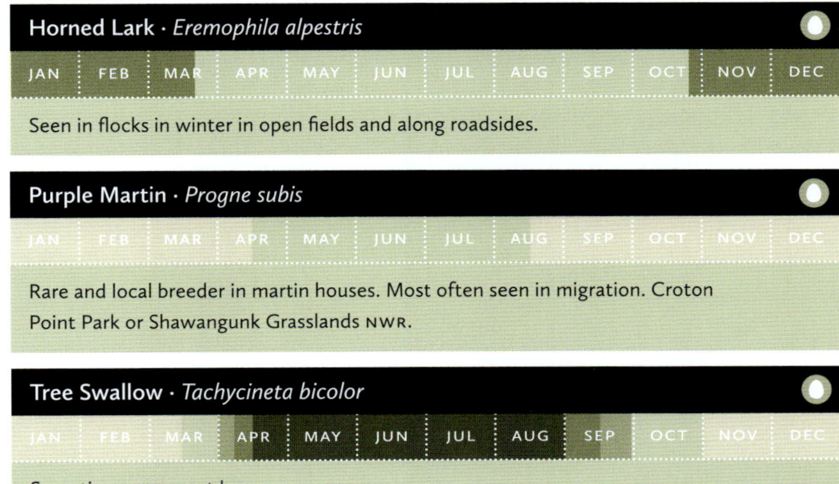

Horned Lark · *Eremophila alpestris*

| JAN | FEB | MAR | APR | MAY | JUN | JUL | AUG | SEP | OCT | NOV | DEC |

Seen in flocks in winter in open fields and along roadsides.

Purple Martin · *Progne subis*

| JAN | FEB | MAR | APR | MAY | JUN | JUL | AUG | SEP | OCT | NOV | DEC |

Rare and local breeder in martin houses. Most often seen in migration. Croton Point Park or Shawangunk Grasslands NWR.

Tree Swallow · *Tachycineta bicolor*

| JAN | FEB | MAR | APR | MAY | JUN | JUL | AUG | SEP | OCT | NOV | DEC |

Sometimes uses nest boxes.

Northern Rough-winged Swallow · *Stelgidopteryx serripennis*

JAN	FEB	MAR	APR	MAY	JUN	JUL	AUG	SEP	OCT	NOV	DEC

Near lakes and rivers.

Bank Swallow · *Riparia riparia*

JAN	FEB	MAR	APR	MAY	JUN	JUL	AUG	SEP	OCT	NOV	DEC

Nests colonially in bluffs and banks along rivers and lakes, and in sand and gravel pits. Stockport Flats.

Cliff Swallow · *Petrochelidon pyrrhonota*

JAN	FEB	MAR	APR	MAY	JUN	JUL	AUG	SEP	OCT	NOV	DEC

Distinctive, gourd-shaped nest of mud pellets built on walls.

Barn Swallow · *Hirundo rustica*

JAN	FEB	MAR	APR	MAY	JUN	JUL	AUG	SEP	OCT	NOV	DEC

Open nest of mud and straw placed on inside rafters of barns, sheds, and porches.

CHICKADEES, TITMICE, NUTHATCHES, AND CREEPERS

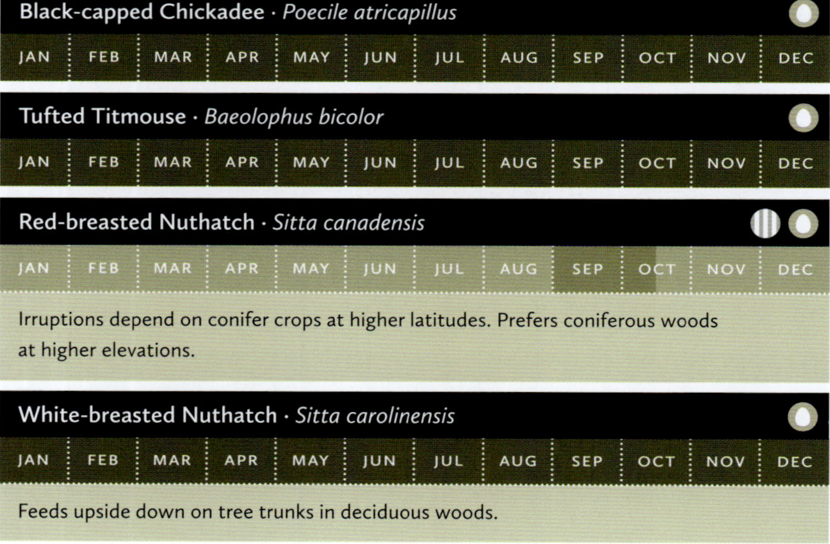

Black-capped Chickadee · *Poecile atricapillus*

JAN	FEB	MAR	APR	MAY	JUN	JUL	AUG	SEP	OCT	NOV	DEC

Tufted Titmouse · *Baeolophus bicolor*

JAN	FEB	MAR	APR	MAY	JUN	JUL	AUG	SEP	OCT	NOV	DEC

Red-breasted Nuthatch · *Sitta canadensis*

JAN	FEB	MAR	APR	MAY	JUN	JUL	AUG	SEP	OCT	NOV	DEC

Irruptions depend on conifer crops at higher latitudes. Prefers coniferous woods at higher elevations.

White-breasted Nuthatch · *Sitta carolinensis*

JAN	FEB	MAR	APR	MAY	JUN	JUL	AUG	SEP	OCT	NOV	DEC

Feeds upside down on tree trunks in deciduous woods.

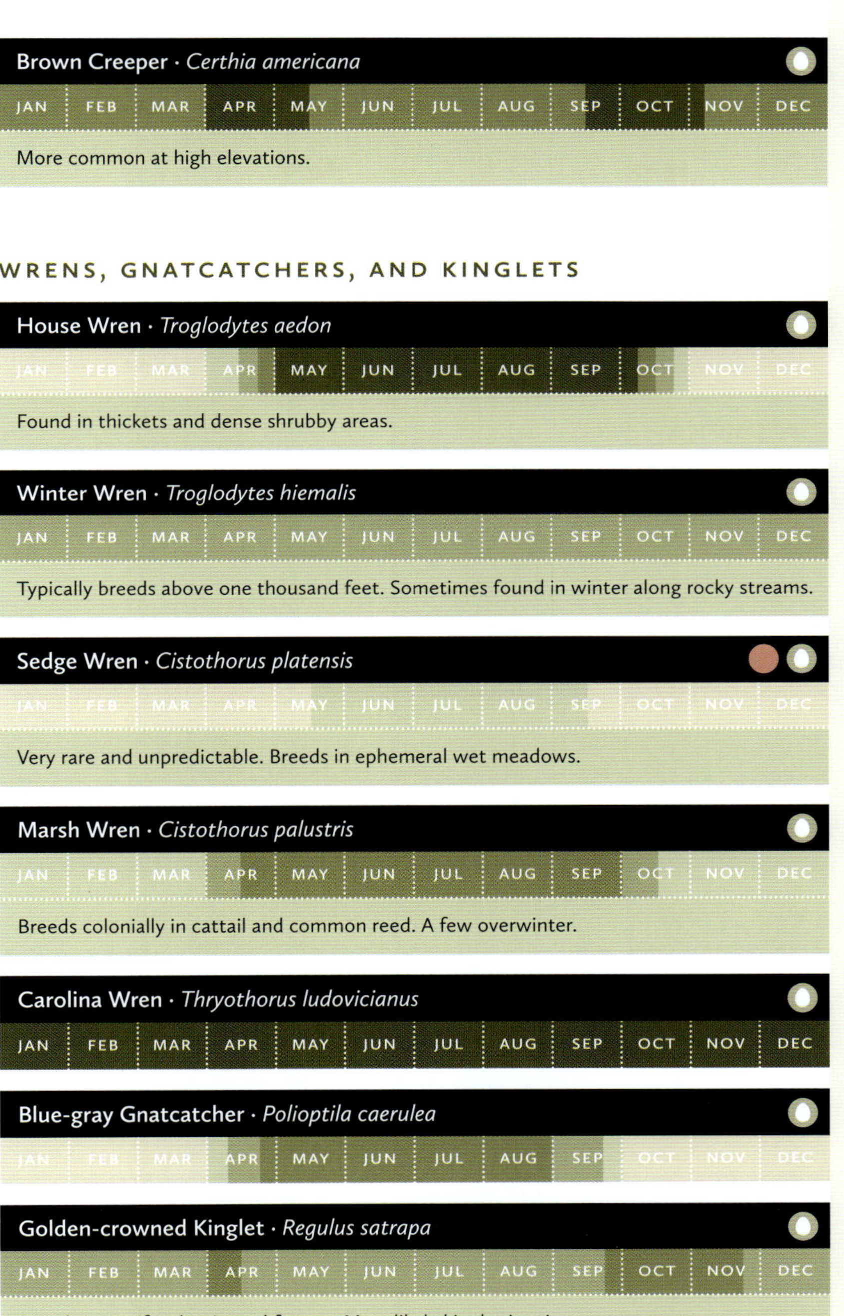

Brown Creeper · *Certhia americana*

JAN	FEB	MAR	APR	MAY	JUN	JUL	AUG	SEP	OCT	NOV	DEC

More common at high elevations.

WRENS, GNATCATCHERS, AND KINGLETS

House Wren · *Troglodytes aedon*

JAN	FEB	MAR	APR	MAY	JUN	JUL	AUG	SEP	OCT	NOV	DEC

Found in thickets and dense shrubby areas.

Winter Wren · *Troglodytes hiemalis*

JAN	FEB	MAR	APR	MAY	JUN	JUL	AUG	SEP	OCT	NOV	DEC

Typically breeds above one thousand feet. Sometimes found in winter along rocky streams.

Sedge Wren · *Cistothorus platensis*

JAN	FEB	MAR	APR	MAY	JUN	JUL	AUG	SEP	OCT	NOV	DEC

Very rare and unpredictable. Breeds in ephemeral wet meadows.

Marsh Wren · *Cistothorus palustris*

JAN	FEB	MAR	APR	MAY	JUN	JUL	AUG	SEP	OCT	NOV	DEC

Breeds colonially in cattail and common reed. A few overwinter.

Carolina Wren · *Thryothorus ludovicianus*

JAN	FEB	MAR	APR	MAY	JUN	JUL	AUG	SEP	OCT	NOV	DEC

Blue-gray Gnatcatcher · *Polioptila caerulea*

JAN	FEB	MAR	APR	MAY	JUN	JUL	AUG	SEP	OCT	NOV	DEC

Golden-crowned Kinglet · *Regulus satrapa*

JAN	FEB	MAR	APR	MAY	JUN	JUL	AUG	SEP	OCT	NOV	DEC

Breeds in conifer-dominated forests. Most likely kinglet in winter.

Ruby-crowned Kinglet · *Regulus calendula*

JAN	FEB	MAR	APR	MAY	JUN	JUL	AUG	SEP	OCT	NOV	DEC

Breeds at higher elevations in spruce-fir forest.

THRUSHES

Eastern Bluebird · *Sialia sialis*

JAN	FEB	MAR	APR	MAY	JUN	JUL	AUG	SEP	OCT	NOV	DEC

Uses nest boxes.

Veery · *Catharus fuscescens*

JAN	FEB	MAR	APR	MAY	JUN	JUL	AUG	SEP	OCT	NOV	DEC

Generally less common than Wood Thrush. Prefers moist woods.

Gray-cheeked Thrush · *Catharus minimus*

JAN	FEB	MAR	APR	MAY	JUN	JUL	AUG	SEP	OCT	NOV	DEC

Seen only as a migrant and difficult to distinguish from Bicknell's Thrush.

Bicknell's Thrush · *Catharus bicknelli*

JAN	FEB	MAR	APR	MAY	JUN	JUL	AUG	SEP	OCT	NOV	DEC

Found above three thousand feet in spruce-fir forest. Hunter Mountain.

Swainson's Thrush · *Catharus ustulatus*

JAN	FEB	MAR	APR	MAY	JUN	JUL	AUG	SEP	OCT	NOV	DEC

Breeds at high elevations slightly below Bicknell's Thrush.

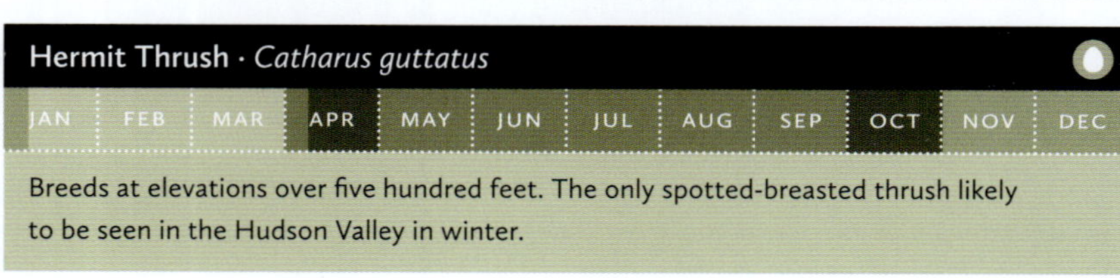

Hermit Thrush · *Catharus guttatus*

JAN	FEB	MAR	APR	MAY	JUN	JUL	AUG	SEP	OCT	NOV	DEC

Breeds at elevations over five hundred feet. The only spotted-breasted thrush likely to be seen in the Hudson Valley in winter.

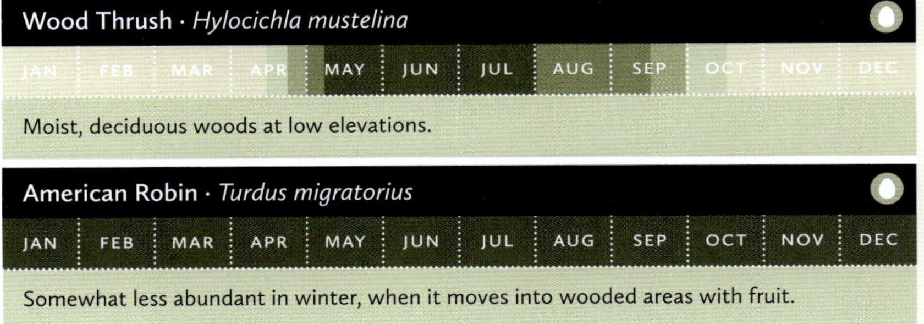

Wood Thrush · *Hylocichla mustelina*

JAN FEB MAR APR MAY JUN JUL AUG SEP OCT NOV DEC

Moist, deciduous woods at low elevations.

American Robin · *Turdus migratorius*

JAN FEB MAR APR MAY JUN JUL AUG SEP OCT NOV DEC

Somewhat less abundant in winter, when it moves into wooded areas with fruit.

MIMIDS AND STARLINGS

Gray Catbird · *Dumetella carolinensis*

JAN FEB MAR APR MAY JUN JUL AUG SEP OCT NOV DEC

Most migrate.

Brown Thrasher · *Toxostoma rufum*

JAN FEB MAR APR MAY JUN JUL AUG SEP OCT NOV DEC

Most winter records are from the Lower Hudson.

Northern Mockingbird · *Mimus polyglottos*

JAN FEB MAR APR MAY JUN JUL AUG SEP OCT NOV DEC

Uses multiflora rose and other fruits in winter.

European Starling · *Sturnus vulgaris*

JAN FEB MAR APR MAY JUN JUL AUG SEP OCT NOV DEC

Introduced cavity nester.

WAXWINGS, HOUSE SPARROWS, AND PIPITS

Bohemian Waxwing · *Bombycilla garrulus*

JAN FEB MAR APR MAY JUN JUL AUG SEP OCT NOV DEC

Erratic winter visitor sometimes found among Cedar Waxwings.

BREEDS IN THE HUDSON VALLEY
COASTAL
IRRUPTIVE
THREATENED
ENDANGERED

NONE
RARE
UNCOMMON
UNCOMMON TO FAIRLY COMMON
COMMON TO ABUNDANT

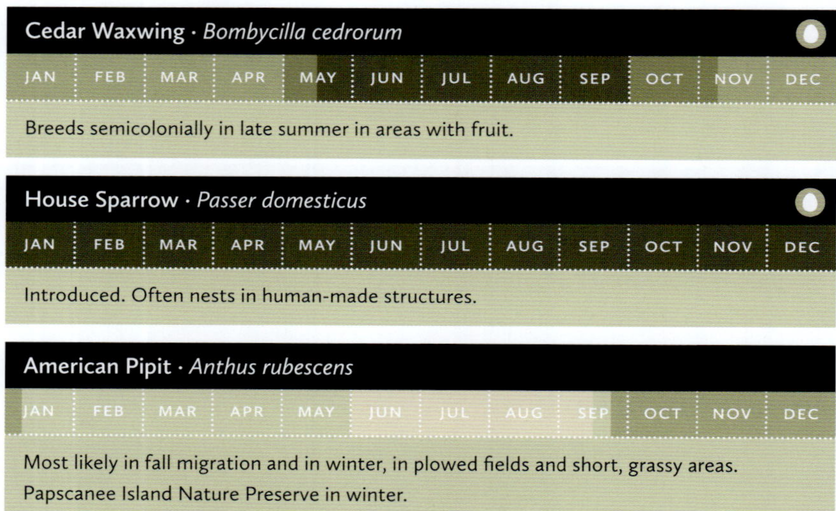

Cedar Waxwing · *Bombycilla cedrorum*

JAN	FEB	MAR	APR	MAY	JUN	JUL	AUG	SEP	OCT	NOV	DEC

Breeds semicolonially in late summer in areas with fruit.

House Sparrow · *Passer domesticus*

JAN	FEB	MAR	APR	MAY	JUN	JUL	AUG	SEP	OCT	NOV	DEC

Introduced. Often nests in human-made structures.

American Pipit · *Anthus rubescens*

JAN	FEB	MAR	APR	MAY	JUN	JUL	AUG	SEP	OCT	NOV	DEC

Most likely in fall migration and in winter, in plowed fields and short, grassy areas. Papscanee Island Nature Preserve in winter.

FINCHES AND CROSSBILLS

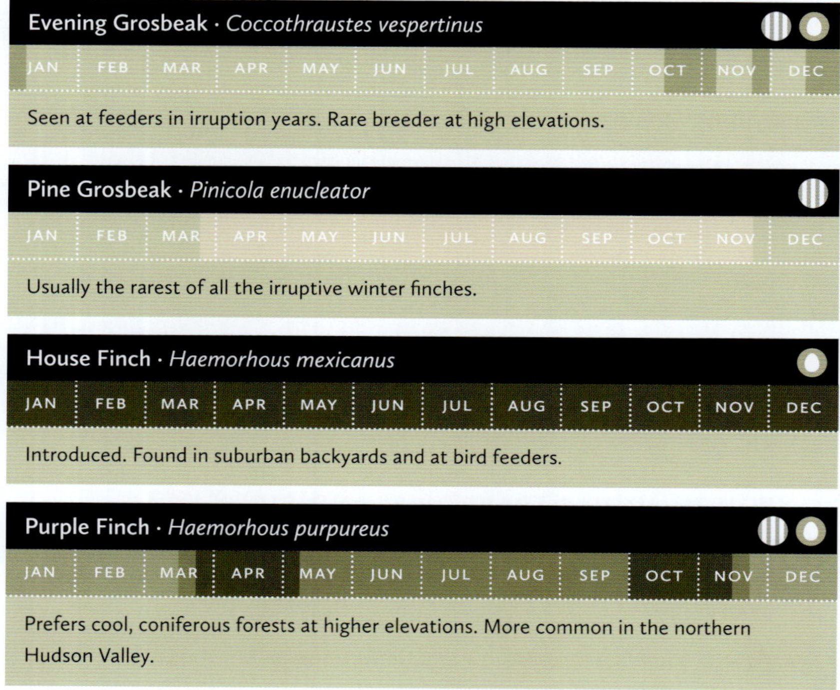

Evening Grosbeak · *Coccothraustes vespertinus*

JAN	FEB	MAR	APR	MAY	JUN	JUL	AUG	SEP	OCT	NOV	DEC

Seen at feeders in irruption years. Rare breeder at high elevations.

Pine Grosbeak · *Pinicola enucleator*

JAN	FEB	MAR	APR	MAY	JUN	JUL	AUG	SEP	OCT	NOV	DEC

Usually the rarest of all the irruptive winter finches.

House Finch · *Haemorhous mexicanus*

JAN	FEB	MAR	APR	MAY	JUN	JUL	AUG	SEP	OCT	NOV	DEC

Introduced. Found in suburban backyards and at bird feeders.

Purple Finch · *Haemorhous purpureus*

JAN	FEB	MAR	APR	MAY	JUN	JUL	AUG	SEP	OCT	NOV	DEC

Prefers cool, coniferous forests at higher elevations. More common in the northern Hudson Valley.

Common Redpoll · *Acanthis flammea*

JAN · FEB · MAR · APR · MAY · JUN · JUL · AUG · SEP · OCT · NOV · DEC

Seen at feeders in irruption years.

Red Crossbill · *Loxia curvirostra*

JAN · FEB · MAR · APR · MAY · JUN · JUL · AUG · SEP · OCT · NOV · DEC

Breeds in coniferous forests with ripe cones almost any time of year. More likely in the Upper Hudson. Taconic Crest Trail, Petersburg Pass to Berlin Mountain.

White-winged Crossbill · *Loxia leucoptera*

JAN · FEB · MAR · APR · MAY · JUN · JUL · AUG · SEP · OCT · NOV · DEC

Prefers spruce, fir, and larch forests. More likely in the Upper Hudson.

Pine Siskin · *Spinus pinus*

JAN · FEB · MAR · APR · MAY · JUN · JUL · AUG · SEP · OCT · NOV · DEC

Seen at feeders in irruption years.

American Goldfinch · *Spinus tristis*

JAN · FEB · MAR · APR · MAY · JUN · JUL · AUG · SEP · OCT · NOV · DEC

Seen in flocks at feeders. Late nester, typically June to August.

LONGSPURS AND SNOW BUNTINGS

Lapland Longspur · *Calcarius lapponicus*

JAN · FEB · MAR · APR · MAY · JUN · JUL · AUG · SEP · OCT · NOV · DEC

Sometimes found among Horned Larks and Snow Buntings in winter.

Snow Bunting · *Plectrophenax nivalis*

JAN · FEB · MAR · APR · MAY · JUN · JUL · AUG · SEP · OCT · NOV · DEC

Seen in flocks after snow, on plowed edges of roads or feeding in fields.

NONE
RARE
UNCOMMON
UNCOMMON TO FAIRLY COMMON
COMMON TO ABUNDANT

BREEDS IN THE HUDSON VALLEY
COASTAL
IRRUPTIVE
THREATENED
ENDANGERED

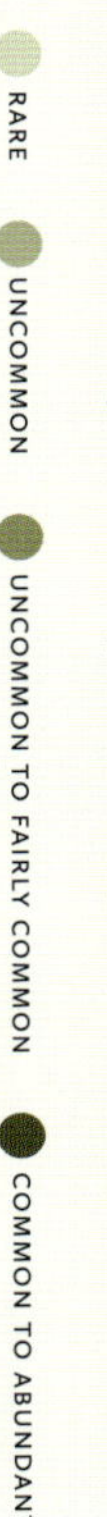

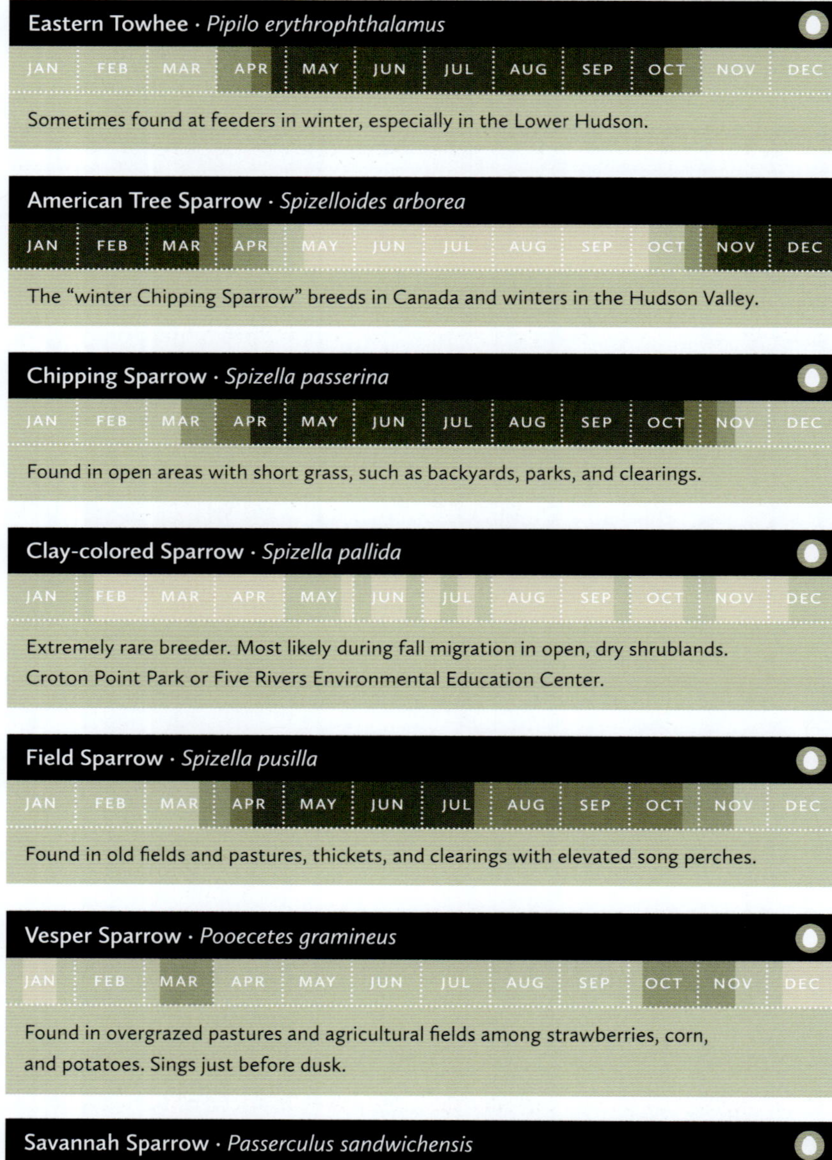

Eastern Towhee · Pipilo erythrophthalamus
JAN FEB MAR APR MAY JUN JUL AUG SEP OCT NOV DEC
Sometimes found at feeders in winter, especially in the Lower Hudson.

American Tree Sparrow · Spizelloides arborea
JAN FEB MAR APR MAY JUN JUL AUG SEP OCT NOV DEC
The "winter Chipping Sparrow" breeds in Canada and winters in the Hudson Valley.

Chipping Sparrow · Spizella passerina
JAN FEB MAR APR MAY JUN JUL AUG SEP OCT NOV DEC
Found in open areas with short grass, such as backyards, parks, and clearings.

Clay-colored Sparrow · Spizella pallida
JAN FEB MAR APR MAY JUN JUL AUG SEP OCT NOV DEC
Extremely rare breeder. Most likely during fall migration in open, dry shrublands.
Croton Point Park or Five Rivers Environmental Education Center.

Field Sparrow · Spizella pusilla
JAN FEB MAR APR MAY JUN JUL AUG SEP OCT NOV DEC
Found in old fields and pastures, thickets, and clearings with elevated song perches.

Vesper Sparrow · Pooecetes gramineus
JAN FEB MAR APR MAY JUN JUL AUG SEP OCT NOV DEC
Found in overgrazed pastures and agricultural fields among strawberries, corn,
and potatoes. Sings just before dusk.

Savannah Sparrow · Passerculus sandwichensis
JAN FEB MAR APR MAY JUN JUL AUG SEP OCT NOV DEC
Breeds in grasslands. In winter, it is more likely in the Lower Hudson.

Grasshopper Sparrow · *Ammodramus savannarum*

| JAN | FEB | MAR | APR | MAY | JUN | JUL | AUG | SEP | OCT | NOV | DEC |

Breeds in large grasslands and pastures. Croton Point Park or Shawangunk Grasslands NWR.

Henslow's Sparrrow · *Ammodramus henslowii*

| JAN | FEB | MAR | APR | MAY | JUN | JUL | AUG | SEP | OCT | NOV | DEC |

Extremely rare. Breeds in large, open grasslands and pastures with dead, woody vegetation. Shawangunk Grasslands NWR.

Nelson's Sparrow · *Ammodramus nelsoni*

| JAN | FEB | MAR | APR | MAY | JUN | JUL | AUG | SEP | OCT | NOV | DEC |

Nests in Canada and winters along the coast. More common during fall migration.

Saltmarsh Sparrow · *Ammodramus caudacutus*

| JAN | FEB | MAR | APR | MAY | JUN | JUL | AUG | SEP | OCT | NOV | DEC |

Breeds in small colonies in coastal marshes dominated by cordgrass. Marshlands Conservancy.

Seaside Sparrow · *Ammodramus maritimus*

| JAN | FEB | MAR | APR | MAY | JUN | JUL | AUG | SEP | OCT | NOV | DEC |

Found in coastal high and low salt marshes. Marshlands Conservancy.

Fox Sparrow · *Passerella iliaca*

| JAN | FEB | MAR | APR | MAY | JUN | JUL | AUG | SEP | OCT | NOV | DEC |

In winter, more common in the Lower Hudson.

Song Sparrow · *Melospiza melodia*

| JAN | FEB | MAR | APR | MAY | JUN | JUL | AUG | SEP | OCT | NOV | DEC |

Fewer in winter, when they sometimes visit feeders.

Lincoln's Sparrow · *Melospiza lincolnii*

| JAN | FEB | MAR | APR | MAY | JUN | JUL | AUG | SEP | OCT | NOV | DEC |

Breeds north of the Hudson Valley. Most likely to be seen during fall migration in the Upper Hudson Valley.

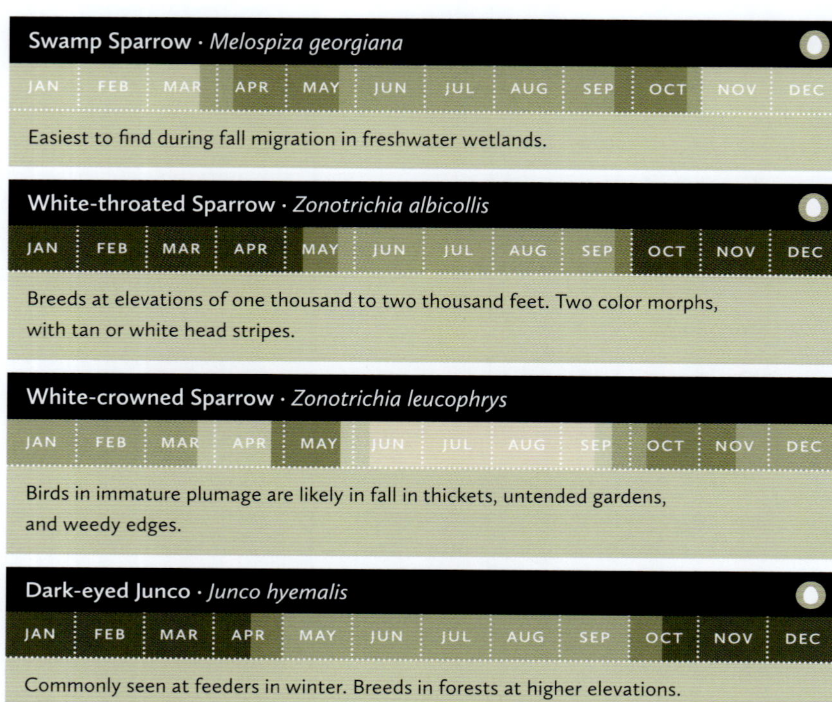

Swamp Sparrow · *Melospiza georgiana*

JAN	FEB	MAR	APR	MAY	JUN	JUL	AUG	SEP	OCT	NOV	DEC

Easiest to find during fall migration in freshwater wetlands.

White-throated Sparrow · *Zonotrichia albicollis*

JAN	FEB	MAR	APR	MAY	JUN	JUL	AUG	SEP	OCT	NOV	DEC

Breeds at elevations of one thousand to two thousand feet. Two color morphs, with tan or white head stripes.

White-crowned Sparrow · *Zonotrichia leucophrys*

JAN	FEB	MAR	APR	MAY	JUN	JUL	AUG	SEP	OCT	NOV	DEC

Birds in immature plumage are likely in fall in thickets, untended gardens, and weedy edges.

Dark-eyed Junco · *Junco hyemalis*

JAN	FEB	MAR	APR	MAY	JUN	JUL	AUG	SEP	OCT	NOV	DEC

Commonly seen at feeders in winter. Breeds in forests at higher elevations.

CHATS AND BLACKBIRDS

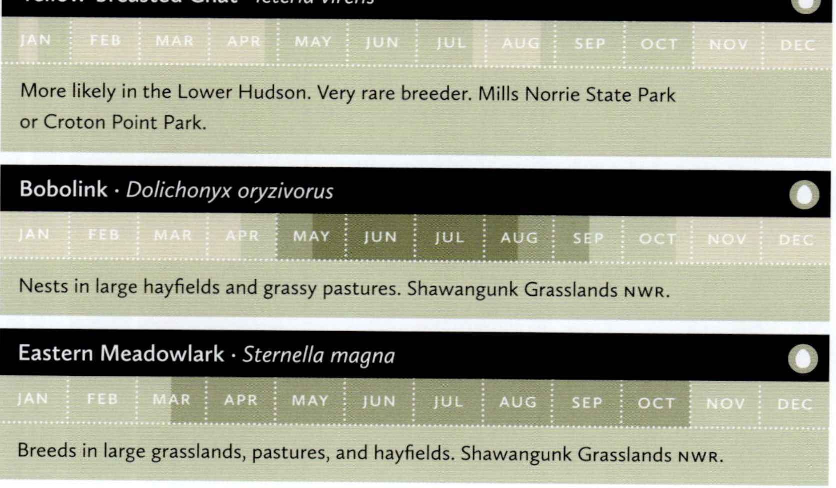

Yellow-breasted Chat · *Icteria virens*

JAN	FEB	MAR	APR	MAY	JUN	JUL	AUG	SEP	OCT	NOV	DEC

More likely in the Lower Hudson. Very rare breeder. Mills Norrie State Park or Croton Point Park.

Bobolink · *Dolichonyx oryzivorus*

JAN	FEB	MAR	APR	MAY	JUN	JUL	AUG	SEP	OCT	NOV	DEC

Nests in large hayfields and grassy pastures. Shawangunk Grasslands NWR.

Eastern Meadowlark · *Sternella magna*

JAN	FEB	MAR	APR	MAY	JUN	JUL	AUG	SEP	OCT	NOV	DEC

Breeds in large grasslands, pastures, and hayfields. Shawangunk Grasslands NWR.

Orchard Oriole · *Icterus spurius* 

Absent from higher elevations, and more likely in the southern part of the Hudson Valley. Peach Hill Park.

Baltimore Oriole · *Icterus galbula*

Nests in tall deciduous trees that hang over roads and water.

Red-winged Blackbird · *Agelaius phoeniceus*

Migrates in large flocks, with males arriving before females. In winter, found in large roosts among cattails on the Lower Hudson.

Brown-headed Cowbird · *Molothrus ater*

Lays its eggs in the nests of many small birds, where host parents raise its young. Sometimes seen at feeders.

Rusty Blackbird · *Euphagus carolinus*

Breeds north of the Hudson Valley. Found in small groups in swamps and on river shorelines during migration.

Common Grackle · *Quiscalus quiscula*

Present in winter in mixed blackbird flocks.

Boat-tailed Grackle · *Quiscalus major*

Wanders from the Atlantic Coast. Edith G. Read Wildlife Sanctuary.

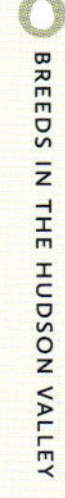

Ovenbird · *Seiurus aurocapilla*

JAN	FEB	MAR	APR	MAY	JUN	JUL	AUG	SEP	OCT	NOV	DEC

Nests and feeds on the floor of mature deciduous forests.

Worm-eating Warbler · *Helmitheros vermivorum*

JAN	FEB	MAR	APR	MAY	JUN	JUL	AUG	SEP	OCT	NOV	DEC

More common in the Lower Hudson. Breeds on wooded hillsides in deciduous or mixed forest with patches of dense understory. Doodletown.

Louisiana Waterthrush · *Parkesia motacilla*

JAN	FEB	MAR	APR	MAY	JUN	JUL	AUG	SEP	OCT	NOV	DEC

Migrates early. Found near rocky, clear, fast-flowing streams in wooded ravines. Hannacroix Creek Preserve.

Northern Waterthrush · *Parkesia noveboracensis*

JAN	FEB	MAR	APR	MAY	JUN	JUL	AUG	SEP	OCT	NOV	DEC

Breeds in bogs, swamps, beaver ponds, and slow-moving streams.

Golden-winged Warbler · *Vermivora chrysoptera*

JAN	FEB	MAR	APR	MAY	JUN	JUL	AUG	SEP	OCT	NOV	DEC

Very rare, but most likely in May. Sterling Forest, Ironwood Drive.

Blue-winged Warbler · *Vermivora cyanoptera*

JAN	FEB	MAR	APR	MAY	JUN	JUL	AUG	SEP	OCT	NOV	DEC

Abandoned farmland and shrubby fields on the edges of forests.

Black-and-white Warbler · *Mniotilta varia*

JAN	FEB	MAR	APR	MAY	JUN	JUL	AUG	SEP	OCT	NOV	DEC

Early to arrive, and late to depart. Prefers unfragmented forest tracts with a well-developed understory.

Prothonotary Warbler · *Protonotaria citrea*

JAN FEB MAR APR MAY JUN JUL AUG SEP OCT NOV DEC

Extremely rare breeder. A southern species most often seen in the Hudson Valley as a spring overshoot.

Tennessee Warbler · *Oreothlypis peregrina*

JAN FEB MAR APR MAY JUN JUL AUG SEP OCT NOV DEC

Spruce budworm specialist that migrates through the Hudson Valley on its way north.

Orange-crowned Warbler · *Oreothlypis celata*

JAN FEB MAR APR MAY JUN JUL AUG SEP OCT NOV DEC

Most likely in fall and early winter in thickets and weedy fields.

Nashville Warbler · *Oreothlypis ruficapilla*

JAN FEB MAR APR MAY JUN JUL AUG SEP OCT NOV DEC

More likely west of the Hudson River at higher elevations. Minnewaska State Park Preserve.

Connecticut Warbler · *Oporonis agilis*

JAN FEB MAR APR MAY JUN JUL AUG SEP OCT NOV DEC

Extremely rare fall migrant.

Mourning Warbler · *Geothlypis philadelphia*

JAN FEB MAR APR MAY JUN JUL AUG SEP OCT NOV DEC

Very rare breeder in dense vegetation at higher elevations. Albany Pine Bush in late May or early June.

Kentucky Warbler · *Geothlypis formosa*

JAN FEB MAR APR MAY JUN JUL AUG SEP OCT NOV DEC

Most likely in the Lower Hudson. Doodletown or Rockefeller State Park Preserve.

Common Yellowthroat · *Geothlypis trichas*

JAN FEB MAR APR MAY JUN JUL AUG SEP OCT NOV DEC

Found near the ground in thickets and shrubby edges. Responds to pishing.

BREEDS IN THE HUDSON VALLEY
COASTAL
IRRUPTIVE
THREATENED
ENDANGERED

NONE
RARE
UNCOMMON
UNCOMMON TO FAIRLY COMMON
COMMON TO ABUNDANT

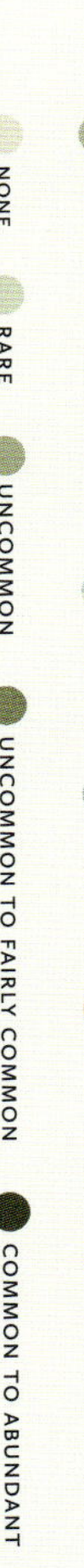

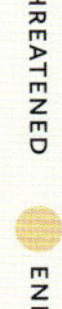

Hooded Warbler · *Setophaga citrina*

| JAN | FEB | MAR | APR | MAY | JUN | JUL | AUG | SEP | OCT | NOV | DEC |

More common in the Lower Hudson Valley, especially the Hudson Highlands, in forests with a dense understory. Common at Doodletown.

American Redstart · *Setophaga ruticilla*

| JAN | FEB | MAR | APR | MAY | JUN | JUL | AUG | SEP | OCT | NOV | DEC |

Found in moist, second-growth deciduous forest with a shrubby understory.

Cape May Warbler · *Setophaga tigrina*

| JAN | FEB | MAR | APR | MAY | JUN | JUL | AUG | SEP | OCT | NOV | DEC |

Spruce budworm specialist that breeds to the north and passes through the Hudson Valley. Peach Hill Park in May.

Cerulean Warbler · *Setophaga cerulea*

| JAN | FEB | MAR | APR | MAY | JUN | JUL | AUG | SEP | OCT | NOV | DEC |

In the Hudson Valley, found in open-canopy riparian forests with an open understory and dry, oak-dominated ridge tops and hillsides. Doodletown or Schodack Island State Park.

Northern Parula · *Setophaga americana*

| JAN | FEB | MAR | APR | MAY | JUN | JUL | AUG | SEP | OCT | NOV | DEC |

Most breed north of the Hudson Valley.

Magnolia Warbler · *Setophaga magnolia*

| JAN | FEB | MAR | APR | MAY | JUN | JUL | AUG | SEP | OCT | NOV | DEC |

Breeds at higher elevations in the understory of hemlock-northern hardwood forests. Minnewaska State Park Preserve.

Bay-breasted Warbler · *Setophaga castanea*

| JAN | FEB | MAR | APR | MAY | JUN | JUL | AUG | SEP | OCT | NOV | DEC |

Spruce budworm specialist that breeds to the north and passes through the Hudson Valley. Peach Hill Park.

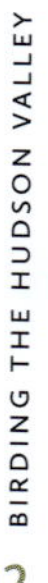

Blackburnian Warbler · *Setophaga fusca*

JAN FEB MAR APR MAY JUN JUL AUG SEP OCT NOV DEC

Typically found above one thousand feet in stands of mature hemlock or conifer plantations. Hunter Mountain.

Yellow Warbler · *Setophaga petechia*

JAN FEB MAR APR MAY JUN JUL AUG SEP OCT NOV DEC

Nests in thickets, shrubbery, and willows.

Chestnut-sided Warbler · *Setophaga pensylvanica*

JAN FEB MAR APR MAY JUN JUL AUG SEP OCT NOV DEC

More common in the Upper Hudson Valley and on the east side of the Hudson River.

Blackpoll Warbler · *Setophaga striata*

JAN FEB MAR APR MAY JUN JUL AUG SEP OCT NOV DEC

Typically breeds above two thousand feet in stunted spruces and firs. Hunter Mountain.

Black-throated Blue Warbler · *Setophaga caerulescens*

JAN FEB MAR APR MAY JUN JUL AUG SEP OCT NOV DEC

Breeds in large tracts of cool, shady, mature deciduous and mixed forests above eight hundred feet.

Palm Warbler · *Setophaga palmarum*

JAN FEB MAR APR MAY JUN JUL AUG SEP OCT NOV DEC

Among the first warblers to appear in spring migration.

Pine Warbler · *Setophaga pinus*

JAN FEB MAR APR MAY JUN JUL AUG SEP OCT NOV DEC

Early migrant. Sometimes comes to bird feeders. Breeds in pine woods.

Yellow-rumped Warbler · *Setophaga coronata*

JAN FEB MAR APR MAY JUN JUL AUG SEP OCT NOV DEC

Abundant in migration. Breeds at high elevations. In winter, feeds on poison ivy and bayberry near the coast.

BREEDS IN THE HUDSON VALLEY
COASTAL
IRRUPTIVE
THREATENED
ENDANGERED

NONE
RARE
UNCOMMON
UNCOMMON TO FAIRLY COMMON
COMMON TO ABUNDANT

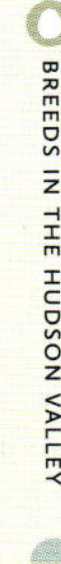

Prairie Warbler · *Setophaga discolor*

| JAN | FEB | MAR | APR | MAY | JUN | JUL | AUG | SEP | OCT | NOV | DEC |

Breeds in cedar fields and open scrub, power line right-of-ways, and successional habitats.

Black-throated Green Warbler · *Setophaga virens*

| JAN | FEB | MAR | APR | MAY | JUN | JUL | AUG | SEP | OCT | NOV | DEC |

Breeds in fairly large tracts of coniferous (particularly hemlock) or mixed forest.

Canada Warbler · *Cardellina canadensis*

| JAN | FEB | MAR | APR | MAY | JUN | JUL | AUG | SEP | OCT | NOV | DEC |

Breeds in forests above one thousand feet with a well-developed understory along wet areas. Minnewaska State Park Preserve.

Wilson's Warbler · *Cardellina pusilla*

| JAN | FEB | MAR | APR | MAY | JUN | JUL | AUG | SEP | OCT | NOV | DEC |

Breeds north and west of the Hudson Valley. Seen in migration in scrubby, wet habitats. Albany Pine Bush Preserve.

TANAGERS, CARDINALS, GROSBEAKS, AND RELATIVES

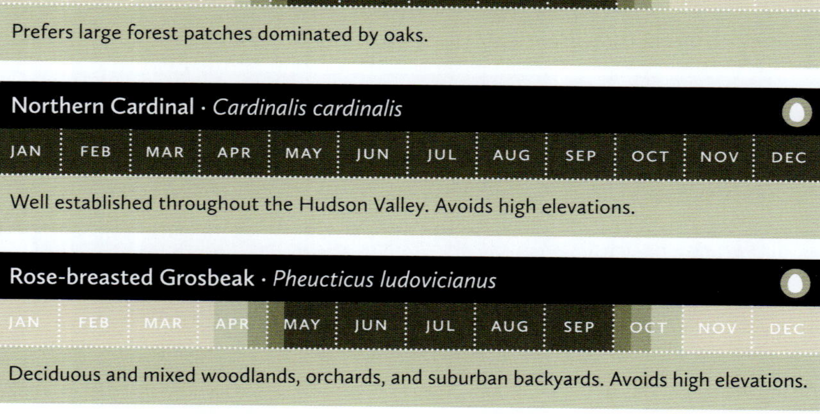

Scarlet Tanager · *Piranga olivacea*

| JAN | FEB | MAR | APR | MAY | JUN | JUL | AUG | SEP | OCT | NOV | DEC |

Prefers large forest patches dominated by oaks.

Northern Cardinal · *Cardinalis cardinalis*

| JAN | FEB | MAR | APR | MAY | JUN | JUL | AUG | SEP | OCT | NOV | DEC |

Well established throughout the Hudson Valley. Avoids high elevations.

Rose-breasted Grosbeak · *Pheucticus ludovicianus*

| JAN | FEB | MAR | APR | MAY | JUN | JUL | AUG | SEP | OCT | NOV | DEC |

Deciduous and mixed woodlands, orchards, and suburban backyards. Avoids high elevations.

Blue Grosbeak · *Passerina caerulea*

JAN	FEB	MAR	APR	MAY	JUN	JUL	AUG	SEP	OCT	NOV	DEC

Very slowly extending its range north through the Hudson Valley.

Indigo Bunting · *Passerina cyanea*

JAN	FEB	MAR	APR	MAY	JUN	JUL	AUG	SEP	OCT	NOV	DEC

Open areas, scrubby old fields, forest edges, and power lines.

Snow Geese showing their mountainous flight formation in the background.
© Deborah Tracy-Kral.

Appendix

Rarities, Vagrants, and Extinct Species

This appendix includes birds that have been recorded from the Hudson
Valley but are not seen regularly. These species are exceedingly rare for a
variety of reasons. Some were historically present in greater numbers, but
have declined over time because of habitat changes or other factors. A few,
including the Passenger Pigeon and Carolina Parakeet, have become extinct.
Others are vagrants, birds that appear irregularly, far outside their normal
migration route or breeding range. The vast majority of these are so rare that
the acceptance of new records requires review by the New York State Avian
Records Committee (nybirds.org/NYSARC). The records listed here reflect the
committee's decisions through 2012. Birds listed as historical were recorded
in our area before the formation of NYSARC in 1977. A few birds on this list
are rare in the Hudson Valley, but are not rare in other parts of New York
State and are therefore not subject to NYSARC review. In addition, some
reports submitted to eBird, listservs, local bird clubs, and rare bird alerts do
not reach the committee. Credible reports, usually with photos, are included
here. Birds marked with an asterisk have been reported from the Hudson
Valley but not reviewed by NYSARC.

Black-bellied Whistling-Duck, *Dendrocygna autumnalis*—one record,
   Orange County, March 2011
Fulvous Whistling-Duck, *Dendrocygna bicolor*—one record, Dutchess
   County, April 1981
Pink-footed Goose, *Anser brachyrhynchus*—multiple records, increasing
Barnacle Goose, *Branta leucopsis*—authentic records difficult to distinguish
   from escapes from captive flocks
Trumpeter Swan, *Cygnus buccinator*—multiple records

Tufted Duck, *Aythya fuligula*—one record, Ulster County, April 2009

King Eider, *Somateria spectabilis*—wanders from coastal Long Island

Common Eider, *Somateria mollissima*—one record, Dutchess County, October 1979

Harlequin Duck, *Histrionicus histrionicus*—regular in winter on coastal Long Island

Eared Grebe, *Podiceps nigricollis*—regular in winter on coastal Long Island

Western Grebe, *Aechmophorus occidentalis*—two records: Rockland County, January 2009, January 2016*

Eurasian Collared-Dove, *Streptopelia decaocto*—one record, Orange County, December 2003

Passenger Pigeon, *Ectopistes migratorius*—extinct

Rufous Hummingbird, *Selasphorus rufus*—multiple fall records

Calliope Hummingbird, *Selasphorus calliope*—one record, Westchester County, November 2004

Yellow Rail, *Coturnicops noveboracenis*—two records: Albany County, May 1984; Dutchess County, September 1992

Black Rail, *Laterallus jamaicensis*—one record, Westchester County, June 1986

Corn Crake, *Crex crex*—historical record

King Rail, *Rallus elegans*—multiple scattered records

Purple Gallinule, *Porphyrio martinicus*—historical records

Black-necked Stilt, *Himantopus mexicanus*—one record, Westchester County, August 2011

American Avocet, *Recurvirostra americana*—multiple records, Lower Hudson

Northern Lapwing, *Vanellus vanellus*—one record, Albany County, March 1991

Hudsonian Godwit, *Limosa haemastica*—fall records

Marbled Godwit, *Limosa fedoa*—fall records

Ruff, *Calidris pugnax*—scattered spring and fall records*

Baird's Sandpiper, *Calidris bairdii*—one record, Dutchess County, May 1979

Western Sandpiper, *Calidris mauri*—scattered fall records, difficult to distinguish from Semipalmated Sandpiper

Wood Sandpiper, *Tringa glareola*—one record, Westchester County, October 1990

Red Phalarope, *Phalaropus fulicarius*—scattered fall records

Long-tailed Jaeger, *Stercorarius longicaudus*—historical records
Dovekie, *Alle alle*—historical records
Thick-billed Murre, *Uria lomvia*—historical records
Black Guillemot, *Cepphus grylle*—historical records
Atlantic Puffin, *Fratercula arctica*—historical record
Black-legged Kittiwake, *Rissa tridactyla*—historical records
Ivory Gull, *Pagophila eburnea*—two records: Orange County, January 1981; Rockland County, February 2007
Sabine's Gull, *Xema sabini*—one record, Westchester County, September 1990
Black-headed Gull, *Chroicocephalus ridibundus*—scattered records, Lower Hudson
Little Gull, *Hydrocoloeus minutus*—one record, Albany County, July 2013*
Mew Gull, *Larus canus*—one record, Westchester County, March 2010
California Gull, *Larus californicus*—two records: Rockland County, October 1978 and 1981
Slaty-backed Gull, *Larus schistisagus*—one record, Dutchess County, January 2012
Sooty Tern, *Onychoprion fuscatus*—two records: Dutchess County, September 1979; Westchester County, August 2011
Roseate Tern, *Sterna dougallii*—historical record
Royal Tern, *Thalasseus maximus*—one record, Rockland County, June 2014*
Sandwich Tern, *Thalasseus sandvicensis*—historical record
White-tailed Tropicbird, *Phaethon lepturus*—one record, Rensselaer County, August 2011, storm-driven bird
Pacific Loon, *Gavia pacifica*—one record, Rensselaer County, October 1998
Yellow-nosed Albatross, *Thalassarche chlororhynchos*—one record, Westchester County, August 1976
Northern Fulmar, *Fulmarus glacialis*—one record, Westchester County, September 1985
Black-capped Petrel, *Pterodrama hasitata*—historical record
Great Shearwater, *Ardenna gravis*—one record, Albany County, September 1989
Manx Shearwater, *Puffinus puffinus*—one record, Dutchess County, August 2013*
Wilson's Storm-Petrel, *Oceanites oceanicus*—one record, Rockland County, August 1986

Wood Stork, *Mycteria americana*—one record, Putnam County, August 1985*

Magnificent Frigatebird, *Fregata magnificens*—one record, Columbia County, August 2011

American White Pelican, *Pelecanus erythrorhynchos*—multiple scattered records

Brown Pelican, *Pelecanus occidentalis*—one record, Westchester County, November 2011

Tricolored Heron, *Egretta tricolor*—two records: Orange County, September 1982; Dutchess County, April 1994

White Ibis, *Eudocimus albus*—several late summer and fall records, all Lower Hudson

Swallow-tailed Kite, *Elanoides forficatus*—multiple scattered records

White-tailed Kite, *Elanus leucurus*—one record, Dutchess County, April 1983

Mississippi Kite, *Ictinia mississippiensis*—multiple scattered records

Swainson's Hawk, *Buteo swainsoni*—multiple scattered records

Great Gray Owl, *Strix nebulosa*—multiple records, Upper Hudson in irruption years

Lewis's Woodpecker, *Melanerpes lewis*—one record, Westchester County, November 1954

American Three-toed Woodpecker, *Picoides dorsalis*—one record, Westchester County, December 1984

Black-backed Woodpecker, *Picoides arcticus*—one record, Westchester County, December 1962

Crested Caracara, *Caracara du Nord*—two records: Rockland County, January 2015*; Orange County, April 2015*

Gyrfalcon, *Falco rusticolus*—multiple scattered records

Carolina Parakeet, *Conuropsis carolinensis*—extinct*

Hammond's Flycatcher, *Empidonax hammondii*—one record, Westchester County, November 2006

Say's Phoebe, *Sayornis saya*—multiple scattered records

Ash-throated Flycatcher, *Myiarchus cinerascens*—historical record

Western Kingbird, *Tyrannus verticalis*—multiple scattered records

Gray Kingbird, *Tyrannus dominicensis*—one record, Rensselaer County, October 1992

Scissor-tailed Flycatcher, *Tyrannus forficatus*—two records: Westchester County, July 2003; Ulster County, August 2008

Fork-tailed Flycatcher, *Tyrannus savanna*—historical record

Loggerhead Shrike, *Lanius ludovicianus*—historical records

Gray Jay, *Perisoreus canadensis*—historical records

Black-billed Magpie, *Pica hudsonia*—historical records, some possibly escaped captive birds

Cave Swallow, *Petrochelidon fulva*—one record, Westchester County, December 2004

Boreal Chickadee, *Poecile hudsonicus*—two records: Greene County, January 2006; Albany County, November 2010

Bewick's Wren, *Thryomanes bewickii*—historical record

Northern Wheatear, *Oenanthe oenanthe*—multiple scattered records

Mountain Bluebird, *Sialia currucoides*—multiple scattered records

Townsend's Solitaire, *Myadestes townsendi*—multiple scattered records

Fieldfare, *Turdus pilaris*—one record, Westchester County, winter 1973

Varied Thrush, *Ixoreus naevius*—one record, Orange County, February 2007

Brambling, *Fringilla montifringilla*—one record, Dutchess County, March 1984

Gray-crowned Rosy-Finch, *Leucosticte tephrocotis*—one record, Greene County, December 2011

Hoary Redpoll, *Acanthis hornemanni*—multiple winter records, mostly Upper Hudson

Chestnut-collared Longspur, *Calcarius ornatus*—one record, Dutchess County, November 1968

Smith's Longspur, *Calcarius pictus*—one record, Ulster County, April 2013*

Lark Sparrow, *Chondestes grammacus*—multiple scattered records

Lark Bunting, *Calamospiza melanocorys*—historical records

Le Conte's Sparrow, *Ammodramus leconteii*—one record, Dutchess County, October 2011

Harris's Sparrow, *Zonotrichia querula*—two records: Orange County, December 2013*; Albany County, November 2015*

Yellow-headed Blackbird, *Xanthocephalus xanthocephalus*—multiple records

Western Meadowlark, *Sturnella neglecta*—historical record

Bullock's Oriole, *Icterus bullockii*—two records: Ulster County, spring 2007; Columbia County, January 2009

Swainson's Warbler, *Limnothlypis swainsonii*—one record, Ulster County,
    June 2006
Yellow-throated Warbler, *Setophaga dominica*—multiple scattered spring
    records
Townsend's Warbler, *Setophaga townsendi*—historical record
Summer Tanager, *Piranga rubra*—multiple spring records
Western Tanager, *Piranga ludoviciana*—multiple records, usually fall
Black-headed Grosbeak, *Pheucticus melanocephalus*—historical record
Painted Bunting, *Passerina ciris*—one record, Dutchess County,
    August 1992
Dickcissel, *Spiza americana*—multiple scattered records

References

Able, Kenneth P. 2004. "Birds on the Move: Flight and Migration." In *Handbook of Bird Biology*, edited by Sandy Podulka, Ronald W. Rohrbaugh Jr., and Rick Bonney, 5-1–5-100. Ithaca: Cornell Lab of Ornithology.

American Birding Association. "American Birding Association Code of Birding Ethics." Accessed November 7, 2017. http://www.aba.org.

American Ornithological Society. *Checklist of North and Middle American Birds*. Last modified through suppl. 58. http://checklist.aou.org/taxa/.

Bochnik, Michael. 2013. "A Guide to the Birds of Westchester County." Revised January 14. http://www.hras.org/birdguide.html.

Brittingham, Margaret Clark, and Stanley A. Temple. 1988. "Impacts of Supplemental Feeding on Survival Rates of Black-capped Chickadees." *Ecology* 69(3):581–89.

Burger, Michael F., and Jillian M. Liner. 2005. *Important Bird Areas of New York*. 2nd ed. Albany: Audubon New York.

Calandro, Daniel. 2005. "Hudson River Valley Ice Houses and Ice Industry." Hudson River Valley Institute. http://www.hudsonrivervalley.org/library/.

Carver, Erin. 2011. *Birding in the United States: A Demographic and Economic Analysis*. Arlington, VA: US Fish and Wildlife Service.

Centers for Disease Control and Prevention. 2017. "Ticks." Updated April 17. https://www.cdc.gov/ticks/.

Clemson University. "Clemson University Radar Ornithology Laboratory (CUROL)." Accessed February 24, 2017. http://virtual.clemson.edu/groups/birdrad/.

Collins, M. J., and D. Miller. 2011. "Upper Hudson River Estuary (USA) Floodplain Change over the 20th Century." *River Research and Applications* 28:1246–53. doi:10.1002rra.1509.

Cornell Lab of Ornithology. 2013. "Our Review: Best IPhone Apps for Learning Bird Songs." All About Birds, December 5. https://www.allaboutbirds.org/.

———. "Project Feeder Watch." Accessed February 7, 2017. http://feederwatch.org/.

Cronon, William. 1983. *Changes in the Land: Indians, Colonists, and the Ecology of New England*. New York: Hill and Wang.

Day, Gordon M. 1953. "The Indian as an Ecological Factor in the Northeastern Forest." *Ecology* 34(2):329–46.

Deed, Robert F. 2010. *Birds of Rockland County, NY and the Hudson Highlands 1844–1978* (with 1983 Addenda). New City, NY: Rockland Audubon Society, Inc. https://www.rocklandaudubon.org/.

DeOrsey, Stan, and Barbara A. Butler. 2016. *The Birds of Dutchess County New York*. Poughkeepsie, NY: Ralph T. Waterman Bird Club, Inc. http://watermanbirdclub.org/publications/.

Dickinson, N. R. 1979. "A Division of Southern and Western New York State into Ecological Zones." Unpublished report. New York State Department of Environmental Conservation, Wildlife Resources Center, Delmar, NY.

———. 1983. "Physiographic zones of Southern and Western New York." Unpublished report. New York State Department of Environmental Conservation, Wildlife Resources Center, Delmar, NY.

Dunn, Jon, and Jonathan Aldefer. 2011. *National Geographic Field Guide to the Birds of North America*. 6th ed. Washington, DC: National Geographic Society.

eBird. 2017. eBird: An Online Database of Bird Distribution and Abundance. Web application. Ithaca, NY. Accessed March 17, 2017. http://www.ebird.org.

Edinger, Gregory J., and Timothy G. Howard. 2008. "Habitats of New York State." In *The Second Atlas of Breeding Birds in New York State*, edited by Kevin J. McGowan and Kimberley Corwin, 43–57. Ithaca, NY: Cornell University Press.

Farnsworth, Andrew, and Benjamin Van Doren. 2013. "A Spring Overshoot Discussion (but not Necessarily a Forecast!)." BirdCast, March 6. http://birdcast.info/.

Glitzenstein, Jeff S., Charles D. Canham, Mark J. McDonnell, and Donna R. Streng. 1990. "Effects of Environment and Land-use History on Upland Forests of the Cary Arboretum, Hudson Valley, New York." *Bulletin of the Torrey Botanical Club* 117(2):106–22.

Haas, John. 2013. *A Birding Guide to Sullivan County New York*. Self-published.

Harris, Wendy Elizabeth, and Arnold Pickman. 2000. "Towards an Archaeology of the Hudson River Ice Harvesting Industry." *Northeast Historical Archaeology* 29(1):49–82.

"Hurricane Irene Redux." 2011. eBird, September 1. http://ebird.org/.

Hutton, George V. 2003. *The Great Hudson River Brick Industry*. Fleischmanns, NY: Purple Mountain Press.

Kilgannon, Corey. 2001. "Putnam's Mysterious Chambers of Stone." *New York Times*, April 22.

Levine, Emanuel, ed. 1998. *Bull's Birds of New York State*. Ithaca, NY: Cornell University Press.

McGowan, Kevin J., and Kimberley Corwin, eds. 2008. *The Second Atlas of Breeding Birds in New York State*. Ithaca, NY: Cornell University Press.

Miller, Daniel, John Ladd, and William C. Nieder. 2006. "Channel Morphology in the Hudson River Estuary: Historical Changes and Opportunities for Restoration." In *American Fisheries Society Symposium*, vol. 51, p. 29. American Fisheries Society.

National Audubon Society. 2010. "The Christmas Bird Count Historical Results." Accessed March 17, 2017. http://www.christmasbirdcount.org.

New York State Avian Records Committee. "NYSARC Reports and Decisions through 2012." New York State Ornithological Association. http://nybirds.org/NYSARC/.

New York State Department of Environmental Conservation. "Bears and Bird Feeders." Accessed February 7, 2017. http://www.dec.ny.gov/.

——— . "Bird Conservation Area Sites." Accessed May 12, 2017. http://www.dec.ny.gov/.

——— . "List of Endangered, Threatened and Special Concern Fish and Wildlife Species in New York State." Accessed June 8, 2017. http://www.dec.ny.gov/.

New York State Ornithological Association. 1973–2015. "Historical Waterfowl Count Data." Updated September 23, 2016. http://nybirds.org/ProjWaterfowl.htm.

Peterson, Roger Tory. 2010. *Peterson Field Guide to Birds of Eastern and Central North America*. 6th ed. New York: Houghton Mifflin Harcourt.

Schlossberg, Scott, and David I. King. 2008. "Are Shrubland Birds Edge-Specialists?" *Ecological Applications* 18:1325–30.

Sibley, David. 2011. "The Proper Use of Playback in Birding." Sibley Guides, April 11. http://www.sibleyguides.com/2011/04/.

——— . 2016. *The Sibley Field Guide to Birds of Eastern North America*. 2nd ed. New York: Knopf.

Smith, Charles R., and Peter L. Marks. 2008. "Land-Use Changes and Breeding Birds." In *The Second Atlas of Breeding Birds in New York State*, edited by Kevin J. McGowan and Kimberley Corwin, 59–68. Ithaca, NY: Cornell University Press.

Stalter, Elizabeth. 1996. *Doodletown: Hiking through History in a Vanished Hamlet on the Hudson*. Palisades Interstate Park Commission Press.

Stephenson, Tom, and Scott Whittle. 2013. *The Warbler Guide*. Princeton, NJ: Princeton University Press.

——— . 2015. "How to Listen to Bird Song—Tips and Examples from *The Warbler Guide*." All About Birds, May 1. https://www.allaboutbirds.org/.

Strayer, David L. 2012. *The Hudson Primer: The Ecology of an Iconic River*. Berkeley: University of California Press.

Sullivan, Brian, Marshall Iliff, Andy Farnsworth, and Chris Wood. 2011. "Understanding Birds and Weather: Fall Birding Basics." eBird, September 15. http://ebird.org/.

Swaney, Dennis P., Karin E. Limburg, and Karen Stainbrook. 2006. "Some

Historical Changes in the Patterns of Population and Land use in the Hudson River Watershed." *American Fisheries Society Symposium* 51:75–112.

Titus, Robert, and Johanna Titus. 2012. *The Hudson Valley in the Ice Age: A Geological and History Tour*. 1st ed. Delmar, NY: Black Dome Press.

US Department of Agriculture. 2010. "Management Considerations for Grassland Birds in Northeastern Haylands and Pastures." Washington, DC: Natural Resources Conservation Service.

Walton, Richard K., and Robert W. Lawson. 2002. *Birding by Ear: Eastern/Central (Peterson Field Guides)*. Audio CD. New York: Houghton Mifflin Harcourt.

——— . 2002. *More Birding by Ear: Eastern/Central* (Peterson Field Guides). Audio CD. New York: Houghton Mifflin Harcourt.

Index

Note: Page numbers in *italics* refer to illustrations.